Literature and Society in Germany 1918–1945

D1131491

HARVESTER STUDIES IN CONTEMPORARY LITERATURE AND CULTURE

GENERAL EDITOR Patrick Parrinder, Department of English, University of Reading

This is a new series of original, full-length studies of modern literature and its cultural context. Although a variety of historical, theoretical and critical orientations will be encouraged, each title will aim to illuminate the common themes and conditions of twentieth century writing, rather than to explicate the work of an individual author. Taking 'literature and culture' to indicate the whole of organized verbal expression, the series will extend to include studies of modern criticism, the press and the communications media, as well as offering new and stimulating approaches in the fields of English and comparative literature.

Also by Ronald Taylor
The Songs of Neidhart von Reuental (with A. T. Hatto), 1958
E. T. A. Hoffmann, 1963
Die Melodien der weltlichen Lieder des Mittelalters, 1964
The Art of the Minnesinger, 1968
The Romantic Tradition in Germany, 1970
The Intellectual Tradition of Modern Germany, 1973
Richard Wagner: His Life, Art and Thought, 1979

Literature and Society in Germany 1918–1945

RONALD TAYLOR

Professor of German, University of Sussex

THE HARVESTER PRESS·SUSSEX

BARNES & NOBLE BOOKS·NEW JERSEY

First published in Great Britain in 1980 by
THE HARVESTER PRESS LIMITED
Publishers: John Spiers and Margaret A. Boden
16 Ship Street, Brighton, Sussex

and in the USA by
BARNES & NOBLE BOOKS
81 Adams Drive, Totowa, New Jersey 07512

British Library Cataloguing in Publication Data
Taylor, Ronald, *b. 1924*
    Literature and society in Germany, 1918–1945.
    (Harvester studies in contemporary literature
&culture:3)
    1. German literature—20th century—History
and criticism
    2. Literature and society—Germany
    1. Title
    830′.9′00912   PT401

Barnes & Noble Books
ISBN 0–389–20036–0

Printed in Great Britain by
St Edmundsbury Press, Bury St Edmunds, Suffolk

FOR B

CONTENTS

PREFACE

It has become increasingly popular in recent years to set the study of literature into a context of social history, to attach special importance to seeing the dramas, the poetry and the novels of a given age against the values, the challenges and the pressures of the society in which they were born. Inasmuch as an artist is as subject to the social realities of his day as his contemporaries from other walks of life, and inherits the same constellation of social and cultural circumstances as they do, there is a necessary interaction between him and his environment, whether he eagerly seeks the raw material of his art from this environment or whether he withdraws from it in fear, in anger, in despair, or in the name of realities of a different order.

It would be perilous to assume that an artist can be fully understood in terms of the conditions around him, for if he is a true artist, his work will have something of the timelessness of all art, that something which distinguishes the artist from the reporter, the creator from the spectator. Equally he cannot be understood apart from these conditions. Michelangelo is as inseparable from Renaissance Italy as Shakespeare from Elizabethan England, or as Wagner from nineteenth-century Germany. The background is not just background—it has its dwelling within the artist's mind and soul, and is as integral to his art as the religious, the aesthetic, the formal or any other dimension of his creativity which scholars may isolate for study. Just as the historian needs to listen to the responses of the artist to life around him in order to understand the movements of society, so the student of art and culture needs a knowledge of the social and political scene out of which the work of art emerges.

In a period of agitation such as that covered by the present volume, as Germany dragged herself out of one war and slithered apparently irresistibly towards another, the interplay between literature and society—one might almost say, between art and the survival of the German nation—needs no labouring. The years of free political manoeuvring under the Weimar Republic produced a state of almost constant crisis. When the smoke of the crisis blew away, Germany was seen to be clamped in the barbaric grip of a dictator. And only four years after the hydra of Hitler's Tausendjähriges Reich had been slain, there grew up the heads of two Germanies instead of one. All this in the space of three decades.

To study literature in this '. . . . and society' mode has two particular consequences. The first is that the material to which one turns is often of the second or third rank, in which there is little of interest left to discuss after one has considered what binds it to its historical and social setting. Indeed, it is by nature the less-than-great works of any age which are swallowed up in the concerns of that age, and which acquire the epithets 'typical' and 'characteristic'. What is contemptibly typical and characteristic of the literature of National Socialism, moreover, while manifest, is beyond comment. This is part of the price one pays for studying such an age.

The second consequence is tantamount to a danger, a danger of which I have been uncomfortably aware at more than one moment. In any context-building enterprise, be it in the name of social or political significance, of movements of the *Zeitgeist*, of aesthetics or of some other activity of the classifying intelligence, one looks to abstract from the chosen works the elements that can be channelled into that context. This exposes one to the hazard of presenting partial, that is, distorted views of the works, and of the authors of the works, with which one deals. In fact one is tempted to say, the greater the artist, the greater the violence done to his creative personality by this, as by any other exercise in selectivity.

In the end, to my relief but not, in retrospect, to my surprise, this difficulty solved itself. For having discussed the plays of a Hasenclever or the novels of a Fallada, and turning to the works of Brecht, of Kafka, of Hermann Hesse, of Thomas Mann, I found that the context widened of its own accord, leaving, to be sure, the original area of socio-political relevance but quickly creating a world in which other, greater issues arise and other, higher values reign. The specifically social and political substance carries us further in Brecht or Thomas Mann, for instance, than in Kafka or in Hermann Broch. But although one takes what one finds, one must be at pains not to take it too far. One must preserve the artist's unique personality *in toto* and ensure, however fascinated one may become by one particular aspect of it, that one retains the organic, biographical unity of his creative work. The artist of genius and of power, as I gratefully discovered, will not permit one to do otherwise.

I have not set out to give a general account of German literature between the two World Wars. Still less have I tried to mention all those writers and works which would find their place in a chronological or encyclopedic survey. Rather, I have worked thematically, setting the social scene, first of 1918 and the Weimar Republic, then of Hitler's Germany down to the defeat of 1945, and discussing literary portrayals of, and responses to, the realities that make up that scene. I have then considered these responses in the generic framework of drama, poetry and novel.

Many names are missing that could have been included, and some,

I fear, that should have been. However, once I had identified certain dominant social phenomena, my principal task was to show how representative works of literature responded to them. The response, to this extent, mattered more than the respondent. Kafka, Brecht, Hesse, Thomas Mann, Stefan George, Döblin, Ernst Jünger—such figures are present *ex officio*, as it were. With the multitude of others the problem was whom to leave out. Whatever names I have unpardonably overlooked, I have tried not to omit a characteristic reaction to the concerns of contemporary society, or a representative train of thought to which these concerns gave rise.

Since I hope that readers other than German specialists may also find areas of interest here, I have quoted most sources in English and provided translations of any material, such as poems, quoted in the original German.

Although I have worked by theme and by genre within both parts of the book, there cannot but be a certain subjectivity, even arbitrariness, in the arrangement of the themes themselves and in the succession of the chosen authors. A strict chronology of works did not seem to me appropriate, since it is the sequence of historical realities that is primary, rather than an order of publication. I have moved associatively from one author to another in the discussion of a particular theme; one theme then leads, also by association, to another. A group of writers may share a common provincial or philosophical heritage, a common political alignment, a common religious confession; or they may be thrown together to suffer a common fate—in exile, for example, or in prison. In these and other ways smaller contexts formed within the overall context. It happened almost willy-nilly that individual chapters, with the discussion of the more time-bound, more society-bound writers behind them, moved towards the great names whose importance stretches beyond any 'literature and society' framework—Kafka, Hesse, Broch and Thomas Mann in the fiction of the 1920s, Brecht among the dramatists and poets in exile, Thomas Mann again among the exiled novelists.

The Bibliography carries the same limitations as the book itself. I could not hope to include more than a handful of literary studies of the authors whose work I have drawn upon. Instead I have looked to the diaries and memoirs of men who lived through these times—contemporary writings which, though not necessarily what historians like to call 'accurate', convey what the 1920s and 1930s 'felt like'—and to works that examine the society of Weimar Germany and of the Third Reich, together with the ways in which cultural life related to this society. Studies of the work of writers exiled from Nazi Germany have also been included.

Within these socio-literary parameters I have sought to put together a pattern which will help the social historian to bring the literary life of the time into his purview, and offer the student of German and European culture a picture of how artistic creativity moves with the swell of political and social events. Above all, I hope that this integrated approach may enable the literature of this most turbulent, most desperate, most tragic of periods in German history to be seen against the realities of its social environment, yet without being made to sacrifice the non-social, 'non-real' spiritual realities that make all art, and *a fortiori* all great art, what it is.

Acknowledgements

PERMISSION to quote from Harry Graf Kessler's *Tagebücher 1918–1937* and from Carl Zuckmayer's *Als wär's ein Stück von mir* was kindly given by Insel Verlag, Frankfurt and S. Fischer Verlag, Frankfurt respectively.

It is my great pleasure to thank the Deutscher Akademischer Austauschdienst for enabling me to study aspects of my subject at various institutes in the German Federal Republic. I should also like to acknowledge the help of friends and erstwhile colleagues in the German Democratic Republic, where I gathered much of my source material. I am deeply grateful to Mrs Erika Poole for typing the manuscript, and to my old friend Mr K. C. J. Case for helping me at the proof-reading stage, while Miss Angela Rutter did me the great service of compiling the index.

The dedication conceals a feeling I shall never be able to express. At the end I can only say, in joy and profound gratitude; 'Thank you.'

R.T.

PART ONE

CHAPTER ONE

Emergence from Defeat: German Society and the Weimar Republic 1918–1933

NOVEMBER 11 1918 is a date with many meanings. At the time it meant different things to different countries, and different things to different groups in each country. Since then it has gone on acquiring meanings, as new events have had their roots traced to it, later policies made to find their justification in it, and new historical perspectives constructed to incorporate it. As the present is conditioned by the past, so the past is changed by the supervention of events in the present, each bringing in its train a new pattern of meaning for the historical sequence of which it is the latest element.

Obviously and essentially, 1918 meant in the first place the end of bloodshed on an international scale. The factories stopped producing armaments, the soldiers went home, leaving eight million of their comrades behind them on the battlefields. But it was not only the fighting that had come to an end. The values and assumptions of pre-war life, in Edwardian England, in Tsarist Russia, in Wilhelminian Germany, in the French Third Empire, in the lands of the Habsburgs, were among the most spectacular casualties of the war—although, recalling the long-standing morbidity of the victims, one might regard the war itself as a moment rather of euthanasia than of murder. The Allies emerged from the conflict with the cognomen 'Victor'; Germany and what had been the 'dual monarchy' of Austria-Hungary, with the stigma 'Vanquished'. For no country that had experienced the war—and not excluding the United States of America—could there be a return to the pre-1914 world.

The German Empire of William II had entered the war in a blaze of confidence and self-righteousness. Maybe, in Lloyd George's words, 'the nations slithered over the brink into the cauldron of war' in 1914. Maybe German war aims developed in the course, and as a result, of military operations, as A.J.P. Taylor maintained in *The Struggle for Mastery in Europe*. Maybe, as Fritz Fischer interpreted the evidence in his *Griff nach der Weltmacht*, the Kaiser and his government had clear annexationist intentions from the beginning. These are questions that cannot be examined here. Moreover when one is concerned with the social scene, the 'atmosphere' of a given period as the environment in which the cultural manifestations of that period were conceived, it is not so much what may be subsequently demonstrated to have been 'official' policies at the highest diplomatic levels that is important, but rather what people *thought* those policies were, or ought to have been.

This gulf between government intention on one hand and popular knowledge and belief—and the public will, if there was such a thing—on the other, was strikingly apparent during the crisis preceding the outbreak of the Great War. The constitution of the Second Reich dictated by Bismarck to Lothar Bucher on 13 December 1866 imposed no obligation on the Chancellor to consult with the Bundesrat (the assembly consisting of representatives from the individual states within the Empire) on matters of major political importance, and Theobald von Bethmann Hollweg consulted neither Bundesrat nor Reichstag during the events that led to the Kaiser signing the mobilisation decrees on 1 August or the declarations of war against Russia on 2 August and against France on 3 August. So when, on 4 August, the Reichstag was asked to vote for the war credits, both the German states and the German people, unprepared for the irreversible position in which they now found themselves, no longer had any decision to consider: it had already been taken. To be sure, the thought of war was not novel, and there had been a number of false alarms in recent years. But being at war at that particular moment was a reality for which they were psychologically unprepared, and this unpreparedness exposed a politically unschooled, unsophisticated public opinion to the propaganda of which those in power were to make full use. True, the gulf between secret diplomacy and public knowledge also characterised the conduct of British affairs in these critical moments. But the German invasion of Belgium on 3 August united British opinion in a more democratic, and therefore more comprehending, spirit than that which prevailed in Germany at the time, and the wave of patriotic fervour that is released in moments of national emergency had not in Britain that sometimes brutal, sometimes hysterical, sometimes whining tone heard from the apologists of the German cause.

The conviction of having embarked on a just war, and in particular of having nothing to be ashamed of in violating Belgian neutrality, quickly took root in all sections of the German population. That the middle-class parties in the Reichstag, conservative and liberal alike, held to this conviction is what one would expect, for here the interests of landowners, industrialists, shopkeepers, public employees, and the army—an ever-present force in German politics—coincided. Furthermore, the authority of confessional allegiances, above all that of Roman Catholicism, consolidated this meeting of interests, and the power of the Catholic *Zentrum*, the second largest party in the Reichstag, was a strong influence in favour of consensus politics, both inside and outside parliament.

But the Social Democrats, too, the largest single party in the Reichstag, who automatically voted against each and every Government bill to appropriate funds for military purposes, decided that 'national survival' was at stake, and joined the other parties in approving of the war credits in the historic debate of 4 August 1914. (When Lenin, who had always believed that Germany was the logical site for the first socialist society, was given the news he refused to believe it.) The Socialist declaration talked of 'the terrible threat of enemy invasion' and assured the country that the Socialists would 'not abandon the Fatherland in its hour of danger'. The danger was represented as coming from Tsarist Russia. By concentrating its hatred on the despotism of what Marx had called 'the dark Asiatic power', the Social Democratic party was able temporarily to close its ranks and pose as a body which, in the defence of the common national interest, had waived its principles of international class-struggle and suspended its tactics of dividing the nation by the dogma of class-distinction. As a result, the anti-Socialist measures on which the military authorities would have insisted as part of their mandate for the prosecution of the war were dropped. The party newspaper *Vorwärts* was again allowed to be freely sold, while the trade unions, for their part, agreed not to call strikes—a kind of industrial truce to match the political *Burgfriede* in the Reichstag, by which the parties pledged themselves not to carry on their traditional sectional feuds as long as the war lasted.

This unanimity was short-lived. The Social Democratic party itself had always nursed a dualism between the 'grass roots' proletarian reform movement represented by Bebel and Lassalle, and the idealistic *edelkommunistisch* visions of the intellectuals; it now had to contain the radicalism of Karl Liebknecht, Kautsky and the Marxist wing of the party within a predominantly evolutionary, rather than revolutionary, framework. So when in March 1915—the month that Italy entered the war on the side of the Allies—some 25 per cent of the Social Democrats in the Reichstag refused to vote for the renewal of the war credits, and when Liebknecht, a few weeks later, wrote his violent anti-war pamphlet *Der Hauptfeind steht im eigenen Land*[1], the cracks were seen to be too wide to paper over. As the war went on, the gap between nationalists and internationalists within the socialist ranks, far from being bridgeable by an appeal to common interest at a moment of common danger, widened. But 1914 was an instant of unity, when German socialists could feel what bound them to their fellow-countrymen.

No less emphatic in defence of the German cause in 1914 were the intellectuals. With them, however, it was not, as with the Social Democrats, the despotism of Tsarist Russia that was used as the rallying-point but the 'infamies' perpetrated by perfidious Albion. Rarely has modern history seen so bewildering, yet so revealing a spectacle as that presented by the distinguished philosophers, scholars, scientists, poets, composers, painters, Jews and Gentiles, Catholics and Protestants who united behind a conviction of the evil intentions of Britain and the moral purity of Germany. The theologian Adolf Harnack and the economist Werner Sombart were among the outstanding thinkers of the day who found intellectual patterns to justify the German resort to arms.

In an essay called *Über Gesinnungs- und Zweckmilitarismus*, written in 1916, the philosopher Max Scheler distinguished between the inborn, 'ethical' militarism which is a true expression of the German psyche—*Gesinnungsmilitarismus*, as he called it—and the pragmatic *Zweckmilitarismus* of other nations, a forced posture of aggressiveness adopted for the achievement of a morally indefensible military victory. German—Scheler really means Prussian—*Gesinnungsmilitarismus* manifests itself in the virtues of service, correctness and discipline, but it carries no threat of aggression, whereas *Zweckmilitarismus* is liable to erupt into violence whenever a nation—and it is Britain that Scheler has in mind—fears a threat to its interests or senses a territorial advantage to be gained.

One of the most striking manifestations of support for the war in intellectual circles is the so-called *Aufruf der 93* of 4 October 1914. In this 93 famous scholars, scientists and artists, of all religious and political persuasions, put their signatures to a declaration defending the German invasion of Belgium and asserting the solidarity of the people behind the policies of the General Staff.[2] When one encounters in this company the philosopher Rudolf Eucken, the actor and producer Max Reinhardt, the authors Hermann Sudermann, Richard Dehmel and Gerhart Hauptmann, the scientists Max Planck, Wilhelm Röntgen and Paul Ehrlich—all three, like Eucken and Hauptmann, Nobel Prize Winners—one realises that this is no private statement from some extreme intellectual coterie but the expression of an attitude adopted by men of otherwise totally different backgrounds and beliefs. 'How shall we react to the war?' asked Harnack, and gave his own proud answer: 'Calmly, resolutely, and with exultation. Petty egoisms will disappear, and there will only be room for the broad view of life. We are entering a period that will fill us with the joys of sacrifice.'[3]

It is in utterances like this—and there were many declarations like the *Aufruf der 93* on behalf of national pride and morale—that one recognises the continued dominance of Prussian values and modes of thought in German national affairs. The effects of centuries of particularism would not disappear overnight, and as German unification had been belatedly and painfully achieved under the leadership of Prussia, which had risen to power through a long series of wars and therefore appeared to hold the secret of successful growth and self-assertion, it was not surprising that apprehensive, self-conscious eyes should look to Prussia for the qualities that the national situation of 1914 seemed to demand. In any case the general expectation was that the war would be over by Christmas, which was even more reason to support the elements that seemed able to guarantee that end.

This expectation contributed not only to the chauvinistic propaganda now being enthusiastically unloaded on to the nation but also to the ineffectuality of what little anti-war sentiment there was. A group of pacifist professors, among them a professionally respected but at that time generally unknown physicist in Berlin called Albert Einstein, founded the *Bund Neues Vaterland* the following year in order to try and bring the war to an end, but they were as voices crying in the wilderness. Hermann Hesse, already a voluntary exile from the Fatherland to which he never returned, made little impression with his earnest appeals to humanist Christian values and man's nobler emotions. Germany did not want to hear at this moment that love was better than hate, sympathy better than anger, peace nobler than war, and the German writers, publishers, even former friends he was seeking to influence branded him as a traitor, a man for whom the country had no use.

At the other end of the anti-war spectrum stood the Marxist revolutionaries Karl Liebknecht, Rosa Luxemburg and Franz Mehring, whose concern was not national survival, which they saw as synonymous with the perpetuation of capitalist exploitation and imperialism, but the promotion of the international working-class movement. It was the common situation in which one sectionalism confronts another. When in December 1914 the Government asked for fresh war credits, Liebknecht was the only member of the Reichstag to vote against. His stand brought him no friends. The most that could be said was that he might have been doing the right thing for the wrong reasons.

To be sure, when the Schlieffen Plan for a quick German victory was seen to have failed and the inevitability of a prolonged struggle became evident, questions began to be asked about war aims, about the ultimate interests of the German nation, about the relationship between political rights and the power of the military. The longer the war continued, the greater the unease over the outcome became. By 1917, particularly in the aftermath of the Russian revolution, events such as the mutiny on board the battleship *Prinzregent Leopold* revealed a rapidly disintegrating national morale, and on 19 July of that year an alliance of the Social Democrats and the Progressive People's Party, together with a number of representatives of the Catholic Centre Party, resulted in the passage through the Reichstag of an 'all-purpose' resolution declaring a desire for an honourable peace.

But 1917 was not 1914, nor did the resolution necessarily imply anything more than a realistic reappraisal of the military situation and an admission of the failure of the General Staff's aggressive war policy. Indeed, it returned to the 'self-defence' plea of August 1914, continued to talk of 'enemy governments' which 'threaten Germany and her allies with annexations and violence', reiterated the oneness of the people with their army and proclaimed that the nation would 'hold fast and fight on until it has secured for itself and its allies the right to live and to develop'. This is again—or still—the world of 1914.

So we are back in a Germany which looked for, and was envious of, the Prussian qualities which the hour seemed to demand. These qualities were most discursively, yet most specifically described by Arthur Moeller van den Bruck—whose later work *Das dritte Reich* (1923) was to bring him into favour with Hitler and the rising Nazi movement—in *Der preussische Still*, first published in 1916. After a Prussian interpretation of German history since the Middle Ages, and a presentation of the Prussian spirit as the necessary complement and corrective to the Romanticism that lies at the root of the German character, Moeller reaches the climax of his argument, with an abundance of illustrations from literature, art and architecture, in a chapter called 'Das preussische Schicksal':

Prussianism represents the political will of the German people. The strength of Prussianism has always been, and still is, the strength to bring together and to unite. Germany stands or falls by the resolution to fight for unity. All Germans who are thus resolved today are Prussians. And Germany is to be found wherever this resolution prevails in Prussia.'[4]

If most of Germany stood behind the Kingdom of Prussia, Prussia stood behind the image of her greatest ruler, the 'first servant' of his State, the epitome of 'enlightened despotism', Frederick the Great. Not only did the glorification of Frederick produce popular ephemera like the dramas *Friedrich Kronprinz von Preussen* (1915) by Emil Ludwig and *Preussengeist* (1915) by Paul Ernst, and novels like Walter von Molo's best-selling *Fridericus* (1918). 'Germany today *is* Frederick the Great. It is *his* struggle that we are concluding, *his* struggle that we are being made to wage all over again, and *his* soul that has been reborn in us'—words written, not by Moeller van den Bruck or some aristocratic, nationalist Prussian historian but by the later anti-militarist democrat, supporter of the Weimar Republic and refugee from Hitler's Reich, the greatest German novelist of the twentieth century—Thomas Mann.[5]

In August 1916 the Kaiser, confronted with a patently unsuccessful German war effort on the western front, appointed Field Marshal Hindenburg and General Ludendorff, successful commanders on the eastern front, to control the affairs of the General Staff. Since the civilian political government was now virtually without power, this amounted to control of the fate of the nation itself. 'Hindenburg will take care of everything', people said in relief.

In December Hindenburg and Ludendorff demanded that Reichskanzler Bethmann Hollweg should declare a policy of unrestricted submarine warfare so as to starve Britain into surrender. No incident shows more clearly how the conduct of national affairs had passed out of the hands of the government and into the control of the military. Bethmann Hollweg strenuously opposed such a policy, convinced that it would bring America into the war, and his fears were shared by many intellectuals, among them Max Weber in his essay *Der verschärfte U-Boot-Krieg*. Hindenburg and Ludendorff, on the other hand, argued that without such an extension of war-operations to stimulate the drive to success, the morale of the armed forces would decline, with inevitable consequences. When Bethmann Hollweg pointed out that unrestricted submarine warfare would mean attacking neutral as well as enemy ships, and that this could only follow a change in foreign policy for which he, not the General Staff, was solely responsible, Hindenburg retorted that he felt 'complete responsibility for the successful outcome of the war' and would 'very naturally . . . . insist that such military measures be taken as I consider appropriate for that purpose'.[8]

Even before this exchange of animosities the Catholic Centre Party in the Reichstag had agreed to support a declaration of unrestricted submarine warfare if the General Staff saw fit to adopt this course, so that the Chancellor's authority was already partly undermined from within. The war between the political leaders and the High Command was over before it started. Kaiser William II gave way to Hindenburg and Ludendorff, and presented his Chancellor with a *fait accompli* by signing, without reference to him, the order that from 1 February 1917 'unlimited submarine warfare was to be waged with all-out effort'. So, as Bethmann Hollweg and Max Weber had foreseen, America declared war on Germany a few months later and the final acts of the German disaster followed. The *de facto* domination of the High Command remained virtually unchecked almost to the end, and if there was little disposition outside a few extreme groups, such as the Independent Socialists, to challenge it, still less was there the power to do so. When, after the war, a committee of the National Assembly investigated the causes of the German collapse, a majority report concluded that the government had had at its disposal no personality capable of opposing the will of the High Command.

The cruellest irony in Bethmann Hollweg's position—and this epitomises the state of the nation—came six months after his ignominious treatment over the question of submarine warfare and military policy. Had he reacted to the snub by resigning, he would at least have drawn public attention to the fact that the country was no longer ruled by its elected government, with the Chancellor at its head, but by the Imperial General Staff; it would have been a stand on principle, even if the country as a whole were inclined to put its trust in generals rather than in politicians. Instead he stayed in office, only to find a few months later that, having sown the seeds of opposition to him in the minds of key politicians and of the Kaiser himself, Hindenburg and Ludendorff suddenly threatened to resign if he were not dismissed from the chancellorship. William II capitulated to the blackmail and hastily accepted Bethmann Hollweg's resignation. The ex-Chancellor knew that his days of political influence were numbered, but when his demise came, not through the will of the Reichstag but by the intrigue of military leaders and the moral weakness of the Kaiser, the impotence of constitutional government became clear for all to see. 'If', said the conservative, nationalist and thoroughly Prussian historian Hans Delbrück to the *Untersuchungsausschuss über die Weltkriegsverantwortlichkeit*—'if the supreme military commander (i.e. the Kaiser) had had General Ludendorff brought before a court martial in July 1917 and charged with mutiny, we should have been saved'.[9]

So the U-boats were given *carte blanche* to extend their 'defensive' activities, America duly entered the war, the German economy deteriorated further and the people faced another winter of misery like that of 1916–17. The implications for Germany and for Europe of the March revolution in Russia were being realised. There were hunger-strikes—incited by the Independent Socialists—on board a number of naval vessels in June. The Reichstag peace resolution of 19 July showed the direction of thought of the left-of-centre parties, and Pope Benedict XV's message to the belligerents on 1 August reiterated the possibility of a negotiated peace.

Against this background of portents of the direction in which German affairs were moving, and would have to move, the High Command continued to behave as the *de facto* government of the country. In so doing, it carried with it a large proportion of public opinion which still thought—and why should it not?—in terms of national honour and the preservation of traditional national interests. Ludendorff was not the man to be deflected from his policies by President Wilson's Fourteen Points of 8 January 1918, and the negotiations that led to the Treaty of Brest-Litovsk two months later were dominated by the High Command's view of what was politically and militarily desirable at that moment. After the failure of his do-or-die offensive of March 1918 Ludendorff still had the power to force Prince Max von Baden and the Kaiser to sue for the armistice which he naively thought to use as a respite before throwing his decimated, demoralised troops into the attack yet again. But a few weeks later, with the military situation seen to be hopeless, he was finally ousted. Hindenburg, who had managed to retain a degree of official remoteness and was less personally identified with the military collapse, was left in his post; he was even consulted over whether the terms of the armistice should be accepted.

On October 29 the Kaiser left Berlin for ever. On November 9 he abdicated, but not before Prince Max, in the only honourable course open to him, had handed over the chancellorship to the Social Democrat leader Friedrich Ebert, and Philipp Scheidemann had triumphantly (if a little prematurely) proclaimed the birth of the German Republic to the cheering crowds gathered around the Reichstag building. The House of Hohenzollern had ceased to rule and the German monarchy had come to an end. Two days later the armistice was signed.

To the shock and confusion, among civilians and soldiers alike, caused by the fact of final and irrevocable military defeat was added the remarkable event—or rather non-event—of the November revolution. For it was not just the Hohenzollern monarchy that had come to an end with the abdication of William II but the whole concept of monarchist government. Count Harry Kessler wrote in his diary on November 15:

A week ago, when monarchist attitudes were taken as a matter of course, the idea of a 'Foreign Ministry of the German Republic' would have appeared grotesque. Yet I believe that the true attitudes are those which are appearing now. In the face of the Kaiser's utter inadequacy, especially during the war but also for many flamboyant yet uneasy years beforehand, the concept of the monarchy had been slowly eaten away.[10]

Perhaps it had, but the sad course of the revolution does not suggest that the people, apart from a small number of strident revolutionaries, led by Karl Liebknecht, Rosa Luxemburg and the other members of the Spartacus League, had any confident notion of what to put in its place. The prevailing spirit was one of resignation and disillusionment rather than of enthusiastic anticipation. In bleak, grey mood, Rilke, in one of his rare moments of political utterance, looked back from his Swiss retreat at the year of the collapse in a letter to his 'Junge Frau', Lisa Heise, dated 1923:

Speaking for my own part, with an objectivity resulting from my heterogeneous background and education, I have no doubt that, by not recognising her true self, Germany is holding the entire world back. In 1918, in the hour of her defeat, she could have put the whole world to shame by a single act of honesty and repentance, by a forthright public renunciation of her spurious prosperity—in short, by a humility which is a very real part of her true nature and dignity, and which could have forestalled the humiliation imposed on her from without. For a moment I thought, and hoped, that that long-lost trait of humility which gives Dürer's drawings so positive a quality would reappear in the strangely submissive yet stubborn features of the German personality. Perhaps there were a few men at that time who did feel this, and who hoped for—even confidently expected—a conversion of this kind, but the truth is now emerging that it did not happen, and we are paying the price. What Germany failed to do was to re-establish her pristine purity and former standards, to undergo an inner conversion or re-think her fundamental position. She did not develop that dignity which springs from profound humility but was only concerned, in a hasty, superficial, grasping and suspicious way, with her own salvation. Instead of following her truest nature and seeking to endure, to overcome, and to prepare herself for the miracle that would have happened, she chose to assert herself, to escape responsibility and to strive for success. She preferred to stay as she was rather than to change. So, as I say, there was something missing.[11]

Whatever was missing was certainly not provided by the November revolution. There is, of course, an internal history of the revolution itself—the history of the agitation fomented by the Independent Socialists and the Spartacists, particularly during the last two years of the war; of the naval mutinies in Kiel and other ports, and of the general strike; of the proclamation of a Socialist Republic in Bavaria, the assassination of its leader Kurt Eisner and the ensuing civil war; of the establishment of Workers' and Soldiers' Councils and their relationship to the provisional government; the history of the dissension between the pragmatic, constitutionally-minded Majority Socialists and the Marxists pledged to the dictatorship of the proletariat and to the creation of soviets on the Russian model.

All this agitation cannot disguise the fact that, in terms of basic attitudes, awareness and values, the people as a whole were barely touched by the revolution. Lenin regarded it as a tragedy that there was no revolutionary party in Germany in November 1918 capable of taking up the leadership of the class struggle. The basic question in all revolutions is the question of power. In Germany at this moment there would have had to be, if a Communist revolution were to succeed, a determined, clear-sighted proletarian party able to seize power, and then, having dismantled the organs of bourgeois government, to establish its own apparatus of state control. The revolution left its permanent mark in the foundation of the German Communist Party in January 1919. But at the time it could not find the revolutionary masses to lead.

Ebert did not see himself as the leader of a revolutionary government; if he had, Prince Max von Baden would not have handed over the chancellorship to him in the way he did. And when social democracy, in the person of Gustav Noske, called on the army—which had been concerned to preserve itself intact as far as possible in the midst of the political upheavals—to put down the Spartacist rebellion in Berlin in January 1919, when Karl Liebknecht and Rosa Luxemburg were murdered, the realities of the situation became even plainer. It was a situation that recurred the following month in Bavaria, when the Social Democrat Prime Minister Johannes Hoffmann brought in the *Freikorps* to stamp out the rival Communist government, thus provoking a civil war in which hundreds were killed and imprisoned.

Of the beginning of the revolution in Berlin Count Harry Kessler, ex-Eton schoolboy and first republican ambassador to Poland, wrote in his diary on November 10, 1918:

In spite of the shooting the people behaved in an exemplary manner during the first few days; they were orderly and disciplined, they did not lose their *sang froid*, and they almost invariably acted honestly and fairly towards each other. A great contrast to 1914, when everyone was waiting to sacrifice himself.

Then, in a *cri de coeur* which so many, both inside and outside Germany, have uttered at so many junctures in German history, he added: 'If only a sense of political awareness were not such a rare thing!'[12]

But it was such a rare thing. The flurry of popular anti-militaristic enthusiasm that followed the proclamation of the republic was brief and superficial. In Berlin officers who walked about in uniform ran the risk of being set upon and having their insignia torn off, but in mid-December, a mere month later, Count Kessler records that most of the officers and other ranks he saw in Berlin were already wearing their epaulettes and cockades again: 'It is a big difference from mid-

November.'[13] As the difference continued to grow, so the forces which had nominally been defeated in the German military collapse reasserted themselves, and on 15 January 1919, only two months after the revolution, the Berlin correspondent of the *Manchester Guardian* wrote:

The formidable military machine, which seemed to have been crushed for ever, has risen again with astounding rapidity. Prussian officers are stalking the streets of Berlin, soldiers marching, shouting and shooting at their command .... The coalition between Government, Socialists, the middle-classes, Pan-Germans and militarists is for the moment perfect, and Germany is now under the control of the same elements which applauded and carried on the war. They have crushed, or are in a fair way of crushing, the political sections which combated the German war party for years. It is a fact that will scarcely fail to affect Germany's international position at the present juncture. At the same time there is no reason at all to believe that the Government's military victory will make for internal peace, order and stability. Everything points to the contrary.[14]

'Thursday, May 1, 1919. A national holiday,' noted Count Kessler. 'Everything closed, even restaurants and bars. An atmosphere of national mourning for the revolution that came to naught.'[15] More trenchantly, Oswald Spengler described the episode a few years later as 'the stupidest, emptiest, most cowardly and most dishonourable revolution in the whole of human history.'[16] For, said Spengler, the war had taught Germany nothing: she had failed to find her true, that is, Prussian, self, with the qualities on which alone the true German state could be built, and attempts to import such alien traditions as those of English liberalism and French democracy, let alone the ponderous superficial principles of Marxist class-warfare, would quickly be shown up for the irrelevancies that they were. The agitation, the bloodshed, the bitterness had all been to no avail. Rudolf Wissell, Social Democrat minister in the first Republican government, declared in June 1919:

We have been governing in the old ways, and there has been little sign of a new spirit infusing the old procedures ... The essential character of German culture and social life has hardly changed, and even the few observable changes have hardly been for the better. The people believe that the achievements of the revolution are purely negative in character, that the only difference is in the set of officials who exercise military and bureaucratic control, and that the principles of the present government do not differ in essence from those of the former régime ... It is my belief that the verdict of history on the National Assembly and on us, the members of the government, will be harsh and bitter.[17]

The coalition of forces to which the *Manchester Guardian* correspondent had referred, the revival of the never-disbanded military machine, and the persistent underlying yearning for national unity which the war had only served to intensify were welded even more firmly together by national reaction to the Treaty of Versailles, signed on 28 June 1919, just two weeks after Wissell's speech. Wilson's Fourteen Points had seemed, above all through their underlying principle of the self-determination of peoples and through the envisagement of universal disarmament, to offer Germany the chance to turn her back on the discredited imperial past and regain her self-respect. This meant that they both conditioned the politicians' and the people's minds to an acceptance to national defeat, and aroused expectations, realistic or otherwise, of what would follow this acceptance.

But when the peace terms came to be presented—for signature rather than for negotiation—the country found itself confronting a different sort of reality. The disagreement between Clemenceau on the one hand and Lloyd George and Woodrow Wilson on the other over the extent of the 'punishment' to be meted out to Germany belongs to the general political history of the time. More important, in the national German context, was the general conviction that, whatever the Fourteen Points had seemed to mean, the peace terms reflected a deliberate policy of humiliation and repression. Individual items such as the loss of colonies—in itself a matter of little economic consequence—and the claim for reparations became festering symbols of Allied viciousness and duplicity. John Maynard Keynes' *The Economic Consequences of the Peace*, published in 1920, seemed to prove Wilson's guilty weakness in allowing his Points to be whittled away, and the atmosphere became increasingly conducive to the spread of the *Dolchstosslegende* assiduously cultivated by the commanders of an army which, they now asserted, had never really been defeated. What rankled above all was the forced admission that Germany and her allies were the 'aggressors' who had caused the war and who had to bear the sole guilt for its consequences. It was not the facts of the Treaty of Versailles that mattered but the myths that surrounded it. And as interpreted myth has a readier access to the popular ear than a corpus of uninterpreted fact, so the German people carried into the era of their new republic a smouldering sense of resentment which grew ever more irrational and destructive as the realities of the post-war situation emerged.

Since it was the new republican leaders who, although there was as yet no new republican constitution, had had to sign the armistice, the most obvious political result as far as the public at large was concerned was the equation of republican government with weakness and lack of principles. This naturally strengthened the hand of the conservative groups—industrialists, army officers, nationalists of various kinds—in the country. Here lie the roots, not only of the failure of the republic as such but also of the stultification of the political education and development of the German people at large. This in its turn leads directly to the moment when, a dozen or so years later, Germans of all classes and generations were to hail Hitler as the saviour of their nation. Of the Treaty of Versailles the historian G.P. Gooch wrote: 'Its unexpected severity struck the frail Weimar Republic a blow from which it never recovered, for democracy was identified in many German minds with humiliation and defeat.'[18] And how many other 'German minds', one might ask, neither rhetorically nor cynically, transferred their allegiance to republican democracy mainly because it seemed to offer the best chance of a lenient peace settlement?

The new government was soon tested. On the economic front they faced the problem of inflation, which had already become an alarming factor by the end of the war and was exacerbated by the cost of demobilisation. On the political front the right-wing Kapp *Putsch* of March 1920 collapsed after a few days, partly from internal dissensions and weaknesses but more encouragingly through a combination of the loyalty of public servants to the government and a general strike of workers in Berlin. For a moment it looked as though the republic might capture the popular will.

But there was little cause for optimism. The spirit of national consensus forged by defeat and revolution was quickly eroded by forces from both left and right: the Communists and Independent Socialists weaned away large numbers of workers, while the middle classes moved back to the right, their true spiritual home. In the Reichstag election of 6 June 1920 the government coalition parties—the Social Democrats (SPD), the Catholic Centre Party (Zentrum) and the liberal *Deutsche Demokratische Partei* (DDP)—lost a great deal of ground to the parties on the left and right of them. For the first time in history there were Communists in the Reichstag, one of them the formidable Clara Zetkin, and the Independent Socialists (USDP) enjoyed a spectacular but short-lived increase in their representation from 22 to 84 seats. On the other side of the political fence the *Deutsche Demokratische Partei*, party of Friedrich Naumann and Max Weber, polled less than half the number of votes they had received in the election for the National Assembly 18 months earlier, losing most of their support to Gustav Stresemann's monarchist *Deutsche Volkspartei* (DVP), which had campaigned under the slogan:

Von roten Ketten macht Euch frei
Allein die Deutsche Volkspartei.

(The People's Party sets you free
From the shackles of a red tyranny)

Still more indicative of the swing to the right was the success of the openly nationalist *Deutschnationale Volkspartei* (DNVP) and the *Deutsche Volkspartei*, both of which attracted support from responsible intellectual circles. On top of this the Social Democrats, though still the largest single party in the Reichstag, temporarily withdrew from the government and went into opposition.

One need not delve into the details of the to-ing and fro-ing of the various groups in the political life of the Weimar Republic to realise that the successive governments neither attracted the enthusiasm and loyalty of a broad spectrum of the German public nor set the country on a definable, let alone acceptable, course. 'Social change' was a phrase few Germans were able or willing to interpret, and the groups who persistently used it were too raucous or too violent to capture middle-of-the-road opinion. A threat of disorder would drive the solid middle class into the arms of authoritarianism and cast the military in the role of saviours of the national interest. The officer class still claimed respect, and military values of loyalty and discipline were preserved by veterans' organisations, chief among them the *Stahlhelm*, whose sinister attraction was to grow as the internal dissensions of the republic became more frustratingly obvious. Smarting under what they had been persuaded were the vindictive terms of the Versailles Treaty, on which they blamed all national ills from the shortcomings of the constitution to inflation, the middle classes found comfort in the various 'stab-in-the-back' myths put about by nationalist groups, and set their sights on the restoration of 'true' German virtues.

The mood is perfectly caught in a scene from Edwin Erich Dwinger's novel *Wir rufen Deutschland*. A ship bringing a group of the last prisoners-of-war home from Russia in 1921 has just docked, and a much-decorated officer delivers an address of welcome on the quayside. 'Even if we were finally beaten by superior numbers,' he cries, 'we fought bravely to the end! And if you now find we have been sold into slavery for years to come, don't put it down to us! *We* only lost the war—the peace has been lost by others!'[19] The same path—from the ruthlessness and corruption of ruling Wilhelminian society, through the misery of the working classes in the pre-war years, to national defeat in the Kaiser's war and the implied calamity of the ensuing peace—is chronicled in the bitter pages of Heinrich Mann's *Kaiserreich* trilogy (*Der Untertan*, 1914; *Die Armen*, 1917; *Der Kopf*, 1925).

It was in Berlin, inevitably, that the pressures, the contradictions, the expectations, the tragedies of these years were at their most extreme. 'This city', wrote Carl Zuckmayer in his memoirs, 'ravenously devoured people's talents and energies, masticated them, digested them—then spat them out again.' But more and more artists, actors, writers, intellectuals of all kinds masochistically presented themselves to the monster for sacrifice. For why dally with minor monsters when the jaws of the greatest were always ready to receive you? 'Once you had Berlin, you had the world.'[20]

And what did you have, if you had Berlin? 'It bore the marks of the war that had been lost. The people were irritable and bad-tempered, the streets were dirty and full of crippled beggars—men blinded in the war or with their legs shot off—while passers-by in elegant shoes or bootees walked hurriedly past,'—the sort of scene shown in the drawings of George Grosz and Otto Dix. As to intellectual life:

The press was cruel, merciless, aggressive, full of savage irony—yet not demoralising, for behind all its viciousness there was still a sense of standards, a desire for quality, a readiness to reveal and encourage new and original creative work . . . The public too was a force to be reckoned with, a dangerous, unpredictable force which would not let itself be muzzled or made fun of, since it had on the one hand a strong sense of tradition, and on the other a great deal of curiosity about unfamiliar things.

In sum: 'Berlin had a taste of the future about it, and as a result people were only too willing to put up with the cold and the dirt of the place.'[21]

The inflation that had been gnawing at Germany's attempts to bring some stability to her economic situation finally reached its destructive climax in 1923, the year that Stresemann, the only politician of international standing to emerge from the Weimar Republic, became chancellor. In the climate produced by the Treaty of Versailles it was not difficult for the Germans to blame the inflation on to the reparations they were being made to pay, principally to the French. If this was what was undermining the economy, so the argument ran, one was only doing one's patriotic duty by opposing any increase in taxation—although taxation was the obvious means of raising, from the industrial concerns ideally equipped to afford it, the money the state needed.

But the coalition government was too weak to impose such a policy on the industrialists. Indeed, the Reichsbank itself encouraged the inflation by extending huge credits to industry and commerce at low rates of interest, thus enabling them to buy up real estate and capital equipment with money whose value was declining almost hourly. In

1914 the German mark stood at 4.2 to the American dollar, and in 1919 at 8.9. On 1 July 1923, it stood at 160,000 to the dollar, and by November 1, 130,000,000. Helplessly the Reichsbank went on printing more and more banknotes of higher and higher de-nominations, though mark-values were meaningless and only goods, property or foreign currency provided a basis for fixing real prices and values. A day's work would earn a factory worker a pound of margarine, six weeks' pay would buy him a pair of boots, and twenty weeks' pay, a suit.

Stefan Zweig lived through these times in Berlin:

There were days when a newspaper cost 50,000 marks in the morning and 100,000 marks in the evening. Anybody who needed to exchange foreign currency spread his transactions over the day, for he got much more for his money at 4 o'clock than at 3 o'clock, and more again at 5 o'clock than at 4 o'clock. I sent my publisher a manuscript on which I had been working for a year, thinking that I would be covering myself if I asked for an immediate advance on 10,000 copies. But by the time I received the cheque, it hardly covered my postage on the manuscript a week earlier . . . . You could buy whole rows of six-storey apartment blocks on the Kurfürstendamm for $100, and what used to buy a wheelbarrow now bought a factory. Some youths who had found a crate of soap lying near a jetty lived like lords for months by selling one cake of soap a day, while their parents, once well-to-do, hobbled about like beggars.[22]

These were the conditions in which industrialists waxed fat, paying their workers in ever more worthless paper marks, while selling their products abroad for solid foreign currency. The most striking success-story of these years is that of Hugo Stinnes, who had already achieved prosperity before the war through coal, mining, shipping, hotels and other interests, and who now could not help becoming even richer. 'He soon owned a quarter of Germany,' said Stefan Zweig, 'and the perversity of the situation was that the German people, always swept off their feet by displays of public success, hailed him as a genius.'[23] It is easy, and has long been fashionable, to revile such men as 'profiteers' and 'tycoons'. But Stinnes, a man who spurned the extravagancies usually associated with the wealthy, and worked to retain a genuinely personal control over the fortunes of his companies, had national German interests at heart and did not look solely to his own personal profit. His activities as a Reichstag deputy of the Deutsche Volkspartei—Stresemann's party—and a member of the Reparations Commission hardly showed him to be the most liberal of politicians, but given the economic system of which he was both a product and a pillar, one must beware of presenting him merely as the biggest ogre in a scene rich in ogres.

Inflation, which reaches to the heart of a nation in a way no purely political event can, undermined the whole of German society. Neither the war, nor the revolution, nor the Treaty of Versailles had struck so deep, and the republic never recovered from it, politically or socially. The urban middle classes—office workers, civil servants, teachers, owners of small businesses, retail tradesmen, etc.: the concept is far from static—traditional exemplars of thrift and custodians of family welfare, had their savings wiped out. They, the most loyal and reliable elements in society, as they saw themselves, looked to the state for economic and social stability and found themselves let down, their legitimate claim to security shattered. The minority—some small tradesmen, for instance—that owned real estate retained something of capital value and watched inflation pay off their mortgages, but investment was out of the question, and the money earned and saved for it was lost with the rest. Attempts by the government to prevent 'excessive' price rises and profits by legislation only succeeded in discriminating against the small trader and the small firm, leaving the wholesalers and other middle-men, together with the industrialists, with their access to large-scale loans from the banks, untouched.

What was more, the victims knew that they were victims, and this knowledge found political expression in a disillusionment not only with the parties and their promises but with the whole democratic Weimar state as such. A conservative journalist, one Albert Erich Günther, spoke for large sections of the middle class when he said in December 1923: 'The greatest tragedy is that we have lost our confidence in the Republic.'[24]

Such disaffected elements in society became increasingly responsive to strident voices ranting against Versailles, against the republican government that had accepted it, against the Allies, against the Jews—in short, against anything and anybody that would serve as a scapegoat and condition people's minds to accept authoritarian, militant, nationalistic alternatives. Virtually any member of an identifiable group, whether racial, religious, social or political, could be made the target of attack in the name of national unity and national pride. When Josef Wirth, Centre Party chancellor in 1921, and Walther Rathenau, Minister of Reconstruction and later Foreign Minister, both of them convinced republicans, announced that it was Germany's duty to carry out the terms of the Versailles treaty, whatever its injustices, they found themselves accused not only of betraying the national cause but of doing so because one of them was a Catholic and the other a Jew:

> *Knallt ab den Juden Rathenau,*
> *Die gottverdammte Judensau-*

(Knock off that wretched Rathenau,
The miserable Jewish sow)-

ran the jingle in 1921. The following year Rathenau was assassinated by two blond, blue-eyed, middle-class young men who themselves met a violent death a few weeks afterwards before they could be brought to trial. The Nazis were later to erect a monument to the two 'patriots'.

A striking portrayal of the lives and the mentality of these two men is given by Ernst von Salomon in his novel *Die Geächteten* (1930). Salomon, an anti-revolutionary nationalist who had joined the Freikorps Ehrhardt in 1919, was an accessory to the murder of Rathenau, and in 1922 he was sentenced to five years imprisonment. On his release he became involved with the anti-republican disturbances of 1928–9 among the farmers of Schleswig-Holstein—the scene used by Hans Fallada for his novel *Bauern, Bonzen und Bomben* (see below p. 129f.). Salomon was not a Nazi, but his militaristic and anti-democratic attitudes enabled him, rather as they did Ernst Jünger, to survive the Nazi era without serious trouble. A sharp, staccato tone brings us a commentary on 'the higher meaning of battle', as Salomon recounts his experiences of the end of the war, the revolution and the events leading to the assassination of Rathenau, experiences shared by his comrades as they fight to create that conservative 'Prussian socialism' preached by Oswald Spengler and Moeller van den Bruck. Men of all levels of intelligence found their way into the patriotic organisations which sprang up after the abortive revolution, and Salomon's novel shows what it was that swept these men along, even to the point of murder.

From the same period, covering the years 1915–1924, and also described through the eyes of a group of former prisoners-of-war struggling to find something worth living for, comes an absorbing trilogy of novels by Edwin Erich Dwinger: *Die Armee hinter Stacheldraht* (1929), *Zwischen weiss und rot* (1930) and *Wir rufen Deutschland* (1932), collected under the title *Die deutsche Passion*. These books, with their panoramic sweep and their power to enable readers of all ages and all kinds of experience to feel that it was *their* Germany about which they were reading, were immensely popular in the 1930s. The cult of *Frontgeist* which he shares with Jünger and Ernst von Salomon, together with the militant anti-Communism born of his own years as a prisoner of war in Siberia, made Dwinger *persona grata* with the Nazis, but this does not make his novels any the less valuable as material for helping one understand the intellectual and spiritual world both of the immediate post-war years and of the decaying republic.

At the beginning of the crisis year of 1923 nationalist propaganda had received a God-given boost through the French occupation of the Ruhr. Ostensibly provoked by a default in German reparations payments, this reaction was in reality an outburst of that French hatred of the conquered enemy which no peace settlement, however harsh, could have quenched. Aware of English and American disapproval of the French invasion, German nationalists gleefully played on Allied dissension to rally national sentiment behind a policy of passive resistance to the French demands. No doubt there was more talk than action on the matter of passive resistance, but the psychological realities were no less harsh for that.

Small wonder that these years should mark the beginning of the vogue of that work which, though published in the last year of the war, was to become a special possession of the Weimar Republic—Spengler's *Der Untergang des Abendlandes*. A defeated and humbled Fatherland, disillusioned with ideals and distrustful of moral values, offered a receptive market for a powerfully-argued plea that western European culture could be demonstrated by historical analogy to be in a state of decay, and was moving towards totalitarianism, control by technology and the cult of relativity. 'There are no eternal truths', said Spengler. This being so, he concluded, why act so unhistorically and pointlessly as to oppose the workings of fate in the name of liberalism and humanity? Why indeed, echoed the Germans of the Weimar Republic.

Spengler's message ministered to a ready-made self-pity that flourished in conditions of disintegration. But the Weimar years also led various intellectual circles, above all in the universities, to assert their involvement in the spiritual regeneration of their country and to show that the concerns of the academic community, contrary to a not unfounded general assumption, had a universal relevance. Metaphysical and sociological contexts were sought for the pursuit of scientific research. Scholarly works acquired such titles as *Die Bedeutung des Waldes und der Forstwirtschaft für die Kultur im Wandel der Zeiten* (by V. Schüpfer, 1928) and *Sprachwissenschaft und Zeitgeist* (F. Schürr, 1922), while the 'crisis years' of the 1920s provided the background for heart-searching investigations into the crisis in medicine, the crisis in philology, the crisis in jurisprudence and so on. The emphasis lay on relatedness, on integration, on the organic wholeness of human life, on the acceptance of a communal spiritual responsibility and a rejection of individualism, naturalism and mechanism. We are confronting, in a word, that tendency to the spiritualisation of reality that is so persistent a feature of German intellectual and cultural life.

Although it would be difficult to think of an author less like Spengler, these same questions underlie many of the writings of Ricarda Huch during these years. Her concern to define a relationship between the individual and society which should respect the rights of both, sustains her study *Michael Bakunin und die Anarchie* (1923), while in the centre of *Entpersönlichung* (1921) stands the familiar modern problem of the loss of personal identity in a Western world increasingly governed by the values of mass-production and technological efficiency. Ricarda Huch was already a woman of 54 when the Great War ended. She was to stay in Germany throughout the years of the Third Reich and World War II, and is one of the few well-known writers to retain a firm Christian conviction in the face of all the inhumanities that the Germany of the first half of the twentieth century inflicted on her own people and on the world.

As one would expect, the decay of moral values in post-war Germany was at its most spectacular in Berlin. 'I think I can claim to know history fairly thoroughly', wrote Stefan Zweig,

but to my knowledge there has never been a period in which madness reached such gigantic proportions. All values changed—and not only material values. Laws were ridiculed and conventional morality scorned . . . Night clubs, fun fairs and bars sprang up all over the place. What we had seen in Austria turned out to be merely a mild, innocent prelude to this Witches' Sabbath, for the Germans indulged in perversities with all the systematic determination for which they are famous. Boys—and not only professionals—walked up and down the Kurfürstendamm wearing make-up and false waistlines; every schoolboy was out to earn money, and senior civil servants and bankers could be seen flirting shamelessly with drunken sailors. Even Rome in the days of Suetonius did not experience orgies like the transvestite balls in Berlin, at which hundreds of men in women's clothes and women in men's clothes danced together under the approving gaze of the police. In the general collapse of values a kind of insanity gripped those middle-class circles which had always seemed unshakeably respectable. Girls boasted of their perversity, and to be suspected of still being a virgin at 16 would have been a disgrace in every school in Berlin. They all wanted to talk about their exploits—and the wilder, the better.[24]

A remarkably direct reflection of prevalent attitudes in this age, as perhaps in any age since its invention, comes from the cinema, while a more distorted, but often equally revealing reflection is given by political cabaret. The films of a nation, as Siegfried Kracauer pointed out in a well-known book[26], reflect that nation's mentality in a peculiarly immediate way; firstly, because they are the products not of a single but of a collective mind, and therefore represent the agreed result of the creative energies of many different minds focused on a common enterprise; and secondly, because, as a mass medium with a *raison d'être* that is basically commercial, it depends for its success on mass, and therefore anonymous, appeal. When the tastes of a mass market change, those who cater for that market must change their product if the market is not to be lost. And although it may be true that mass media lead and create, as well as follow, public demand, the continued consumption of the finished product preserves the justification for regarding it as what matches general expectation and satisfies general need. The perpetually prying photographic eye—the Germans, incidentally, were the first to evolve the fully mobile studio camera—seeks out the long-range and the short-range psychological realities of a chosen situation, revealing what the age would expect characters to feel in that situation.

Films with titles like *Frauen, die der Abgrund verschlingt, Verlorene Töchter, Hyänen der Lust* and *Das Mädchen und die Männer* belong to the same salacious world as the activities described above by Stefan Zweig. The underlying nihilism of the films of Ernst Lubitsch (*Madame du Barry*, 1919; *Danton*, 1921); the gruesome expressionism of *Das Cabinet des Dr. Caligari* (1920), followed by Fritz Lang's *Dr. Mabuse, der Spieler* (1922) and Paul Leni's *Das Wachsfigurenkabinett* (1924); massive, opulent UFA productions like *Fridericus Rex* (1922); the social criticism of the Heinrich Zille films (*Die Verrufenen*, 1925; *Mutter Krausens Fahrt ins Glück*, 1929) and the early socialist films of the Prometheus company—this mélange tells its own story of a society without a sense of direction—or rather, with so many senses of direction that the result was a centrifugal dissipation of energies and values.

The arrival of talking films in 1929 coincided with the years of depression and the 'softening-up' period that led to Hitler, and the sense of national psychological confusion showed itself in the juxtaposition of socio-personal studies like *Der Blaue Engel* (1930) and *Berlin Alexanderplatz* (1931), and appeals to nationalistic sentiment, often in historical guise, like *Luise Königin von Preussen* (1931) and *Der Rebell* (1933). These nationalistic appeals, set round with lavish spectacle and the emotive associations of Germanic mythology, invoked both the *Führerprinzip* and the complementary virtue of subservience to the common interest. They were thus calculated to capture both the imagination of youth seeking an outlet for its energies and the allegiance of a bewildered and betrayed middle-class.

The nightmare year of 1923 held one more portent of what was to come—Hitler's abortive coup in Munich on 8 November. The *Putsch* itself was a fiasco, but the trial of Hitler and nine others, including Ludendorff, three months later was given front-page coverage in the German press and attended by many foreign correspondents. Hitler made no attempt to defend himself. On the contrary, posing as the champion of the national interest, he addressed his speeches of self-defence to all those, from the army to the 'working masses', who would respond to an appeal to regain a lost German unity and a true sense of honour. 'I feel myself the best of Germans', he cried, 'who wanted the best for the German people.'[27] *Mein Kampf*, written during his imprisonment in Landsberg jail, expounds what he considered 'the best for the German people'.

The leniency of Hitler's sentence is an ironic comment on the administration of the law during the 1920s. Some of his fellow-conspirators, among them the S.A. leader Ernst Roehm, received a mere 15 months imprisonment, while Ludendorff claimed he had only been present at the time of the *Putsch* 'by accident' and was not tried at all. Zealousness to protect the young republic had created a body of legislation full of provisions for dealing with activity said to be against the interests of the State. The decision as to what constituted an offence against these interests came to rest more and more frequently on the interpretation of the presiding judge—in other words, on servants of the state whose attitudes and values were those not of the republic but of the Kaiser's Reich. For a variety of reasons, partly economic and partly social, the Reichstag never really possessed the political power which the republican constitution gave it, while the judiciary, a self-perpetuating force with its own traditions, and not answerable to the National Assembly, came to exert an ever-increasing influence. Indeed there were moments when the political power wielded by the courts through their interpretation of the law was the equal of that which issued from the Assembly itself.

Thus while left-wing agitators, whether peaceful or violent, were severely dealt with, those involved in right-wing movements such as the Kapp-*Putsch* of 1920 and Hitler's Munich *Putsch* of 1923, were treated lightly or even acquitted.[28] In December 1922 the Jewish editor Maximilian Harden was attacked and almost beaten to death. The attacker himself escaped; his accomplices, who belonged to the same gang as the men who had murdered Rathenau six months earlier, received a total of two years' imprisonment between them. The Munich court that tried the conspirators of 1923 decided to ignore that article in the Law for the Protection of the Republic which ordered that any alien convicted of treason—as Hitler had been—should be deported. Hitler was Austrian, not German. However, in his defence at the trial he convinced everyone that because he 'felt' as a German, he should be treated as a German. So, as a German, he was sentenced to a mere five years imprisonment and released after serving only 13 months.

At the end of 1923 the Dawes Plan laid down principles for settling the question of reparations, and the German currency was stabilised with the introduction of a new unit, the *Rentenmark*. Ironically, inflation left Germany, as a nation, virtually free from debt, as though it had emerged from the war as conqueror rather than conquered. Similarly German industry had cleared its debit account and was left in possession of more capital plant, property, equipment and so on than ever before. The post-inflation 1920s saw the striking growth of cartels and trusts stimulated by foreign, above all American, investment. I.G. Farben, the giant concern embracing chemicals, paints, pharmaceuticals, fertilisers, films, rayon yarn and a mass of synthetic products, was formed in 1925; Vereinigte Stahlwerke, compounded of the already large, diversified companies of Stinnes, Thyssen, Otto Wolff and the Phoenix A.G., was constituted in 1926, as was the Vereinigte Oberschlesische Hüttenwerke. The Siemens-Konzern dominated the electrical industry, the Wiking-Konzern created a virtual monopoly in cement, shipping lines were gathered into the folds of a few giants like Hapag and the Norddeutsche Lloyd, while Hugenberg, Mosse and Ullstein built up their publishing empires. The economic life of the country was governed by industrial magnates.

But the small man, above all of the thrifty middle-class, the bastion of stable respectability, had lost everything. Caught between the resurgent confidence of the state and the entrenched power of monopoly capitalism, and seeing himself as the *Deutscher Michel* who had carried the weight of war and defeat, the disgruntled and disillusioned *Bürger* had only the asset of his capacity for work by which to regain his material standards and a sense of community purpose. The Germans have demonstrated this capacity time and again, both in prosperity and adversity. But as an end in itself—and it has often been made such—it has contributed to political sterility, to the stultification of moral and political education, and to national disaster. The middle classes in Germany, being newer than those in England and France, had shallower roots and a less secure, less influential position in society. What little sense of purpose and cohesion they had had was now destroyed, and while venting their anger on the political machine that had watched, even helped to precipitate, their downfall, they became prey to any demagogic pseudo-saviour with a message that promised to restore their position and their morale.

As national prosperity slowly grew, so did the promise of a period of stability. The Dawes Plan was put into operation in 1924, 'passive resistance' in the Ruhr was called off, and French troops began to leave the follwing year. The temporary, stabilising *Rentenmark* gave way to the *Reichsmark*, which remained the unit of German currency down to 1948. Trade union power increased, the social security system was extended, most notably in the field of unemployment benefit, and wage levels rose steadily. Even the death in 1925 of Friedrich Ebert, respected first President of the republic, was successfully weathered, and whatever fears might have been aroused by the election of 'the wooden Titan', old Field Marshal Hindenburg, as his successor were quickly dispelled by Hindenburg's thoroughly correct execution of his office. In the field of foreign affairs the Treaty of Locarno in 1925, Germany's admission to the League of Nations in 1926 and the Kellogg-Briand declaration of 1928 condemning war as an instrument of political policy, all added to the impression of stability and the mood of optimism. Germany appeared to have become a good neighbour. Ironically the first movement towards the disintegration of this euphoria came from abroad. Equally ironically the principal agent of this disintegration was the same as that which had been largely responsible for the initiation and consolidation of the economic success of the preceding years, *viz.* the dependence on foreign, above all American, capital in the form of short-term loans. 'We have been living in recent years on borrowed money', said Stresemann before the Reichstag in November, 1928. 'If a crisis were to arise and the Americans called in their short-term credits, we should be faced with bankruptcy.[29]

A year later they were. In October 1929 Wall Street collapsed, precipitating the Great Depression. The depression was a world-wide phenomenon, but it struck most disastrously at countries whose economy rested on investment from abroad rather than on home-owned, independent sources of wealth and productivity. As the better-off countries hastened to protect their own positions, withdrawing their capital from uncertain foreign investments and reducing their imports, Germany found herself both deprived of investment capital and unable to sell her products abroad. Numerous companies went bankrupt, unemployment rose from a little over one million in early 1929 to over three million in 1930, and the state, receiving less in taxes and paying out more in social security benefits, grew poorer. By 1932 unemployment was to stand at over six million.

In such conditions anti-democratic movements, both on the left and on the right, were bound to flourish. The republican régime had all along been tolerated rather than supported by the majority of Germans of all classes, and now the frailty of its hold over the minds of this majority became sadly apparent. Political parties and their programmes had seemed irrelevant in the face of the need for a strong, single national line free of superfluous subtleties. The Communists offered their own brand of one-party state on the left, and in the election of 14 September 1930 they gained 50 per cent more votes than in the previous election. Hitler and his National Socialist German Workers' Party also promised to abolish the nuisance of political parties, and in the same election of 1930 the Nazi representation in the Reichstag went from 12 to 107, second only to the Social Democrats, who, with the Catholic *Zentrum*, were the only party to retain more or less the same measure of support.

This was the new, forward-looking nationalism that took the place of the old nationalism that looked back to the monarchy and the age of Bismarck. Being both new and militant, it had a ready-made claim on the young, who had nothing to thank the Republic for and were waiting to be given a sense of direction. It also had its appeal for those in the army and para-military organisations, in intellectual circles and among the disillusioned middle-class who upheld the classic Prussian virtues of discipline, national loyalty and self-sacrifice to the common weal.

The theme of national solidarity sustained a number of the intellectual journals of the time. *Deutsches Volkstum*, for instance, successor to *Bühne und Welt* in Hamburg, cultivated a fulsome neo-romanticism based on a text from Treitschke: 'The Germans are always in danger of losing their German-ness', while *Die Tat* made great play with the concept of *Volksgemeinschaft*.

The most intensely intellectual of these journals, stood, however, not on the right of the political scene but on the left—the incomparable *Die Weltbühne*. In 1905 Siegfried Jacobsohn had founded *Die Schaubühne* in Berlin, a journal committed to a conception of the theatre as an institution with a primarily social relevance. Increasingly involved in political issues—it could not be otherwise—*Die Schaubühne* was renamed *Die Weltbühne* in April 1918 and subtitled 'A Weekly Journal for Politics, Economics and the Arts'. Shortly after Jacobsohn's death in 1926 the editorship passed to Carl von Ossietzky, at his side Kurt Tucholsky.

Full of sharpness and wit, publishing fiction and poetry, social comment and political satire, *Die Weltbühne* was *the* organ of progressive intellectual opinion throughout the Weimar Republic, a rallying-point for an astonishing variety of writers, Marxists and non-Marxists alike, who saw some form of socialism as the only hope for the salvation of the Republic. Ernst Bloch, Walter Benjamin, Döblin, Feuchtwanger, Heinrich and Thomas Mann, Karl Kraus, Huelsenbeck, Erich Mühsam, Ringelnatz, Toller, Zuckmayer, Arnold Zweig, Erich Kästner—the list of its contributors is as endless as the nuances of their political and artistic personalities are infinite. It was banned in 1933, the year in which Karl Kraus' *Die Fackel* also came to an end. Becoming increasingly Marxist in alignment, it survived from 1933 to 1939 in Paris, Zurich and finally in Prague, as *Die Neue Weltbühne*. It still appears weekly, again as *Die Weltbühne*, in the German Democratic Republic today. Tucholsky went into exile in 1929 and committed suicide in 1935. Ossietzky was arrested in 1931, again in 1933, and his works burned; he died in 1938 as the result of his three years in the concentration camp of Papenburg-Esterwegen. Two years earlier, to Hitler's fury, he had been awarded the Nobel Peace Prize.

Yet the intellectualism of the *Weltbühne* circle did not include a denigration of true patriotism, and they were as concerned as any right-wing nationalist to see the restoration of German well-being and self-respect. It depended on where one sought these qualities. As Tucholsky subtly put it: 'Kurt Tucholsky hates "Germany". Kurt Tucholsky loves Germany.'[30] It was to be the tragedy of *Die Weltbühne* to hear its voice of reason swamped by the bawling of rabble-rousers, and to fail, like almost all the republicans of the 1920s, to forestall the destruction of the constitutional state from within, the victory of 'Germany' over Germany.

The feeling of solidarity among the politically-conscious youth of the time, who, while accepting the republican constitution as a step forward, were far from regarding it as the ideal tool for repairing the nation's fortunes, emerges strongly in the formation of the Deutsche Studentenschaft in 1919. For despite the many shades of political opinion represented in this body—and there will never be a general student organisation in which political extremes are not noisily prominent—there was little opposition to its conception of itself as a 'Pan-German student community' of universal appeal and relevance. One reason why such organisations could attract liberal intellectual support was that the concept of nation absorbed and neutralised the energy otherwise consumed by the class struggle. Students, over 95 per cent of whom in the years of the Republic were from the upper and middle classes, were expected to recognise their community of interest with the working class, and to explain to the workers what united all Germans in a *Volksgemeinschaft*; in this way one could draw the fangs of much propaganda that was socially divisive in intent or in effect.[31]

Influential works of educational philosophy such as *Der Aufbau des preussischen Bildungswesens nach der Staatsumwälzung* (1923) by Otto Bölitz, Prussian Minister of Education from 1921 to 1925, had a nationalist emphasis accepted as being in keeping with the needs of the time, and the ideals behind the famous school of Salem, founded by Prince Max von Baden in 1920, rested on a conviction of the necessity of bringing about a spiritual renewal of the defeated Fatherland. Rediscovery and idealistic reassertion of the unifying values of the past—which was what was often meant by talk of 'reform'—also dominated the philosophy of university education contained in *Gedanken zur Hochschulreform* (1919) and *Vom Wesen der Universität* (1925) by Bölitz's successor at the Prussian Ministry of Education, Carl Heinrich Becker. And both Bölitz and Becker were Social Democrats.

Becker was also involved in an incident with students which showed one of the more unpleasant aspects of German life in the 1920s as well as in the Nazi period—anti-Semitism. In 1927 over three-quarters of all students in Prussia voted for a form of university government that excluded non-Aryans from student corporations. Racial discrimination of this kind was clearly intolerable in any public body, whatever rights of self-determination it claimed, and Becker was forced to intervene in order to prevent the democratic rights of the student body being used for undemocratic ends. In Austrian universities anti-Semitic feeling ran even higher—indeed it was Austria, rather than Germany, that set the pace in the popularisation of racialist doctrines. (By one of the ironies of history it had also been in Austria, a quarter of a century earlier, that Theodor Herzl founded the World Zionist Organisation.) The national sentiments which, as many liberal-minded intellectuals of the time knew, had much in them that was sound and inspiring, all too easily spilled over into the intolerant and the destructive. As early as 1931 there was twice as much support for the Nazis in the universities as in the population as a whole.[32]

Extremism, indeed, from both the left and the right, was insistently wooing the youth of the time to its destructive cause. And youth, with little stabilising political experience to be derived from its forebears, and slight cause to believe that the Weimar constitution had finally set the nation's fortunes on their true course, had little idea which way to turn. If a sufficient number could be made to turn in one direction, the sometimes terrifying enthusiasm that youth brings to its actions could help sweep a would-be ruler to power. Hitler did not need to be told this.

The problems facing the youth of the Weimar Republic were defined in the issues of *Die Neue Rundschau*, liberal-democratic journal of the S. Fischer Verlag, that appeared in 1932. Here Jakob Wassermann, Ernst Robert Curtius, Peter Suhrkamp and others sought to direct the energy of the student generation into channels of

humanism, liberalism and historical awareness, and to wean it from
the false allurements of unbridled emotionalism, irrational commitment and self-sacrifice to the demands of a *Führerprinzip*. If a young
man looks back, says Wassermann, he sees the war; if he looks ahead,
he sees the collapse of society: 'The Communist tugs him to the left,
the Nationalist tugs him to the right. Nowhere is there a trace of
honesty or rationality, and all his good instincts are being perverted
into hate.'[33] But although he understands the psychology of this hate,
Wassermann pleads with the young not to turn this into a pretext for
waging an equally irrational generation-war by rejecting everything
their fathers had lived by: 'Not every man of 40 is an idiot or a
criminal just because he is 20 years older than you are. Nor is every
man of 50 or 60 a reactionary and an enemy. Not every father is a
fool—nor is every son a hero or a martyr.'[34]

As for the Jews—Wassermann was one—let it only be said here
that the seeds of many horrors perpetrated in Nazi Germany were
already sown in the Weimar Republic. As the effects of the Wall
Street crash of October 1929 reached Germany and millions of dollars
of American capital were withdrawn, unemployment soared, credit
became scarce, and people looked around for scapegoats among those
who managed the country's banks and finance houses. Many of these
were Jews. So began the hysterical identification of the Jews with all
the misfortunes that befell the country—the practical expression of
the racial principles enunciated by Count Arthur Gobineau, Julius
Langbehn, Houston Stewart Chamberlain, Paul de Lagarde, Alfred
Rosenberg and other purveyors of the ideas from which National
Socialism drew its dogma. And because it was so easy to couple with
the Jews the liberal-democratic politicians and intellectuals who were
responsible for founding the republic, with its 'un-German' values
that national propaganda said had proved so disastrous for the
country, a general atmosphere of intolerance and even persecution
prevailed, in which Hitler was to be in his element. Few newspapers
and journals—Carl von Ossietsky's *Weltbühne* was a shining
exception—dared to face 'the Jewish Question' head-on and speak
out against the crude irrationality that was gaining ground on all
sides.

One of the most revealing documents on the predicament of the
liberal European Jew at this time is Wassermann's *Mein Weg als
Deutscher und Jude* (1921), a fragment of autobiography written by a
man who knew both popular success as a novelist and, like Alfred
Döblin, Franz Werfel, Lion Feuchtwanger, Franz Kafka, Max Brod
and a host of others, the personal antipathy that greeted a Jew. It was
a subject to which, often with bitterness and sarcasm, but never

without dignity, he frequently returned in essays and open letters. One of these, addressed to an American magazine in 1925, conveys in its few lines more of the tragic reality of the situation than pages of description by outsiders:

A person who looks impartially at the question of racialism in Germany will not cherish great hopes for the future. The search for whipping-boys is in full swing, and when one sees, day in, day out, the methods used in political propaganda, one has to force oneself to realise that this really is the twentieth, not the sixteenth or the seventeenth century, when all manner of superstitious beliefs were directed against a virtually defenceless people, and governments, consciously or unconsciously, but with invariable success, turned their nations' discontent against the Jews. Such, roughly speaking, is the situation. Our country, ravaged by the war, weakened by hunger and blockade, demoralised by years of disappointment, has lost its sense of perception and its power of judgment, and is at the mercy of all the inflammatory lies of demagogues and desperadoes . . .

When I published my autobiographical work *Mein Weg als Deutscher und Jude* four years ago, I received from the opposing faction hundreds of letters, some of them quite remarkable. Some shocked me by their expression of amazement, even of revelation: professors, aristocratic ladies, young men all wrote with a strange naiveté, assuring me they had no idea things were like that, saying I had opened their eyes to the truth, they would now have a completely different view of the situation, etc. etc. My hopes rose. I will not say that they have been utterly dashed, since that would be to despair of human nature, but there is at the moment a great black cloud above our heads. The name of the phantom that threatens us was coined by the historian Gothein in his investigations into the Spanish Inquisition: he called it racial arrogance (*Blutdünkel*). In this concept lies the source of all the chauvinism and racial conflict that hangs over the world today.

In 200 years people will look back on our age with the same astonishment as we now look back on witchhunts. But this does not exonerate me, or anyone else, from the clear duty to strive with all the power of my mind and heart to make men more humane and to prevent the white race from succumbing to this self-administered poison.[35]

Slowness to recognise, and, if recognised, reluctance to confront political issues directly is not a novel feature of German public life. One form of compensation for this lack has often been the transference of a problem from the practical to the intellectual realm, the conversion of a socio-political issue into a metaphysical exercise. The years following the end of World War I released a climate particularly favourable to the growth of thought about cosmic purpose, about the powerlessness of man to escape from the shackles of his alienated condition. The influence of the nineteenth-century Danish thinker Søren Kierkegaard, spiritual father of modern existentialism and source of the modern concept of *Angst*, grew apace, and the novels and short stories of Franz Kafka came to be seen as the characteristic statement in literature of the modern human predicament.

To these years belongs also the philosophical investigation of the nature of contemporary existence by Martin Heidegger, whose key works *Sein und Zeit* (1927), *Kant und das Problem der Metaphysik* (1929) and *Vom Wesen des Grundes* (1929) are of central importance in the development of modern European existentialist thought. The basic concepts with which Heidegger operates—*Existenz, Angst, Nichts*, the ontological search for what he calls 'das Sein des Seienden'—also reflect in their own way the spirit of transcendentalism and the urge to conceptualisation which so often find their way to the surface of German intellectual life. For Heidegger the question of human existence and human nature is inseparable from the question of Being itself, and his quest leads beyond the subjective and the psychological, but in the context of the German 1920s his analysis of personal existence, of the agencies of freedom and responsibility in a world that has lost its way, also reflects on its own plane the *Zeitgeist* of a society whose tensions are barely disguised and ultimately so destructive. Heidegger's unhappy contribution to this destruction, a few years later, was to put his authority as Rector of the University of Heidelberg behind Hitler and the Nazi cause.

It has always been recognised that Hitler rose to power on the shoulders of industrialists like Hugenberg and Thyssen; of the aristocracy, represented by Chancellor Franz von Papen; and of the army, personified by the aged President Hindenburg. It was Hindenburg who dissolved the Reichstag in June 1932, and in the election of 31 July the Nazis won a huge victory, holding more seats (230) than any party had ever held in the history of the German parliament. The victory of the new nationalism was complete, and the steps leading to the subsequent creation of a one-party state, with supreme power residing in the hands of the dictator of that one party, were mere formalities.

But long before this it had become evident that popular confidence in republican government had virtually disappeared, and that the massive swing of votes to the National Socialists in September 1930 involved the capture of the allegiance of large numbers of the Protestant middle-class (the strength of the Catholic Centre Party remained almost unchanged at around 12 per cent of the votes cast in all the Reichstag elections between 1920 and 1933). Chancellor Brüning, whose dissolution of the Reichstag had led to the election of September 1930, had already cut deeply into the supremacy of parliament by having recourse to the emergency executive powers which the constitution provided, saying that he viewed these powers as 'a means for educating the German people to political thinking'.

The disarray of the parties in the Reichstag can be gauged from the fact that the opposition to Brüning's act took the form of a vote of no-confidence in which Social Democrats, Communists, Nationalists and Nazis all enthusiastically joined.

Yet the Reichstag only reflected the divisions and contradictions in the country itself. After 1930 the Nazis began systematically to infiltrate the Prussian police and other organs of civilian power, and to provoke violence against the Communists, the Jews and any other groups which could be portrayed as 'enemies of the people'. Hitler's consciousness of purpose was unmistakable, though many failed to see it. He could even claim that he had come to power not *via* revolution (the revolution was still to come) but *via* the ballot-box, and that he was made Chancellor by Hindenburg in 1933 without offending any item of the constitution. And had he not sworn the same oath as his 20 predecessors in the office of Chancellor of the Republic?

It may be more strictly accurate to talk of Hitler's *Machtergreifung* in terms of pseudo-legality than of true legality, but for the people involved at the time, and for the subsequent development of the Third Reich, it was an academic distinction. Certainly, as the collapse of political parties and intellectual and moral values showed, the constitutional state offered little resistance. Maybe in 1932 Hitler's triumph was not yet absolutely inevitable, but the fall of the Republic was. And the only power to offer a viable alternative to the Nazis was that of conservative nationalism, backed by the army.

The official pronouncement of the death of the Weimar Republic came on March 21, 1933, when President Hindenburg, Chancellor Hitler and the Reichstag deputies, (except the Communists, who had not been invited) assembled in the Garnisonkirche in Potsdam to hear the proclamation of the Third Reich. But the obituaries had already been written, and the cause of death was open to public scrutiny—not one single attack from without—but prolonged internal bleeding. The Garnisonkirche has since been razed to the ground by the efforts, first of British bombers, then of the new city council. The legacy of March 1933 has proven less easy to dispose of.

NOTES

1. To be found in K. Liebknecht, *Ausgewählte Reden, Briefe und Aufsätze*, (Berlin, 1952), 296 ff
2. The full text, with a complete list of signatures, is given in H. Kellermann, *Der Krieg der Geister* (Weimar, 1915), 64 ff
3. See K. Schwabe, *Wissenschaft und Kriegsmoral* (Göttingen, 1969), 38

4. Moeller van den Bruck, *Der preussische Stil* (Breslau, 1931),

5. *Friedrich und die Grosse Koalition* (Berlin, 1915), 16

6. This number has not been used.

7. This number has not been used.

8. *Untersuchungsausschuss über die Weltkriegsverantwortlichkeit. Zweiter Unter-Ausschuss* (Berlin, 1920), 214

9. *Untersuchungsausschuss über die Weltkriegsverantwortlichkeit. Vierter Unterausschuss. Die Ursachen des deulischen Zusammenbruchs im Jahre 1918*, ed. A. Philipp (12 vols. Berlin, 1925–9), 1, 153

10. Harry Graf Kessler, *Tagebücher 1918–1937* (Frankfurt, 1961), 32–3

11. Rilke, *Briefe an eine junge Frau*, (Leipzig, n.d.), 43 ff

12. *ibid.* 27

13. *ibid.* 4

14. quoted in K.S. Pinson, *Modern Germany* (2nd ed. New York/London, 1966), 384–5

15. op. cit., 182

16. O. Spengler, *Politische Schriften* (Munich/Berlin, 1934), vii

17. A. Rosenberg, *Geschichte der deutschen Republik* (Karlsbad, 1935), 105

18. *Studies in Diplomacy and Statecraft* (London, 1942), 163

19. E.E. Dwinger, *Wir rufen Deutschland* (Leipzig, 1932), 16

20. C. Zuckmayer, *Als wär's ein Stück von mir* (Vienna, 1966), 311

21. *ibid.* 312, 313, 314

22. Stefan Zweig, *Die Welt von Gestern* (1944), 286

23. *ibid.* 286

24. H.A. Winkler, *Mittelstand, Demokratie und Nationalsozialismus*, (Köln, 1972), 78

25. Stefan Zweig, *ibid.* 286–7

26. *From Caligari to Hitler* (Princeton, 1947) 5 ff

27. *Der Hitler-Prozess.* Record of the court proceedings in Munich in 1924. (Deutscher Volksverlag, Munich, 1924, 28)

28. see the works of E.J. Gumbel, *Vier Jahre politischer Mord* (Berlin, 1922) and *Verräter verfallen der Fehme* (Berlin, 1929). Gumbel, a professor at the University of Heidelberg and a well-known pacifist, was one of the objects of nationalist student demonstrations during the last years of the Republic against academics of 'liberal' sympathies. For an account of such incidents see Helmut Kuhn, *Die deutsche Universität im Dritten Reich* (Munich, 1966), 37 ff.

29. see K.S. Pinson, op. cit. 452

30. *Gesammelte Werke 1907–1932* (Reinbek, 1960–1), II, 1009

31. cf. J. Melzer, 'Die völkische Studentenbewegung auf den deutschen Hochschulen' (*Akademische Turnbundesblätter* XXXIV, Heft 3, 1921, 26 ff) and J. Schwarz, *Studenten in der Weimarer Republik* (Berlin, 1971), 338 ff.

32. cf. A. Flitner, *Deutsches Geistesleben und Nationalsozialismus* (Tübingen, 1965), 33 ff.

33. 'Rede an die studentische Jugend über das Leben im Geiste; Zum Goethetag 1932' (*Die Neue Rundschau* XLIII, 1. Teil, 1932, 530

34. *ibid.* 544

35. Wassermann, *Lebensdienst: Gesammelte Studien, Erfahrungen und Reden aus drei Jahrzehnten* (Leipzig/Zurich, 1928), 178–9

CHAPTER TWO

The Trail of Expressionism

OUR world must be made new, but this can only come about in agonised convulsions—there is no other way. The days of serenity, of gracefulness, of reticence, of modesty are over. God does not come to us ill-starred mortals on the wings of a gentle breeze. Expressionism has a mission in which beauty plays no part. When expression has become the sole will and principle of an age, and when the naked soul kneels down and cries out to God, beauty is like a robe that has been consumed by flames, while despair manifests itself in forms filled only with the sound of screams and prayers.[1]

Nowhere have aesthetic values and the principle of art-for-art's sake been so flouted as in this poetry, which has come to be called 'modern' or 'expressionist' because it erupts, explodes, has an intensity which it must have in order to break through the hostile crust of aestheticism . . . One cannot emphasise too often that this poetry is characterised by its intensity. Never in world literature have the screams, the disasters and the yearnings of an age reverberated with such vehemence, such poignance, such destructiveness, as from this savage band of prophets and martyrs whose hearts were pierced, not by the romantic shafts of Eros but by the agonies inflicted by their own condemned youth, by a society they detested and by the years in which acts of murder had been forced upon them.[2]

The first of these utterances was made in 1918 by the critic Margarete Susman, the second in 1920 by the one-time avant-garde poet and publicist Kurt Pinthus. Both characterise the mingled moods of disillusion, intolerance and thrustful self-assertion that settled upon many who had been born into the Second Reich, been dragged through the experience of the Great War and now found themselves in a directionless world whose pseudo-values they angrily rejected.

Or, from a quite different source:

The war made deep inroads into art. Man cried out in his agony; racked with pain, tortured, crippled, he mounted the pulpit and preached with the tongues of men and of angels . . . Artists expected everything of the suffering man who was 'good'.

—a retrospective glance by a man whose career was just beginning at that time: Bertolt Brecht.[3]

The impulses that came to be assembled under the banner of expressionism had been felt in all the arts—painting and music as well as literature—well before the Great War. Indeed, what issued in the national violence and hatred of 1914–18 had already been acted out in the aesthetic realm where poets, dramatists, artists and critics projected in their own ways the forces of disruption that led to the catastrophe of war and the final collapse of a way of life. In Germany the term 'Expressionism' itself seems to have been first used in 1911,[4] but the tendencies it was called upon to define had long been evident, as had its points of conflict with the beliefs and values that had sustained the nineteenth century. In fact, this opposition to the past, above all in the forms of naturalism and impressionism, was virtually the only point on which the heterogeneous 'expressionist' groups agreed: the world was out of joint, life had become degraded and empty, man an ignoble creature of animal instincts, immoral urges and crude, despicable ambitions. But though the diagnosis was unanimous, the prescriptions for cure were legion. Some, like Reinhard Sorge and Franz Werfel, sought the solace of religion, others, like Georg Trakl, of drugs and states of ecstasy; some, like Ernst Toller and Johannes R. Becher, saw salvation in political commitment, others, like Gottfried Benn and Alfred Döblin, preached a negative statement of the human condition as the only positive truth; some found the roots of the crisis in the individual personality, others in the state of society.

Divergent as these tendencies were, they found expression in a violence of tone common to all who aligned themselves with the new attitudes. The characteristic sound became *der expressionistische Schrei*, an agonised scream of protest at the cheapening of human life and the soullessness of human institutions, an emotional, at times hysterical outburst against the older generation, against social inequality, against the stultification of human potentialities, against the denial of human dignity. The cry is not for a new 'expressionist' artist but a new 'expressionist' man, a man who would re-establish the reality of his divine origin and reassert his true creative powers. 'Expressionism believes in the all-possible,' wrote Friedrich Markus Huebner in 1920. 'It is the philosophy of utopia. It puts man back in the centre of creation, giving him the power to fill the void as he wishes with lines, colours, and sounds, with plants and animals, with God, with space and time, with his own ego.'[5]

There was a kind of desperate enthusiasm in the air, an atmosphere of intolerance and *Rausch* expressed already in the names of the pre-war journals in which the new mood and the new principles were first made public, journals such as *Der Sturm, Aktion* (both founded in 1910) and *Revolution* (1912). Flamboyant claims were made in the name of the rights of the individual personality, and sonorous phrases filled the air. We await the advent, wrote Otto Flake, of 'a higher intellectuality and an increasing emphasis on the total personality as a determining and integrating force . . . the ultimate source of vital energy . . . . We are the moderns—it is we who recognise the vital, animal, dynamic facts of life.'[6]

Already in its programmatic stage, both before, during and after the Great War, the expressionist movement had plainly identifiable antecedents. Its subjectivity, its passionate commitment, its emphasis on the emotional and the irrational rather than on calculated poise and intellectual refinement recall Baroque, Sturm und Drang, Romanticism. Lyric poets looked on the one hand to the effusiveness of Klopstock, on the other hand to the concentrated 'expressive' power of the language of Hölderlin and Goethe. Dramatists embraced the soul-revealing intensity of Strindberg and the violence of Kleist and Büchner. And dominating the entire scene stood the figures of Dostoevsky and Nietzsche:—Dostoevsky, through his radical morality and his religious power, 'a divine power that rises like a giant from out of the crater of events', as Kurt Pinthus put it;[7] and Nietzsche, through his intoxicating Dionysianism, his overthrow of nineteenth-century morality and values, and the steely penetration of his remorseless language.

Expressionism, both as a movement and as a mood, belonged to youth, a youth in revolt. The oldest among them, like Alfred Döblin, Georg Kaiser and Otto Flake, were in their thirties at the outbreak of the war; the majority were of an age to be sent immediately to the front, and many—Reinhard Sorge, Alfred Lichtenstein, Gerrit Engelke, Ernst Stadler, August Stramm, the painters Franz Marc and August Macke—died in action. And as 'youth's a stuff will not endure', so much of the work of expressionist *littérateurs*, in so far as they were circumscribed by the principles of the movement, remained a body of youthful ephemera. For them expressionism was both a beginning and an end, a goal in itself, and much of this literature, above all the lyric poetry, is an undifferentiated mass, a kind of communal product by a faceless assembly. Only a few—Döblin, Werfel, Toller, Gottfried Benn, Johannes R. Becher, Georg Kaiser—of those who had thrown in their lot with the expressionist cause succeeded in surviving its hold over them and emerging with personalities strong enough to respond to new situations and create significant new works of art.

Benn and Becher, indeed, reveal in their very different ways how the apocalyptic claims of expressionism, having failed to substantiate themselves, came to be converted into other promises of spiritual and aesthetic salvation. Benn found refuge in moments of irrationality and cultural disillusionment, affecting a nihilistic distaste for emotion and a brittle scepticism of the possibility of meaningful human relationships—one form of the expressionists' hatred of the industrial society that has degraded human life. For him the motto of the expressionist generation was to be found in the last line of Rilke's *Requiem* for Graf Wolf Kalckreuth:

Wer spricht von Siegen? Überstehn ist alles.

The world of 1910 to 1920 was an *'untergangsgeweihte Welt'*, as Benn called it, a world doomed to destruction, and what united the Futurists, the Cubists, the Surrealists and the German expressionists was 'a basic urge to destroy so-called reality, to pierce relentlessly to the heart of things. . . . It is not a matter of presenting a subject in a finite form but of establishing a context of emotional excitement, of mystical bonds forged by pure, transcendental forces.'[8]

Becher, on the other hand, looked for a quasi-metaphysical power which, like the Christian Church, gave a promise of salvation and a form of authority that would preserve man from anarchy—and found it in Marxism. An indefatigable champion of the cause of proletarian revolution and of the interests of the Soviet Union, he spent 10 years in exile in Moscow from 1935 to 1945 and was Minister of Culture in the German Democratic Republic from 1954 until his death four years later. And what Becher found in one form of authoritarianism, a fellow one-time expressionist, the poet and dramatist Hanns Johst—S.S. Brigade-führer, President of the *Reichsschrifttumskammer* and the *Deutsche Akademie der Dichtung* under Hitler—found in another.

Far more telling in the context of political involvement, and of far greater intrinsic interest than such political poetry is the graphic and plastic art of the period. In various individual ways painters, among them many of those who shortly before had helped to project expressionism as a movement, were turning from the ideal to the physical reality and the social function of art, from the 'expression' to the object. This *Neue Sachlichkeit*, or 'Neo-Realism'—a convenient term, but one which, like expressionism, encompasses a variety of sometimes conflicting tendencies—retained on the one side a certain abstraction, a social utopianism, and a functional formalism found at its most powerful in the artists and teachers associated with the Bauhaus.

On the other side it struck out in the cause of social revolution, unsentimental in its pity and with a savage bitterness that often issued in caricature. Cold-hearted employers, slimy profiteers, the frivolous pleasure-seekers of a degenerate bourgeois society, set against the downtrodden worker, the social outcast, the grimy misery of back-street slums and the degradation of poverty—such tabloid contrasts, drawn from the urban industrial scene, above all in Berlin, make up a great deal of this art, art used as a political weapon. The paintings and drawings of Oskar Nerlinger, Otto Dix and George Grosz, together with the graphics and sculptures of Käthe Kollwitz, show at its most powerful the social situation of the 1920s seen in terms of the class struggle, as do the photomontages of John Heartfield (Helmut Herzfelde). Others, like Otto Nagel and Carl Hofer, felt an equal social commitment but expressed it in less radically political ways.

Pledged to the social function of art in a very different way were the members of the Bauhaus, a public institute of arts and crafts founded in 1919 by the architect Walter Gropius in Weimar and transferred to Dessau in 1925. For Feininger, Paul Klee, Gerhard Marcks, Kandinsky and the other artists Gropius engaged, the Bauhaus was an educational project in which aesthetic ideals and the techniques of practical craftsmanship, including those of modern industry, should together provide a basis for the function of art in society. During its brief existence (it was closed down by the Nazis in 1933, when Mies van der Rohe was its director), the Bauhaus left an influence in form and design (schools, housing projects, furniture, industrial and domestic textiles) that has been felt all over the world, and its principles of functional art in society have become part and parcel of modern educational programmes.

For many artists, however, whether of expressionist, neo-realist or any other persuasion, art had little to do with political involvement. Paul Kornfeld coined the terms *metapolitisch* to define their position. The painter Max Beckmann, looking back in middle age at the 1920s, said: 'I was never politically active in any way'[9], while his older contemporary Emil Nolde, painter of some of the most striking and best-known expressionist pictures, found himself in an anti-Semitic, anti-intellectual stance only as a result—and this was true of many—of his attraction to allegedly non-political concepts of chthonic Nordic values and irrational appeals to *Blut-und-Boden* virtues. (For the record one should add that this did not save Nolde from assignment by the Nazis to the class of 'decadent' artists, and from 1938 onwards he was forbidden to paint.)

Given the intensity with which the new message was preached, and the enthusiasm with which the avant-garde journals were received, one could be forgiven for thinking that these expressionist writers had a monopoly of authenticity of emotion and seriousness of purpose. In truth their art was made no more 'expressive' by the theoretical claims that underpinned it, nor did its subjectivity differ in kind from that of earlier, spiritually kindred movements. Moreover there was at the time a ground-swell of attitudes and tendencies that for a while carried many writers along with it. Inevitably, the greatest are those who were carried the shortest distance.

It was not only literary activity that felt this ground-swell. Indeed, whereas one may compare German literary expressionism with an explosion, violent but short-lived, the course of the visual arts, of music, and perhaps most striking of all, of the production techniques of theatre and cinema, underwent radical and lasting change. The Munich *Blauer Reiter* group of painters, led by Kandinsky and Franz Marc, built on the new attitudes towards art of the Dresden group—Ernst Ludwig Kirchner, Erich Heckel and Karl Schmidt-Rottluff—founded in 1905 with the name *Die Brücke*. The notion of 'objective' reality, which rested on a faith in the power of human perception, came to be seen as a chimera, and the portrayal of visible objects in a spirit of representationalism as a betrayal of the artist's vocation. In its place came the depiction of subjective realities, experimentation with the psychological effects of forms and colours and the relationships between them, non-figurative, non-representational exercises in the realm of absolutes and supra-personal realities. This is the birth of modern abstract art, the statement of the condition to which Kandinsky, in his book *Über das Geistige in der Kunst* (1910), claimed that painting would ultimately and inevitably attain. In this perspective a development such as Cubism, for example, emerges in its abstraction and anti-realism as basically expressionist; so also does an extreme movement like Dada. Expressionism in painting was not a prerogative of German art, but its effects have probably been more profound and its achievements more striking in Germany than elsewhere, and its content of abstraction and subjective idealism makes it a phenomenon peculiarly expressive of the German cultural and intellectual tradition.

By the same token it is appropriate that expressionism in music too emerges in a German—or more properly Austrian—context. In 1911, a year before Kandinsky's *Über das Geistige in der Kunst*, Arnold Schoenberg published his *Harmonielehre* in Vienna. Three years earlier he had written the Three Piano Pieces, Op. 11, his first published exercises in atonality, a radical negation of the principles on which all Western music had been built. These short, stuttering pieces have the same revolutionary impact, the same determination to seek other forms of 'reality' than those which had sustained the nineteenth century, including the current impressionism of Debussy and the young Stravinsky, as the paintings of Kandinsky, Klee and Feininger. Schoenberg himself also painted oils and pastels which were exhibited alongside those of the *Blauer Reiter* painters. His overthrow of classical tonality is the counterpart of Kandinsky's rejection of representationalism: the old laws have lost their validity, the old conventions no longer apply. Expression has become its own justification.

The greatest work of musical expressionism—among the operas, songs, etc. of Arnold Schoenberg, Kurt Weill and Ernst Křenek (*Jonny spielt auf*, 1927), and with the possible exception of Schoenberg's *Moses und Aaron*, which was not completed until 1951—is both an epitome of the European 1920s and one of the masterpieces of twentieth-century music: Alban Berg's *Wozzeck*. The sordid, tragic story told in Büchner's fragmentary drama *Woyzeck*, with its lurid cruelty and sentimentality, the smouldering violence of its atmosphere and the ejaculatory harshness of its tone—this is the stuff of expressionism. To this Berg brings music of an almost unbearable intensity. Classical in the details of its formal structure, atonal in musical language, that is, based on the enthronement of disintegration and relativity as structural principles, *Wozzeck* is the same shattering experience today as it was at its first performance in Berlin in 1925. The world's great operas—*Don Giovanni*, *Fidelio*, the *Ring des Nibelungen*, *Otello* and so on—are not remembered for the achievements of da Ponte, Sonnleithner, Wagner the poet, or Boito. Their greatness is a greatness in music. But Büchner's tragedy itself has an impact as powerful and as modern as Berg's music. *Wozzeck* is perhaps the nearest we have yet come to a 'total experience' of opera in a work of overwhelming power and genius.

In the theatre the dominant personality, from the time he took over the Deutsches Theater in Berlin from Otto Brahm in 1905, was Max Reinhardt, whose long reign and immense influence stretched from the neo-Romanticism of the early years of the century through the years of expressionism and the Weimar Republic down to 1933, when, as a Jew, he was driven into exile. In Reinhardt's wake came two influential producers: one was the revolutionary Erwin Piscator, with his left-wing agitprop theatre and his technical innovations in the use of film, loudspeakers, posters and simultaneous scenes; the other was Leopold Jessner, a determined innovator who introduced what to many were alarming 'expressionist' techniques into the production both of classical and modern dramas in the 1920s.

These techniques were to show themselves especially strikingly in the realm of the cinema. The nightmarish plot and, even more, the story of the genesis and creation, of the famous *Cabinet des Dr. Caligari*, made in 1919 and released in Berlin the following year, mirror the extraordinary compound of disillusionment, cruelty, moral earnestness and light-headed hedonism left in Germany at the end of the war. The demonic qualities of this film, expressed in sentiments of protest and revolt, and through techniques of shock and mystery, set the tone for Fritz Lang's *Dr Mabuse, der Spieler*, Paul Leni's *Das Wachsfigurenkabinett*, Lupu Pick's *Scherben* and many other films of undisguised expressionist derivation.

In all these realms of activity the roots of what came to be seen as the characteristic moods and achievements of the culture of Weimar Germany had been firmly planted in the pre-war years. Although expressionism in literature, painting, sculpture, architecture (the Einstein observatory in Potsdam, built 1920–1, is one of the classic examples), music and the theatre is inseparable from the ethos of the Republic, the declarations of aesthetic and philosophical intent were issued in the days of Empire. The war, and the revolution that followed it, inevitably shaped the course of intellectual life and offered new motifs to writers and artists, but the radical change of direction had already been made. Likewise the disintegration of the pre-war social and political order, utter and irreparable by 1918, is clearly mirrored in pre-war art and literature.

Although during the war and the years that followed there may have been certain common impulses in the various arts, there was little by way of concerted, programmed action. One sphere in which many of the divergent interests converged, however, was the new-found science of psychology and its revelations. When Freud's first work, *The Interpretation of Dreams*, appeared in 1900, it attracted little attention. But with the publication of *The Psychopathology of Everyday Life*, the *Three Essays on Sexuality* and other studies in the years that followed, together with the academic following that Freud's lectures in Vienna were beginning to attract, the whole intellectual world, scientific and artistic, critical and creative, realised that a new area of human reality was opening up before them. Freud offered a new theory of the mind, making explicit, as he put it, 'the scientific method by which the unconscious could be studied' and exposing a bewildering new range of human situations and motifs which liberated in all the arts, but especially in literature, revolutionary new views on the nature of human conduct and human responsibility. In 1910 a branch of the International Psychoanalytical Association was found in Berlin. The name Freud became a household word, and the epithet Freudian applied, often indiscriminately, to extravagant and irrational behaviour which there now appeared no need either to justify or, if confessedly unjustifiable, to amend.

Writers of the expressionistic persuasion opposed any thought of a positivistic science of the mind, governed by the laws of causality, as they rejected the positivistic biological and economic claims of the nineteenth century, but the shift away from environmental, that is, peripheral, considerations towards the 'inner man', Man of the mind, matched their own scheme of values. The human personality claimed the right to 'express' itself in its uniqueness and its infinite variety, without recourse to rationalisation or conformism. And in these depths of personality lay the roots of the New Man invoked by the expressionists, 'man set in the centre of creation', in Huebner's words, man as the touchstone of meaning and the measure of achievement. Such attitudes persisted in much German literature, art and thought in the years following the war.

NOTES

1. M. Susman, 'Expressionismus' (*Die Masken. Blätter des Düsseldorfer Schauspielhauses,* Jahrgang XIV, 1918–9, 96)
2. K. Pinthus, from the Preface to the anthology *Menschheitsdämmerung ; Symphonic jüngster Dichtung* (Berlin, 1920), XIV–V
3. 'Offener Brief an Heinrich George', 1933
4. R. Samuel and R. H. Thomas (*Expressionism in German Life, Literature, and the Theatre,* Philadelphia, 1971, 10) trace it to the art critic Wilhelm Worringer; J. Bithell (*Modern German Literature 1880– 1950,* 1959, 154) credits it to the poet Otto zur Linde, editor of the literary review *Charon.* But in both cases it is the year 1911. It appears earlier in France and earlier still in England (see G. Kaiser, *Die Koralle, Gas I* and *Gas II,* ed. B. J. Kenworthy, 1968, xx)
5. 'Der Expressionismus in Deutschland' (*Preussische Jahrbücher* 173, May 1920; reproduced in *Expressionismus. Der Kampf um eine literarische Bewegung,* ed. P. Raabe, Munich, 1965, 136)
6. 'Von der jüngsten Literatur' (*Die Neue Rundschau* 26, II, 1915; reproduced in *Expressionismus. Der Kampf um eine literarische Bewegung,* 61, 65
7. 'Zur jüngsten Dichtung' (original version in *Die weissen Blätter* 2, 1915; revised version reproduced in *Expressionismus. Der Kampf um eine literarische Bewegung,* 71
8. From an Introduction written in 1955 to *Lyrik des expressionistischen Jahrzehnts* (Wiesbaden, 1955), 10
9. Quoted in B.S. Myers, *The German Expressionists: A Generation in Revolt* (London, 1963), 254

CHAPTER THREE

'The lady doth protest too much, methinks': Drama from Hasenclever's *Antigone* to Brecht's 'Lehrstücke'

WHEN a new literary programme is asserted, inspired by ideals that lie outside the field of literature, the problem at once presents itself of how to accommodate the new impulses to the existing genres of literary expression. The demands of prose fiction, for example, are different from those of lyric poetry, and however novel a work of art may be, its meaning, both in formal and substantial terms, rests on its relationship to the body of art-works upon which it has supervened — its relationship, in other words, to the tradition of which it is itself the latest moment. That one can only approach the new in terms of the old, or seek to understand the unknown in terms of the known, is a truism. But it is no less true for that.

All artists confront this reality, however they assess their position in the continuum to which they belong. But it is the protesters, the radical innovators, the 'angry young men', of whatever period, who set themselves the hardest task. Their new visions have to be given coherent form, while at the same time the finished work, as a product of the imagination, has to offer a measure of aesthetic satisfaction. And the more clearly defined the contours of the form in which the artist chooses to cast his work, the more difficult the accommodation becomes. Narrative fiction and lyric poetry are less prescriptive, less circumscribing; with drama come more conditions and expectations that encroach, persist, impose, above all through the activity of actors, designers, directors and all the other intermediaries between the work and its public. Here, perhaps, the challenge is at its greatest; equally great is the immediate reward for success.

The naturalists had presented man as subject to the laws of material nature, as conditioned by forces against which it was pointless and meaningless to rebel, forces which by definition constituted 'reality'. The expressionists preached the absolute inner freedom of man, man as the agent of humanism which would lead to the establishment of the new Jerusalem. Behind the utterly committed but generally doomed attempts of their heroes to reform the world stand the dramatists themselves, manoeuvring their *dramatis personae* into pre-determined postures and making them the spokesmen of their own world-view.

The early *loci classici* of expressionist tragedy such as Reinhard

43

Johannes Sorge's *Der Bettler* (1912), Paul Kornfeld's *Die Verführung* (1913) and Hasenclever's *Der Sohn* (1914) have their centre of gravity in the domestic and personal spheres, specifically in the conflict between father and son, symbolising the clash between the old and the new, between the worldly wisdom of the establishment and the impatient ideals of the young. A strong strand of sexuality, recalling Frank Wedekind, whose dramas anticipate those of the expressionists in many ways, also runs through these situations. The figure of Freud is not far away either. Probably Hans Henny Jahnn, who acquired the title 'Prophet der Unzucht' for his obsession with incest (*Pastor Ephraim Magnus*, 1919; *Der gestohlene Gott*, 1923) and other abnormal sex relationships (*Der Arzt, sein Weib, sein Sohn*, 1922) represents this concern at its least edifying. It was a concern that was to stay with Jahnn through the 1920s, through his exile in Denmark during the Third Reich—perhaps his really was 'degenerate art'—and on to his late play *Armut, Reichtum, Mensch und Tier* (1948), with its uneasy motif of a relationship between a man and a horse.

The war, and the revolution that followed it, gave the conflict of generations a social and political twist, and the uncomprehending, oppressive power that stood in the way of the realisation of human ideals came to be identified with the state. 'Official policy', 'the national interest', 'political expediency' and similar slogans, argued the young generation, were mindless Shibboleths, mechanically invoked in justification of acts of inhumanity and immorality. As society itself was rotten at the roots, so all forms of social organisation were diseased, the infection showing itself at its most virulent in the largest of such organisations, the nation-state. Modern capitalist society rested on the exploitation of human beings for the economic advantage of the few, with an accompanying depersonalisation and dehumanisation of life—what Karl Marx called 'alienation'—and the activities of this society could only issue in imperialism and war. Without surrendering their principle that a new society pre-supposed a new man, writers sought to stir public opinion to transform the discredited values that had brought Europe to disaster.

What better medium through which to accomplish this than the theatre, time-honoured institution for the graphic presentation of moral issues and for inculcating beliefs and values in the public mind? In an essay called 'Das Theater von Morgen', published in Siegfried Jacobsohn's journal *Die Schaubühne* in 1916, Walter Hasenclever demanded a 'theatre for art, politics and philosophy' to be established 'on that foundation we need in order to move the world.' And standing on that foundation, they would proclaim their cosmic message, a message that would transcend all personal limitations. 'A proclamation that is uttered six times will penetrate even the deafest ear', says the Billionaire's son in Georg Kaiser's play *Gas*.

So Hasenclever makes his *Antigone* (1917) an attack on war and on the classes he believes responsible for it, and a call to rebellion in the name of the values of the world to come. This is no simple re-telling of the classical story but an impassioned, sometimes hysterical outburst against violence, against tyrants whose rule rests solely on their control of that most despicable of the agents of government—the army. Only the troops obey Creon's order to seize Antigone, whose crime is to have given decent burial to her fallen brother Polynices: the people of Thebes refuse to lay hands on her, and when she sees this, she knows that the values for which she stands have won the day:

> Die Liebe hat gesiegt.
> Gott ist uns gnädig.

> (Love is victorious.
> God has been merciful to us.)
>   (II 5.)

Not for nothing is the list of *Dramatis personae* headed by 'The People of Thebes'

Behind the figure of Creon, King of Thebes, stands Kaiser Wilhelm II, less an individual tyrant than the chief executive of what Hasenclever portrays as a desperate, ruthless régime (a later parallel is Brecht's *Antigone des Sophokles*, a free adaptation of Hölderlin's translation, set in the final year of World War II, with Creon cast as a murderous tyrant and Polynices hanged by the S.S. as a deserter). Yet the masses over whom Creon rules are no idealised victims, with a latent virtue and nobility waiting only for the opportunity to display themselves, but fickle, easily led, sometimes cruel. At one moment he can whip them into a frenzy of hate against Antigone, making them scream 'Stone her!' At the next he turns proudly to the audience to announce: 'This is the voice of the people!' Only minutes later Antigone, with a speech denouncing the futility of violence and appealing to the power of love and compassion, has the starving masses kissing her feet and shouting at Creon to release her:

> Paläste wanken. Die Macht ist zu Ende.
> Wer gross war, stürzt in den Abgrund;
> Die Tore donnern zu.
> Wer alles besass, hat alles verloren;
> Der Knecht im Schweiss seiner Hände
> Ist reicher als er.
> Folgt mir! Ich will euch führen.
> Der Wind steigt aus den Trümmern,

Die neue Welt bricht an . . . .
Brot und Früchte für jedermann.
Blut ist geflossen.
Der Krieg versinkt.
Völker reichen sich die Hände.

(Palaces totter. Power is at an end.
Those who were once great will plunge into the abyss,
The gates crash shut behind them.
Those who owned everything have lost everything;
The slave sweating at his job
Is richer than they.
Follow me! I shall lead you.
The wind stirs among the ruins;
The new world dawns . . . .
Food and rewards for everyone;
Blood has flowed;
War will perish;
Nations will stretch out their hands in friendship.)

(V. 3.)

Whereas the Son, in Hasenclever's earlier drama of that name, recalls the hero as social protester familiar from the run-of-the-mill tragedies of *Sturm und Drang*, Antigone, as the spokesman of a new personal and political morality, belongs in the line of revolutionary heroes from Karl Moor in *Die Räuber* and Marquis Posa in *Don Carlos*. As Hasenclever's own convictions drive Antigone forwards, leading her to sacrifice her life in the knowledge that it is her values, not Creon's, that will prevail, so Schiller stands behind his revolutionary heroes, whose hubris brings their downfall but whose humane principles represent the hope for the salvation of the world. Kaiser's *Hölle, Weg, Erde* (1919) and Hanns Johst's *Thomas Paine* (1927) are other expressionist dramas in the same revolutionary mould. Indeed, the very titles—August Stramm's *Erwachen* (1915) and *Kräfte* (1915), Paul Zech's *Empor* (1916), Toller's *Die Wandlung* (1918) and *Die Maschinenstürmer* (1922), Kaltnecker's *Die Opferung* (1918), Hasenclever's *Die Menschen* (1918) and *Jenseits* (1920), Barlach's *Die Sintflut* (1924)—reveal the blend of apocalyptic fervour and reforming determination which invoked the terms 'Erlösungsdrama', 'Verkündigungsdrama' and 'Wandlungsdrama' to define these works. Less flatteringly, it is these same qualities, in their more naive, more lurid, more extravagant manifestations, that led such programmatic dramas of revolution and innate human goodness in the post-war period to be sardonically dubbed 'O Mensch' plays.

This is an inescapable consequence of the expressionist view of life. Since tragedy, in their eyes, emerged not from a conflict between man and some exterior force, such as his environment, but from the nature of man himself, their portrayals of individual characters became synecdochic searches for the essential and the typical, and tended towards an abstraction and an unreality which stage-drama does not willingly bear. Characters are called 'The Son', 'The Father', 'The Patriot', 'The Old Man', 'The Nameless One'—we recall 'The Stranger', 'The Beggar' and 'The Doctor' in Strindberg's *To Damascus*. Whatever wider representative quality a stage-character may have, he must in the first instance stand as a credible individual within the circumstances into which he has been set. The expressionist hero, mouthpiece of his creator, loses himself in an eloquent lyricism through which the great human issues are rhetorically reviewed, and we miss the philosophical and aesthetic satisfaction which the story of a truly individual human character would give.

The free-verse style of Hasenclever's *Antigone*, ranging from hard, staccato ejaculations to the emotional, almost Baroque oratory by which Antigone sways the masses, matches that of the expressionist lyric poetry of the period and brings to the work a certain tense dignity which the more melodramatic *Der Sohn*, cast in prose, does not have. In *Die Menschen* (1918), and again in *Jenseits* (1920), the sharp rattle of short words and phrases becomes deafening, inducing that numbness by which the mind was to be made receptive to a mystical message—a message rooted in Hasenclver's new experience of Swedenborg. Stylistically the timelessness and spacelessness of *Die Menschen*—the scene of the action is given as 'The World', the time as 'The Present'—remind one of the dream-sequence in Strindberg's *Dream Play* and the religious universalism of *To Damascus*, while the spoken dialogue is so clipped and bare, the thought so cryptic, that the course of the action has to be followed from the stage-directions rather than from the characters' words and deeds. This reduction of the verbal content, like the juxtaposition of contrasting, psychologically-linked scenes, led Hasenclever to the new medium of the film, and in 1925 he wrote what he later called 'the first German film to be published in book form', the scenario of the silent movie *Die Pest*. In 1930 this interest in films took him as a German script-writer to Hollywood.

But in the early years of the Weimar Republic Hasenclever, like many of his contemporaries, turned away from the tragic contemplation of the human lot, exclaiming 'We are now ripe for comedy'. He contributed a number of social satires to the repertoire, gentler exercises in the genre for which Carl Sternheim had become famous during the last years of the Wilhelminian era, and which reached its *ne plus ultra* in Karl Kraus' *Die letzten Tage der Menschheit*. In 1933 Hasenclever left Germany and after a restless exile in Italy,

England and France finally committed suicide in the internment camp of Les Milles near Aix-en-Provence in June 1940. German newspapers saw no reason to draw particular attention to the event. A few months later the Nazi journal *Der Stürmer* compared him to Judas Iscariot and called his suicide 'the only thing one can put to his credit'.

The revolutionary anti-war spirit takes a different turn in the works of Fritz von Unruh. An aristocrat and an officer in the Prussian army, he turned against his background and his career when confronted with the realities of war, leaving his early Kleist-like plays on military duty and obedience (*Offiziere*, 1912; *Louis Ferdinand Prinz von Preussen*, 1913) for works of passionate protest against the degradation of the human spirit which war brings in its train. His highly emotional dramatic poem *Vor der Entscheidung* led to a court-martial on the charge of undermining the war-time morale of the army by preaching the brotherhood of man. The full force of his humanitarian message, however, came with the one-act expressionist tragedy *Ein Geschlecht* (1917), the first part of a planned trilogy, the second part of which, *Platz*, followed in 1920.

The effectiveness of *Ein Geschlecht* rests to a large degree on its compactness—a small central group of characters all of one family, the restriction of the time-span to a single night, and the compression of the story into a single act. The burial by the Mother of the Son killed in action (again the use of nameless, representative characters); the rebellion of the two remaining Sons, in the name of conscience and individual responsibility, against an intolerable military discipline; the Mother's execution by the army commanders; the one Son's suicide and the other's call to revolt against an oppressive, war-ridden régime—from these motifs Unruh assembled his picture of a corrupt, immoral society, proclaiming his message of hope through the Mother's final *credo* of love and the youngest Son's commitment to a nobler future.

For Unruh's concern, unlike Hasenclever's, was less with social and political change than with the spiritual rebirth of the individual. Man's struggle is not against impersonal external forces, nor even against his fellow-men, but against himself, and the root of human tragedy lay, for Unruh, in the dynamic forces that welled up within the individual heart and mind, forces that had quite literally to be 'expressed'. Material reality receded before the higher reality of subjective knowledge and the higher claims of personal responsibility, and the tragic hero's physical environment becomes, as in Strindberg's *To Damascus*, a solipsistic projection of his own inner realities. Personality prevails over plot, as it had done in the days of the *Kraftmenschen* of *Sturm und Drang*.

Written in blank verse and in a highly-coloured language whose extravagancies it is now difficult to take seriously, *Ein Geschlecht* and *Platz* roused vital issues of conscience in the minds of German audiences during the years following the Great War, and brought their author great acclaim. He received one literary prize after another, making speeches denouncing the false loyalties that caused men to kill each other and behave like animals, and calling on his people to set about rebuilding the moral, social and political life of the nation in the only possible place—in their own hearts. 'Where are the men and women we can trust?' he cried at a meeting of the Republikanische Partei which he, Carl von Ossietzky and a few others founded in 1924 in a forlorn attempt to influence political events. 'The question need not be asked—for we ourselves are these men and women. Let us leave the moaning and grumbling to others!'[1]

Unruh's striving to make his fellows into 'men and women we can trust' led him to probe the deepest, fullest of human relationships, that of the love between man and woman, as the informing power of his ideal society. *Platz*, which picks up the situation left at the end of *Ein Geschlecht*, describes the progress of the youngest son from his position at the head of the revolutionary troops to his realisation that the new order cannot rest on mere social and political change but demands a transformation of the whole personality; in this transformation the love of man and woman is the prime catalyst. A third drama was to have shown this love-ruled society in action. As the mood of the immediate post-war years began to change, however, and the melodramatic appeal of the expressionist dramatists gave way to a more sober, less despairingly idealistic view of the German condition, Unruh found that he had lost his audience, and the conclusion of the trilogy was never written. Indeed, throughout the 50 years that lie between *Platz* and his death in 1970, both during his exile from the Nazis and after his return to Germany in 1948, the audience never returned. There were occasional performances of later plays, but the characteristic Unruh, preacher to a demoralised people during their emergence from defeat, remained a *Zeiterscheinung*.

A *Zeiterscheinung* of a very different order, a dramatist whose name has not died with the expressionist age in which his reputation is rooted, is Ernst Toller, whose response to the conditions created by, and responsible for, the war was to embrace a radical socialism that called, not like Unruh, for the rebirth of the inner man, but for salvation by political organisation. Nor was Toller a mere armchair revolutionary. He joined the Independent Socialist Party in 1917 and was jailed at the beginning of 1918 for advocating pacifism and supporting a strike of munition workers in Munich. During his imprisonment he wrote his first play, *Die Wandlung*, a half-realistic, half-symbolic autobiographical presentation of how the hero rouses the masses to revolution by making each man realise the nature of the true humanity within him. This optimism never returned. In 1919, as an independent member of the Soviet-style *Räterepublik* in Munich, he was imprisoned for five years for incitement to violence. By the time he was released he had written *Masse Mensch* (1920), an expressionistically stylised statement of disillusionment with the masses and their worthiness to achieve revolutionary ends, *Die Maschinenstürmer* (1922), a play based on the Luddite uprising of 1815, and the bitterly realistic 'Heimkehrerdrama' *Hinkemann* (1924). So when he emerged from prison he found that he had taken his place alongside Brecht and Georg Kaiser as one of the most talked-of dramatists of the day. Leading directors like Piscator and Karlheinz Martin, revelling in the new expressionist designs and techniques, were producing his plays, and translations were appearing in more and more countries.

But his pessimism and disillusionment only grew deeper. In 1927 appeared *Hoppla, wir leben!*, his most savage portrait of what he saw as the soulless materialism, the treachery, the cynicism and the sinister militaristic chauvinism that governed German society during the era of the Weimar Republic. 'In times of violent social conflict the theatre will reflect this conflict', he wrote,[2] and he followed his own precept. Or in personal terms, expressed in a letter written in prison but confiscated by the authorities: 'I do not feel my fate as a personal misfortune but as the expression of the present conditions of political power.' His conflict with society had always been political; with the establishment of the Nazi state it also became racial. As a Jew and a Communist sympathiser he escaped from Germany in 1933 and sought refuge, first in London, then in the United States, where he gained the respect and friendship of Einstein, Klaus and Erika Mann, Döblin and other refugees from Nazism. Without heroics, without intimation or explanation, a few days before the outbreak of the war he had known for years would come, he hanged himself.

Toller was a revolutionary idealist, a man with a burning message. 'His true role', said Humbert Wolfe, 'was that of the author of the *Marseillaise*. He interpreted men to themselves in verse and plays, and this gave to them the unexpected freedom of this illumination.'[3] In the plays in which he proclaimed this 'unexpected freedom' his tone is expressionistically strident, rough, often cruel, and became the more so with the deepening of his tragic disillusionment. He stands for social revolution yet despairs of its achievement. For the Marxist he represents a transition—a significant step forwards but still a transition—to true socialist literature, a man to be characterised by the moving couplet with which he prefaced his later play *Feuer aus den Kesseln*:

> Der die Pfade bereitet, stirbt an der Schwelle,
> Doch es neigt sich vor ihm in Ehrfurcht der Tod.

(He who blazes a trail dies at the threshold,
Yet Death bows its head in reverence before him.)

For the uncommitted observer his five dramas from *Die Wandlung* of 1918 to *Hoppla, wir leben!* of 1927 make up a left-wing view of political and social life in the 1920s, a literary counterpart to chronicles such as the diaries of Graf Harry Kessler and memoirs like Stefan Zweig's *Die Welt von gestern*, Zuckmayer's *Als wär's ein Stück von mir* and Fritz Kortner's *Aller Tage Abend*. His poetry, much of it equal in power to Brecht's, and mottoes like

> Wer keine Kraft zum Traum hat,
> hat keine Kraft zum Leben

(If you have no strength to dream,
You have no strength to live)
(from *Hinkemann*)

—show that we are dealing with a truly poetic nature, an affirmer of life in its fullness, not with a mere propagandist. Appreciation of his work does not depend on acceptance of his politics.

In its characteristic full-blooded manifestation expressionism, together with related phenomena like Dada and Vitalism, was an affair of the young—or at least of the young in heart. A bond of opposition to the philosophical, social and aesthetic values of the Wilhelminian age held this generation together, a generation intoxicated with the Nietzschean appeal to the instinctive and the irrational and the Nietzschean call for the 'revaluation of all values'. No man of culture in Germany at the turn of the century could escape from Nietzsche, but it was inevitably on the young and impressionable, united in an anti-positivist, anti-naturalist bias, if in little else, that his impact was greatest, and in them that the manifestations of his influence were at their most extreme.

It is perhaps chiefly this factor of age, coupled with the circumstances which condition the time and the nature of an artist's rise to maturity, that distinguishes Hasenclever, Unruh, Toller, and others born in the later 1880s and 1890s from those whose literary careers were further advanced when the force of expressionist ideals was at its height. One of these latter is Carl Sternheim, most of whose characteristic works, satirical comedies at the expense of bourgeois society in Wilhelminian Germany, belong to an earlier age. Another is Georg Kaiser, whose career as a dramatist began well before the war, but whose central output falls into the years when expressionism was at its height. These works have acquired a pivotal significance in this context without, however, displaying the extreme violence of reaction which was a commonplace with younger contemporaries, or being totally absorbed within the phenomenon of expressionist drama.

From an undistinguished group of dramas in conventional realistic style written in the first decade of the century, Kaiser suddenly exploded on the theatrical scene with *Von Morgens bis Mitternachts*, produced in 1916. This frenzied *Stationsdrama* portrays the stages by which a bank clerk breaks out of his petit bourgeois environment, uses the money he has stolen from his bank to buy himself, Faust-like, all those experiences denied him in his humdrum life, and finally kills himself in an agony of disillusionment with the world whose pleasures he had bought and whose values he had come to despise. Expressionist is the reduction of the characters (Kaiser calls them 'Figuren') to their social functions—The Bank Clerk, The Mother, The Wife; the wildness of individual scenes such as the bicycle-race, with the language of the crowd and the spectacular lighting effects; and above all the principle, here given a tragically satirical, grotesque twist, of regeneration and self-fulfilment.

Kaiser's *Die Bürger von Calais*, first performed in 1917 and belonging to the large body of contemporary anti-war plays, was one of the first real successes in expressionist drama—a success, moreover, both in dramatic and in expressionistic terms. It presents in historical guise the 'new man' demanded by the expressionists as the prerequisite of the 'new society', man prepared for, and worthy of, the ultimate sacrifice which symbolises the victory of true humanity.

But the most revealing of Kaiser's plays in the twin contexts of expressionism and the immediate post-war cultural scene are the *Gas*-trilogy (*Die Koralle*, 1917; *Gas I*, 1918; *Gas II*, 1920) and *Hölle, Weg, Erde* (1919), for here we face at its most powerful a statement of the condition of man in a defeated nation and a decayed society.

Gas is a statement of utter pessimism, reiterated in the fate of three successive generations. In *Die Koralle* the Billionaire, suffering pangs of conscience over his privileged position and deserted by his children, tries to find a new and happier identity by killing the Secretary in order to acquire the latter's happy childhood. He is condemned to death, but his crime has brought him a contentment he has never before experienced, giving him the strength, as he explains to the chaplain before his execution, 'to force my way back into the paradise that lies behind us'. But the agony of life is all-besetting: 'We are all drifters—exiles from our paradise of tranquillity, broken pieces of glowing coral—all born with a wound. The wound will never heal: it burns, and the agony drives us through life' (Act V). Although there are rumblings of social revolution at the beginning of the play, the climax is the hero's satirical achievement of his own *nirvana*. 'We expected Karl Marx', commented a contemporary critic, 'but we got Schopenhauer.'[4]

The central figure of *Gas I*—gas being the symbol both of capitalist industrial society and of the dynamic power that impels man to action, often thoughtless, senseless action—is the Billionaire's Son. A humane and progressive employer in a ruthless capitalist economy, he seeks not just the birth of the 'new man', as his father had done, but the regeneration of the whole of society. And how does society receive him? As it receives all prophets—by killing him. Men return to their soulless, meaningless existence, producing more and more gas in order to demonstrate their vitality and their domination of nature.

But over and above its character as an *Erneuerungsdrama*, a 'drama of regeneration', with a full complement of expressionist linguistic extravagancies, stylised emotionalism and elaborate scenic and lighting effects, the first part of *Gas* has a terrifying meaning which has no less force today than it had in the years after, and even before, World War I. That meaning originates in the most important event in the whole drama: not a human action or the calculated outcome of a human decision but a symbolic moment of profound catastrophe—the explosion that wrecks the factory. The explosion leads the Billionaire's Son to embark on his vain crusade against the dehumanisation of life and work; it also sends the scientists and workers back to rebuild the same blind, soul-destroying pattern of existence that had caused the explosion. Man has become the servant of the machine, not its master, and destruction, unpremeditated yet inevitable, belongs to the nature of machine-dominated society. Each man sees and knows only that little patch of existence from which he derives his livelihood: he has lost sight of the total context which is the only true unit of meaning. He thus falls an easy prey to the predatory gods of Efficiency and Scientific Progress, and the nightmare of an uncontrollable mechanical artefact—the fantasy conjured up in Lucian's *Philopseudes*, from which Goethe took his *Sorcerer's Apprentice*, and a recurrent theme in literature from E.T.A. Hoffmann's *Der Sandmann* to Karel Čapek's *R.U.R.*—becomes more and more real.

For Kaiser, as for many others before and since, the only hope for the future lay in the restoration of the 'whole man' in his full expressive humanity and personality.

In *Gas II* private capitalism has been swept away, the state controls all production, and industry, resting on the labour of lifeless men who have become mere minders of machines, serves one single end: war. From the generations of the Billionaire and the Billionaire's Son we have moved to the era of the Billionaire Worker, the idealist who, like the Billionaire's Son before him, seeks to draw the torpid masses away from the path of destruction along which the spokesman for materialistic science—here represented by the Master Engineer who has invented a poison-gas that will annihilate the entire enemy—enthusiastically seeks to lead them. The masses, of course, heedless of the call to morality and salvation, vote for poison-gas and destruction. But it is the Billionaire Worker, fulfilling on a cosmic scale the death-wish that had made the Billionaire in *Die Koralle* kill the Secretary, who throws the gas-bomb that leads to the holocaust in which the terrifying drama ends. The only realistic philosophy is despair, the only certain fulfilment of life is self-destruction. Only once, in *Hölle, Weg, Erde* (1919), did Kaiser permit himself an optimistic outcome of the struggle for self-renewal, and this at a moment of misplaced hope in the regenerative stimulus of the 1918 revolution.

With its terseness and violence of diction, its passionate outbursts (with liberal use of double, triple and quadruple exclamation marks), its neologistic rhetoric and its extravagance of stage-direction and scenic effect, Kaiser's *Gas*-trilogy has come to occupy a central position in expressionist drama. But the enthusiasm with which the advent of the 'new man' had been proclaimed in the manifestoes of the movement has turned sour. 'Expressionism is the philosophy of utopia!' cries Friedrich Markus Huebner in the year that *Gas II* is produced. 'It puts man back in the centre of creation![15] The Billionaire, the Billionaire's Son and the Billionaire Worker, powerless philosophers of an illusory faith in mankind's ability to envisage any form of utopia, discover that the centre of creation is the centre of destruction, and that man is intent on nothing so much as demonstrating how little different he is from the animals.

'Yes! I found the new kingdom!' cries the Billionaire Worker to the masses. 'No! Set fire to the gas!' shrieks the Master Engineer, spokesman of scientific progress. There is a terrifying silence. Then comes a single plaintive cry: 'The gas!' A few more voices join in: 'The gas! The gas!' Finally the whole crowd screams in hysterical unison: 'The gas! The gas! The gas!' But the idealist is no martyr. Once the will of the mob is clear, it is he who leads the rush of the Gadarene swine.

Significantly, in the midst of the intensity of the *Gas*-trilogy Kaiser turned from full-blooded expressionist social drama to a quieter form of personal drama, still on the theme of regeneration but now in the form of the purification of a man's emotions through the love of a woman (*Das Frauenopfer*, 1916; *Gilles und Jeanne*, 1922; *Oktobertag*, 1927). This subject informed much of his subsequent work through the 1920s and 1930s. It is as though the force of social expressionism in him were quickly spent, giving way to a less ostentatious, albeit no less intensely-felt concern with intimate personal relationships.

In as much as expressionism, as an historical phenomenon, was an explosive outburst, often merely impressionistic about its ends and impulsive about its means, it has tended to be the noisier subscribers to the movement who have attracted the most attention. And perhaps, given the events, culminating in the war, the revolution and the foundation of the republic, that surrounded their activity, and given also their youthful crusading zeal, one expects a spirit of aggressiveness and intransigence to predominate. At the same time there were other, quieter voices, often religious in tone, no less concerned to express in dramatic form essential truths about the unchanging inner nature of man. One was that of Ernst Barlach, a man more readily remembered today as a sculptor (likewise the characteristic achievement of Oscar Kokoschka, who also wrote dramas during the 'expressionist decade', lies in painting). Barlach's dramas, which are as reflective and slow-moving as Kaiser's and Toller's are excited and violent, rest on an intense yet serene Christianity as the source of all timeless truths about man. Of similar inspiration are certain of Franz Werfel's plays of this period, notably *Spiegelmensch* (1920), a strange, symbolical presentation of the career of a kind of latter-day Faust, while Stefan Zweig's *Jeremias* (1917) uses an Old Testament subject to preach the message of the futility and immorality of war. Zweig was Viennese, an heir to the heritage of Hugo von Hofmannsthal. Hofmannsthal's own world disappeared with the collapse of the Austro-Hungarian Empire in 1918, but the spirit of *Das Salzburger grosse Welttheater* (1922) and the rambling symbolical *Der Turm* (1925–7) is close to that of Zweig's, as is also that of lesser neo-romantic dramatists like Richard Beer-Hoffmann.

Of all the social dramas of wartime and the years that followed, whether stridently calling the people to action, like Hasenclever's *Antigone* and Toller's *Die Wandlung*, or urging the regeneration of personal morality and values, like Unruh's *Ein Geschlecht* and Barlach's *Die Sintflut*, the most colossal, extraordinary and horrifying is the Viennese satirist Karl Kraus' *Die letzten Tage der Menschheit*, completed in 1921. It comprises a 10-scene Prologue, Act I of 30 scenes, Act II of 33 scenes, Act III of 46 scenes, Act IV of 45 scenes, Act V of

55 scenes and a 40-page Epilogue. It requires a cast of hundreds, drawn from every corner of wartime Viennese society. Needless to say, it has never been performed, and never will be. Kraus' characteristic introductory note laconically and unemotionally concedes as much: 'This play, which in terrestrial terms would fill some ten evenings, is intended for a theatre on Mars. Audiences on this earth could not stand up to it.'[6]

Indeed they could not—and not for physical reasons. For Kraus subjects mankind to a merciless satirical assault—an assault on modern morality, on the futility of war, on the corruption of society, on individual self-delusion, and above all on the discrepancy between the profound meaning of the metaphysical drama that was being played out in the Vienna—by implication the Europe—of the day and the puny stature of the men who had cast themselves as the *dramatis personae*. These were 'the nightmare years', wrote Kraus of the period in which *Die letzten Tage der Menschheit* is set, 'in which the tragedy of mankind was enacted by characters from musical comedy.'[7]

His drama presents a bizarre succession of men and women from the decadent society of imperial Austria-Hungary, most of them designated as types—A Journalist, An Intellectual, An Invalid, Two Admirers of the Postal Service, etc. Contemporary personalities appear under their own names—writers like Hofmannsthal and Alfred Kerr, army commanders like Hindenburg and Ludendorff. Even Kaiser Wilhelm II is present. The scene of the action moves from battlefront to nightclub, from War Ministry to field-hospital, from Berlin and Weimar to Constantinople and the Vatican. Throughout the work two figures give a running commentary on the events. One is 'Der Optimist', the reasonable and balanced observer. The other is 'Der Nörgler' (The Grumbler: Kraus himself), who sees things *sub specie aeternitatis*, applying absolute moral standards to a world that takes refuge in pleas of relativity and appeals to psychology. In a steely polemical language the Grumbler exposes the falsities of contemporary life and stands by to witness the death-throes of a world which God cannot help and from which the unborn child begs to be spared:

> *Wehlust irdischen Getues!*
> *Liebend hinterlässt die Lues*
> *mir mein Vater, dieser Schuft.*
> *Ruft uns nicht in diese Reiche!*
> *Wir entstammen einer Leiche.*
> *Ungesund ist hier die Luft.*

> (V. 55)

(O joyous agony of earthly doings! Lovingly my scoundrel of a father bequeathed his syphilis to me. O do not call us into such realms! We are the progeny of a corpse. The air here is unhealthy.)

Die letzten Tage der Menschheit, which draws on innumerable press reports and other contemporary documents, opens with the news-paper vendor shouting the headline of the assassination in Sarajevo of the Archduke Franz Ferdinand, heir to the Austrian throne, on 28 June 1914. It ends with the Voice of God uttering the words attributed to the dying Austrian Emperor Franz Joseph, as he looked out on a Europe at war: 'Ich habe es nicht gewollt!' This is the tragedy in which Karl Kraus' mankind will end: the insulated comfort of our mediocrity has blinded us to the destructiveness latent in that lack of moral fibre which we deck out with euphemisms like 'seeing the other side to the question' and 'taking the matter in its context.' For Kraus morality was a matter of black and white. The evidence of his day proved to him that people had said no, and would go on saying no. The victory was Satan's, and the annihilation of Kraus' world by the invaders from Mars is as inevitable as that of George Kaiser's world through the suicide of the masses.

A creed of art and life that challenges tradition so outspokenly and makes such revolutionary demands as expressionism did, places a special strain on the relationship between the content of the work of art and the form in which it is cast, that is to say, between the formal characteristics and demands which have grown up round a particular genre and the new ideas that the artist has used this genre to express. A writer may initially propose a form unsuited to the nature of his thoughts: literary history has many examples to show of the second thoughts that turned a drama into a novel, or a narrative into a drama. In an inappropriate form the thoughts can be stifled or distorted; they can also shatter the mould that has tried to contain them, leaving the dissatisfaction of aesthetic formlessness. Either way one will be conscious of an incompatibility, and either way the incompatibility will impair the work of art. In extreme cases it can even destroy it.

This is not to reassert the schoolman's dogmatic insistence on a comprehensive and prescriptive definition of form, but merely to recall that form moulds content just as content creates form. Indeed, inasmuch as content rests on ideas, and form itself is an idea, the interaction is inescapable. As ideas evolve, so form evolves with them. There is no form without ideas, and no art without form. And the artist communicates with his public through both.

Before referring these questions to the phenomenon of expressionism, and to add a new perspective to them we may turn for a moment from dramas of rebellion and unrest to one of the last works of a writer whose fame had long been established, and whose values were those of pre-war society—Hugo von Hofmannsthal's *Der Schwierige* (1921).

A discussion of this superb comedy of manners in Hofmannsthal's development as a whole—the same would apply to his second morality *Das Salzburger grosse Welttheater* (1922) and his last play *Der Turm* (1925–1927), with its tragic vision of a world ruled by evil—lies outside our concerns. *Der Schwierige* itself, however, has an importance in the post-war period on two separate counts: firstly in its portrayal of the social conflict between the old and the new, between the quiet, considerate, conservative values of pre-war Viennese society and the spirit of self-assertion, rationalisation and pragmatism in the proud upper classes of a defeated Prussia; and secondly in its central theme of the nature, limitations and ultimate impossibility of true communication between individuals, in so far as this communication depends on speech.

Although *Der Schwierige* is the only play of Hofmannsthal's to have a contemporary setting, it is not a play of social comment but formally a Viennese *Konversationsstück* in the line of Bauernfeld and Schnitzler, a genre whose *raison d'être*, as the name says, lies rather in its dialogue and wit than in its plot or its characters. In *Der Schwierige*, moreover, it is 'the difficult man' himself, Hans Karl Bühl, who holds the centre of attention, not the society in which he lives.

Yet Hans Karl, precisely through his difficult-ness, gives the play a social as well as a personal tension, and faces the choice between the elegant, orderly world of a past that survives only as an attractive anachronism, and the graceless 'real' world of the present, full of churlishness and pretentious intellectualisation. As Baron Neuhoff, the Prussian spokesman for the modern world, puts it, surveying what he sees as the cultured trivialities of a Viennese soirée: 'Nobody found in these drawing rooms belongs to the real world where the intellectual crises of the country are resolved.' (II. 2.). Neuhoff is the twentieth-century German, Hans Karl the nineteenth-century Austrian, the two men embodying the incompatible characteristics described by Hofmannsthal in his essay *Preusse und Österreicher* (1917). The result is a miniature of life in Viennese high society in the years of the collapse of the monarchy, with changing social attitudes reflected not only among the aristocrats and intellectuals but also among the servants. For the old and the new are no less vividly contrasted in the figures of Lukas, the master's faithful old retainer, and Vincenz, the new valet who is concerned only to get as much out of his employer as he can.

Neuhoff, of course, is right: 'All the people you see here don't really exist any more' (*loc. cit.*). At the same time—and in such interplays lies much of the charm, as well as of the deeper social and personal meaning of the comedy—what in itself seems right becomes less so in the mouth of a Neuhoff. 'I suppose things are much as he says', muses Hans Karl, 'but there are people who cannot help altering all the emphases. He has a keen intellect, yet somehow it makes one feel uncomfortable'. And he adds, with the old-world gentleness and Christian tolerance paramount in Hofmannsthal's own set of values: 'Basically, I suppose, one ought to feel sorry for a man like him.' (I. 13) And as for whether new 'realities' should prevail over old 'illusions', it is Hans Karl that Helene loves and marries, not his rival Neuhoff.

'Speech is the product of an immodest over-assessment of one's own abilities', says Hans Karl to Helene (II. 14). At the end of the play he is even more convinced: 'Everything one expresses is immodest. The very fact that one expresses something is immodest . . . I [am] a man who is gripped by one fact in this world—that it is impossible to open one's mouth without creating the most terrible misunderstandings' (III. 13.). It is this knowledge that makes Hans Karl 'difficult'. Man, being man, is bound to open his mouth and to communicate, and therefore to perpetuate misunderstanding, hence the decay of language as a means of communication and as a vehicle of man's moral sense. And with the decay of language goes the decay of society. Small wonder that Hans Karl should say: 'I understand myself far worse when I speak than when I stay silent' (II. 14.).

In Kafka's parable *Eine kaiserliche Botschaft* a messenger rushes through the world trying to deliver a message from the dying emperor. In the first place he cannot fight his way through to the person for whom the message is intended; in the second place, even if he eventually did get through, who would want to listen to a message from an emperor who had now died? It was a situation that had been with Hofmannsthal from the time of his *Chandos Letter* of 1902. And in the year that *Der Schwierige* was published, there appeared Wittgenstein's *Tractatus Logico-Philosophicus*, fountainhead of the modern conception of philosophy as the philosophy of language, and of the logical syntax of language as the source of the *a priori* element in knowledge. Where this power of language ends, there meaningful philosophy, in Wittgenstein's anti-metaphysical sense, also ends. The rest is silence. Or, as he puts it in the famous last sentence of the *Tractatus*: 'What one cannot speak about, one must be silent about.'

Hans Karl Bühl knows what Wittgenstein meant. He also knows that the inexpressible—'das Mystische', as Wittgenstein calls it—is no less real for being inexpressible.

As ideas have a history, so also do forms, and the artist has to acknowledge both these histories, for he himself is part of them. Whatever the originality of his thoughts, the moment he decides to commit them to a poem, a novel or a drama, he submits himself to criteria of judgement that have grown up round the form in question, and this is the point at which the relationship, appropriate or otherwise, between his message and his chosen medium for conveying it becomes the focus of attention. The thought; the chosen form; the aesthetic demands of that form and its standing in the cultural life of the community; the relevance of the thought in its philosophical and social context: between these facets of the complete work is generated the tension which is the life-blood of artistic creation. But each facet will also attract critical attention in its own right, and if the tension provokes strain or discord, the reason will be sought out.

We thus find ourselves asking: what was the nature of the relationship between expressionism, as a movement with declared principles, however heterogeneous, and drama? To what use did these expressionist playwrights put drama? And was it a medium congenial to their purposes?

Possible answers to such questions have in part been anticipated in the works already considered, and are also implied in the subsequent careers of their authors. After *Jenseits* (1920) and *Mord* (1926) Hasenclever abandoned serious drama for fashionable comedy. The third part of Unruh's trilogy was never written. After *Hoppla, wir leben!* (1927) Toller exchanged his burning commitment to social issues for realistic political plays, and the same return to realism characterises the post-expressionist dramas of Kaiser from the mid-1920s. An undercurrent of naturalistic drama, indeed, persisted throughout the years when expressionism was at its height. It found its way not only into comedy but also into historico-political works on subjects that readily came to mind during the years of the war and the revolution. Among such works are Paul Ernst's *Preussengeist*, Hermann von Bötticher's *Friedrich der Grosse* and Joachim von der Goltz' *Vater und Sohn*—all of which take Frederick the Great as their hero—Emil Ludwig's *Bismarck* (Wedekind also wrote a drama with this title) and Reinhard Göring's *Scapa Flow*.

To face these questions directly is to become aware of the limitations in drama *qua* drama which the expressionist philosophy imposes. Expressionism is in essence egocentric. The dynamism of expressionist drama is man-centred and man-generated, and the independent reality of the external circumstances that press upon the individual is removed from the centre of concern. Circumstances no longer have their own character and force, their own power to generate dramatic action and mould the fate of the hero, but merely provide the setting. The source of the dramatic tension is the hero's own psyche.

Furthermore the hero is so often not an individual but the unnamed representative of a class or a social function, an almost abstract figure that spurns the flesh-and-blood relationships and the processes of action and reaction that make up the life of a particular person in a particular environment. Deprived of a human cause-and-effect framework of events, such drama acquired a self-generating rhetorical momentum that paid little heed to inner dramatic satisfaction and owed more to the lyrical than to the dramatic impulse. The theatre has become half-pulpit, half-confessional. Spiritual biographies are unfolded in successions of scenes—the so-called *Stationsdramen* influenced by the techniques of the film—whose unity is not historical or dramatic but emotional, 'expressive'. And since 'expression', in this lyrical sense of self-projection, follows unpredictable though self-justifying paths, a sense of formal dramatic satisfaction is hardly to be expected. The tragedies of Georg Kaiser and the comedies of Carl Sternheim stand out in this context largely by virtue of their concern for dramatic values *per se*.

Among the comedies of the 1920s, as successful in their day as Hofmannsthal's *Der Schwierige*, but now, with one prominent exception, little heeded, were the comedies of Carl Zuckmayer. Before this exception—*Der Hauptmann von Köpenick* (1931)—Zuckmayer had made his mark on the Berlin theatre with *Pankraz erwacht oder Die Hinterwäldler* (1925) and especially with *Der fröhliche Weinberg* the following year. The overnight success of this knockabout dialect comedy, both with the public and with the press—at the premiere even the dreaded Alfred Kerr, doyen of Berlin critics, was seen to smile twice—made Zuckmayer's reputation once and for all through its sharpness of dialogue and its often vulgar raciness. That clerics, innkeepers, ex-servicemen and other pillars of conservative society should take offence at the way they were pilloried, was not surprising. But so did the students. Incensed by the drunken speech of the would-be 'academic' Knuzius, with its mocking use of 'Wehrhaftigkeit', 'Pflichttreue', 'Rassenreinheit' and similar items of nationalist verbiage, they felt that they were being held up to ridicule, and in a number of German cities they broke up performances of the play by chanting and throwing stinkbombs.

As to the comic realism of *Der Hauptmann von Köpenick*, a Till Eulenspiegel satire on authority and the cult of military trappings, it had the political effect Zuckmayer meant it to have, both on friend and foe. Uniforms, above all Nazi uniforms, filled the streets at this time, and the exploits of the little cobbler Wilhelm Voigt might have been expected to cause an uproar. But the discrimination of Zuckmayer's satire lifts it above the level of crude propaganda. The Nazi press, led by Goebbels' *Angriff*, raged and threatened, but performances continued all over Germany down to the beginning of 1933. Lightweight though it may be, it has acquired an exemplary status among works that set out on that task of unfailing popularity—popular, that is, with all but the victims—the task of holding authority up to ridicule.

Although the stage seemed to many an ideal vehicle for preaching a new message—any new message—few had the sense of dramatic unity that would couch that message in a convincing form. The expressionists laboured under their own shortcomings. But where the expressionists had passion with little sense of stage drama, the socialist realist plays of Friedrich Wolf, by contrast, are efficiently turned but lack emotional fire. Wolf had been a member of the Independent Socialist Party in 1918 and joined the German Communist Party in 1928; he emigrated in 1933, spent most of the war in Moscow and returned to East Germany in 1945, becoming the German Democratic Republic's first ambassador to Poland in 1950.

As he made clear in his declaration of intent, *Kunst ist Waffe* (1928), Wolf saw literature not merely as an exercise in 'realism' but as an instrument in the class struggle. The hero of *Der arme Conrad* (1924), a play about the Peasants' Revolt, is the toiling masses who are fighting their way towards their historical destiny, while in *Cyankali* (1929) he uses the abortion laws of the Weimar Republic to expose the hypocrisies of capitalist society. The revolutionary play *Die Matrosen von Cattaro* (1930), which has the common sailors as its hero, has been hailed as the 'first throughgoing socialist-realist drama in Germany', but has little more than socio-historical interest. *Professor Mamlock* (1934), on the other hand, a powerful play on the persecution of the Jews, with a man of true humanistic greatness as the focus of attention, has kept his name before a wider public. Drama needs great men before it needs great causes.

Socialist in more personal terms are the best dramas of the Viennese Franz Theodor Csokor, who first drew attention to himself in the years immediately following the war with expressionist plays written under the shadow of Strindberg. In the mid-1920s Csokor discovered the figure of Büchner, and though he remained a Catholic throughout his life, he made this atheistic social revolutionary of the nineteenth century his hero as a fighter for humanitarian ideals. He wrote a 'completion' of *Woyzeck* in 1928, and in the same year a play on Büchner as revolutionary called *Gesellschaft der Menschenrechte*. From the twentieth-century world of his own experience—which included exile from Austria in various countries of Eastern Europe and his liberation from an internment camp by Yugoslav partisans—he composed a trilogy of dramas published in 1952 as *Europäische Trilogie*. The first of these, *Besetztes Gebiet* (1930), deals with the issues of conscience provoked by the French occupation of the Ruhr in 1930; the second, *3 November 1918* (1936), describes in terms of events in a hospital the last days of the Austro-Hungarian army; while the third, *Der Verlorene Sohn* (1947), returns to the struggle of the partisans against their military oppressors, as in *Besetztes Gebiet*.

In these and his many other plays, as in his novels and lyric verse, Csokor shows himself, like Büchner, a fighter for human rights and one for whom the achievement of these rights must involve the supersession of a played-out capitalist social order by a new pattern of humanitarian ideals. But modern German drama was still waiting for a man who had both a burning conviction of the need for new, humane values in his heart and the instinct of the true man of the theatre in his head, creator of a new, sustained realism, passionate yet critical. Which leads us to Brecht.

When the Great War ended and the revolution broke out, Bertolt Brecht was 20. He had spent the last two years as a medical orderly, and his experiences in a military hospital in Augsburg are the source of the savage pacifism, sometimes almost cynical in its savagery, that persisted throughout his life, cheek by jowl with a characteristic justification of violence in a politically righteous cause. It was a pacifism partly productive of, partly nurtured by, his hatred of the capitalist society whose *raison d'être* he saw as resting on the preparation for war, a society manipulated, above all in his own country, by military leaders and their civilian henchmen.

But as well as its political side, his pacifism had a strong, inflexible moral content. For if it is wicked to plan destruction, it is also wicked to carry it out, and Brecht's accusations are levelled as much at the man in the street who allows himself to be used as the instrument of an immoral purpose, as at the military and political leaders who have incorporated that purpose into their political plans. Brecht's is the moral intransigence of the believer in collective responsibility, and both the matter and the manner of his work, plays and poetry alike, are calculated to keep this responsibility before our eyes.

The fierceness of his morality in the 1920s, however, does not detract from his condemnation of the conditions in which he demands its application. Like the expressionists whose strident voices filled the air during his school and student days, he violently rejected the decadent culture of the time, preaching a nihilistic disillusionment with the achievements of sophisticated society and affecting a crude, *épater le bourgeois* preference for what are usually regarded as the baser aspects of human nature. This is the world of his first play, *Baal*, (1918–19) written in a style, sometimes coarse, sometimes vicious, sometimes surprisingly lyrical, that recalls Georg Büchner. Büchner was one of the most important influences on expressionist diction and manner, and was regarded by Brecht as the greatest German dramatist of all time.

Brecht's reaction to the post-war situation in Germany, and in particular to the moral issues thrown up by the revolution, is the subject of *Trommeln in der Nacht*, first produced, like *Baal*, in 1922. It was a play that fascinated the great Max Reinhardt, earned Brecht the Kleist Prize for that year and gave him a position in the public eye which he never lost. For here was a writer with drama in his blood, a writer as intense as Hasenclever, or Kaiser, or Toller and with expressionistically-coloured characters and language, but without the frenzied self-centredness of the expressionists, a writer who struck home with a clean, merciless, coolly disillusioned diction as spare and athletic as that of the expressionists was passionate and rhetorical.

Originally called *Spartakus*, after the name of the international socialist faction led by Karl Liebknecht and Rosa Luxemburg, *Trommeln in der Nacht* belongs to the sub-genre of *Heimkehrerdramen*, plays describing the return of the demobilised soldier to the world in which he has to make a new start. Brecht's pathetic hero Kragler, a soldier who, having been reported 'missing—presumed dead' and thus written off by all who knew him, returns to find his fiancée the mistress of another man, a petit-bourgeois time-server. He throws in his lot with the Spartacus rebels, men who feel, like him, betrayed by the society in whose name they had fought the war. But when the moment of decision comes, he turns his back on the revolution and opts for a comfortable life with his former fiancée, who has come back to him.

When Brecht was preparing his plays for the East German Aufbau-Verlag edition of his collected works in 1954, he not surprisingly found himself embarrassed, living as the star cultural protégé of a revolutionary socialist state, by the nihilistic anti-revolutionary behaviour of his hero. In a new prefatory note to what he now called a comedy, he maintained that Kragler was meant to be seen as a negative character: it was, he said, purely a technical inadequacy on his part—specifically, the absence of a *Verfremdungseffekt*, a technique he had not yet discovered at the time of *Trommeln in der Nacht*—to have failed to make the audience react to the revolution differently from Kragler.[8] In tones reminiscent of the 'confessions' extracted from erring comrades by the custodians of Party orthodoxy, Brecht conceded his error of judgment and sought to rectify it by introducing a new character into the play 'as a kind of counterweight to Kragler'.[9]

This incident reveals the predicament of the politically committed writer faced with the need to interpret, and sometimes justify, his past, and illuminates the nature of Brecht's own convictions, past and present. The writer Arnolt Bronnen said that in the early 1920s Brecht was not interested in revolutions and social causes but only in the promotion of his career as a dramatist,[10] and his poem 'Gesang des Soldaten der Roten Armee' (1919) makes it clear that he had as little confidence in the fighting power of a revolutionary proletariat as did his hero Kragler. Bronnen—one-time expressionist dramatist and poet, then a pillar of the Nazi literary establishment and finally a Communist, with his honoured place alongside Heinrich Mann, Brecht, Arnold Zweig and the other Communist intellectuals in the Dorotheenstadt cemetery in Berlin—is perhaps hardly the most consistent of witnesses. But with evidence in Brecht's own work pointing in the same direction, there seems no reason to doubt the tenor of Bronnen's story. Carl Zuckmayer, too, who came to know Brecht well during these post-war years in Berlin, recalled that the social-revolutionary element in him was born of an 'anarchic vitalism', not of any humanistic or ideological conviction.[11]

The 'Gesang des Soldaten der Roten Armee', a ballad in which the lash of Brecht's tongue already finds its mark, expresses the common soldier's jaundiced view of the ideals for which he is told he is fighting in the Russian revolution, and of the men—'many with fangs like tigers', marching behind the inhuman red flag—in whose blood-stained hands the future lay:

> *Sehr viele Höllen kamen noch,*
> *Die Freiheit, Kinder, die kam nie.*

> (Many hells were yet to come.
> But freedom, fellows, never came.)

So it is fully in keeping that Kragler should shout, at the end of

Trommeln in der Nacht: 'Do you expect my flesh to rot in the gutter so that your ideal can find a place in heaven?' The duplicity, the immorality, the sordidness of life, so persistent a theme among the expressionists—Brecht is close at this moment to Gottfried Benn—outweigh the alleged nobility of the cause. The end does *not* justify the means.

Impersonality and violence come together in Brecht's *Im Dickicht der Städte* (1922–3), a strange, rarefied statement of 'Kampf an sich', as he later described it.[12] It owes an undenied debt to Rimbaud, as *Die Dreigroschenoper*, together with innumerable poems, owes an equally patent debt to Villon, and portrays 'a fight fought for no other reason than pleasure in fighting'. Set in pre-Great War Chicago, it is filled with the manifestations of his cherished love-hate relationship with capitalist society at its biggest and brashest. The two antagonists in the play, Shlink and Garga, seek to make contact with each other by fighting, but even this is beyond them: 'Man's unutterable isolation makes enmity an unattainable goal', says the one to the other. '. . . Indeed, so great is man's loneliness that not even fighting is possible' (Scene 10). The helplessness, the dispensability and replaceability of the individual also make up the substance of the comedy *Mann ist Mann* (1924–5), which pledges itself to demonstrate, in the mock poetic words of the widow Leokadja Begbick at the end of Scene 8—

> *Dass man mit einem Menschen beliebig viel machen kann.*
> *Hier wird heute abend ein Mensch wie ein Auto ummontiert*
> *Ohne dass er irgend etwas dabei verliert.*

(. . . that one can do whatever one likes with a man.
This evening we are reassembling a man like we reassemble a car,
And he doesn't lose a thing in the process.)

Man as an assemblage of bits and pieces that can be dismantled, then put together again in a different order—or even in the same order, if one feels like it—again recalls the disjointed methods of the film—flashbacks, the illumination of a scene from different angles, the sudden transfer of attention from one character to another, and so on—and the surrealist and montage techniques of Max Ernst, Chirico, Duchamp and other painters of the time. As an attitude towards the nature of man, owing something of the behaviourist theories of John Broadus Watson, it marks Brecht's turn from the scornful nihilism of his earlier plays to an admission, however heartless and cynical at this moment, that one man's mind can after all be reached, and thus influenced, by the minds of others.

One of the ironies of the German theatre in the 1920s is that no play by the most powerful left-wing dramatist of the time was produced by the greatest exponent of left-wing political theatre—Erwin Piscator. Piscator was one of the three most influential producers of the day. Pride of place inevitably belongs to the legendary Max Reinhardt, who introduced startling innovations in the 1920s, such as dispensing with curtain and footlights in order to break down the barrier between actors and audience; with the same thought in mind he gave mammoth open-air performances in public settings like the Rathausplatz in Vienna, the Parvis Notre-Dame in Paris and the Domplatz in Salzburg (both Brecht and Zuckmayer worked as dramaturges at Reinhardt's Deutsches Theater in Berlin). The other powerful figure was Leopold Jessner, who evolved non-realist, expressionist productions of classical plays using platforms, cones and—his particular invention—a large central staircase, known as the *Jessnertreppe*.

Piscator came from Königsberg to Berlin in 1920 and at once joined Karlheinz Martin, first producer of Toller's *Die Wandlung* and champion of the involvement of the masses in the whole enterprise of theatre, in Martin's 'Proletarisches Theater'. The 'Proletarisches Theater' was an agency of political agitation. 'We tore the word art completely out of our programme', said Piscator. 'Our plays were calls to action with which we intended to engage in politics and influence everyday life'.[13] The theatre played to steadily dwindling audiences of uncomprehending workers in halls and beer-cellars in the workers' own neighbourhoods, and died a predictable, un-lamented death in April 1921. But two years later Piscator joined with Hans Rehfisch—dramatist, producer and critic, one of the many *literati* forced into exile in 1933, and later founder of the *Club 43*—to acquire the Central-Theater, on the Alte Jakobstrasse in Kreuzberg. Here he found himself compelled to put on a less aggressively avant-garde, though still predominantly modern programme, with greater box-office appeal. The repertory included Gorki's *The Barbarians*, Romain Rolland's *Le temps viendra*, and Tolstoi's *The Power of Darkness*.

This was Piscator's experience of the paradox which Brecht was to witness after World War II during his regimen at the Theater am Schiffbauerdamm with the Berliner Ensemble: that even in a socialist state the patrons of drama with a revolutionary message remain solidly middleclass, while the proletariat in whose name the whole exercise is said to be carried out stays mostly as disinterested as ever. A year before his death Brecht told the film producer Erwin Leiser that he was not surprised that in 1928 his *Dreigroschenoper* had been so enthusiastically applauded by the very people it set out to attack.[14]

A use of the stage for political propaganda of a very different kind was made by Hanns Johst, a minor one-time expressionist who would today enjoy a more-or-less complete oblivion, were it not for the literary role he was to play in Nazi Germany. Where Piscator and Brecht used the theatre to proclaim Marxist revolution, Johst, in his expressionist Luther-drama *Propheten* (1922), in *Thomas Paine* (1927) and above all in *Schlageter*—first performed, with a sinister apposite-ness, on Hitler's birthday in 1933—hurled chauvinistic slogans at his audience in order to arouse national pride. A discussion of the Johst phenomenon belongs to a later period. But one may *en passant* observe that semantics here mischievously unite extreme left and extreme right, and that when Johst writes: 'The true work of art must be totally absorbed into the people, to whom it belongs. True drama is the harbinger of freedom'[15]-Brecht, meaning something very different by 'people' and 'freedom', and especially by 'true', could only have said 'Amen'.

Piscator's tenancy of the Central-Theater provides an amusing example of the unexpected blessings that the inflation of the early 1920s could bring. By 1923 paper money was being churned out by over 2,000 printing establishments working round the clock, and the prices of such goods as were available went up almost hourly. Debts were wiped out overnight. So were savings. This, more than any other factor, both laid the foundation of the industrial fortunes of men like Stinnes and Hugenberg, and destroyed the middle classes on whom depended any chances of success that the Weimar Republic might have had.

When Piscator and Rehfisch took over the Central-Theater the lease, as Piscator's widow told the story, cost three million marks: one million was to be paid at once and the remaining two million three months later. The first million was met from the already inflated subscriptions of the members of the Proletarisches Theater—Piscator's only source of capital. By the time the remainder fell due, all that was required was 'to tear out the heating pipes in the theatre and sell them to a junk dealer'.[16]

In 1924, at the Volksbühne in Berlin, Piscator produced the first play to bear the generic title of 'epic drama'. The play was *Die Fahnen*, a dramatisation by Alfons Paquet of the Chicago trial of the anarchists who instigated the Haymarket Square riot of 1886. By 'epic drama' Piscator meant a loose assemblage of heterogeneous episodes, some spoken, some sung, some hung in front of the audience on placards, some projected on to a screen as still or moving pictures—in short, the antithesis of everything that the European tradition had come to see as logical, homogeneous, systematically planned and developed 'dramatic drama'. To this he then added his Marxist intention to use the theatre as an instrument in the class struggle. As he put it in his book *Das politische Theater*, in 1929, 'the heroic component in this new mode of drama is not the individual, with his own private, personal fate, but the age itself, the fate of the masses. . . The theatre should not just play on the audience's emotions but deliberately appeal to their reason, dealing not in elation, inspiration and emotional abandonment but in education, knowledge and understanding.'[17] Paquet's *Die Fahnen* he regarded as 'in a sense . . . the first Marxist play, and my production of it as the first attempt to uncover the materialist forces that underlie the events.'[18]

In 1927 Piscator took his agitprop theatre to the Theater am Nollendorfplatz, opening with the sensational premiere of Ernst Toller's nightmare *Hoppla, wir leben!* In Piscator's production the 10 years spent in a mental asylum by the former revolutionary hero Toller were reviewed for the audience's benefit in the form of a newsreel presentation of the decade 1917–27, from the Russian revolution through Mussolini's march on Rome and Hitler's Munich *Putsch* to Lindbergh's solo flight across the Atlantic and the expulsion of Trotsky from the Soviet Communist Party. Another of Piscator's premieres was that of Walter Mehring's *Der Kaufmann von Berlin* in 1929, a remarkable revue-like satire on the exploiters and the exploited during the years of inflation after the war.

In the Theater am Nollendorfplatz and the acting studio that complemented it, soon re-christened the Piscatorbühne, the architect Walter Gropius, the satirical artist George Grosz, Max Brod, Brecht, actors like Max Pallenberg, Oscar Homolka, Carola Neher, Helene Weigel (later Brecht's wife), Lotte Lenya (wife of Kurt Weill) and many others met in the common enterprise. The method of 'objective acting' that emerged from the Piscator Studio was a natural counterpart to the theory of 'epic drama', and when in 1936 Piscator escaped from Germany, first to Paris, then to the United States, this approach to the actor's craft gained great influence on the American stage and in drama schools.

For 11 years after his return to Europe in 1951 Piscator, now seen by many as a figure overtaken by history, went from country to country as guest producer of German and other plays, until in 1962, coming full circle, he was appointed director of the new Freie Volksbühne in West Berlin (the original Volksbühne still stands on its old site in the eastern part of the city). The Berliner Ensemble—Brecht himself had died six years earlier—was still at the peak of its fame. So here were two theatres, both in the control of left-wing intellectuals, one-time close friends and associates, who believed

in using the stage as a means of changing society. Yet the Freie
Volksbühne is no more a 'popular' theatre in the capitalist West than
the Berliner Ensemble is a 'popular' theatre in the socialist East. The
Freie Volksbühne on the Schaperstrasse and the Berliner Ensemble in
the Theater am Schiffbauerdamm are three miles apart geographi-
cally and worlds apart politically. Culturally they are closer together
than we might expect—but not for the reasons that we, or their
founders, would think.

Brecht first studied Marx systematically in 1926. At the same time he
formed the opinion that the objective processes of social reality could
not be accommodated within the forms of drama hitherto developed
in the Western world. This meant that, as a new, that is, Marxist-
world would take the place of the old, so a new, Marxist-oriented
drama was needed to stimulate and exemplify the process of historical
evolution. Since this process was inevitable, man's obligation lay in
an objective understanding of what he was witnessing, and of what he
was a part, rather than in an emotional involvement in it. Drawing on
new experiences, like that of the ritualised Japanese No-plays, and
through his technique of estrangement, the much-discussed
Verfremdungseffekt, he introduced a distance between the events of
drama and the spectators of these events, making people think rather
than feel, understand rather than sympathise, make decisions rather
than ponder motives. These qualities make up what he called 'the
active spectator', and the art-form he evolved for his purpose received
the name first used, in this political sense, by Piscator—epic drama.
    Political theatre meant for Brecht the demonstration of how the
world could, and must, be changed in accordance with Marxist
principles. But from the beginning he took an independent view of the
Marxist dialectic, using it, not as the theoretical basis for a code of
party discipline but as the repository of proof that the social changes
in which he believed could in fact be brought about. The seeds of this
independence were sown by Karl Korsch, the man to whom Brecht
ascribed his introduction to Marxism. Korsch had been expelled from
the German Communist Party as early as 1926 for an 'unacceptable'
book on Marx, and this non-conformism passed to the 28-year-old
Brecht.
    A similar influence reached Brecht from the sociologist Fritz
Sternberg, a man whose attitudes reflected the confusion that beset
many an intellectual in the years of the Weimar Republic. He
believed in the class struggle and in the necessity to base the culture of
the future on a classless society, but he saw the great achievements in

German culture as having preceded the present age of epigones absorbed with the class-struggle, while the struggle itself could only be culturally unproductive. Of the contribution of the proletariat to both the socialist revolution and the consolidation of the socialist culture that would follow, Sternberg had a low opinion, and his appeal for action was directed to the intelligentsia. But of the few who heard the appeal, only a handful were outside the Communist Party whose authority Sternberg would not accept, and the intellectual's traditional lack of contact with the proletariat left him in a position of isolation from which he never escaped.

In considering the relationship of men like Korsch, Sternberg and Brecht to the German Communist Party one must recall the economic and political background during these latter years of the Weimar Republic. In the wake of rising prosperity between 1924 and 1929 came, on the one hand, the formation of industrial trusts like Vereinigte Stahlwerke and I. G. Farben, and on the other hand the increased concentration of organised labour into trade unions with an official place in the social and economic system. With the state acting as mediator in conflicts of interest between these two blocs, the economy ran smoothly and efficiently before the depression of 1930 burst the bubble of illusory prosperity. Power, and hence discipline, were of the essence. Pride in national achievements had tangible results by which to justify itself, and self-gratulatory emotions about 'German' virtues led to the rise of nationalist sentiment, both honourable, in the sense of an acceptance of history and of the conditioning influences of tradition, and dishonourable, in the shape of bigotry, militarism and anti-Semitism.

In 1928, the year of Brecht's *Dreigroschenoper*, Hugenberg became leader of the Deutschnationale Volkspartei, whose support came from the *Stahlhelm* (the biggest and most aggressive of the war veterans' organisations), the *Alldeutscher Verband* (Pan-German League) and the great financial and industrial concerns. The following year Hugenberg and Hitler published their Law against the Enslavement of the German People, and 1930, the year of the great depression, marked the emergence of Hitler and the National Socialist Party as a major force in German politics. Fascism was round the corner, and those who had scorned Hitler as a megalomaniac with no hope of gaining popular support were about to experience the tragic consequences of their blindness.

Against such a background the Communist Party was bound to feel all the more determined to close ranks. Born rebels like Korsch, Sternberg and Brecht, who had more than a touch of the anarchist about them, were unwelcome, and assertions of independence were to show themselves throughout Brecht's career, right down to his final years.

The dilemma of the dissenting party member—or, more accurately, of the party faced with the problem of a dissenting member—is presented in *Die Massnahme* (1930), the most powerful of Brecht's openly didactic plays of this period, which also include *Das Badener Lehrstück vom Einverständnis* (1928–9) with music by Hindemith, the two school operas *Der Jasager* (1929–30) and *Der Neinsager* (1930), both with music by Kurt Weill, and *Die Ausnahme und die Regel* (1930; music by Paul Dessau).

Die Massnahme, the first of a number of works for which Hanns Eisler, a pupil of Schoenberg's, composed the music, was performed in the Berlin Schauspielhaus in December, 1930, with Helene Weigel (whom Brecht had married in 1928) and Ernst Busch as two of the 'Agitatoren'. It was three months after the spectacular leap by the Nazi party to become the second largest party in the Reichstag, and a time when, against a background of rising unemployment and political disillusionment, the brown-shirted, jack-booted thugs of Hitler's S.A. were breaking up rival political meetings and preparing the ground for his seizure of power. Since the Communists were one of the prime objects of violent attention, the issue of party solidarity held a crucial and sensitive importance. Brecht sets out in *Die Massnahme* a pattern of action in which a young party member, by having given way to his humane instincts and helped the oppressed labourers, obstructs the work of the party and thus has to be 'liquidated'—with his own consent. In the second volume of his posthumously-published memoirs, the Marxist *littérateur* and critic Ernst Fischer describes how, in exactly the same way, with a conviction that could not have been other than self-generated, the Hungarian Communist 'rebel' Lászlo Rajk acquiesced in his own trial and execution in 1949.

In a note appended to the play Brecht prescribes that the hero's role in his four principal scenes shall be taken by each of his accusing comrades in turn, so that the actors who convey the message can themselves learn what it means:

> *Furchtbar ist es, zu töten,*
> *Aber nicht andere nur, auch uns töten wir, wenn es nottut*
> *Da doch nur mit Gewalt diese tötende*
> *Welt zu ändern ist, wie*
> *Jeder Lebende weiss.*

> (It is terrible to kill.
> But we do not only kill others: if needs be, we even kill ourselves,
> For it is only by force that this killing
> Can be changed, as every
> Living soul knows.)   (Scene 8)

And if a non-committed spectator ventures to wonder about compassion, or justice, or freedom, Brecht immediately cuts off the discussion with a quotation from Lenin: 'Our morality is based on the interests of the proletarian class-struggle.' [20] Morality—as Brecht said of man himself—is at the centre of things. But only relatively.

Brecht's commitment to the Marxist-Leninist cause cannot be doubted. Yet the Party could hardly give its blessing to a play that presented the shooting of a comrade as the normal way of dealing with deviationists. Harsh criticism came from both Berlin and Moscow, pointing out, in addition, the unhistorical nature and bourgeois idealistic irrelevance of the struggle between emotion and reason which gives the work its moral meaning. The intolerability of humane sentiment in a world of violence and selfishness also informs another 'Lehrstück' of this year, *Die Ausnahme und die Regel*, in which the overseer of the coolie sings:

> *In dem System, das sie gemacht haben,*
> *Ist Menschlichkeit eine Ausnahme.*
> *Wer sich also menschlich erzeigt*
> *Der trägt den Schaden davon.*

> (In the system they have made
> Humaneness is the exception.
> So a man who shows he is humane
> Has to suffer for it.)[21]

Yet it cannot be overlooked in *Die Massnahme* as it stands that Brecht shares the humanity of his victim as well as a conviction of its inevitable destruction. For the decision of the accusers to get rid of their young comrade comes, not after he rebels against a soulless and immoral authority by tearing up the works of Lenin, but because, by ripping off his mask and shouting his protest, he endangers their lives. He is as much a revolutionary as they are—'Mein Herz schlägt für die Revolution'—but he is also for freedom, and will not be silenced:

> *Ich kann nicht schweigen, weil ich recht habe.*

> (I cannot keep silent, because I am right)

The play's sympathy, whatever views its author expressed elsewhere, does not lie on the side of the executioners or of the stern orthodoxy in whose name they act. Karl Thieme (see note 22. below) quotes a comment by one who attended a public discussion of the play a week after its first performance: 'It was noticeable that the Marxists present were very much in conflict with their natural emotions' (*ibid.* p. 413).

This is not the only point at which Brecht's uncompromising morality, like his involvement in the plight of the underdog—the social outcast for whose 'immorality' (like that of Shen Te in *Der gute Mensch von Sezuan*) society itself is to blame—recalls the moral challenge of the New Testament, a challenge as studiously avoided by contemporary society as it had been by the contemporaries of Christ. When he was asked by a magazine in 1928 what book had most influenced him, he replied: 'You'll laugh when I tell you . . . the Bible.'[22] And it is more than an affinity of language and imagery that links Brecht the rebellious, intolerant, radical atheist, and Luther the rebellious, intolerant, radical Christian reformer.

Perhaps this juxtaposition of the Marxist and the theological, the radical programmatic and the Lutheran mystical, entitles us to turn for a moment from Brecht to another of what Hemingway called this 'lost generation', a fellow-Marxist from the mid-1920s, a fellow-refugee from Hitler's Germany in 1933, a critic for whom Brecht was the most important figure in the last 10 years of his life, and whose suicide in 1940 Brecht is said to have called the first real literary casualty of Hitlerism—Walter Benjamin. Drawn first to Zionism, then to Marxism, wholly committing himself to neither yet grasping each as a comprehensive statement about the world both as present reality and as product of history, Benjamin looks in one direction towards Kafka, and in the other towards Brecht. His essay on Goethe's *Die Wahlverwandtschaften* appeared in Hofmannsthal's *Neue Deutsche Beiträge* in 1924–5, and his *Ursprung des deutschen Trauerspiels* in 1928, but a great deal of his work, including the original text of *Das Kunstwerk im Zeitalter seiner Reproduzierbarkeit*, has only been published since the 1950s. Attracted by what Brecht called 'plumpes Denken', as opposed to dialectical dogmatism, he found his own, independent Marxist position, though his value judgements are often those of a critic who was a Marxist, rather than of a Marxist critic. For as Schopenhauer's pessimism is not logically necessary, or deducible from the terms of *Die Welt als Wille und Vorstellung*, but a psychological assumption, so Benjamin's Marxism is far from being the *fons et origo* of all the critical conclusions at which he arrives. Something of a cult figure in recent years, he reminds one of what Tucholsky said of Brecht in 1928: 'He is as overrated today as he will be underrated tomorrow.' But he is too challenging a figure to be overlooked.

Brecht's 'Lehrstücke' form a kind of positive counterweight to the destructive, anti-capitalist works of the same period, the two operas *Die Dreigroschenoper* (1928) and *Aufstieg und Fall der Stadt Mahagonny*

(1928–9), both with music by Kurt Weill, and *Die heilige Johanna der Schlachthöfe* (1929–30). The last-named returns to the larger-than-life American capitalist world of Brecht's imagination, a despicable world in which force, not the compassion of the Salvation Army heroine of the play, is needed to effect social change.

Die Dreigroschenoper, a ballad opera adapted from John Gay's *Beggar's Opera* of 1728 and set in the Soho of the Victorian age, enjoyed a huge popular success from the moment of its first performance in the Theater am Schiffbauerdamm. The extraordinary concatenation of events that surrounded this work is a microcosm of the turmoil that attended Brecht's public career. As a satire on modern capitalist society, portrayed as a world in which success equals villainy and corruption, it had the standard-bearers of that society squealing with delight. And there is no more sardonic representation of the slick, sordid, light-headed,don't-want-to-know world of the tottering Weimar Republic than the spiky yet sentimental, bitter-sweet music of Kurt Weill, which is an inseparable part of the work.

As a legal *cause célèbre* in which Brecht and Weill sued the Nero Film Company for breach of contract over the film rights of the work (Brecht lost, Weill won), it revealed its author as a litigious figure with a keen eye to self-interest (the publicity proved very remunerative), a dogmatic public confidence in the rightness of his own position and a readiness to invoke any intellectual sophistries to retain it—though to define it would be as tortuous and contradictory a process as to try and trace the international movement of his finances. And as a literary *cause célèbre* in which he was found to have plagiarised 'K.L. Ammer's' German translation of poems by Villon, it gave him a public platform from which to plead 'a basic laxity in matters of literary property'.[23] This, he maintained, accorded with his notions of 'collective authorship'—which can be followed in his *Versuche* from 1930 onwards. There was something of Mackie Messer in Brecht himself.

The mercenary greed of capitalist society is also the object of assault in *Aufstieg und Fall der Stadt Mahagonny*, a portrait of contemporary Berlin and an attack, in its form and its music, on the bourgeois 'black-tie-and-evening-gown' institution that Brecht called 'kulinarische Oper'. Weill's music, cool, detached, parodistic in tone, forms both a perfect foil for the text and an independent dimension to the work, the deliberate denial of the fusion of words and music on which the edifice of Wagnerian opera rests.

On the day after the Reichstag fire, as Hitler's stormtroopers, many of them already incorporated by Goering into the Prussian police, were launching the campaign of terrorism that led up to the

Reichstag elections of 5 March 1933, Brecht left Germany for Vienna. With Thomas and Heinrich Mann, Thomas's son Klaus, Arnold Zweig, Ernst Toller, Alfred Döblin, Arthur Koestler, Lion Feuchtwanger and countless other intellectuals, he became one of those whose careers in their native country were at an end for as long as Hitler's regime lasted.

Described in the familiar terms of tendencies of the *Zeitgeist*, Brecht belongs to the movement of so-called 'Neue Sachlichkeit' ('New Objectivity' or 'Neo-Realism') that held sway after the expiry of the expressionist impulse in the mid-1920s. If expressionism emerged as an egocentric protest against the Great War and the values that had led to it, and as a call for a 'new man' with the moral strength to set the world right, then 'Neue Sachlichkeit' can be seen as an acknowledgement—sometimes confident, sometimes resigned, sometimes rebellious—of the material consolidation of the Weimar Republic, as an acceptance of the derivation of art from life, and a statement of the obligation of the artist to his public. In social-revolutionary form it is particularly powerful in the graphics of men like Otto Dix, Alexander Kanoldt and Oskar Nerlinger, in the savage caricatures of George Grosz, and in the use of photo-montage as a political weapon in the cause of the proletariat. In music it has a parallel in the philosophy of *Gebrauchsmusik* ('Utility Music') associated with Hindemith and Ernst Křenek during these years.

That art was part of, not apart from, life was axiomatic to Brecht—not some utopian life seen in a vision, or the life known to our forefathers, but the beautiful, sordid, exciting, depressing, historically-conditioned 'real' world of our present experience. The Swiss novelist and dramatist Max Frisch, who spent a good deal of time in his company in Zurich in 1947, after Brecht's return from America, describes how, coolly, objectively, with the Swabian accent he never lost, he read his moving poem 'An die Nachgeborenen' to a circle of friends. 'His attitude', writes Frisch,

'was that of a man who, cigar in hand, was forced to read the words simply because not everyone had these words in front of him—rather like reading a letter aloud, for the information of others. . . The pause that usually follows the reading of a poem—a situation that reminds me of coming out of church, suddenly leaving the organ behind and being somewhat taken aback on confronting the real world again, which is so different from the world of poetry—this pause is unnecessary. A real poem has no need to shrink from the real world; it can stand up to it, even when the doorbell rings and an unexpected visitor arrives who, while we are still drinking the same cup of coffee, tells us about the four years he has just spent in jail.'[24]

'An die Nachgeborenen' belongs to a later period of Brecht's life, but the blunt commitment to life, above all to its rough, cruel, earthy side, already dominates the balladesque poems of the *Hauspostille*, published in 1927, a repository of Brechtian attitudes from the expressionist-coloured days of *Baal* to *Die Dreigroschenoper*, *Aufstieg und Fall der Stadt Mahagonny* and the early didactic plays.

Brecht has become a classic, and has acquired what Max Frisch called 'the sweeping ineffectiveness of a classic'.[25] The big plays of his later career, from *Mutter Courage und ihre Kinder* to *Der Kaukasische Kreidekreis*, do not belong to this context, but the works written during these final years of the Weimar Republic may lead us to conclude with Frisch that we cannot expect drama to do what direct political propaganda has failed to do: 'Audiences running into millions have seen Brecht and will see him again and again. I venture to doubt whether anyone has as a result changed his political thinking or even seriously examined it.'[26]

Like all works of art, these plays of Brecht's relate to a specific historical situation. But their power, to a greater degree than that of many works of the period, derives directly from this situation. The Western capitalism that Brecht presents no longer exists, and to do justice to these dramas one does not need to make the historical pretence that it does. As Herbert Marcuse once pointed out, the workers of today have a good deal more to lose than their chains.[27]

Martin Walser summed up the matter thus:

One borrows the spittle of history and spits at an historical corpse but still has the satisfying feeling of having spat in the right direction. . . I therefore wonder whether it would not be better to interpret Brecht's plays as documentary records of a struggle in the past: very much for practical use. In this way one can show how things used to be.'[28]

NOTES

1. *Aufruf an die Jugend* (1924) in F. von Unruh, *Politeia. Aufrufe, Proteste, Gedichte, Reden* (Frankfurt, 1968), 32
2. Toller, *Ausgewählte Schriften* (Berlin, 1961), IX
3. see Toller, *No More Peace!*, transl. E. Crankshaw (London, 1937), 105
4. B. Diebold, *Der Denkspieler Georg Kaiser* (Frankfurt, 1924), 65
5. *Expressionismus. Der Kampf um eine literarische Bewegung* ed. P. Raabe (Munich, 1965), 136
6. *Die letzten Tage der Menschheit* (Munich, 1957), 10
7. *ibid.*
8. *Stücke* I (Berlin, 1954), 6–7
9. *ibid.* 8
10. *arnolt bronnen gibt zu protokoll* (Hamburg, 1954), 6–7

11. *Als wär's ein Stück von mir* (Vienna, 1966), 380
12. *Stücke* I (Frankfurt, 1961), 10
13. E. Piscator, *Das politische Theater* (Reinbek, 1963), 47
14. In the symposium *Bertolt Brecht* (Inter Nationes, Bad Godesberg, 1966), 17
15. *Ich glaube! Bekenntnisse* (Munich, 1928), 18
16. Maria Ley-Piscator, *The Piscator Experiment* (New York, 1967), 71
17. M. Piscator, op. cit. 61
18. *ibid.* 57
19. *Schriften zum Theater* I (Frankfurt, 1963), 89–90
20. *Stücke* IV (Frankfurt, 1955), 314
21. *Stücke* V (Frankfurt, 1957), 226
22. K. Thieme, 'Des Teufels Gebetbuch?' (*Hochland* 29, 1, 1932, 402 note 6)
23. see E. Schumacher, *Die dramatischen Versuche Bertolt Brechts 1918–1933* (Berlin, 1955), 242
24. Frisch, *Tagebuch 1946–1949* (Frankfurt, 1958), 225–7
25. 'Der Autor und das Theater', an address to the *Dramaturgentagung* in Frankfurt in 1964 (*Die Neue Rundschau* 76, 1, 1965), 38
26. *ibid.*
27. *The Listener* (London, 9 February, 1978), 170
28. In *Bertolt Brecht* (Inter Nationes, Bad Godesberg, 1966), 41

CHAPTER FOUR

A Vision of Man and the World:
Lyric Poetry

LOOKING back on the Great War and on the watershed that it formed in the history of Europe, Erich von Kahler reflected:

'It marked the end of 40 years of peace, and at the same time the end of what had been a basically middle-class era. The social order had still been preserved by old conventions of class and occupation, with their rigid restrictions and their air of outer respectability. The nobility the middle classes, professional soldiers, politicians, scientists, artists—all had their own separate preserves, established on materialistic principles but rationalised for the benefit of the outside world. And although anybody with the slightest sensitivity realised how intolerable the situation was, a mysterious balance of forces conspired to maintain it. It was still the world of Fontane and Sudermann and the early Schnitzler, though becoming increasingly undermined and insecure. Politics was for the politicians, art was a decorative appendage to life, science served the needs of industry, hygiene and a mechanistic society. Everything had its appointed place. Yet everywhere one sensed a highly-charged atmosphere, the heaviness that precedes a great storm. Today's conflicts, in all their savagery, take place in the open and are left free to run their destructive course, but at that time progressive movements were concealed behind an official mask of approved behaviour and social convention.'[1]

If in literature the more importunate, more spectacular of these 'progressive movements' showed themselves in drama, their most immediate, most concentrated expression came in lyric poetry, where external conventions were at their least pressing and formal values at their most malleable. The expressionist 'new man', seeking the timeless essence of things and rejecting the forms of a contingent reality, intolerantly and violently asserts the absoluteness of the individual personality. As the old Adam dies, and with him the assumptions of naturalism, of the power of conceptual thought and of a demonstrable ethic, so the new generation thinks out its own relationship to God, to nature, to the vital springs of existence.

In this, of course, the poets of expressionism did only what any generation of poets does, defining its originality against the data of contemporary life. The first decade of the twentieth century, together with the Great War, had demonstrated the rottenness of the body politic, the hollowness of social morality and the transience of the much-vaunted naturalistic 'reality' on which art was assumed to depend. The 'revaluation of all values', in Nietzsche's phrase—and all these poets stood in the shadow of Nietzsche—reflected an unquestioned, almost spontaneous urge to rejection and renewal, to

79

the Goethean 'Stirb und werde', the exposure of the decrepitude and decay of an 'untergangsgeweihte Welt', in Gottfried Benn's phrase, and the proclamation of a spiritual regeneration. In the isolation of moments of conflict between the old and the new, and their presentation as a challenge to those with the courage to demand a new future, the public initiative lay with the dramatist. In the intimate, personal sphere, where immediacy of expression is paramount and directness of reception intrinsic, the lyric has the power to reach deepest into the mind and compel a reaction to the new thoughts and the new techniques of form and language. Attitudes come first—subjects come later. The How matters more than the What.

There is still no more authentic or powerful source of this poetry than the anthology published in Berlin in 1920 under the title *Menschheitsdämmerung, Symphonie jüngster Dichtung*. Its editor, Kurt Pinthus, a contemporary of those whose work he assembled, put together some 270 poems by 23 poets in, as he put it,

a collection of emotional schocks and passions, the yearnings, happinesses and sufferings of an age—of our own age. It is a collection of human emotions drawn from the age and transmitted back to the age. It is not meant as an exhibition of poetic skeletons but as a kaleidoscope of all the explosive agitation and confusion of our time.[2]

It is often in lyric poetry that the earliest signs of change in the spiritual climate of an age appear—the lyric, in Pinthus' image, as a barometer of imminent movement in the conditions of life. The mechanistic naturalism of the latter nineteenth century, sustained by a faith in the universal validity of the law of cause and effect and by a confidence in the inevitability of human progress, crumbled under the gaze of Else Lasker-Schüler, Ernst Stadler, Theodor Däubler and other writers in the first decade of the twentieth century, and in the years surrounding the war the gaze became fiercer, the tone harsher and more intolerant, the poetic message more violent. Georg Heym's collections *Der ewige Tag* (1911) and *Umbra Vitae* (1912), Gottfried Benn's *Morgue* (1912) and George Trakl's *Gedichte* published in volumes seven and eight of *Der Jüngste Tag* in 1913 contain some of the most substantial and representative examples of this mood, a mood of cold nihilism and *memento mori* set by the poem 'Weltende' by Jakob van Hoddis (the pseudonym of Hans Davidsohn), which opens *Menschheitsdämmerung*:

> Dem Bürger fliegt vom spitzen Kopf der Hut,
> In allen Lüften hallt es wie Geschrei.

Dachdecker stürzen ab und gehn entzwei,
Und an den Küsten—liest man—steigt die Flut.

Der Sturm ist da, die wilden Meere hupfen
An Land, um dicke Dämme zu zerdrücken.
Die meisten Menschen haben einen Schnupfen.
Die Eisenbahnen fallen von den Brücken.

(End of the World
The citizen's hat is blown off his pointed head, and sounds of screaming rend the air; tilers fall off the roof, their bodies split, and the tide, so one reads, is rising round the shores.

The tempest is here; the savage seas leap on to the land to crush the thick embankments. Most people have colds. The trains fall off the bridges.)

Almost every short, paratactic sentence has its image of movement and agitation—'fliegt', 'Geschrei', 'stürzen ab', 'gehn entzwei'.

Yet the poet's manner is detached, unconcerned, irreverently ironical: is this a time for people to be blowing their noses? It is as though the cataclysm were something of which he were a mere spectator, something which, as he says, he had read about in the paper. A step further leads to the love-hate relationship with the ugly and unpleasant aspects of the life of the here and how, a relationship broached in the very next poem, Georg Heym's 'Umbra vitae', and cultivated especially by Benn and Trakl.

With a handful of exceptions—Trakl, Benn, occasionally Johannes R. Becher and Franz Werfel—the lyric poetry of the expressionist movement has an aura of collectivity about it. That this should be true of the capers of the Dadaists and Surrealists is not remarkable, for so radical and irrational an anarchism could not but issue in a chaos within which differentiation was at best irrelevant and at worst impossible. But it is not markedly less true of the body of expressionist poets as a whole, from Stadler to Bruno Goetz and from Däubler to Karl Otten, and this poetry is more aptly approached through its common themes and attitudes than through the study of the *oeuvre* of individual poets.

Thus Pinthus assembled his *Menschheitsdämmerung* not chronologically or by personality but under four subject-headings expressive of the concerns and moods of a generation that despised the world of its forefathers and, surrounded by the fruits of destruction, looked for a new sense of brotherhood:

Wir schenken einander das Ich und das Du -
ewig eint uns das Wort:
MENSCH.
Immer
Können wir glücklich sein.

(We give our own selves to each other;
we are united for ever by one word—
MAN
We can be happy
eternally.
(Kurt Heynicke, 'Freundschaft')

The first section of poems is headed 'Sturz und Schrei', and dwells
on elements of life in society which symbolise the malaise of the time
and provoke the 'scream' of protest. The senselessness and immorality
of war fill poems by Albert Ehrenstein, August Stramm, Wilhelm
Klemm and Franz Werfel, poems in which man confronts death and
asks himself what meaning his situation has. From this one moves to
studies of sickness, disease and the decay of human bodies—
calculated, sometimes callous essays in the technique of offence and
shock:

> *Komm, hebe ruhig diese Decke auf.*
> *Sieh, dieser Klumpen Fett und faule Säfte*
> *das war einst irgendeinem Mann gross*
> *und hiess auch Rausch und Heimat.*

> (Come on, lift up this blanket.
> Look at that mass of fat and stinking fluid:
> It all used to belong to some upstanding man
> And bear the names of Ecstasy and Homeland.)
> (Gottfried Benn, 'Mann und Frau gehn durch die Krebsbaracke')

Some poems talk of suffering—Ehrenstein's 'Leid' and 'Schmerz',
Heynicke's 'Gethsemane'; others of despair—Stramm's 'Schwermut'
and 'Verzweifelt', Ehrenstein's 'Ich bin des Lebens und des Todes
müde'; others again, in querulous bewilderment, of the apparent
pointlessness and Godlessness of life—Werfel's 'Warum mein Gott',
Klemm's 'Philosophie'. A particular object of bitterness is the city,
symbol of man-made misery and monument to the false gods
worshipped by the nineteenth century. 'O Stadt der Schmerzen in
Verzweiflung düsterer Zeit!' cried Becher to that city which above all
others embodied the vices of the past and carried within it the
certainty of damnation:

> *Einst kommen wird der Tag! ... Da mit des Zorns Geschrei*
> *Der Gott wie einst empört die milbige Kruste sprengt.*
> *Im Scherbenhorizonte treibt ein fetter Hai,*
> *Dem blutiger Leichen Frass aus zackichtem Maule hängt.*[3]

(Some time the day will come when, incensed as once before, the god will break open
the mouldy crust with a scream of rage. On the cracked horizon a pot-bellied shark

will be floating, with its meal of bloodstained corpses trailing from its jagged jaws.)
(Johannes R. Becher, 'Berlin')

The second section of *Menschheitsdämmerung*, 'Erweckung des Herzens', is generally gentler in tone, a collection of emotional reactions to nature, to the passing seasons, to personal relationships and experiences, to the Almighty. Yet here too there is coldness and nihilism, as in Benn's 'O, Nacht!' and 'Synthese', alongside anxious desires to find some ground for hope (Iwan Goll's 'Karawane der Sehnsucht') and moments of confidence in meaningful survival (Hoddis' 'Morgens', Werfel's 'Ich habe eine gute Tat getan', Schickele's 'Ode an die Engel'). The poets are seeking here to define their position *vis-à-vis* the unchanging facts of life, to lay the foundations of what could be called, in the widest sense, their religion. The pantheistic tendency of this religion emerges with particular clarity in the 1920s in the expressionistically-coloured poems and plays of Ernst Lissauer.

In the third section, with the title 'Aufruf und Empörung', the more specifically political programme of the new movement finds expression. Shrill, strident tones dominate:

> *Der Dichter meidet strahlende Akkorde.*
> *Er stösst durch Tuben, peitscht die Trommel schrill.*
> *Er reisst das Volk auf mit gehackten Sätzen.*

> (The poet shuns radiant chords.
> He sounds trumpets, flays the drums deafeningly,
> Stir up the people with staccato phrases)
> (Johannes R. Becher, 'Vorbereitung')

If there was to be a political tendency among these 20- and 30-year-old poets, it could only be towards the overthrow of discredited social institutions which symbolised the forces that had to be overcome if a new Germany was to arise. The 1917 revolution in Russia represented for many the hope for the future of mankind, and the revolutionary impulse behind Hasenclever's *Antigone* and *Die Menschen*, Toller's *Die Wandlung* and *Masse Mensch* and many other dramas of those years also found its way into the lyric. Brecht, who was younger than any of the poets in *Menschheitsdämmerung*, is an obvious example, but many of the expressionists themselves looked in the same direction at this time. Among them was Karl Otten, who, recalling his career as an 'angry young man' in these post-war years, wrote:

I thought I had found in Russia and her revolution a deliverance from evil. I was not the only one to think that. Like me, many believed in those years, 1917 to 1919, that they had made the final cruel, supreme sacrifice in the spirit of Tolstoi and Dostoevsky. History has made us think again, for the horrors of the years that followed reduced those of the war to insignificance.[4]

But at the time faith in the Marxist creed, or at least in parts of it, ran high, encompassing the 50-year-old naturalist poet Richard Dehmel at the one extreme ('Der Arbeitsmann', 'Predigt an ein Grosstadtvolk') and the 20-year-old Brecht at the other, with many highly articulate poets of the expressionist movement between them.

Where the first three sections of *Menschheitsdämmerung* focus on the private and self-justificatory, or on the violently resentful and reformatory, the final section, 'Liebe den Menschen', appeals to the creative humanistic, sometimes religious values that bind men together. Poems are here called 'Hoffnung' (Ehrenstein), 'An die Besiegten' (Otten), 'Freundschaft' (Heynicke), 'Erfüllung' (Klemm), 'Pfingsten' (Schickele), 'Veni creator spiritus' (Werfel). The quivering rage of Becher's 'Hymne auf Rosa Luxemburg', written after the murder of the Spartacist leader in January 1919, is almost incongruous in this company, an incongruity made especially pointed by the eerily sober poem that follows—'Der tote Liebknecht', written by Rudolf Leonhard on the shooting, that same January day, of Rosa Luxemburg's fellow-revolutionary leader.

Thus the expressionist 'new man' would join his brethren to create a 'new mankind', often Christian in conception, even among those, like Otten, who saw the Russian revolution as the harbinger of a new world order:

> Wir wollen warten, bis uns vor Gottes Thron
> Gemeinsam, Hand in Hand,
> Als Brüder, als Brüder, ja als Brüder Flammen der Liebe entzücken.

(Let us await the time when together, standing hand in hand before the throne of God as brothers, brothers, yea, as brothers, we are ravished by the flames of love.)
(Otten, 'An die Besiegten')

And in the final poem in the book, 'Ein Lebens-Lied', Werfel advances 'Anmut des Menschlichen' as the only imperishable value in life, the faith by which to overcome the despair of Hoddis' poem 'Weltende' with which *Menschheitsdämmerung* had opened:

> Doch über allen Worten
> Verkünd' ich, Mensch, wir sind!!

(But surpassing all one can say,
I proclaim, O man—*we are!*)
(Werfel, 'Ein Lebens-Lied')

The mood may have changed, but the style and mode of address is the same: direct, peremptory, insistent, challenging. There is no exposition or extended narration, no schematic unfurling of a programme. Aesthetic values are at a discount, above all any talk of 'beauty', however defined, and new, angular forms emerge to contain the new, anti-conceptual, anti-naturalistic, anti-bourgeois postures. In language as in outlook the figure of Nietzsche dominates. And behind Nietzsche, in terms of what these poets saw as their philosophy of a unity not conceptual and causal but 'expressive', stand Novalis, Kleist (Benn called *Penthesilea* 'a pure orgy of emotional excitement given dramatic form and converted into verse')[7], Hölderlin, the late Goethe, Klopstock, and, still further back in the tradition of *Rausch*, the poets of the Baroque, Jakob Böhme and the mystics of the Middle Ages. The image, the vision, has become absolute, born in, and identical with, the action of expression. The word does not convey an image or vision 'of something', but has become absolute. There is to be extreme economy of words, each word rich in overtones, each utterance terse and powerful—the ideal represented by Hölderlin's 'Hälfte des Lebens' and 'Lebensalter'.

Outside the framework of expressionist anthologies like *Menschheitsdämmerung*, *Die Erhebung* and *Verkündigung*, but related to some of the political sentiments to be found there, lies a proletarian lyric poetry—Heinrich Lersch, Max Barthel, Gerrit Engelke, Karl Bröger—based on themes from working-class, predominantly urban, life and using the everyday attitudes and everyday modes of speech of the working-class community. The grand-scale utopianism of the expressionist vision here gives way to the concrete presentation of social reality in terms of the class-struggle, and to the definition of a distinctive working-class ethos in the conduct of life, of work and of personal relationships:

> *Wir stehen an glühenden Feuern*
> *und hämmern,*
> *Wir stehen an sausenden Bänken*
> *und drehen. . .*
> *Doch wir feilen in aufgelegter Fron,*
> *wir feilen zu unserem eigenen Hohn,*
> *und in jedem wilden Hammerschlag*
> *stöhnt und dröhnt es:*
> *Wann kommt der Tag der Freiheit?*

(We stand by the glowing furnaces and hammer. We stand and work by the roaring lathes. . . . But in our forced labour we are only perfecting our own derisive state, and with each savage hammer-blow booms and pounds the message: when will the day of freedom come?)

(Kurt Klaeber: in
Das proletarische Schicksal
ed. H. Mühle, Gotha, 1929.)

But times will change:

> *Ihr im Kontor, in der Fabrik und in der Grube,*
> *am Rad, am Werk und in der Erde, ihr alle hört:*
> *die Frühlingsherrlichkeit ist auch für euch!*

(You in your office, in your factory, in your mine, you at the wheel, at your work and in the ground—you all will hear that the glory of spring is for you too.)

(Max Barthel: in *Das proletarische Schicksal*, 167)

Hans Mühle's *Das proletarische Schicksal*, the best-known anthology of working-class verse from the 1920s, contains scarcely a handful of memorable poems, yet it has its interest—a social rather than a literary interest—as a presentation of the attitudes and aspirations of this *Arbeiterdichtung* in particular and of the often ambivalent character of political poetry in general. Starry-eyed, rhetorical appeals to man's better nature in the cause of humane ideals are portrayed as the privileged intellectual's substitute for the direct action seen by the depressed classes as the only realistic course before them. Yet as the ideals faded before the manifest imperfectibility of the world and the limitations of human power, so also the patent absence of any political initiative with even a faint hope of success brought its own cynicism and disillusionment, and by 1930 liberal intellectuals and working classes were once more united in defeat. Neither was the proletariat going to assume the cultural mantle of the bourgeoisie, nor had it demonstrated a power to evolve its own cultural values and convince society that the future rested on these values.

Working-class poetry could readily incorporate a commitment to socialism, but as the best-known to these *Arbeiterdichter*, Heinrich Lersch, shows in his self-conscious proletarian nationalism, this is by no means to be taken for granted. Lersch's ideal lay not in workers' control of factories and the dictatorship of the proletariat but in the nobility of the artisan's labours and the uniqueness of his service to the community. It is an ideal which is closer to that of William Morris than to that of Karl Marx, reflecting a stubbornly naive, local, almost parochial conception of the cooperation and mutual respect of the different classes within society, far removed—the same is true of Lersch's autobiographical protest novel *Hammerschläge* (1930)—from the dictatorship of the proletariat. It was also an ideal that was to lead Lersch into the arms of National Socialism 10 years later.

The group calling itself the 'Werkleute auf Haus Nyland' drew Lersch, Engelke and others into its orbit, and as early as 1914 the leader of the group, Josef Winckler, had published his *Eiserne Sonette* to proclaim the imminent fulfilment of his cooperative ideals. Lersch's

Mensch im Eisen (1924) took up Winckler's message. In 'Bekenntnis', from the collection *Deutschland* (1918), Lersch had cried:

> *Ich glaub an Deutschland wie an Gott!*
> *Er gab uns, Mensch zu sein!*[5]

> (I believe in Germany as I do in God.
> It is He who made us men.)

And in 1934, in the collection *Mit brüderlicher Stimme*, he still struck the simple, loyal attitude which was to attract him to Hitler:

> *Ich bin, wie du, ein armer Knecht,*
> *Bin ein Prolet von Gottes Gnaden.*
> *Mit allem, was da gut und schlecht,*
> *Bin ich ein Mensch, von Gott beladen.*

(I am a poor servant, like you—a worker, by the grace of God. I am a man, with all the good things and bad that God has laden upon me.)

He was nothing if not consistent.

The ideology of this working-class poetry could have embraced an internationalism and a set of domestic priorities that would have averted attention from the disgraced values of the past. For whereas the intellectual tradition had to carry with it the detritus of its past failures, the 'Werkleute auf Haus Nyland', Lersch, Barthel, Bröger and the other proletarian poets carried no such historical encumbrances. That instead they thought in narrow, national terms and became a willing prey to the Nazis is one of the many sad pieces of the jigsaw puzzle of 1930 and the years that followed.

In contrast both to the committed poetry, personal or political, of the expressionists and to proletarian verse, the post-war situation also produced its sceptical, anti-idealistic attitudes, and at the fringes of expressionist lyric poetry itself, where anti-conceptualism and the cult of random word-association move into the extravagancies of Dada and surrealism, there is an acute awareness of the grotesque and the bizarre. Items are wrenched from their context, contexts are exploded, the discrepant and the incongruous become the paths to the new knowledge.

Dadaism grew out of the 'Cabaret Voltaire' in Zurich as an iconoclastic, anti-bourgeois movement dedicated to unsettling and scandalising the public in literature and the visual arts. The German practitioners of literary Dada in the 1920s—Hans Arp, Richard Huelsenbeck, Hugo Ball, Raoul Hausmann, Kurt Schwitters (they were also active in the visual arts)—were provoked by the chaotic, the incongruous, and the fortuitous to assume a mocking, frivolous tone which scorned the utopianism of much expressionist writing and deliberately outraged conventional, middle-class 'consumers' of the work of art. The result was poems like Arp's untranslatable 'Opus Null':

> Ich bin der grosse Derdiedas
> das rigorose Regiment
> der Ozonstengel prima Qua
> der anonyme Einprozent.
> Das P.P. Tit. und auch die Po
> Posaune ohne Mund und Loch
> das grosse Herkulesgeschirr
> der linke Fuss vom rechten Koch.
> Ich bin der lange Lebenslang
> der zwölfte Sinn im Eierstock
> der insgesamte Augustin
> im lichten Zellulosenrock.

The same dedication to the arbitrary and the experimental, the same anarchistic urge of *épater le bourgeois*, sustained the surrealists of the period, with Freud looking over their shoulders. The figure of Marx could also be seen in the background at times. Literary surrealism, however, had its headquarters in France (André Breton, Louis Aragon), and although both Dadaism and surrealism caused ripples on the surface of literary life in many European countries, their most striking influence was felt in the visual arts. Here too most of the leading artists associated with surrealism at one time or another in their career—Chirico, Masson, Picasso, Magritte, Joan Miró, Giacometti—belong to the Romance, not the Germanic world. Max Ernst was German by birth but worked in France and became a French citizen, while Paul Klee, having worked in Germany in the 1920s, went back to his native Switzerland when Hitler came to power.

Such symptoms of a decaying culture as the convulsions of Dadaism and surrealism are, however, not found only in the work of extremists, nor do they distinguish solely the generation of 20- and 30-year-olds who sustained the expressionist and other movements as a whole. The satirical world of Karl Kraus, for instance, above all of his drama *Die letzten Tage der Menschheit*, has its qualities of the hyperbolic and the bizarre. And have not 'bizarre' and 'macabre' become commonplace epithets to apply to the world of Franz Kafka? So in the lyric, in the wake of Gumppenberg and Morgenstern—the latter's *Galgenlieder* were published as early as 1905—comes the *Bänkelsänger* Joachim Ringelnatz, with the poems he recited in the cabarets of Munich, Leipzig and Berlin.

Ringelnatz (his real name was Hans Bötticher), with features and facial expression uncannily reminiscent of E.T.A. Hoffmann's grotesque sketches of Kapellmeister Johannes Kreisler, is a typical phenomenon of the 1920s. Sentimental yet irreverent, sensitive yet mockingly satirical, wittily superficial yet profoundly sympathetic, he embraces the contradictions of commitment and detachment, sincerity and disillusionment so familiar to the intellectuals of the Weimar Republic. Dressed as his favourite character of a sailor with open collar and bell-bottom trousers, he recited and acted his piquant *Moritatenlieder* and satirical verses before motley audiences of elegant middle-aged ladies, sharp-minded intellectuals and impecunious students. Often his tone had the roughness and calculated offensiveness of the intolerant moralist:

> *Wie seine eigene Spucke schmeckt,*
> *das weiss man nicht.*

> (One does not know what
> one's own spittle tastes like)

His gentler moods also had the power to make one feel uneasy:

> *An einander vorbei*

> *Irgendwo: Zwei Barfussmädchen winken.*
> *Wissen selber nicht, warum sie's tun,*
> *Lassen ihre arbeitsharten Hände*
> *Für Momente ruhn.*

> *Wissen nicht, dass deine Hände sinken.*
> *Winken,*
> *Grüssen,*
> *In den ganzen langen Zug hinein,*
> *Ahnen nicht, dass du die Scholle sein*
> *Möchtest unter ihren schmutzgen Füssen.*

> *Angelangt, ergibst du mittelgross*
> *Dich der Höflichkeit, dem Stande und dem Gelde,*
> *Nachts im Bette träumst du hoffnungslos*
> *Von den beiden Mädchen auf dem Felde.*

> (Passing by

Somewhere, two barefooted girls wave, not knowing themselves why, giving their work-hardened hands a few moments' rest.

Not knowing that your hands drop, they wave, say hallo down the whole of the long train, having no idea that you would like to be the soil beneath their dirty feet.

> When you arrive, you surrender yourself in your mediocrity to politeness, to
> class and to money; despairingly you dream in your bed at night of the two girls
> in the field.)

His use of everyday language in his poetry brings him close to
Brecht, particularly in parodistic vein. Rilke's 'Herbsttag', for
instance, ends with the well-known lines:

> *Wer jetzt kein Haus hat, baut sich keines mehr,*
> *Wer jetzt allein ist, wird es lange bleiben,*
> *Wird wachen, lesen, lange Briefe schreiben*
> *und wird in den Alleen hin und her*
> *unruhigwandern, wenn die Blätter treiben.*

Ringelnatz's version is:

> *Der Schnee ist schwarz und traurig*
> *In der Stadt.*
> *Wer da keine Unterkunft hat,*
> *Den bedaure ich.*
>
> (from the poem 'Schnee')

'Some of his poems', said Paul Claudel, 'have a Goethean
grandeur; others have a macabre humour. But how close to each
other seriousness and humour really are.' It is this last thought that
led people to couple his name with that of Charlie Chaplin. One
might say of Ringelnatz what Tucholsky said of Chaplin: 'Like all
great clowns, he is a philosopher.'[8]

The world of cabaret to which Ringelnatz belonged is deeply
rooted, like the world of the cinema, in the social, political and
cultural life of the time. But whereas the cinema is a mass medium, a
large-scale commercial enterprise depending for its existence on
broad public approval and representing the concerted activities of
many different craftsmen, cabaret is a refined, intimate milieu that
rests on the talent of the individual. Within the German-speaking
realm, above all in Berlin, Munich and Vienna, satirical social
comment has always been a staple ingredient of cabaret, and this
made places like the *Corso* and the *Distel* in Berlin and *Simplicissimus* in
Munich centres of intellectual discussion and political activity.
Indeed, political cabaret already flourished in the years before 1914,
when Frank Wedekind, Christian Morgenstern, Ludwig Thoma and
Otto Julius Bierbaum were the leading figures, singing their own
songs. Erich Mühsam, a Berliner who joined the Bavarian *Räterepublik*
after the war, spent six years in jail in the 1920s and died in the
concentration camp at Oranienburg in 1934, was also performing at
the *Hungriger Pegasus* and the *Cabaret zum Peter Hille* in Berlin at this

time, as well as at the *Simplicissimus* and in Vienna.

On the surface the aim is entertainment. Save for the intrusion of this commercial element, they might be considered a latter-day Bohemian equivalent of the early nineteenth-century salons in Berlin and elsewhere, where progressive intellectuals assembled to discuss the political and cultural issues of the day. Fundamentally, however, the intention is didactic, whether in musingly philosophic vein, like the great clown Karl Valentin in Munich (an early influence on Brecht), in literary and character satire like that of Max Pallenberg, or in mordant political sketches and songs in the tone set by men like Walter Mehring, Brecht—and Tucholsky.

Kurt Tucholsky is one of the most fascinating and attractive minor figures in the literature of the 1920s. By profession and by temperament he was a journalist, a Jewish intellectual with the keenness of perception to sense the political and social malaise in the body of the Weimar Republic, and with the integrity to make public the symptoms that he found. Like all independent left-wing intellectuals, he had to face the opposition both of the right and of the Communists, and as an intolerant crusader for truth, he was driven more and more into a position of loneliness and isolation. By 'truth' he meant, not an acceptable ideology to which to submit one's decisions but the pragmatic, experienced reality of the particular moment. In over 2,000 contributions, some in verse, some in prose, to the satirical journals *Simplicissimus* and *Ulk*, but above all to *Die Weltbühne*, he appealed for intellectual honesty and a sense of national decency in order to clear away the ruins of 1918 and bring honesty and respect into the conduct of public affairs.

From 1933 onwards he did not publish a single word. He was deprived of his German citizenship in that year, and his works, along with those of Marx, Freud, Heinrich Mann, Erich Kästner, Carl von Ossietzky, Erich Maria Remarque and other 'enemies of the Fatherland', were ceremonially burned. Tucholsky had seen it all coming, and had already written off the Weimar Republic as a forlorn episode in German history. In 1931, in a review of Hans Fallada's novel *Bauern, Bonzen und Bomben*, he wrote in resignation:

After one has read this book, one realises the enormous guilt of the republic which we once had and which now lies in pieces, broken by its unbelievable cowardice, its feebleness and the lack of instinct of its middle classes, paramount among them those champions of social democracy who sanctioned the use of armoured cars. The will of the others was stronger, and those who are stronger are entitled to claim their victory. You have no ground for complaint.[9]

'Those who are stronger' were the industrialists, the army and para-military organisations like the *Stahlhelm*, and right-wing nationalist opportunists like Hitler. These were the prime targets of Tucholsky's merciless scorn and invective. More aggressive, more bitter than Ringelnatz, and more deliberately political in commitment and intent, he addressed himself in his poems and prose pieces to rousing the social conscience of the people and making them aware of the realities to which they were happy to blind themselves:

> *O hochverehrtes Publikum,*
> *sag mal: bist du wirklich so dumm,*
> *wie uns das an allen Tagen*
> *alle Unternehmer sagen?*
> *Jeder Direktor mit dickem Popo*
> *spricht: 'Das Publikum will es so!'*
> *Jeder Filmfritze sagt: 'Was soll ich machen?*
> *Das Publikum wünscht diese zuckrigen Sachen!'*
> *Jeder Verleger zuckt die Achseln und spricht:*
> *'Gute Bücher gehn eben nicht!'*
>> *Sag mal, verehrtes Publikum,*
>> *bist du wirklich so dumm?*

> (Tell me, gentle readers all,
> Why our commercial masters call
> You stupid, rate your taste so low.
> *Are* you stupid? *Is* it so?
> Directors say: 'It is our task
> To give the people what they ask.'
> And fat-bummed film men, sly enough,
> Make out we want their treacly stuff.
> The publisher just turns away:
> 'No one reads good books today!'
>> Is the people's taste so low?
>> *Are* you stupid? *Is* it so?)

(ed. cit. III, 889)

This sort of thing is, of course, nothing more than journalistic versifying, and has no place in the history of 'serious' poetry—though in tone and technique it could count Heine and Wilhelm Busch among its antecedents. The political Heine, indeed, was a very obvious source of inspiration to Tucholsky at many points. But, like Carl von Ossietzky and the circle of *Weltbühne* contributors as a whole, he embodies the spirit of independent left-wing intellectual opinion during the years of the Weimar Republic and is a man through whom one gains many insights into the tensions of those years. In a sense the social historian needs him more than does the student of literature, for he is almost completely encompassed by the events of his time, but as a shrewd commentator on human affairs, with a wit familiar in style to

Anglo-Saxons but rare among Germans, he has his corner in any study that seeks to set literature in its social context.

Part of the poetic originality of Ringelnatz and Tucholsky lies in their rejection of an elevated, philosophical, 'poetic' diction in favour of the flat, familiar language of everyday. The hyperboles of expressionism were as far from them as were the solemn intensities of Rilke and George, and they neither made messianic claims for their 'message', nor expected schools of admiring disciples to congregate round them. They were poets of the here and now, not of the eternal; of the particular, not of the cosmic; of the reality of relativity, not of the ideality of the absolute. Their eyes were on man rather than on Man, thus on imperfection, failure and disillusion rather than on progress, confidence and vision.

These qualities combine at their most powerful in Brecht. Already in the poems of his schooldays, some of which he later re-worked for inclusion in the collection *Bert Brechts Hauspostille* (1927), there is the directness of manner and coarseness of tone characteristic of all his mature work, and the early influences of Kipling's *Barrack-Room Ballads* and the poems of François Villon nurtured the same tendencies. The society of Kipling's ballads is a society of adventurers, rough-and-ready 'soldiers of the Queen', whose bluff exterior belied the sense of comradeship and honesty that lay within. The blunt, unsentimental, almost impersonal language of these men, with the pounding rhythm of Kipling's ballad metres and refrains, was just what the young Brecht wanted to hear, and its presence in his own poetry and drama is clearly felt through the mid-1920s.

In Villon, whose poems had been translated into German in 1907, and whose influence on Brecht was to prove even more durable than that of Kipling, Brecht found a paradigm of rebellious irreverence, a perfect opponent of the quiet and ordered life in which each man knew his place, and kept it. Villon deliberately put himself beyond the social pale and filled his poems with accounts of his amoral exploits at the expense of bourgeois convention:

> *François Villon, den nie ein Bett bedeckte,*
> *Fand früh und leicht, dass kühler Wind ihm schmeckte.*

(François Villon, who never slept between the sheets, quickly discovered that the cool breeze was what he liked.)

—wrote Brecht in his poem 'Vom François Villon' from the *Hauspostille*. His Baal is cast in the same mould.

The influence of the newly-discovered poetry of Rimbaud provides almost the only point of contact between Brecht and his expressionist contemporaries. Rimbaud, like Villon, was a born rebel, violently anti-establishment, amoral, seeking an unconventionality of poetic expression to match the unconventionality of his philosophy of life. Such an opposition to the values of contemporary society met the sympathy both of the pre-Great War expressionists and of the younger Brecht, who was little more than a schoolboy when the war ended, but who already uttered the disillusioned '*J'accuse*' that was to remain his hallmark.

But antagonism to the world of middle-class values was not in itself a sufficient basis for making common cause. Many of the expressionists held to visions of moral and spiritual regeneration, of the brotherhood of man in a world of gentleness and goodness. To Brecht this was moonshine. He saw no grounds for believing in the innate goodness of man, or even in man's desire to lift himself out of his present baseness, and he distrusted rallying-cries for the creation of 'a better life'. His materialism gave him a conception of reality utterly different from that which underlay the expressionist manifestoes, and what to them was revolutionary was to him mere intellectual play, a bogus compromise between equally discredited claims. Even Ernst Toller, an active revolutionary who was a member of the *Räterepublik* in Munich in 1919, did not match Brecht's standards. Toller's play *Die Wandlung*, in which each man is to be 'transformed' by realising the true humanity within himself, Brecht saw as a piece of idealistic abstraction: 'Pallid visions, eminently forgettable. Cosmos weak. Man as object and proclamation, instead of just man; man in the abstract, man as the singular of mankind. His cause is in weak hands.'[10]

Likewise the intense, high-flown language of the expressionists ran counter to Brecht's cool matter-of-factness. The poems of the last phase of impressionism and expressionism he characterised as consisting of 'pretty pictures and sweet-smelling words', not without their attractions but too much like monologues: 'They simply get too far away from the activity of conveying an idea or a feeling in which the outsider can share. All great poems have the quality of documents'.[11]

Art as communication, and as such embedded in, not set apart from, the rest of life, remained an unshakeable principle for Brecht. Max Frisch's account, related above (p. 76), of Brecht reading 'An die Nachgeborenen' in Zurich in 1947 compares Brecht's attitude to that of a man reading a letter aloud, 'for the information of others'. And his later reflections on a suitable inscription for his gravestone set up a context of communication between him and us without which, and *pace* his ironical tone, the *raison d'être* of his work would be lost:

Ich benötige keinen Grabstein, aber
Wenn ihr einen für mich benötigt
Wünschte ich, es stünde darauf:
Er hat Vorschläge gemacht. Wir
Haben sie angenommen.
Durch eine solche Inschrift wären
Wir alle geehrt.

(I require no tombstone, but if
You require one for me,
I should like it to say:
He made proposals. We
Accepted them.
An epitaph like that would
Do us all credit.)

('Ich benötige keinen Grabstein': 1955)

As artist and public face each other on the same plane—the only plane there is, says Brecht—so the work of art must be seen by the 'consumer' as an object worthy of penetration and study, not as some wonderful creation to be worshipped from afar, inviolate, unapproachable. In a short piece called 'Über das Zerpflücken von Gedichten', written in the 1930s but not published until 1964, he wrote: 'The layman who considers poetry inaccessible forgets that although the poet may well share his light-hearted moods with him, to formulate them in a poem is a job of work. The poem is thus something fleeting whose passage has been arrested, something tangible and relatively substantial'. One need therefore have no fear that by subjecting a real work of art to scrutiny, one will destroy it: 'Pluck a rose—and each petal is beautiful'.

The qualities which attitudes like these would lead one to expect in lyric poetry characterise Brecht's first published collection, (if one excepts the 25 privately-printed copies of the *Taschenpostille* of 1926), with its ironic title *Bert Brechts Hauspostille*. Though it bears the date 1927, the idea of a *Hauspostille*, arranged as a kind of domestic breviary, goes back to the years immediately after the war, and the collection even contains reworked versions of poems from the war years themselves. Most of the 50 poems are ballads, and most of the remainder are balladesque in character. All owe a debt, not only to Kipling and Villon but also to Frank Wedekind, whose cabaret performances inspired Brecht to sing his own ballads to guitar accompaniment (Melodies to a dozen or so are given in an appendix to the *Hauspostille*: they do not suggest that in Brecht we have lost a great song-writer).

True to the association of his chosen title, Brecht applies liturgical terminology to the division of his collection into five *Lektionen*, starting with *Bittgänge* and *Exerzitien*, and gives characteristic prefatory instructions to the reader on how to approach the work. His opening remark is: 'This collection of homilies is intended for the reader's use. It is not meant to be thoughtlessly soaked up'. Then, in sober, unsentimental style he lays his ballads before us, ballads on men and women in everyday situations, on love, hate, friendship and the other emotions that bind us, on man as soldier ('Gesang des Soldaten der Roten Armee'; 'Lied der drei Soldaten'), as professional adventurer ('Ballade auf vielen Schiffen'; 'Ballade von den Seeräubern'; 'Ballade von den Abenteurern') and as member of other social groups, past and present. Almost all the poems are written in regular stanzas, all except two are rhymed—always simply and sometimes care-lessly—and many have a refrain. The diction is plain yet emphatic, the rhythm crisp yet free, with frequent enjambment and with a deliberate avoidance of decorative elements. Yet it is still lyric verse—a kind of lyrical anti-lyricism found at its most striking in the 'Choral vom Manne Baal', a part of that grotesque complex of pieces which has Brecht's drama *Baal* at its nub.

A microcosm of these qualities, and of the world of Brecht the poet in the 1920s, lies in what is probably the best known of the poems in the *Hauspostille*, 'Vom armen B.B.'. This remarkable strophic monologue, balladesque in manner but not in form, and eminently unsingable, conveys the thoughts of Brecht in the guise of an American who calmly and fatalistically foretells the destruction of civilisation. Statement and negation confront each other, the firmest of physical realities gives way dialectically before the force of earthquakes, while the 'American' Brecht seeks the strength to envisage his own survival. At the very beginning the '*schwarze Wälder*' of his birth, with their coldness that he will never lose, are set against the '*Asphaltstadt*' in which, with his newspapers, his cigarettes and his liquor, he is now content to live:

1

Ich, Bertolt Brecht, bin aus den schwarzen Wäldern.
Meine Mutter trug mich in die Stadt hinein
Als ich in ihrem Leibe lag. Und die Kälte der Wälder
Wird in mir bis zu meinem Absterben sein.

2

In der Asphaltstadt bin ich daheim. Von allem Anfang
Versehen mit jedem Sterbsakrament:
Mit Zeitungen. Mit Tabak. Mit Branntwein.
Misstrauisch und faul und zufrieden am End.

1

(I, Bertolt Brecht, come from the dark forests.
My mother carried me into the town
As I lay in her womb. And the cold in the forests
Will stay in me till I expire.

2

I live in the asphalt city. They gave me
The whole last sacrament right at the start—
Newspapers, cigarettes, alcohol.
Suspicious, lazy, content for my part.)

Similar paradoxes follow. Having invited a group of women to his home, he tells them, as they sit cosily in his rocking-chairs:

In me you've got a man you can't depend on.

In the evening, when the men come to have a drink with him, they are confident that things will get better:

But I don't ask when.

Men used to carouse together in houses 'that were reckoned to be indestructible', but the future has other plans:

What will be left in these cities will be what went through them—the wind.

Outwardly the nine strophes, with their prosaic diction, their casual, irregular rhymes and their flat, dead-pan manner, make up a sequence of autobiographical episodes. But they tell us nothing that a third party, looking in on these episodes from outside, could not describe equally accurately. The character of the first-person subject emerges from his confrontations with people and events and from the opinions he expresses on the future of life, not from personal revelations of emotions or desires. 'People's views interest me more than their feelings', he once said in an interview.[12]

He is just one of the 'Vorläufige', as he calls mankind in the eighth strophe, and since 'nothing worth mentioning' will come after us, to express emotion or cherish desire would be sheer irrelevance. The only reasonable possibility is a kind of personal impersonality.

All this accords with Brecht's view of poetry as communication, that is to say, as reflection on objects or ideas in the tone and atmosphere of everyday life, which is the only life there is:

Ihr sterbt mit allen Tieren
Und es kommt nichts nachher.

(You die, like all the animals, and there's nothing to follow.)

('Gegen Verführung')

' "Vom armen B.B." contains everything that makes the *Hauspostille* valuable for us', wrote Tucholsky,

'including all those external trappings like the poet's posturing, his despair and genuine suffering, his affected coldness that pretends to be emotion where he has a genuine coldness, and his splendid lyrical language ... I think he must be spiteful by nature and rather deceitful—and he won't leave off. He and Gottfried Benn seem to me the greatest lyrical talents in Germany today.'[13]

'In der Asphaltstadt bin ich daheim', Brecht sang in 1922, and he remained a man of the city to the end, a compulsive lover of that supreme manifestation of the capitalist way of life he loved to hate. The city had also been a central object of hate to the expressionists, and in his concern with social outcasts and amoral drop-outs—again Villon and Rimbaud come into the picture—Brecht shares with Benn, Heym, Wolfenstein, Max Herrmann-Neisse and others an anti-bourgeois stance. The expressionists depicted the world in terms of men *in extremis*. Brecht too chooses as his spokesmen the murderer, the robber, the prostitute, the dipsomaniac—characters living on the fringes of society, whether through their own nature, like the asocial, sex-crazy Baal, or through the force of circumstance, like the pathetic cuckolded Kragler in *Trommeln in der Nacht*.

But whereas the expressionist poets used the sordidness of city life to make an emotive statement about man and the cosmos, sending out a passionate call for total spiritual regeneration, Brecht coolly dissects the picture to produce a diagnosis of a specifically social and economic malady with a materialistically identifiable cause. As his play *Mann ist Mann* had already shown, he denies the possibility of a metaphysical position, since man as the product of his environment is not the possessor of a unique, immutable self but can be modified, re-formed and reassembled like a reconditioned automobile.

In a review of Brecht's *Hauspostille* for *Die Weltbühne* in 1928 Kurt Tucholsky wrote: 'He is as overestimated today as he will be underestimated tomorrow. As a dramatist this man has very considerable talent; as a lyric poet he has even more'.[14] What Tucholsky called the 'herrliche lyrische Diktion' of the *Hauspostille* poems is the source of this talent, a talent magnified by the narrowness of the limits within which it operated. The trinity of 'Ansichten', 'Erfahrungen' and 'Verstand' on which he built his poetic *credo*,[15] and of which the concept of epic theatre is also a reflection, represents the antithesis of the whole tradition of German bourgeois *Gefühlskultur*, a tradition bitingly mocked in the 'Liturgie vom Hauch', with its parody of Goethe's *Wandrers Nachtlied*:

> *Da schweigen die Vögelein nicht mehr*
> *Über allen Wipfeln ist Unruh*
> *In allen Gipfeln spürest du*
> *Jetzt einen Hauch.*

The didactic poems of Brecht's *Lesebuch für Städtebewohner* (1927), which belong to the period that culminates in *Die Dreigroschenoper* and *Aufstieg und Fall der Stadt Mahagonny*, show an almost nihilistic cynicism towards contemporary life and values. The money-grabbing immorality which he saw as the product, then as the basis, of capitalist society, dominates the *Lesebuch* and other poems of 1927–30, such as 'Vom Geld', with its final thrust:

> *Dem Geld erweisen die Menschen Ehren.*
> *Das Geld wird über Gott gestellt.*
> *Willst du einem Feind die Ruhe im Grab verwehren*
> *Schreibe auf seinen Stein: Hier ruht Geld.*

(Men pay their respects to money. Money is set higher than God. If you want to prevent an enemy from lying peacefully in his grave, write on his tombstone: 'Here Lies Money'.)

So through lapidary prophecies of the doom of capitalist society, primarily that of the United States, and through a mocking review of the technological and other 'benefits' bequeathed by that society, he found his way by 1930 to a committed Marxist position. Together with his fellow-convert Hanns Eisler, composer of the music to *Die Massnahme*, *Die Mutter* and others of his plays, he wrote political songs in the proletarian cause and performed them to working-class audiences in Berlin bars and clubs. But these political poems—the 'Solidaritätslied' (1930) for example, the 'Lob der Partei' from *Die Massnahme* (1930), and the 'Ballade vom Reichstagsbrand' (1933)—are a far cry, both from the incisive verses found in the *Hauspostille* and from the broader, wiser, but no less forceful humanism of his works written during and after World War II. The urge to power is stronger, humanitarian values less in evidence; the appeal has become sectional, the didacticism cruder, the polemic and satire coarser. Born fighter that he was, and like all social critics from Molière and Swift to Bernard Shaw and George Orwell, he found his true character in opposition, not defence, in a posture of negation, not of affirmation, while his abrasive manner sets him in the tradition of German polemical writers from Luther and Murner through Lessing, Heine, Büchner and Nietzsche to Karl Kraus.

But these poems in praise of revolution, of Communism, of dialectics have a cramped feel about them. It is as though the subject were too confined to allow his poetic diction to rise to that of those earlier works in which he had revelled in destroying the values he so affectionately detested. The opening of his 'Lob des Revolutionärs' from *Die Mutter* (1932), for example, comes close to banality:

> *Wenn die Unterdrückung zunimmt*
> *Werden viele entmutigt*
> *Aber sein Mut wächst.*
>
> *Er organisiert seinen Kampf*
> *Um den Lohngroschen, um das Teewasser*
> *Und um die Macht in Staat.*
>
> *Er fragt das Eigentum:*
> *Woher kommst du?*
> *Er fragt die Ansichten:*
> *Wem nützt Ihr?*

(When oppression grows, many become discouraged, but *his* courage grows greater. He plans the struggle for his pittance, for water to make his tea, and for power in the state. He asks property: 'Where do you come from?' He asks opinions: 'What use are you?')

His anti-Nazi poems, from 1930 onwards, among them six 'Hitler Charades' for 'congregational' singing, reveal a sad, often overlooked, response to the rise of Nazism. The two poems 'Das Lied von der Tünche' and 'Das Lied vom Anstreicher Hitler' were both written in 1930, the year when the Grand Coalition in the Reichstag collapsed, when street fighting between Hitler's storm troops and the Communists became the order of the day, and when in the general election the Nazi party increased its share of the vote by 800 per cent. These poems show Hitler as a demagogue, a false prophet, a dangerous deceiver—but not as an evil power-seeker of whose policies terrorism, concentration camps and war were an integral part. Moreover, apart from an insensitivity to the moral issues, Brecht shows a tragic unawareness at this time of the political consequences of Hitler's success. It has long been fashionable to blame the German intelligentsia, conservative and liberal alike, for failing to take Hitler seriously until it was too late. After 1933, indeed, when it *was* already too late, most of Europe, together with America, was still reluctant to believe that some form of accommodation with the Nazi régime could not be arranged. But Brecht saw no further than did the liberals whom he now spurned as 'reformers' rather than 'revolutionaries'.

In fact, he did not see as far. Tucholsky, Ossietzky and others of the *Weltbühne* had a far more acute prescience. Early in 1930 Tucholsky wrote a poem called 'Deutschland erwache!'. The climax of successive strophes comes in the lines:

> . . . *dass der Nazi dir einen Totenkranz flicht;*
> *Deutschland, siehst du das nicht?*
>
> . . . *dass der Nazi für die Ausbeuter ficht;*
> *Deutschland, hörst du das nicht?*
>
> . . . *dass der Nazi dein Todesurteil spricht;*
> *Deutschland, fühlst du das nicht?*[16]
>
> (The Nazis are plaiting a wreath for your grave;
> Germany, can't you see what's happening?
>
> The Nazis are siding with those who exploit you;
> Germany, Can't you hear what's happening?
>
> The Nazis have uttered your sentence of death;
> Germany, can't you feel what's happening?)

And in the *Weltbühne* of October 21, 1930, warning of the freebooting Nazi terrorists who had made their influence felt in the recent elections, Ossietzky bitterly concluded: 'The electorate may have very mixed views, but it has shown it believes that force is the only thing that matters, both at home and abroad.'[17] Brecht, meanwhile, was writing poems on 'Hitler the house-painter' ('Anstreicher Hitler'), presenting a ridiculous little man busily papering over the cracks in the German body politic.

From the protests, the fine phrases and the extroversions of the expressionists, through the bizarreries of Dada, the quiet sincerities of a Carossa and a Hesse, the satires and parodies of a Ringelnatz and a Tucholsky, to *Arbeiterdichtung* and socio-political commitment, the lyric in the years of the Weimar Republic produces only the name of Brecht to set among the new poets of lasting fame. The end of the Great War saw no surge of new lyric poetry to match that at the turn of the century—Hofmannsthal, Rilke, George, and with Liliencron, Dehmel and others still active—or that of Benn, Heym, Trakl, Loerke and the many others who made their mark in the early years of the 'expressionist decade' of 1910 to 1920. The last of Rilke's *Duineser Elegien* and the *Sonette an Orpheus* were written in 1922, but their world—if it is a world of temporal definition at all—is that of imperial pre-1914 Central Europe, not of post-war republicanism. George, whose *Blätter für die Kunst* had come to an end in 1919, published no poetry between *Der Stern des Bundes* (1914) and *Das neue Reich* (1928).

Yet these poets of an older generation, paramount among them the contrasting figures of Rilke and George, remained powerful forces during the Weimar years. The poet, like the philosopher, held a privileged position in the eyes of German society from the early nineteenth century onwards, and by the early 1900s, especially in the wake of the rediscovery of Hölderlin, Kleist and Büchner, the influence of the *Dichter und Denker* was at its height. Young German and Austrian soldiers went to the front in 1914 with copies of Rilke's *Weise von Liebe und Tod des Cornetts Christoph Rilke* and *Requiem* in their packs, and many of his more sentimental early poems became the special property of the *Wandervogel* youth movement. In the *Fünf Gesänge* of 1914 he even added his voice to the chorus of military sentiment:

> Dich will ich rühmen, Fahne. Immer von Kind auf
> sah ich ahnend dir nach, grüsste dich ahnend.

(Thee, flag, will I glorify. From my childhood I always gazed after thee expectantly, saluted thee expectantly.)

(Fünf Gesänge, V)

But the Prussia-dominated urge to conquest quickly turned him against Germany—he was born into the Austro-Hungarian empire—and after the war he disowned any affinity with, or indebtedness to, the German spirit in its modern formative characteristics. From the time he finally settled in Switzerland in 1921 until his death five years later he estranged himself more and more from the German literary tradition and increasingly adopted French as the medium of both practical and poetic communication. Paul Valéry described the Rilke of the 1920s as 'the most international mind conceivable',[18] while nationalist Berlin periodicals accused him of betraying German interests at the moment when the need was for unity and loyalty.

Yet to many, as Stefan Zweig bore witness in his *Abschied von Rilke* in 1927, Rilke was the great poetic visionary of the age, the inheritor of the great tradition of nineteenth-century philosopher-poets. His realm was a *Weltinnenraum*, a world of inwardness, of poetic values, enticing the mind away from the concerns of social reality into a rarefied, inner world of symbolic verities and metaphysical absolutes. 'He revealed himself at all times', wrote Zweig, 'as the pure, eternally questing artist. We know of not one single moment in his life when he was not a poet.'[19] But the demands of the Orphic *Duineser Elegien* and *Sonette an Orpheus*, poetry which makes on its readers the total claims of a Hölderlin or a Novalis, went beyond the understanding of his age: 'The Germans could not keep pace with him, and only a few were capable of experiencing the spiritual abandonment to which his creative mind surrendered itself in these last, most mysterious poems.'[20] Yet the poet whose work Zweig described as 'a dialogue with the eternal' did not have to wait so long for recognition, national or international, as the poet of *Hymnen an die Nacht*, or of *Brod und Wein* and *Patmos*.

As for George, his utter rejection of the world around him, and the fact that, unlike Rilke, he was attended by a close-knit group of determined disciples—many of whom gained their own individual fame and influence—gives him his own importance at a time when German material prosperity was nurturing a rising national self-confidence.

Das neue Reich was George's last collection of poems, containing everything he had written since 1914. But it is not, like Rilke's *Duineser Elegien* and *Sonette an Orpheus*, the achievement of a profound new originality; rather, it has the character of an assemblage of occasional pieces from isolated moments in the past. Indeed 1914, the year of publication of the *Stern des Bundes*—originally to be given the significant title *Lieder für die heilige Schar*—marks the beginning of the disintegration of the close inner circle of acolytes round the master: Heinrich Friedemann and Norbert von Hellingrath (editor of Hölderlin) were killed in action; the *Blätter für die Kunst*, journal of the George circle, came to an end in 1919; in 1921 came the final break with Gundolf, George's favourite disciple; and from 1925 onwards George himself withdrew completely from the world, moving from place to place, often without a word to those closest to him. Max Kommerell finally left him in 1930, and the young poet Johann Anton committed suicide the following year, leaving Karl Wolfskehl as virtually the only figure of significance still faithful to him.

At the core of George's 'new kingdom' lies an esoteric faith in a spiritual world of which the privileged poet (George himself) is the only true prophet. Prophecy here has the form of compulsion: there is nothing to question, nothing to explain—the need is simply to obey. 'Ein volk ist tot wenn seine götter tot sind', he writes in 'Der Krieg'; and the gods of Greece would join with the gods of Germania to show Germany the path to spiritual victory. This poetic utopia, with its points of reference to events and personages in the contemporary world, and its confrontation between false material values and the values of the true poetic vision, fills the poem 'Geheimes Deutschland', which concludes:

> *Wer denn, wer von euch brüdern*
> *Zweifelt, schrickt nicht beim mahnwort*
> *Dass was meist ihr emporhebt*
> *Dass was meist heut euch wert dünkt*
> *Faules laub ist im herbstwind*
> *Endes-und todesbereich:*
> *Nur was im schützenden schlaf*
> *Wo noch kein taster es spürt*
> *Lang in tiefinnerstem schacht*
> *Weihlicher erde noch ruht -*
> *Wunder undeutbar für heut*
> *Geschick wird des kommenden tages.*

> (Who then, who of you brothers
> Doubts, unshocked by the warning,
> That what most you acclaim, what
> Most you value today is
> Rank as leaves in the fall-wind,
> Doomed to perdition and death!
> Only what consecrate earth
> Cradles in sheltering sleep
> Long in the innermost grooves,
> Far from acquisitive hands,
> Marvels this day cannot grasp
> Are rife with the fate of tomorrow.)
> (transl. O. Marx and E. Marwitz, University of North Carolina, 1949)

Like many others who, in the shadow of Nietzsche, set irrationality, authoritarianism, elitism and mysticism at the heart of their philosophy, George inevitably became linked in people's minds with the National Socialist movement. He himself ignored the Nazis' overtures to him, saying 'Spiritual laws and political laws are very different,'[21] but even before his death in 1933 articles were appearing with insinuating titles like 'Stefan George est-il précurseur d'Hitler?' (Francus in *La Grande Revue* XXXVIII, Paris, 1933) and 'Das Schweigen Stefan Georges' (Klaus Mann, writing in the first volume of the exile periodical *Die Sammlung* in 1933). Perhaps he is yet one more example of a figure the constituent elements of whose personality first unwittingly prepared the ground for the Nazi takeover of the national destiny, and then, once the Nazi hold had become unbreakable, could be torn from their context and made to support what Nazism stood for.

At the same time it seems unhappily true that no member of the

George-Kreis, let alone the master himself, declared an open opposition to Hitler during the vital years when opposition was still possible. Unquestioning obedience to a 'Führer'; a basic conservatism; disapproval of modern 'experimental' art and literature; a xenophobic rejection of contemporary foreign literature of whatever persuasion; a preference for the aesthetic message of a Schopenhauer and a Nietzsche over the analytical philosophy of a Descartes or a Spinoza: such characteristics were all that the Nazi predator could wish for. In 1933 Ernst Bertram, formerly a member of George's innermost circle, delivered a lecture at the University of Cologne called 'Deutscher Aufbruch: Rede an die akademische Jugend', in which he specifically traced the roots of the 'German [i.e. Nazi] awakening' to George's poetry.[22] And the minor poets and writers Woldemar Uxkull and Friedrich Wolters, who stayed loyal to George to his death, did in fact find their own 'neues Reich' in Hitler's 'drittes Reich'. On the other hand, devoted to George and his memory was Claus von Stauffenberg, the man who planted the bomb in the ill-fated attempt on Hitler's life on 20 July 1944.

Against the more dubious characteristics of the George circle must be set the ascetic intellectual discipline, the cultivation of Classical humanistic values and the critical faculties that found their outlet in historical and philological study, which show the noble, undistorted aspect of the group. Though George himself wrote less and less as the 1920s passed, the influence of some of his followers reached new heights. Gundolf followed his *Shakespeare und der deutsche Geist* (1911) and *Goethe* (1916) with *George* (1921), *Heinrich von Kleist* (1922), *Caesar im neunzehnten Jahrhundert* (1926) and *Shakespeare. Sein Wesen und Werk* (1928), powerful works of criticism and exposition centred on men of power and destiny, born leaders, vital figures in the history of the modern European mind. In these studies Gundolf pledged himself to demonstrate that the true European tradition rested on the reconciliation of Christianity and the ideals of Classical Greece. Among the numerous translations done by members of the *George-Kreis* those by Gundolf of Shakespeare are among the most distinguished. The same concept of leadership inspires Max Kommerell's *Der Dichter als Führer in der deutschen Klassik* (1928), which owes its philosophical premises to George and its critical methodology to Gundolf. The literary scholarship of Norbert von Hellingrath and Friedrich Wolters also belongs in this context.

Perhaps the most striking single work of scholarship to come from the George circle in these years was Ernst Kantorowicz's *Kaiser Friedrich II* (1927), a biography of one of the supermen of history, *stupor mundi et immutator mirabilis*, as he was called, the Hohenstaufen ruler whose thirteenth-century empire stretched from Germany to Sicily and Palestine. In this great leader and conqueror, Kantorowicz—like Gundolf, Wolfskehl and many others in the George circle, a Jew—found the qualities so conspicuously absent from the Germany of the Weimar Republic yet so imperative for the regeneration of the German people. Turning away from a dry, rationalistic historiography, he drew into his narrative the myths that had collected round the great Emperor. For in order to penetrate the *Geist* of such a man and his epoch, Kantorowicz believed, with historians of culture like Herder, Spengler, Toynbee and Curtius, that myths, the repository of a people's unspoken and often irrational assumptions about life, were as much part of the historian's raw material as documented material event. In short, he aimed at a Gestalt interpretation of Frederick II's personality and activity within the complete context of his age, a work of scholarly empathy and total commitment. Like Gundolf's *Goethe* and *Shakespeare*, this is *Geisteswissenschaft* at its most challenging. In its philosophical premisses and its methodology it stands, again with Gundolf, Curtius and Leo Spitzer, in the spiritual line of Dilthey.

Unlike Rilke, who was widely read, even if considerably less widely understood, in the 1920s, Stefan George and the poets of his circle were not. Nor were they meant to be. Heedless of public appeal, they wrote for a coterie, pursuing their own intellectual values as the expression of their own definition of *Geist*. These values, together with the private and public attitudes of the *George-Kreis*, are no less an expression of the escapist irrealities of the late Weimar years for being restricted in their currency. George's world, like Rilke's, represents a withdrawal from external pressures and from the obligations that these pressures impose. It was probably this withdrawal, leading to a sense of irrelevance, that led to the progressive defection from the circle of those whose horizons were wider, and whose sense of social responsibility was more insistent.

The development of post-war Europe, and above all the stultification of hopes for a Franco-German *rapprochement*, made George's imperious isolationism and aesthetic paganism appear more and more irrelevant. Looking back on these years in 1931, in an essay for *Die Neue Rundschau* ominously called 'Abbau der Bildung', the humanist scholar Ernst Robert Curtius wrote: 'The George circle, which promised so much and seemed to bring a breath of spring into our lives, had exhausted its energies and taken refuge in the slogans of a curious dogmatism.'[23] Curtius' new hero, 'the last legitimate herald of a new unity of nationhood and poetic vocation', was Hugo von Hofmannsthal.[24]

Another noble figure to acknowledge, though never to succumb to, the power of the *George-Kreis*, was Theodor Heuss, historian and first President of the German Federal Republic. Heuss drew an interesting distinction between the *guru* and his disciples. 'I did not find myself drawn to him,' he wrote in his memoirs; 'I was probably put off by the esoteric trappings and self-consciously artistic language of his poetry. Subsequently, however, the achievements of his disciples showed me something of the power and the discipline that he possessed both in his use of language and in the whole grandeur of his conception.' Heuss concludes: 'One's high assessment of him rested not on what one could learn from him—though this was considerable—but on the measure of the demands that he made on one.'[25] One recalls Goethe's remark about Winckelmann: 'One does not *learn* anything when one reads him. But one *becomes* something.'

The elements of irrationality, authoritarianism and *Rausch* in George's *Das neue Reich* provide a link with the Gottfried Benn of this period. During the years immediately after the war Benn wrote little, most of it setting him in the company of the polemical sceptics whose position was almost completely nihilistic. His poem 'Bolschewik', for instance, turns loose an almost bizarre extravagance of language and allusion against the Russian revolution. By the time of the little cycle *Betäubung* (1925) he has turned his gaze away from the world around him and taken refuge in a private world of fantasy, a mythical world in which time stands still and the imagination can pursue its visions of a life free from the tensions and causalities of earthly existence. In the inducement of this blissful state of heightened awareness, and of the creativity that accompanies it, drugs have their part to play:

> *Es stehen Krüge, Tische*
> *vor Schatten, traumgewillt,*
> *Schlafdorn und Mohnkelch, frische,*
> *daraus das Weisse quillt*
> *der Lippe zu.*

(Jugs and tables stand before shadows,
ready to dream—belladonna and opium, fresh jugs,
from which foam rises to the mouth.)

('Betäubung')

This period of Benn's career, dominated by thoughts of unreal worlds to which it was the poet's task to introduce his fellow-men, is on the one hand an evasive response to the joyless circumstances of the post-war years—and as a doctor, Benn knew some of the most depressing manifestations of these realities. On the other hand it is a sinister prelude to his welcome of the Nazi regime in 1933. Thus 'Der Sänger', which opens his poems of 1919–25 collected under the title *Spaltung. Neue Gedichte*, revives in mocking, distorted form the concept of *poeta vates*, the poet as seer, as intellectual leader—a concept prominent in German literature from Klopstock through Hölderlin to Stefan George. Again the power of dreams is invoked as Benn depicts the modern poet as a 'Zersprenger mittels Gehirnprinzip':

> *Stündlich webt er* [sc. *der Sänger*] *im Ganzen*
> *drängend zum Traum des Gedichts*
> *seine schweren Substanzen*
> *selten und langsam ins Nichts.*

(Hour by hour, pressing forward to the dream-world of poetry, the poet slowly and with scant success blends his ponderous material into the void.)

It is the poet's task, first to reveal, then to pierce, the chaotic reality of earthbound contingencies and create a new world through the poetic rearrangement of the 'facts' of existence, whereby time will be transformed into eternity, the sense of human transcience and impotence into an awareness of the transcendental values of myth. A concern with the appropriate poetic form for the expression of these thoughts led Benn to the half-lyric, half-epic eight-line strophic pattern in which the poems in *Spaltung* are cast, and which, in sequences of between four and eight strophes, persists also into his later lyrics. In this form too, in his *Gesammelte Gedichte* of 1927, he consolidated the tendencies of these years with a number of poems ('Trunkene Flut', 'Osterinsel', 'Orphische Zellen') that reflect on Jung's psychological theories of the collective unconscious in the myths, cults and rituals of Western man and of primitive peoples, and on the thesis of Spengler's *Untergang des Abendlandes*.

This latter work, the first volume of which appeared in 1918 and the second in 1922, had a profound effect on German intellectual opinion in the 1920s. A widespread disillusionment with ideals and a distrust of moral values provided a ready receptivity to a philosophy of decay which took the German defeat in the Great War out of the realm of military disaster and national shame, and made it part of a statement about the future of the whole of Western civilisation. Spengler claimed to have evolved 'a philosophy of fate—the first of its kind . . . . a German philosophy'. Benn, in his *Urgesicht* of 1920, had already given expression to a bitterly negative view of culture and society, and he was only one of many who found themselves confirmed in their nihilism by Spengler's apparently unanswerable historico-scientific case.

> *Dunkler kann es nicht werden*
> *als diese Stunde, die sinkt,*
> *mit allen Lasten der Erden*
> *in fremder Nacht ertrinkt . . .*

(Things can become no blacker than in this fading hour which, bearing all the burdens of the earth, is drowning in a strange darkness. . .)

The same conviction informs his most difficult, most intellectual lyric work of these years, the text of the oratorio *Das Unaufhörliche* (1931), set to music for soloists, choirs and orchestra by Hindemith. The cultural pessimism of this work is mercilessly summarised in uncomfortably modern phrases (which translation would destroy) from Benn's essay 'Fazit der Perspektiven':

Immer formelhafter das Individuelle, immer genormter der Betrieb . . . Auf den alten Schlössern der Grossmogule klatschen die Antennen; Vernichtung des Raums: an den Hängen des Himalaya, am Rand Tibets, im Anblick des Mount Everest steht der Achtröhrenapparat und hier diktiert Grimsby und Königswusterhausen. Erst die Piraten, dann die Militärs, jetzt die Wissenschaftler . . . Die weisse Rasse ist zu Ende. Technische Magie, tausend Worte Rebbach, Text genormt, Partitur aus Zahlen, das war ihr letzter Traum . . . Das Unaufhörliche, von Meer zu Meer, mondlose Welten überfrüht, hinan, hinab.[26]

So as the Weimar Republic tottered into its final years, this significant and highly intellectual poet secreted in his own attitudes and activities many of the elements that burned away the roots of social democratic republicanism and drove millions of Germans into the arms of the National Socialists. Benn had his medical practice in the Belle-Alliance-Strasse in Berlin during these years, and saw for himself the gangs of Nazi thugs that roamed the streets, smashing the windows of Jewish shops and beating up 'suspicious' passers-by. If Hitler was to be the popular candidate for the role of saviour of the German people, what sort of a salvation was one to expect? It was not difficult for Benn to rationalise the nihilism he professed. The myths of other cultures led him to a world of poetic fantasy, and his drug-poems ('O Nacht!', 'Kokain', 'Betäubung' and others) similarly invoke the experience of new, timeless realities.

This blend of disillusionment, *Rausch* and unreality was the perfect soil for the cultivation of National Socialism. Intellectuality and poetic imagination gave no immunity from infection—Nazism was not the prerogative of the lower classes. And in 1933, less than three months after Hitler's accession as Reichskanzler, Benn gave on the

Berlin radio a talk called *Der neue Staat und die Intellektuellen*—a call to the intelligentsia to have done with pondering and criticising, to stop talking about reconciliation and understanding between nations, and to join in the creation of the new German *Machtstaat*. This infamous piece, from which Benn's reputation and moral standing never fully recovered, is a striking example of the perversion of a subtle, cultured mind by the barbaric crudities and inhumanities of Nazism. As such it will concern us again in a later context. So too will the question: does such a phenomenon represent a passing moment of blindness—or is it a predictable climax of long-known tendencies?

NOTES

1. H. Steffen (ed.), *Der deutsche Expressionismus* (Göttingen, 1965), 162
2. K. Pinthus, Preface (written in the autumn of 1919) to *Menschheitsdämmerung* (repr. Hamburg, 1959), 22
3. It is interesting to note the frequency with which the shark, predator of the sea, also appears in the roughly contemporary early poetry of Brecht ('Ballade auf vielen Schiffen', 'Ballade von den Geheimnissen jedweden Mannes', 'Vom Schwimmen in Seen und Flüssen').
4. To Kurt Pinthus; see *Menschheitsdämmerung*, ed. cit. 357
5. Lersch, *Deutschland* (Jena, 1918), 28
6. Lersch, *Klinge hinaus, schlagender Schall* (Berlin, 1940), 179
7. 'Expressionismus' (*Gesammelte Werke* I, Wiesbaden, 1959, 244)
8. Tucholsky, *Gesammelte Werke 1907–1932* (Reinbek, 1960–1), I, 1005
9. Tucholsky, ed. cit. III, 824
10. 'Dramatisches Papier und anderes', 1920 (*Schriften zum Theater* I, Frankfurt, 1963, 48)
11. 'Kurzer Bericht über 400 junge Lyriker', 1927 (*Schriften zur Literatur und Kunst* I, Frankfurt, 1967, 69)—a note by Brecht on why, having been appointed to judge a competition for young lyric poets, he found none of the entries worthy of the prize. That, as he goes on to say, he has little sympathy for Rilke, George and Werfel, may reveal the characteristic limits of his appreciation, but in so far as his context at this moment is 'art as communication' as opposed to 'art as monologistic self-expression', his attitude is far from idiosyncratic.
12. *Die literarische Welt*, July 30, 1926
13. ed. cit. II, 1065
14. ed. cit. II, 1062
15. cf. Bernard Guillemin, 'Was arbeiten Sie?', a conversation with Brecht in *Die literarische Welt*, July 30, 1926
16. ed. cit. III, 417
17. *The Stolen Republic*. Selected Writings of Carl von Ossietzky, ed. B. Frei (London, 1971), 120
18. see E.C. Mason, *Rilke, Europe and the English-Speaking World* (Cambridge, 1961), 4 and 98
19. S. Zweig, *Abschied von Rilke* (Tübingen, 1927), 8
20. *ibid.* 23

21. see C. Hildebrandt, *Erinnerungen an Stefan George und seinen Kreis* (Bonn, 1965), 272ff
22. see M. Winkler, *Stefan George* (Stuttgart, 1970), 62
23. *Deutscher Geist in Gefahr* (Stuttgart, 1932), 19
24. cf. Curtius' later essay, 'George, Hofmannsthal und Calderon', included in his *Kritische Essays* (Bern, 1954)
25. *Erinnerungen 1905–1933* (Tübingen, 1963), 354
26. ed. cit. I, 127–8

CHAPTER FIVE

Social Realities and Private Realities: Novels of War and—Peace?

'THE novel only breathes freely when it has its roots in society', wrote C.P. Snow in *The New York Times Book Review*, 30 January 1955. From Richardson, Fielding, Smollett and Sterne, from Rousseau's *La nouvelle Héloise* and *Emile*, from Gellert's *Schwedische Gräfin*—all these lying between 1740 and 1760—through Goethe, Stendhal, Balzac, Manzoni, Dickens, Flaubert, Zola, Tolstoi and Dostoevsky down to Henry James, Galsworthy, Conrad, Arnold Bennett, Thomas Mann's *Buddenbrooks*, Gide's *L'immoraliste* and almost all other works of prose fiction in the pre-Great War era, the social roots were firm. And because society, with the lives of the people who compose it, is real, and can thus be made the object of observation and analysis, the novel has acquired the cachet of being 'realistic', of dealing with life 'as it really is'.

In this sense the novel, as a distinctive literary genre, emerges late in the development of a culture, since it presupposes the existence of an established society with acknowledged personal and social conventions, an organism with its own mode and momentum of evolution. Sometimes this evolution may itself be made the object of attention; at other times the writer's gaze may be focused on the position of individual elements within this evolution, that is, on the relationship to it of particular men and women. The novelist looks round him and sets his imagination to work on characters and situations inspired by, and thus relating to, the 'real' social world of his experience.

This remains true in whatever role *vis-à-vis* society the novelist casts himself and his characters. He may praise the virtues of that society or he may expose its evils: in either case there is an objective situation as the point of reference. His hero may be an outcast from society, or feel himself in a state of alienation from it: but there must be a defined social context from which he has been cast out, or to which he finds himself alien. The public life of society, the private and public lives of the characters, the position of the writer in the world that he has created through his imagination—the novelist makes his artistic statement in the synthesis of these forces. It will not be a simple statement, for life is not simple. And although it must be a statement true to the life it describes, it must also be true to the canons of art—more particularly, to the essence of the literary form whose

112

tradition it has inherited and of whose history it is the latest part.

Of all literary forms the novel is the least susceptible to dogmatic definition in terms either of subject-matter or of structure. One recalls the conclusion of Abel Chevalley made famous by E.M. Forster: 'A novel is a work of prose fiction of a particular length.' But if an unsatisfactory one-sidedness is to be avoided, and respect paid to the complexity of life, which the freely discursive genre of the novel has a peculiar power to present, there must be a fusion of three realms: the social, as the 'real' setting from which the material and moral lives of the characters receive their meaning; the psychological, through which we enter the minds of the characters and come to understand their relationship to the external facts of their existence and to each other; and what one may variously call the abstract, the religious, or the universal—source of the power of the book to make us see the general in the particular by lending the events and personages a paradigmatic significance, and to implicate in some way the intangible, irrational realities behind the world of appearances.

As life is neither pure order nor utter chaos, but presents a kaleidoscope of the predictably recurrent and the predictably unpredictable, so art, in its search for form, must draw on both the ordered and the apparently chaotic to produce the intellectually considered structure without which the work of art can give no aesthetic satisfaction. E.M. Forster talks in *Aspects of the Novel* of the 'fertile muddle' of life out of which it is the artist's task, through vision and the exercise of choice, to fashion meaning. 'Neither the wholly inchoate nor the wholly conceptualised tallies with what we know of life', as Paul West puts it.[1]

Throughout the nineteenth century the forces of the inchoate had been contained within the firm boundaries of the social framework. But an eventual disruption of this framework by concentration on the psychological, the contingent, the irrational and other forces that nurture the private, social realm of the individual consciousness was predictable. Proust, Joyce, Virginia Woolf and the stream-of-consciousness novelists mark this reaction in its most radical form, and although the elevation of this change of perspective to a technique appears to have led into an aesthetic *cul-de-sac*, one can hardly blind oneself to the achievements and novelties that it exhibits *en route*. But all retreats into art have a certain sameness about them, whereas the social circumstances of life are continually changing, forcing the individual into ever new physical and moral predicaments.

Although the key moments in the emergence of the 'new' novel—the first form of *A la recherche du temps perdu* (1912), Joyce's

Ulysses (1922), Virginia Woolf's *Jacob's Room* (1922) and *Mrs. Dalloway* (1925)—fall within the space of a dozen years or so, there is no simple chronology of a linear movement from 'old' to 'new'. The novel of firm social reference never leaves the stage. Indeed, whatever awe has come to surround these famous works which explore a segment of the individual private consciousness, they represent but a small part of the total field of modern prose fiction. Virginia Woolf's conception of the novelist's task as to convey 'the varying, the unknown and uncircumscribed spirit' of life 'with as little mixture of the alien and external as possible'[2] excludes the external world with a radicalism which deprives the novel of a vital source—perhaps *the* vital source—of its power and meaning.

The German novel of the 1920s was not short of challenging social realities on which to draw. The first in time, and the most profound in impact, was the Great War.

'War is the father of all things', said Heraclitus. In the situations of war—moments of personal glory and tragedy, of moral responsibility and desperate decision, of national survival and social obligation—painters, sculptors, writers, even composers, have through the ages found a host of qualities to capture and to illuminate.

The historical circumstances of the conflict which the writer makes his point of departure may themselves dominate the narrative, and the work present an historical panorama in which a sequence of events becomes the epic *raison d'être*. In such a case, as in the despatches of a war reporter, it is the physical reality of attack and defence, of victory and defeat, of strategy, morale and the hundred other observable phenomena that make up the events of battle, which is the writer's concern. The history must be sound, the motivation plausible, and the demands on the novelist are akin to those on the writer of documentary drama.

In modern times, however, war, like so many other things done in the name of society, has become an object of individual moral concern, and participation in fighting has involved a confrontation with the moral principles in whose name one is called upon to fight. One cannot imagine a Roman legionary questioning the rightness of the Punic Wars, or a Norman foot-soldier debating the propriety of William the Conqueror's invasion of Britain. Throughout the centuries of European feudalism fighting formed part of a man's obligation to his lord, and in the wars of religion the principle of *cuius regio eius religio* continued to inhibit the emergence, on any substantial scale, of private moral scruples. But with a sense of democratic representation and responsibility came a desire to reflect on the things one was being called upon to do in the name of the state, and to understand why one consented, or declined, to do them. Thus whatever degree of realism, or naturalism, that novels on the Great War may possess, they tend to form contexts held together by the novelist's experience of, and judgement on, the historical circumstances of 1914 to 1918 and the phenomenon of war *an sich* as a liberator of basic human qualities, laudable or otherwise.

The reality was all too apparent in a country that had suffered military defeat and whose economy was slithering towards disaster. The human sacrifices that the war demanded had propitiated no gods, and when the German people asked where the imperial promises of national glory and the sweat and blood of four years had brought them, they received no answer. Small wonder that this disillusionment should infuse the work of novelists who pledged themselves to preach the futility and immorality of war through stories rooted in the action of war itself. Two of the best-known of these works, the one very different from the other, are Ludwig Renn's *Krieg* (1928) and Erich Maria Remarque's *Im Westen nichts Neues* (1929)—the same years, incidentally, that saw the publication of Robert Graves' autobiographical *Goodbye to All That* and the war novels *Undertones of War* by Edmund Blunden and *Death of a Hero* by Richard Aldington.

It is given to very few writers to enjoy the sort of success that came to Remarque (a 'romanticised' form of Remark, i.e. Kramer, his real name, spelt backwards). Although he had written a couple of novels in the earlier 1920s and was to write nine more over the following 30 years, his reputation rests alone on *Im Westen nichts Neues*—indeed, as *Der Weg zurück* (1931), *Drei Kameraden* (1937) and the later novels followed, it became uncomfortably clear that he was a one-book author.

But it was a remarkable book. Not many such instantaneous successes stand the test of time. Remarque had gone straight from school into the army in 1916, been wounded, then demobilised into an empty civilian world for whose activities he had had neither practical nor psychological preparation. Out of tune with the present, and with no responsibility for the events that had led up to it, he made his estrangement from the society around him into the cornerstone of his self-projection as spokesman for a 'lost generation'.

And it was because it did indeed speak for so many of this generation that its success was so phenomenal. 'I suffered bouts of acute despair', Remarque said in an interview at the time *Im Westen nichts Neues* was published,

. . . . and in my attempts to overcome them, I began deliberately and systematically to look for the source of my depression. This led me back to my war experiences, and I noticed the same was true of many of my friends. We were, and often still are, restless, aimless, sometimes enthusiastic, sometimes indifferent, but fundamentally joyless. The shadow of the war still hung over us, even though it was far from our thoughts.[3]

By the end of its year of publication *Im Westen nichts Neues* had been translated into 12 languages and sold a total of a million-and-a-half copies. Bernhard Kellermann (author of *Der neunte November*), Bruno Frank and Fritz von Unruh were prominent among those who acclaimed it, and it caught the attention of the world in a way that Scott Fitzgerald's *This Side of Paradise*, e.e. cummings' *The Enormous Room*, Hemingway's *The Sun also Rises* and other 'lost generation' novels of the 1920s did not. Hollywood acquired the film rights for £40,000, at that time the largest sum ever paid for a foreign work, and there was even talk of proposing Remarque for the Nobel Prize for Literature.

The success of *Im Westen nichts Neues* aroused the suspicion that the book was merely a clever exercise in sensation-mongering, a piece of jumped-up journalism. In fact it has an honesty and a directness of tone which penetrate beyond the theme of war into an area of consciousness to which the Germans were especially responsive. Through its first-person narrative and its sober, though also lurid, diary-like record of the thoughts and actions of the hero, his comrades and their enemies in war, it penetrates to the meaning of life, the moral essence of common humanity, the worship of an absolute, ideal, almost mystical concept of life in the train of Schopenhauer, Nietzsche and Spengler. War turns men into animals, but there are still moments when a flash of our true humanity breaks through and lights up the scene of crushed ideals and false values.

'Forgive me, brother,' says Paul Bäumer to the French in-fantryman he has just killed. 'We always see things too late. Why do people not go on telling us that you poor devils are just as badly off as we are, that your mothers worry just like ours, that we all have the same fear of death, and that we shall all die and suffer together?' The events of war have changed them: 'We are soldiers. Only after that, and then in some strange, embarrassed way, are we still individuals.' And as he sits in the sunshine recuperating from a poison-gas attack, he ponders: 'If we had gone home in 1916, the intensity and agony of our experiences would have unleashed a storm. But when we go back now, we shall be tired, crushed, bled white and without hope. We shall have lost our way, people will not understand us . . . . .'

Paul Bäumer need not have worried. He was never to return. 'He was killed in October 1918,' runs the unemotional report with which the novel ends, 'on a day so quiet and uneventful that the army communiqué was restricted to a single sentence: "All quiet on the western front." A man's death had no power to contradict the global observation that "all was quiet." Moreover, the expression on his face was one of such composure that one felt he was almost satisfied things had ended this way.'

Perhaps things ended this way too for another non-heroic hero, Thomas Mann's Hans Castorp, who also volunteered for the front, and whom we leave at the end of *Der Zauberberg* tramping grimly across the muddy battlefield. But *Der Zauberberg*, published five years before *Im Westen nichts Neues*, is not concerned to portray the reality of war or the emotions of those who fought in it, and although he 'would not put much money on the possibility that [Castorp] would return to tell the tale', Mann is 'fairly indifferent' to the question, only musing on whether 'this cosmic festival of death' might ultimately give way to love.

Like the poets and dramatists of expressionism, most of whom were half a generation his senior and had made their characteristic contribution to literature that much earlier, Remarque appealed above all to his own and younger generations. The war-comrades in his narrative are all of his own age, except for one, Landwehrmann Katczinsky—and Katczinsky, ironically and significantly, is the only fully-rounded personality we encounter, the man whose death clinches for Paul Bäumer his realisation of the pointlessness of the existence to which they are all committed. Expressionist also is the jagged style which conveys the book's underlying reproach to a society that has brought man to this pass—a reproach audible despite the author's claim that his book was meant neither as an accusation nor as a confession. At the same time it was the naturalistic traits of the *Neue Sachlichkeit* of the middle and later 1920s that turned *Im Westen nichts Neues* into a piece of realism which, as Heinrich Mann pointed out in an essay on the book,[4] touched that sense of the objective and the real in which a disillusioned younger generation was desperately trying to put its trust. There is a link in these terms, substantial as well as stylistic, between *Im Westen nichts Neues* and Theodor Plievier's *Stalingrad* (1945), one of the few successful German novels inspired by the experience of the Second World War.

The portrayal of war as a dehumanising, soul-destroying irrelevance, and of those forced to experience it as a dispirited, betrayed generation, captured the minds of thousands in Germany, but it also provoked the anger of militaristic and nationalist organisations, prominent among them the already rampant National Socialists. To such groups, not all of which were by any means as crude and barbaric as the Nazis, war was an ethical force and a means of true self-fulfilment—what Wilhelm Müller-Scheld, in an essay on Remarque's book, called 'war in a higher sense'.[5] It was also an inevitable and legitimate means of preserving the national values for which the Fatherland should stand.

So when in 1930 the film of *Im Westen nichts Neues* was due to be shown for the first time in Berlin, groups of Nazi thugs, led by a certain Dr Joseph Goebbels, broke up the performance by starting fights in the audience, throwing stink-bombs and setting loose white mice. A few weeks later the film was banned from exhibition over the whole of Germany. In 1933 Remarque, who had moved to Switzerland, was deprived of his German citizenship and his books were burned 'for their betrayal of the soldiers of the war'; in 1939, now rich from overseas sales of his books and from film rights, he emigrated to the United States and, like many fellow-exiles, became an American citizen. With his second wife, the film star Paulette Goddard, he returned to Switzerland after World War II and lived in Locarno until his death in 1970. A certain interest followed the semi-autobiographical novel *Der schwarze Obelisk* (1956), a story set in the year 1923, which gives a picture of the desperation of the early years of the Republic, and he continued writing down to within a few months of his death, but nothing came close to rivalling *Im Westen nichts Neues* in either quality or popularity.

Like Remarque, and in direct line of descent from the earliest reportage-novel of the Great War, Henri Barbusse's *Le feu* (1916), Ludwig Renn adopts an 'objective' chronicle style in the first person for relating his experiences. Also like Remarque, he depicts the events in his *Krieg* (1928) through the eyes of a private soldier. But the real author of *Krieg* was a Saxon aristocrat called Arnold Vieth von Golssenau, who had been through the war as company and battalion commander, studied art, archaeology and oriental history after his demobilisation, become a Marxist and joined the German Communist Party in the year that *Krieg* was published under the pseudonym of Ludwig Renn. Twice imprisoned by the Nazis, he escaped to Spain in 1936 to fight in the International Brigade; having spent the war years in Mexico, he returned to East Germany in 1947 and became a much-honoured figure in the German Democratic Republic, where he died in 1979.

As for Remarque, Arnold Zweig, Lion Feuchtwanger, Bertolt Brecht and others of a highly-developed socio-political consciousness, so also for Renn the war—the private's war, that is, not the battalion commander's—determined the course of both his career and his intellectual development. But unlike Remarque, Renn was politically committed, and his opposition to the senselessness of war rests less on a sense of outraged humanitarianism than on an interpretation of war as an inevitable concomitant of capitalism in its imperialist phase. Opposition to a war, and even unconditional pacifism, can spring from very different sources and lead to a temporary alliance of very different minds, and the names of Renn and Remarque were often spoken in the same breath at the time their best-known books appeared. In 1961 Renn made a public appeal to Remarque in the columns of the Socialist Unity Party's newspaper *Neues Deutschland*: 'Why do you not say Yes to negotiations, and No to war? It would mean a great deal. And say it so that the world can hear you!' Remarque's answer was a predictable silence.

Indeed, while fostering a hatred of the imperialist war of 1914–18, the Communists of the 1920s were bound to keep the spirit of belligerence alive in the cause of their own war, the class-war. In his preface to the anti-war anthology *Der Krieg* (1929) the former expressionist poet Johannes R. Becher, a member of the German Communist Party since 1919, made this quite explicit: 'War is for us not a matter of "once upon a time" but a living reality in our midst.'[7] Becher had already envisaged in his novel *Levisite oder der einzig gerechte Krieg* (1926) how the Great War would give way to world revolution, 'the only just war'.

While distrustful of the high-sounding ideals of regeneration in which the expressionist poets professed to put their faith, Renn shares with them certain fundamental characteristics of style, most obviously the use of short, ejaculatory phrases and a highly concentrated, vivid diction. But whereas the highly-charged language of the expressionists is the immediate expression of a complex of intense personal emotions, Renn's intention is the transmission of a forceful, unsentimental realism expressive of the objective cruelty and inhuman senselessness of the events he chronicles in firm, logical sequence. A second novel, *Nachkrieg* (1930), which carries the autobiographical narrative of Private Renn into the post-war years, stands in much the same thematic and stylistic relationship to *Krieg* as Remarque's *Der Weg zurück* to *Im Westen nichts Neues*. That is to say, it attempts to capitalise on an initial success by carrying the biographical situation forwards from the terrifying conditions of war to the circumstances of the unhappy peace that followed. But the success of *Krieg* was a unique phenomenon, and *Nachkrieg* added as little to Renn's reputation as *Der Weg zurück* to Remarque's. Except in his own country, little notice was taken of the novels, short stories, essays and other works he wrote after that time.

The war-novels of both Renn and Remarque are what may be

called, in a broad sense, pacifist in tendency. Those who had had to fight the war bore no responsibility for it and had not inherited the promised land 'fit for heroes to live in'. Nor was war anything to be heroic about, for all that it generated a sense of comradeship and loyalty. For others—and not only conservatives at the nationalist-militarist extreme, or those, like the Nazis, for whom violence was a basic instrument of policy—war represented a challenge to man's inner powers, a catalyst of hidden qualities, an education in the school of life. Two such figures, very different from each other in most other respects, are Hans Carossa and Ernst Jünger.

Carossa, like the three most significant prose writers of expressionism who were his contemporaries—Gottfried Benn, Ernst Weiss (a tragic figure, friend of Kafka, Werfel and Kisch in Prague, author of psychological novels on the father-son conflict and the tensions between the sexes, who committed suicide in Paris as the Germans occupied the city in 1940) and Alfred Döblin—was a doctor, and his *Rumänisches Tagebuch* (1924) derives from his experiences as a medical officer on active service in Rumania and on the western front. Remarque's *Im Westen nichts Neues* and Renn's *Krieg* both adopt the form of a documentation of day-to-day events in the manner of a personal diary; Jünger's *In Stahlgewittern* too was originally sub-titled 'Tagebuch eines Stosstruppführers'. Carossa's *Rumänisches Tagebuch*, however, retains the strict diary-form, each entry prefaced by precise statements of time and place. The story of Paul Bäumer in *Im Westen nichts Neues* starts in the summer of 1917 and ends with his death a few weeks before the armistice, while 'Gefreiter Renn's' war lasted the whole four years from 1914 to 1918. In Carossa's book, although the scene of the action stretches from the eastern to the western front, the period covered is a mere two months in the year 1916.

Yet this chronicle form, bearing a sequence of events with no defined or logical course, conceals an artistic inner plan which makes the final diary-entries a climax, and the diary as a whole becomes a novel of imaginative reflection, shot through with lyrical symbolical epigrams, sometimes obscure in meaning, sometimes heavily moralistic in tone. There is no epic sweep, and little sense of the intensity, in either personal or political terms, of the total experience of war. It culminates, not in the death of the young soldier Glavina, the character who comes to dominate the work, yet of whose actions in life we know nothing, but in the poetic reflections and aphorisms found on a piece of paper in his pocket and read aloud to the soldiers huddled together on the Rumanian battlefield. One of Glavina's earlier aphorisms is set at the head of the book as a motto: 'Raube das Licht aus dem Rachen der Schlange!'

Carossa's message is one of moral regeneration, Nietzschean in impulse and akin to that preached by Stefan George in terms of his 'New World' of the spirit. We are in a world of poetic values, of fantasy, of symbols, the same world as that of the lyric poetry Carossa wrote throughout his life, and that of the strangely insubstantial novel *Der Arzt Gion* (1931), into which he weaves his experiences as a Munich doctor in the years following the war. Both the doctor and the poet had in his eyes the task of healing a suffering humanity. To match the sedatives by which he alleviated physical pain he adduced a vocabulary of healing values such as 'Innigkeit', 'Ruhe', 'Traum' and 'Gnade'.

But war, like sickness, can be a test and an education, and Carossa, in poems, in the autobiographical fragment *Kindheit und Jugend* and elsewhere, describes many scenes in which destruction becomes a force with its own spiritual power and beauty, part of the process of creation. He consciously set himself in the line of descent from Goethe's 'Stirb und werde'. War, like all sources of suffering, is not to be sought after for its own sake, still less is it to be glorified. But neither is it to be regretted, or evaded, or cursed. Moreover Carossa was older than the other war-novelists with whom we are concerned here: he was 36 when he joined the army, and his formative years belonged in the period of Wilhelminian decadence on which the war had set its seal. If this was the agent by which the old Adam was to be cast off, it must be confronted and welcomed, not reviled. One step further brings us to the glorification of war as the supreme moment of personal commitment and sacrifice, the sublime means to self-realisation and communal fulfilment. It is the step that leads to Ernst Jünger.

Together with his brother Friedrich Georg, Ernst Jünger has been a polarising influence in German life and letters for over 50 years. Born in 1895, three years before Remarque and Brecht, he made an abortive attempt at the age of 17 to join the Foreign Legion, volunteered for the front at the beginning of the Great War, was commissioned in 1915, fought at the Somme and Langemarck, was decorated with the highest military honour, the *Pour le mérite*, and finally left the army in 1923. In August 1939, now a distinguished writer of 44, he re-enlisted with the rank of captain, serving until late in 1944, a few months before his 50th birthday.

Biographical sketches are often irrelevant, sometimes even misleading, in one's study of a creative artist's work. But they can also convey what he found it important to do in life, and, given the closeness of his life to the things in which he believed, what values he sought to enshrine in his work. With Jünger the coincidence is almost complete. Having chosen the context—war—which is dominated by the sacrifice of human life, he acted as though it were the sacrifice of his own life that would give that context its fullest meaning. Death eluded him in both wars. But his son was killed on the Italian front in 1944 at the age of 18, achieving, as Jünger wrote to General Speidel in a terse, almost emotionless, yet coldly gripping tone, a fulfilment denied to his father: 'It was his first day under fire—a day he had eagerly looked forward to. He always wanted to follow in my path, and now, with his very first step, he has gone so much further than I ever did.'

From Jünger's *Fronterlebnis* between 1915 and the end of the war sprang the characteristically titled *In Stahlgewittern* (1920), originally described as 'Tagebuch eines Stosstruppführers' but subsequently just as 'Kriegstagebuch', and dedicated 'To the Fallen'. Its 20 chapters, written as a first-person narrative and culminating in the announcement that the author had been awarded the *Pour le mérite* for personal bravery, constitute a work which, though based on events recorded seriatim in a diary, has a planned construction which puts it into the genre of the novel, like Carossa's *Rumänisches Tagebuch*. The personality of the novelist, moreover, never leaves the scene, and with the citation from the Kaiser as the last words in the book, the whole work becomes a spiritual biography, a form of *Bildungsroman* in which self-fulfilment is achieved in the higher reaches not of life but of death, and through acts not of creation but of destruction and sacrifice.

On one plane *In Stahlgewittern* is an adventure-story, a formidably brilliant eye-witness account of battles, of moments of relaxation, of soldiers and civilians, of comrades and enemies. In this Jünger's acknowledged stimulus came from *Don Quixote* and Grimmelshausen's *Simplicissimus*. Events are precisely located in time and place, the narrative manner is as harsh and powerful as the weapons of destruction that carry the action, and all outward philosophising and moralising is pared away.

But the morality must needs be implicit in the substance and style of the narration, and the role of war as a testing-ground in *In Stahlgewittern* needs no labouring. Indeed, it is like a practical handbook to illustrate beliefs which Jünger made explicit in other writings from the 1920s. In his study of the philosophy and psychology of war, *Der Kampf als inneres Erlebnis* (1922), we read: 'War is as much a feature of human life as the sexual urge. It is a law of nature, and we shall therefore never escape its grip . . . To live is to kill.'[8] And: 'Fighting is not simply an act of destruction but the masculine form of procreation. Even if a man fights for the wrong cause, he does not fight in vain.'[9] Irrational it may be, and unconcerned with the niceties of right and wrong, but the spirit of combat is what the world, above all the German world, needs at this moment when the Weimar Republic is full of spineless 'liberal' ideas about 'the welfare of the people' and 'social democracy': 'It is war that has made men and ages what they are . . . War, the father of all things, is ours too, and has hammered, chiselled and hardened us into what we are. As long as the dynamism of life still pulsates through our veins, this war will be its generating point. We have been reared to war and shall remain fighters as long as we live.'[10] War is irrational in essence, a law unto itself and not susceptible to moral assessment, being, in Jünger's words, 'not subject to the laws of a passing civilisation but directly governed by the eternal laws of Nature herself.'[11] The aphorism at the head of the novel *Die Geächteten* by Ernst von Salomon—a writer and man of action whose attitudes and style are close to those of Jünger and who also, like Jünger, managed to retain a certain independence during the years of Nazism—might well have come from Jünger himself: 'Blut und Erkenntnis müssen zusammenfallen im Leben. Dann entsteht Geist.'

In the early 1920s such a message was gratefully seized upon, firstly by those in the country at large to whom Germany had not been defeated but 'stabbed in the back', secondly by the *Stahlhelm* and other veterans' organisations, and thirdly by the army itself. The army, having survived the disaster of 1918 and been reconstituted by the National Assembly as a *Reichswehr* more unified in organisation than the *Kaiserheer* had ever been, was to exercise great political power in the Republic and play a vital role in bringing Hitler to power. The concept of the national state which it is the army's task to defend also received Jünger's approval: 'A great and powerful Reich of all Germans will for ever be our ultimate commitment' (*Einsatz* is his characteristic word; 'Der Frontsoldat und die Wilhelminische Zeit' in *Die Standarte. Wochenschrift des Bundes der Frontsoldaten* 3, Magdeburg, 20 September 1925, 2).

Jünger's position after Hitler became Chancellor was equivocal, and alongside his preparedness 'to make a positive contribution to the creation of the new state', as he put it,[12] must be set his allegorical attack on the crudities of the Nazis in his novel *Auf den Marmorklippen* (1939). But in the context of *In Stahlgewittern, Der Kampf als inneres Erlebnis* (1922), *Wäldchen 125* (1924: a kind of sequel to *In*

Stahlgewittern) and other works of this period, one must see Jünger's philosophy of war not as an expression of a lust for power, still less as an act of national self-aggrandisement, rather, as total involvement and sacrifice, both personal and communal, the supreme test of human fibre, an end in itself. Hence the frequency in *In Stahlgewittern* of epithets like 'eisern', 'scarf', 'stählern', and the anti-bourgeois cult of 'man in action' which Jünger shares with Hemingway, Malraux and other novelists of the 1920s and 1930s. His belief in the tragic nature of human destiny, the need for man to face this destiny alone, and the irrelevance to the human condition of beneficent democratic attitudes and institutions, also sets him in the company of D.H. Lawrence.

Jünger is not given to speculation, but he does project the figure of the Unknown Soldier as the hero symbolic of supreme military honour. Later he ranged alongside this figure those of the *Arbeiter*, the technocrat, representing the new élite committed to the absoluteness of 'totale Mobilmachung'—for War and Work make the same demands—and the *Waldgänger*, the loner who carves out his own destiny in the face of the apathy and the herd instincts of the masses. These three are what he calls 'the great figures of our age'[13] and through the 30 years that separate *In Stahlgewittern* from *Der Waldgang* (1951) his vision remains constant: 'I must ask my readers to consider my works as a single unit in which there are two periods but no contradictions. I should not like to be reckoned among those who do not want to be reminded today of what they were yesterday.'[14]

So Jünger remains the most remarkable spokesman in modern German literature for contentious and not always welcome values which have become part and parcel of the intellectual climate of modern Germany. There is a venerable tradition, stretching from Heraclitus and the Spartans down to Hegel and Nietzsche, which sees war as both inevitable and beneficial, and a Martian surveying 3,000 years of history in the Old World would conclude that war was the normal state of affairs between peoples, with brief respites apparently produced by exhaustion. War *an sich*, with its companions, suffering and sacrifice, contains the values which Jünger urges upon the world, qualities of ennoblement which are far removed from the quest for national glory or material gain for which, from behind a smokescreen of high moral sentiments, aggressive wars are fought. Jünger was no Nazi, yet—or perhaps therefore—he refused with characteristic disdain to submit to 'de-Nazification' procedures at the end of World War II. But the values for which he stands, like those of Nietzsche, Stefan George and most of those who stand in the Nietzschean shadow, can readily appear as unhappily welcome allies of inhumanity and tyranny. And after one has sifted his achievements in terms of his own intentions, one is left, again as with Nietzsche and those of his spiritual lineage, with the familiar nagging question of the writer's hidden responsibility for the uses to which his works are put by the later generations he is powerless to influence.

Remarque, Renn, Carossa and Jünger all, in their different ways, make war the subject, the hero, of the works we have discussed. Their novels have been about war itself, the war of the German soldier, located, except for parts of Carossa's *Rumänisches Tagebuch*, on the battlefields of the Western front. Different from these, in that the events of war form a backcloth to an epic narrative, the story of the last months in the life of a Russian prisoner-of-war in the hands of the Germans, is Arnold Zweig's *Der Streit um den Sergeanten Grischa* (1927), one of the finest, most powerful novels of the period. The author intended it as the centrepiece of a triptych called *Trilogie des Übergangs*, which, set in and after the Great War, was to portray the transition from the age of a decadent, discredited imperialism to the new age of socialism. Out of this then grew a plan for a sequence of eight novels on the post-war age, under the general title *Der grosse Krieg der weissen Männer*. Using a true incident as his point of departure, Zweig first wrote a drama, *Das Spiel vom Sergeanten Grischa* (1921), and a few years later the novel. Jewish by birth, he formed his socialist views during active service in the war, and in 1933 his works, with those of Feuchtwanger, Alfred Kerr, Heinrich Mann, Tucholsky and many others, were branded as 'subversive' by the *Börsenverein der Deutschen Buchhändler*.[15] He remained a Marxist through his exile in Palestine during the Nazi period, and returned to East Berlin after World War II. Like Remarque and Renn he lives in the public memory by virtue of one novel, but he was also a prolific writer of essays and short stories, both before the Great War and for 50 years after it.

Der Streit um den Sergeanten Grischa owes its literary position in large measure to its thematic richness and to the vivid realism with which a remarkably broad spectrum of characters is presented. The action covers a mere eight months, from March to November 1917, the period immediately following the abdication of the Tsar, and the rumblings of the Russian revolution are heard in the background. But unlike the novels Zweig wrote in exile and after, which follow more singleminded Marxist paths, *Grischa* has a wider range of relevances, and as with the later plays of Brecht, we find ourselves less concerned with the presentation of a particular world view than with the understanding of a series of moral predicaments. The events of the time, and their challenge, are inextricably bound up with the decisions thrust upon individual characters. As in Brecht's *Die Massnahme* the agitators are as worried about saving their skins as about closing the Party ranks, so Grischa is moved to escape from his prisoner-of-war camp by an urge to see his wife and child, not by a determination to join the revolution.

Grischa is the 'little man', the scapegoat, caught up in a whirlpool of uncontrollable events and made the centre of the 'Streit' between the old Prussian military code, which, though harsh, was just and kept to its rules, and the pragmatic militarism of the win-the-war-at-all-costs leaders in the High Command. In defiance of any decent code of justice, and even after Grischa has been identified as an escaped prisoner-of-war, not a spy, the letter of the High Command's decree concerning Russian deserters is carried out, and he is shot.

The common soldiers and the peasants are the helpless victims of the events of war. But Zweig finds among the aristocratic officers too, especially the younger ones, a disapproval of the conduct of some of their seniors. When young Lieutenant Paul Winfried learns of the Grand Duke of Sachsen-Eilenburg's plan 'to come and shoot a few Russians at some quiet spot in our sector', he does not conceal his contempt:

Since some other Grand Duke started it, somewhere up in the Tirul Marshes, I believe, shooting Russians seems to have become a pastime among the nobility. He drove up to the front, where things are now as quiet as a mouse, and when an unsuspecting Russky passed by on the other side, His Royal Highness just picked him off. It was a novelty for him and, poor chap, for the Russky too. The idiot of a commander who allowed it to happen . . . naturally expected a pretty medal, and he got it. But the man in the trenches, like the supply troops and sappers, paid for it with 107 casualties. The Russkies retaliated with heavy stuff the whole afternoon and gave us a proper pounding. Then our artillery started up, and we almost had a big battle on our hands in the middle of what was virtually peace. The communiqué just referred to 'increased artillery activity'. And now they're trying to introduce this pastime in our sector as well.[16]

This is a young Prussian officer speaking. At the very end of the novel, after Grischa's execution and the birth, symbolically simultaneous, of his illegitimate child to the rough, passionate Mother-Courage-figure of Babka, it is also a young lieutenant who, in response to an older officer's threat to punish an engine-driver for deliberately slowing down his train so that a corporal going on leave could jump aboard, mockingly retorts: 'Then you'd better get on the footplate yourself, my friend. I fancy a man who can drive a locomotive is more indispensable these days than Schieffenzahn.'[17] It is a brazen remark, for General Schieffenzahn—*Grischa* as a whole is something of a *roman à clef*—conceals the figure of Ludendorff.

Over and above his symbolic role as a sacrificial victim of cold injustice, Grischa serves in the novel as a touchstone of the humanity of those with whom he comes into contact. With the prominent exception of Babka, most of those who seek a just solution to his case, from Gerichtsrat Dr. Posnanski down to sympathetic onlookers like Täwje, the carpenter, are Jews. It is a Jewish doctor and a Jewish midwife who deliver Babka's daughter, and the clerk Bertin, poet, novelist and reader of Bergson and Husserl, bears a number of autobiographical traits.

Many years after *Der Streit um den Sergeanten Grischa* Arnold Zweig reasserted in the language of the class struggle the social basis of the novelist's craft: 'The function of the novel in society is to be a messenger from those in the depths to the fortunate few who live on the surface; to tell of the toiling masses and the oppressed who will be the victorious fighters of tomorrow and prove that they can contribute more to the world than their familiar capacity for suffering.'[18] Grischa Ilyitch Paprotkin is one of those who live 'in the depths'. But his story needs no body of doctrine to bolster its significance. It is a rich human story, rugged and uncompromising in style, told with an epic sweep far beyond the reach of a Remarque, or a Jünger, or a Renn. Like the very different story of another 'little man's' war, Jaroslav Hasek's *The Good Soldier Schweik*, it has acquired a position of impregnable popularity among modern war-novels.

Prose fiction, to a greater extent than either the lyric or the drama, is a primary source of information for the social historian. The novelist's interest in the society in which his story is set, be it of his own or of an earlier period, may be only incidental to his principal concerns, but the reader must needs absorb the social setting along with the events of the narrative, and the novelist knows this. The characters may accept their society with gratitude or resignation, they may rebel against it or they may be so perfectly attuned to it that they—and we—are hardly aware of its existence. In any event it is there to be observed, whether as a virtual *dramatis persona* in its own right or as the framework which holds together the actions of the characters.

A novel is not a document of history in the sense of a set of diplomatic papers or an eye-witness account of events. The mirror of art—if one retains for the moment the familiar, though often inappropriate antithesis of 'art' and 'reality'—is a distorting mirror. The images projected by the artist have passed through the filter of his artistic imagination and been modified by the qualities of that imagination. One cannot learn the history of the Plantagenet kings from Shakespeare, or of Joan of Arc from Voltaire or Schiller, and whatever the novels of Christopher Isherwood tell us about the Berlin of the early 1930s belongs to a different plane from that on which one must gather one's basic historical and political facts. But the psychological insights of a writer can add an area of understanding to the events which the 'strict' historian expounds in a different frame of mind and with a different purpose in view. In this sense the two are complementary. The society which the novelist sees may be no less valid than that which the historian uncovers, and from his works one can feel one's way into personal and social situations which the accounts of political and social historians do not penetrate. A kind of middle term between the two is reportage: Egon Erwin Kisch's famous collection *Der rasende Reporter* (1925), with its social criticism from a proletarian-revolutionary stance, is a contemporary *locus classicus* of the genre.

The Great War, European society in turmoil, provided a subject for some, a background for others. In the directionless years of peace that followed, filled with the discrepant and mutually destructive influences of militarism and pacifism, idealism and cynicism, economic self-assertion and spiritual timidity, national aggressiveness and political hesitancy, novelists found a veritable Pandora's box of social motifs. Again one must distinguish between the writer for whom a social situation or movement is a subject in itself, with characters acting out their parts in it, and the writer whose gaze is centred on individuals, or on a set of abstract values. In many cases it may be inappropriate to draw a firm dividing line, and whereas the interest attaching to a lesser writer may lie almost entirely in the social information his work conveys, with the greater writer this aspect is quickly absorbed into a broader and deeper context. Greatness, after all, resides not in the expression of the values of an age but in their transcendence—the source of the timelessness of all great art. But the presence of a social content, historical or contemporary, and whatever its extent and form, is undisturbed, and it is to this that we are looking here in the first instance.

Famous among the lesser, 'typical' writers whose works yield revealing insights into the political and social realities of the Weimar years is Rudolf Ditzen, who wrote under the name of Hans Fallada. At the mention of this name the literary reflex produces the title *Kleiner Mann—was nun?*, the enormously successful novel about life in post-war Germany which has sold millions of copies, been translated into 20 languages and twice made into a film. When the publishing house of Rowohlt launched the literary paperback on the German market in 1950, *Kleiner Mann—was nun?* was given the proud number One in the *rororo-Taschenbücher* series.

But in 1931, a year before *Kleiner Mann—was nun?*, there appeared a work of greater political interest, and perhaps also of greater narrative power, the story of another pathetic 'little man'—*Bauern, Bonzen und Bomben*. This work broke the silence into which Fallada had lapsed since the publication of two expressionistic novels in the early 1920s, and it immediately captured public attention.

In its broadest aspect *Bauern, Bonzen und Bomben* portrays the confusion, the pettiness and the intolerance that bring violence to a small-town community and the peasants in the surrounding country-side under the frustrations generated by a bureaucracy-ridden government. A peasants' demonstration is broken up by the police, bombs are planted in public buildings, countrymen and townsmen are at each other's throats, with the peasants boycotting the local shops and cutting even their own relatives in the town, bands of Communists and Nazis fight in the streets, back-scratching civil servants sit in their offices looking after their own interests—such is the picture that Fallada paints. (A symbolic picture of the way Italian Fascism had moved in on, and German Fascism was on the point of moving in on, just this kind of situation, makes up the broader, public area of significance in Thomas Mann's chilling little story of 'Verwirrung der Gefühle', *Mario und der Zauberer*, published in the same year as *Bauern, Bonzen und Bomben*).

No section of the community, from the peasants of Altholm to the national authorities in Berlin, emerges unscathed from Fallada's story. When the verdict on the rebellious peasant leaders is announced, the judge has harsh words for the almost hysterical violence with which the police broke up the demonstration and decides that leniency must be shown towards the accused. They are not acquitted, however, but given short suspended sentences, because, in the judge's words, 'their actions could have had extremely dangerous consequences'. The Weimar Republic was not unfamiliar with the spectacle of settling political differences in the street. Nor was respect for the law at a premium, and one can hardly miss an overtone of mockery in Fallada's account of how, since the proper courtroom in Altholm was too small for the trial, and to use the tap-room of a nearby tavern would hardly have been appropriate, recourse was finally had to a school gymnasium, in which there was plenty of room but where the wall-bars and ropes 'made it a rather eerie scene'.

But it is the members of the white-collar bourgeoisie, the *Stehkragenproletariat*, as they were cuttingly called by the classes both above and below them, who are made to appear the most pathetic, even despicable. The antics of the staff of the three local newspapers, for instance, with councillors trying to exert political pressure on the owners, and the owners telling their editors what to print and what to sweep under the carpet, reveal the ways in which public opinion was manipulated.

The supreme cynicism over the conduct of public affairs is left for the very last page of the novel. The Social Democrat Bürgermeister who has been at the centre of the furore over the 'peasants' revolt' is not dismissed and taken to court, as public morality would demand, but given an appointment elsewhere. As the train that is to take him away from Altholm draws into the station, hundreds of peasants pour out of the coaches, lured into the town for a further demonstration organised by a scheming politician as an electoral ruse. The demonstration, announced as being in the cause of reconciliation, is banned. The peasants are rounded up by the police and sent back where they came from, while the ex-Bürgermeister, getting into the almost empty train in which the peasants had arrived, sets off to take up his new post.

His verdict on the situation? 'Of course it's right that the peasants shouldn't demonstrate here, today of all days. But everybody does things for the wrong reasons—everybody . . . It's never the issue itself but some paltry private interest.'[19]

Into this scene is woven the career and downfall of Max Tredup, a pitiful, infinitely dispensable clerk in a newspaper office. He will sell his soul for a few hundred marks, and his employers consider him worthy of only the most menial work, yet by spreading slanderous rumours about his editor, he succeeds for a few dizzy moments in holding editorial responsibility in his own hands, only to be sacked for printing a libel on the Bürgermeister in the course of the trial of the peasant leaders. While his meek, helpless wife waits for him at home, he is clubbed to death by one of the peasants.

Nothing can ever work out for Tredup, a predecessor of Johannes Pinneberg in Falladas's *Kleiner Mann—was nun?* 'Tredup is simply one of those people who never have any luck', is the verdict passed on him.[20] And to be unlucky is, of course, one's own fault. Money— more properly, the lack of it—lies at the root of his downfall and eats away his marriage, his last refuge in a world whose values are governed by what money can buy. The same fate awaits the little insurance clerk Max Schreyvogel in Fallada's later Novel *Kleiner Mann—grosser Mann, alles vertauscht* (1939): 'The destructive effect of the money I had inherited was so great that it quickly changed my relationship to Karla and finally jeopardised our whole marriage . . . For one of the curses of money is that it makes the man who owns it a lonely person and threatens to destroy all human ties.'[21] The bond of marriage—in *Bauern, Bonzen und Bomben*, in *Kleiner Mann—was nun?*,as well as in his later novel of life in the Weimar Republic, *Wolf unter Wölfen* (1937)—is the only human tie in Fallada's novels that survives the onslaught of demoralising and degrading circumstance.

'I recommend this novel to everybody who wants to know what Germany is like', wrote Kurt Tucholsky in *Die Weltbühne* in 1931. 'This is Germany—the world of the towns, the world of the countryside, especially in the north, and the world of politics.'[22]

While the scene of *Bauern, Bonzen und Bomben* is rural and small-town, *Kleiner Mann—was nun?* (1932) is set in Berlin, with its *Kleinbürger* non-hero and his newly-wed wife fighting, unsuccessfully, to stave off the threat of unemployment that hung over every German employee's head from the beginning of 1930. The workers at least had their trade-unions to help preserve proletarian solidarity. But the white-collar members of the lower middle-class—clerks, shop-assistants, the service trades in general—had neither nationwide organisations to represent their interests nor, more sadly symptomatic of their condition, a sense of loyalty and common purpose that might have helped preserve some vestige of morale, if not of honour (the latter was a luxury few could afford at such a time).

So Johannes Pinneberg, the *Stehkragenprolet*, belongs nowhere and finally loses his job, betrayed by his so-called colleagues. The workers are nominally his social inferiors, but he has now sunk lower than they. As he slouches along the Friedrichstrasse, he is chased into the side-streets by a policeman who suspects him of being one of the many agitators that roamed the city during those days, and he suddenly sees his true situation:

He no longer belonged here, and they were right to chase him away. He was out of place, finished, sunk without trace. Order and decency?—Things of the past. Work and regular pay?—Things of the past. Promotion and hope?—Things of the past. Poverty is not misery—it's a crime, a disgrace, something to be suspicious of.[23]

As the deterministic hopelessness of Max Tredup's situation lay in his offence of belonging to that category of persons 'who were always out of luck', so poor Pinneberg resigns himself to being a member of a class that will for ever be the whipping-boy, with hardly the strength or the will to murmur a word on its own behalf. In his elegant words: 'Wir haben ewig Schiss.'

The elections of September 1930 had increased the strength of the two extremist parties, the National Socialists and the Communists, and Chancellor Brüning was only able to govern under the emergency decrees which the President had signed under Article 48 of the constitution. Despite their hatred of the Nazis, the Communists stated openly that they would rather see the Nazis in power than do anything to keep the republic alive, and they made their first priority the destruction of the Social Democrats as the rival working-class party. Germany had become familiar with these sectarian squabbles, and also with the strong-arm measures of the police that were inevitably associated with government by emergency decree. Hitler could have wished for no better foundation for his own seizure of power.

So when the innocent Pinneberg—who admits that innocence and poverty are incompatible—is set upon by the police, there are many respectable onlookers who murmur not the slightest protest. It cannot be called a society of thugs, but it might be called a society of connivers at thuggery.

The 'proletarisation of the white-collar workers' during the 1920s was a situation diagnosed and described by the Marxist sociologist Siegfried Kracauer in his essay *Die Angestellten* (1930). This work, whose conclusions provide a sociological framework for *Kleiner Mann—was nun?*, made a great impact on Tucholsky, Walter Benjamin and other prominent intellectuals of the time, who saw in it both a statement of the true social situation of the bourgeoisie as a whole, and a revelation that might shock the middle-class into a state of political awareness.[24]

It did nothing of the kind. The *Bürgertum* continued to think in the terms of traditional morality, right and wrong, just and unjust, and to seek fulfilment in the family, in friends, in nature, in art. They were not induced by the language of class-warfare to see themselves as slaves of a system, still less as agents of revolution. Johannes Pinneberg, as a member of Kracauer's class of *Angestellte*, may feel the degradation and desperation of his position when he is dismissed from the firm of men's outfitters for which he worked. But it is a source of satisfaction to him that his staff manager is also to become redundant, and a further source of pleasure that he was not being fired for inefficiency—indeed, he had been the only one in his department to sell anything approaching the prescribed quota of goods—but because one of his colleagues had denounced him. 'I wrote the book in the afternoons and evenings of the most depressing days of my life', Fallada recalled many years later.[25] At the same time the love story of Pinneberg and his Lämmchen has a sentimentality which, one suspects, was in large measure responsible for its remarkable success at the time.

This same Berlin world, its infiltration by the Nazis and the circumstances which lured the economically and morally vulnerable into the Nazi snare, is the subject of F.C. Weiskopf's racy novel *Lissy oder die Versuchung*, written in 1934–35 in Prague and published in 1937 in Switzerland. With a chilling inevitably the little clerk Elias Fromeyer, made redundant by the economies that accompanied the slump of the early 1930s, slithers into the Nazi morass and becomes an officer in the S.A., living by a creed of hatred, violence and anti-Semitism; his wife Lissy, by contrast, fights off the fascist temptation and makes cause with the Communist opposition.

Conspiracies, street battles, parades, rallies—these and other elements in the social and political life of the Republic of whose sickness Weiskopf had been an eye-witness, are devastatingly portrayed in the naturalistic pages of what, shortly before his death in 1955, Weiskopf said had been 'a contemporary novel when it was first published but now, a bare two decades later, has become an historical novel.' The history, in particular, of how the Nazis exploited the middle-class fear that the Communists were poised to destroy the German *Bürgertum* in the name of the proletariat, is all too true. The National Socialists always claimed to be a workers' party, but in 1930 the middle classes made up 53 per cent of the membership, the workers only 28 per cent, in total disproportion to their numbers in the population as a whole (workers 46 per cent, middle classes 26 per cent). The propagandists of the Nazi party were tragically successful in convincing the electorate that they could be all things to all men.

Another picture of the Berlin of the early 1930s, this time of bohemian life and the moral decay of the bourgeoisie, is given by Erich Kästner in his *Fabian, die Geschichte eines Moralisten* (1931). Kästner, who was twice arrested by the Nazis but managed to survive the Third Reich by writing mainly children's books in the wake of *Emil und die Detektive* (1929), composed in *Fabian* a spicy, satirical, semi-autobiographical novel about an advertising agent whose moral standards are incompatible with those of the society around him. Fabian's disillusionment does not lead him, however, to commit suicide; instead, he is drowned trying to save a boy who has fallen off a bridge into the river. 'Unfortunately,' explains the dead-pan narrator, 'Fabian could not swim.' The inscription above this last chapter of the book is 'Learn How to Swim.'

Fabian, said Kästner, was intended as a warning of impending disaster in Germany and in Europe (its original subtitle was *Der Gang vor die Hunde*). But its Berlin is not the cruel, realistic Berlin of Johannes Pinneberg or Lissy Fromeyer, for the mirror that the moralist—call him Fabian or Kästner—holds up to society is a distorting mirror. Yet caricature can be no less piercing a social weapon than icy bitterness or passionate protest: the 1920s belong as much to George Grosz as to Otto Dix or Käthe Kollwitz. For all that, the playful mockery of *Fabian*—no doubt this is the occupational hazard of the parodist and satirist: Karl Kraus makes it even plainer—leaves a strange insubstantiality, a sensation of not having really come to grips with things, as though our enjoyment of the dexterous manner has distracted our minds from the desperate seriousness of the substance.

Kleiner Mann—was nun?, *Lissy oder die Versuchung* and *Fabian* are all set in Berlin. And Berlin—political and cultural metropolis, enticer of those with ambition and murderer of those who failed, a victim to the entrepreneur and a haven to the beggar, Mecca of art and cesspool of morality—Berlin *was* the Weimar Republic. Expressionist poets—Becher, Rubiner, Lotz, Goll and many others—were held in its merciless fascination, while Brecht, whose *Im Dickicht der Städte* exposed the hollowness and loneliness of Berlin city life, perversely yet compulsively clung to this loneliness. Fortunes were made and lost here, reputations gained and ruined; there was more sentimentality than sympathy, and no welfare state to look after the drop-outs. Writers, artists, actors, musicians, journalists—Berlin clutched at them like an octopus: Brecht, Heinrich Mann and Bruno Walter from Munich, Furtwängler and Erich Kästner from Leipzig, Willy Haas from Prague, Kurt Weill from Dessau, Ernst Ludwig Kirchner from Dresden—all came to join native Berliners like George Grosz, John Heartfield and Otto Nagel, and long-established residents like Ludwig Meidner, while Benn, Döblin and many literary survivors of the expressionist heyday were still living in the city.

Here were published most of the leading political and literary journals of the day—Jacobsohn's (later Ossietzky's) *Die Weltbühne*, Grossmann's *Das Tagebuch*, Willy Haas' *Die Literarische Welt*, Ernst Niekisch's *Der Widerstand*, together with the long-established *Deutsche Rundschau*, *Vossische Zeitung* and *Die Neue Rundschau*; here were the great publishing houses of Ullstein, Mosse and S. Fischer; here were Piscator's agitprop theatre, political cabaret and the centres of social satire. Most of the intellectuals and artists who came, came to stay; others came to create a particular occasion or to make a special mark on the life of the city. But they all came. As in the slogan once coined to characterise a popular English Sunday newspaper, 'All human life is there'.

All human life is also there in that most famous of Berlin novels from the era of the Weimar Republic, Döblin's *Berlin Alexanderplatz* (1929).

To trace the life of Alfred Döblin from his Jewish origins in Stettin, through his long years as a doctor in a working-class district of Berlin, his exile in France and later in the United States, to his return in 1945 to West Germany and his death there in 1957, is to view a panorama of German history in the first half of the twentieth century. And to follow his literary career from the expressionism of the early 1900s (he was a co-founder of the journal *Der Sturm* in 1910) through socialist, psychological and aesthetic phases to the highly personal Catholicism in which he ended his days, is to review almost the whole gamut of intellectual pressures and attractions of these years. The fate of his last significant work, the psychological novel *Hamlet oder Die lange Nacht nimmt ein Ende*, shows the extent to which the post-war literary world had passed him by. Finished in 1946, it attracted no interest from publishers in the West. Ten years later it was finally published—in East Germany; the following year it appeared in West Germany also. Such was the reluctant, almost grudging reception for a man who 40 years earlier had been in the forefront of progressive literary movements, and whose reputation in the early 1930s had made him a focal point of literary discussion.

For Döblin, as for so many artists of his time, the creation of works of the artistic imagination went hand in hand with the establishment of a critical philosophical position. The essays he wrote throughout his literary life give a commentary on the changes of direction taken by his works of fiction, explaining, for example, what lay behind the choice of a Chinese subject-matter for *Die drei Sprünge des Wang-lun* (1915), what led him to write his anti-Utopian novel *Berge, Meere und Giganten* (1924), and how he saw the transition from the 'unreality' of the Indian world in his verse epic *Manas* (1927) to the 'real' Berlin of his own long experience in *Berlin Alexanderplatz*. 'Every one of my large-scale epic works is preceded by a statement of its intellectual groundwork', he wrote in 1932.[26] For *Berlin Alexanderplatz* much of the 'intellectual groundwork' is to be found in the essay *Das Ich über der Natur* (1927).

Particularly revealing in Döblin's critical writings, and of central interest in an age full of pronouncements on the social responsibility of the artist, is his ambivalence in the face of the quarrel between those who asserted the sacred autonomy of the artistic imagination and those who envisaged a single, universal art of, and for, the people. In 1926 we find him saying that works of art 'neither emerge from a community nor return to a community. I claim that they emerge from solitude and return to solitude. They emerge from an ego and return to an ego.'[27] Eminently expressive of this attitude, and of the poet's claim to speak from an elevated plane, is his epic poem *Manas*, published the following year. In 1928 he gave an address before the Preussische Akademie der Künste with the title 'Schriftstellerei und

Dichtung', making it his task to distinguish between 'literature' and an inferior mass-market industry that produces works of fiction 'that descend to the level of the practical, that which people can grasp and make use of.'[28] His own position is clear: 'I have chosen to speak on this subject precisely because I believe that the erection of a barrier between these two—reinforced with concrete, if possible—is one of the most urgent necessities in modern literature.'[29]

But a few years earlier he had been decrying in Marxist terminology the pretensions of the 'bourgeois' class to which he belonged and the 'aesthetic' ends that its literature pursued. In another address to the Preussische Akademic der Künste, given in memory of Arno Holz only a year after 'Schriftstellerei und Dichtung', he again, before a somewhat bewildered audience, took up the stance of the artist as the servant of the proletariat, demanding that control of the media of education and culture be wrested from the hand of the self-perpetuating and self-protecting middle-class. He concluded his speech with a shattering challenge (the emphases are Döblin's own):

Zwei Dinge sind nötig: Verbreiterung der Bildungsbasis durch Beseitigung des Bildungs-monopols *(ein ungeheures Kapitel) und seitens der Autoren:* Hinwendung zur breiten Volksmasse! *Um Naturalismus im echten und vorbildlichen Sinne von Arno Holz zu treiben, haben wir notwending in Deutschland, wo die Literatur schon eine grosse Höhe erreicht hat,* Senkung des Gesamtniveaus der Literatur. *Aus dem Bildungskäfig, in dem unsere heutige Literatur steckt, in dem sie von breiten Volksmassen nur als Attribut der feinen Leute angesehen wird, muss sie heraus.*[30]

(Two things are necessary: to broaden the basis of education *by doing away with educational monopoly* (a huge task); and to get writers *to address themselves to the masses*. In order to pursue a naturalism in the true, exemplary sense of Arno Holz, we need *to lower the overall level of literature* in Germany, where literature has reached great heights. Modern literature must be taken out of that private preserve which the masses see as the property of the privileged classes.)

These two voices within Döblin *are* saying two different things, and no simple, chronological explanation will resolve the difference. It is a conflict revealed by many artists of left-wing persuasion—the conflict between the absolute, urgent demands of the individual creative spirit, and intellectual convictions about the role in society that the artist ought to play, including the manner in which that society should be made to develop. One thinks of Heine, for instance, whose liberal-democratic sentiments clashed with his admiration for Napoleon as a 'mighty man of Destiny', and who uneasily refused to let his concern for the achievement of social reform interfere with the private freedom demanded by, and for, his own creative personality as a poet.

So when Franz Biberkopf, the jailbird hero of *Berlin Alexanderplatz*, finally comes to terms with his fate, and at the same time recognises the need for men to band together in order to change in life what it is in their power to change—for injustice, exploitation and other social evils are not fate—he shrinks from doing what his attitude implies, namely, joining a political party pledged to the achievement of change. What Biberkopf did, or failed to do, was what many thousands of the German working class did, or failed to do, at that time. This reluctance, in 1918 and 1919, was one of the main reasons for the collapse of the November Revolution.

After his years in the Berlin underworld, 'the terrible thing that was Biberkopf's life', as Döblin himself put it, 'acquired a meaning. He was cured by shock treatment.' But as he sits there at the factory entrance in his new job as janitor, and watches a group of demonstrators march by, he reflects: 'If I join the march, I shall end up by laying my head on the block for what others have concocted. That's why I work everything out first. When the time is ripe, and it suits me, I'll join in. Man has the gift of reason—it's only cattle that move in herds.'[31] It might almost be Brecht speaking.

The setting of Döblin's novel is not the fashionable Berlin of Grunewald or Charlottenburg but the seedy proletarian east side, where Döblin had his medical practice. These scenes of life among pimps, prostitutes and criminals are what made the novel into a best-seller, as well as into a film, in which Heinrich George played the part of Franz Biberkopf. But it is not an exercise in the naturalist manner, as we refer the term to the novels of Zola or the early plays of Gerhart Hauptmann, nor, despite the title, is the city of Berlin cast in the role of hero. The story of Franz Biberkopf is a work of didactic literature, more subtly so than the 'Lehrstücke' Brecht was writing at the same time or than the *Dreigroschenoper* with its own set of shady characters, but as frankly committed as any *Bildungsroman* to the exposition of its 'inneres Thema': 'It is a matter of sacrifice, of making a sacrifice of oneself'.[32] And through the agonising, heuristic process of sacrifice which is his life from the moment he leaves Tegel jail at the beginning of the book, Biberkopf finally attains the condition of understanding and 'Zurechtgebogenheit', as Döblin calls it, in which we take leave of him (Döblin hinted more than once at plans for a second volume).

Put another way, Franz Biberkopf acts out his own variation on the theme that had thrust itself into Döblin's mind a few years earlier, when he was writing the epic poem *Manas*. 'The question with which *Manas* confronted me,' he said, 'was: "What happens to a good man in our society?"' 'For Döblin's criminal Franz Biberkopf, like Brecht's prostitute Shen Te, is a 'guter Mensch'. Society is his adversary, for ever dragging him into crime. Only by knowing his enemy, by learning to make a rational assessment of everything that has happened to him, does he come at the end to understand what life—his life—is all about.

As to the manner of the book, Franz Biberkopf's Odyssey is told in a remarkable mixture of realistic and fantastic styles which owes a great deal to the montage technique of the cinema. The juxtaposition of long shot and close-up, the sudden switch of attention and shift of viewpoint, the assembling of partly logical, partly incongruous sequences of scenes—all this comes from the film. Description and explanation are dissolved into action, into dialogue, into interior monologue. Döblin shows an extraordinary range of technique, as the narrator's thoughts swing to and fro in a manner now analytical, now freely associative within the 'stream of consciousness', now expressionistically bizarre in its self-indulgent and sometimes empty extravagance. James Joyce's *Ulysses*, which had appeared in 1922, is often seen as a spiritual forebear of Döblin's novel, although Döblin said that by the time he came across Joyce's work, a quarter of his own book had been already written, and there is no change of direction or style at a given point in *Berlin Alexanderplatz* to make one doubt his word. Closer to Döblin, a *Grosstadtroman* with many of the montage effects and verbal tricks of *Berlin Alexanderplatz*, is John Dos Passos' *Manhattan Transfer*, a naturalist-surrealist-expressionist-futurist story of New York City, published in 1925 and translated into German in 1928.

But in the context of the age it is hardly necessary to look beyond the pervasive influence of Freud and the poetic techniques of the German expressionists, surrealists and Dadaists in order to see what impulses lie behind such virtually untranslatable passages as this:

> *Jedoch aus welchem Grunde (ich küsse Ihre Hand, Madame,*
> *ich küsse), aus welchem Grunde, mal nachdenken, nachdenken,*
> *Herbert in Filzpantinen denkt auf seiner Stube, und es regnet,*
> *es drippelt und drippelt, man kann gar nicht runtergehen,*
> *die Zigarren sind alle, kein Zigarrenfritze im Haus, aus welchem*
> *Grunde regnet es nur im August, der ganze Monat schwimmt einem weg,*
> *der pladdert weg wie nischt, aus welchem Grunde geht der Franz nu zu*
> *dem Reinhold und quatscht und quatscht von dem?*[33]

Playful moments like this are interposed between stretches of highly-coloured dialogue, much of it in the slang idiom of Berlin working-class and underworld circles, with the narrator intervening in the first person from time to time to take stock of his pilgrim's progress and to underline the basic philosophical issues. In consequence the narrative moves forward at an uneven pace. At one moment we are watching a thriller, at the next we are looking into the mind of a psychopath or a prostitute, then reflecting on the social forces that sustain this milieu of parasitic, self-destructive drop-outs. It is picaresque novel, study in psychopathology, social and political commentary, existential state-ment with an underlying moral (some would say Christian) didacticism, and other things besides. 'Aesthetically too it is a pandemonium, embracing both heaven and hell—sublime and ridiculous, shapeless yet majestic, careless yet rigid, anti-artistic yet intoxicated with melodies and rhythms.'[34] There is no common denominator of such values, and the essence of *Berlin Alexanderplatz* lies in a jagged irreconcilability of extremes.

There is too much of what can be called, in the broadest sense, 'spiritual' meaning in *Berlin Alexanderplatz*, too vital a confrontation between the individual and his fate, in a modern existentialist sense, for it to be called simply a social or political novel. Inasmuch as the life of Franz Biberkopf is set contrapuntally against the life of the city in which—one might say, against which—he lives, and given Döblin's own left-wing sympathies at this time, one cannot but discern a political content in the book. But it is not *the* content. At the same time there are novels of the period whose substance and purpose are overtly political, and which set themselves the task of converting readers to a particular point of view on social and political issues. On the political left in this context are the last two parts of Heinrich Mann's *Kaiserreich*-trilogy—*Die Armen* (1917) and *Der Kopf* (1925). On the political right is Hans Grimm's *Volk ohne Raum* (1926).

Heinrich Mann's *Der Untertan*, completed in 1914, had shown the rise to power of the ruthless opportunist and nationalist Diederich Hessling. The workers of *Die Armen* are shown, in contrast to Mann's earlier expectations, as incapable of providing the leadership of the new society which he envisaged as the successor of the discredited and disintegrated society of the Wilhelminian era. At the end of the war Mann stood for the union of proletariat and intelligentsia but rejected the Communist left as uncompromisingly as he had always hated the nationalist right, holding to, though disillusioned by, the democratic, non-revolutionary wing of the Social Democratic Party. Converting the perspective of hindsight into a quality of foresight, *Der Kopf*, which he called in a letter to Félix Bertaux (March 1925) 'a kind of balance-sheet of past and present', transfers to the years leading up to the defeat of 1918 Mann's observation of republican failure in the years between 1918 and 1925.

Der Kopf belongs to that large corpus of works, half art, half social history, that is the joy of the historian and the despair of the lover of literature. As socio-political commentary into which the author has put much of his own pessimistic self, it is a revealing document of the age, standing between the prophetic contemporaneity of *Der Untertan* and the fully historical *Henri Quatre* novels, which were to dominate the next decade or so of Mann's life. But as a socio-political novel, in the line of Stendhal, Dickens, Flaubert, Zola (the last-named one of Mann's heroes), it has neither sustained life nor calculated cohesion, and leaves the aesthetic expectation largely unsatisfied. Confused in style and uneven in pace, it is the novel of a political essayist, an attempt to convey through the medium of prose fiction what in essence is a political analysis of an historical situation and of the dangers that that situation holds for the future.

The discrepancy between the essayist and the novelist remains in Heinrich Mann's subsequent works that treat of life in the Weimar Republic itself. His deep involvement in the issues of the day finds direct expression in the memoirs and occasional pieces from the years 1921 to 1928 published as *Sieben Jahre* (1929), but the novels that draw on the same raw material—*Mutter Marie* (1926), *Eugénie oder die Bürgerzeit* (1928) and *Die grosse Sache* (1930) again lack the quality of convincing fiction. They stand in strong contrast to the *Berlin Stories* of Christopher Isherwood, which focus on the same pre-Nazi society as Mann's novels but strike home in a manner which the Berlin 'insider' Mann, 30 years senior to the young 'outsider' Isherwood, cannot match. Only when, in exile from Nazi Germany, he turned from a contemporary or near-contemporary setting to the thoroughgoing historical novel, did Heinrich Mann restore the narrative strength which had made *Der Untertan* such a success. And by then he had lost much of his audience.

Far cruder and more radical in the context of social novels are the largely autobiographical *Hammerschläge* (1930) by the 'workers' poet' Heinrich Lersch and Willy Bredel's *Maschinenfabrik N & K* (1929). Both are industrial novels of protest against working conditions in the factories, but while Lersch's bitterness stops well short of a call to revolt, Bredel, who escaped to the Soviet Union in 1933, preaches revolution and turns his story into a piece of open propaganda.

It is a far cry from these works of the left to Hans Grimm's *Volk ohne Raum*, a work gratefully seized upon by the Nazis as conveying a nationalistically expansionist message which conveniently under-pinned their racialist chauvinism.

The title *Volk ohne Raum* will never lose these sinister associations. Nor was Grimm himself a mere innocent victim of perverse mis-interpretation. In June 1933, together with Hanns Johst, Werner Beumelburg, Erwin Guido Kolbenheyer, Hermann Stehr and five

other writers prepared to underwrite the régime, he was elected a
senator of the new-style Nazi Deutsche Akademie der Dichtung.
Already in the previous year he had made the sort of statement
guaranteed to secure his position: 'In company with a number of
others I see National Socialism as the first and only genuine
democratic movement of the German *Volk*.'[35] In pursuit of the values
of *völkische Dichtung* he instituted the so-called 'Lippoldsberger
Dichtertreffen' on his estate near Kassel, to which came not only Nazi
sympathisers like Beumelburg and Kolbenheyer but also Carossa,
Rudolf Alexander Schröder and a few others who stayed in Germany
throughout the Nazi era and managed to save their skins without
sacrificing their intellectual and spiritual integrity. Grimm himself,
however, was unrepentently compromised, and continued to the end
of his life to preach a politico-racialist ideal of German-English-
American domination of the world, still pleading after the war that
Hitler and National Socialism had been misunderstood.

From Grimm's years as a trader in South Africa before the Great
War come both the setting and the 'moral' of *Volk ohne Raum*—itself
only one of a number of his stories set in the then German colonies of
southern Africa, and dominated by the trial of strength between the
black and white races.

The question of German colonialism aroused strong feelings both
inside and outside Germany, from the commercial penetration of
Africa by Hanseatic merchants in the mid-nineteenth century down
to the Treaty of Versailles and its confiscation of all German colonial
possessions. Bismarck originally opposed the idea that Germany
should become a colonial power, arguing that a dispersal of interests
around the globe could only distract attention from the more pressing
problems at home, Also, he argued, they would compel Germany to
devote an excessive amount of money to expanding the navy, without
which overseas possessions could not be defended. A rival lobby
insisted that any world power needed colonies as a matter of self-
respect; that they provided an outlet for the restless and the
domestically undesirable; and that they offered a challenge to the
moral and spiritual resources of a nation to prove its ability to
administer and exploit the resources of a foreign land. Under Kaiser
Wilhelm II the imperialist argument prevailed, and the possession of
parcels of foreign soil acquired the quality of an almost sacred right;
without such possessions, it was maintained, the country would lose its
spiritual vitality. A young and growing nation 'must not be hemmed
in', wrote the historian Adalbert Wahl, and the development of
colonies was the natural outlet for its energies.[36]

At the opening of *Volk ohne Raum*, we are told 'that the life-story of a

simple man can at the same time reveal the destiny of his country.'
Shortly after, we are asked the rhetorical question: 'Do you think
there is anything greater than the ultimate destiny of our nation?'
Then we are confronted with the premiss: 'The German needs space
(*Raum*) around him, sun above him and freedom within him, if he is to
be fine and good.'[37] Such emotional appeals inevitably found
expression in nationalistic demands for an extension of the German
sphere of influence in the world. The story of Cornelius Friebott's life
from his emigration to South Africa to his return to Germany after the
Great War covers the years from 1887 to 1923. These are the years
that lie between the imperialist heyday and the nadir of total national
defeat, and as what Grimm himself called 'a political story', it is shot
through with the ideology which was his starting-point.

All the invocations of a Romantic irrationality so familiar in
German life and letters are made in this long-winded, sentimental,
now well-nigh unreadable book. The philosophical parts are dominated by appeals to 'Destiny' and the authority of 'Nature', set
around with emotive phrases like 'a passionate spirit of reverence and
devotion to Germany', 'the intolerable restrictions imposed on
Germany' and 'the burning demand for justice for the German *Volk*
from the world, from God and from history.' In themselves, such
slogans might merely induce an indulgent smile. Put alongside
Grimm's political essays of the Nazi period and after, they assume a
more sinister significance. And relating this to the career of a man
whose political ideas, according to a doctoral dissertation of 1937,[38]
could be shown to coincide with those of Hitler in the principle of
'Aryan' racial supremacy, one finds oneself looking at a case-history
of how readily pervertible ideas can be absorbed into a body of evil
doctrine.

Colonialism seen from a very different standpoint lies behind the
once immensely popular stories of the mysterious character who
published under the name of B. Traven. Anti-imperialist, anti-
militarist, a supporter, under the name Ret Marut, of the Munich
Räteregierung in 1919 and editor of the revolutionary journal *Der
Ziegelbrenner* from 1919 to 1921, he escaped from Munich to London in
1923, thence to Mexico, where he lived till his death in 1969. His first
stories were published in 1924 in the Social Democratic paper
Vorwärts, and in the years that followed, he wrote a series of
fascinating novels (*Das Totenschiff*, 1926; *Der Schatz der Sierra Madre*,
1927; *Die Rebellion der Gehenkten*, 1936: all three became famous films),
describing his adventures as sailor, cotton picker, farmer, gold
prospector, and medicine man among the Mexican Indians. These
and other books sold in their millions and were translated into 32

languages. From his naturalistic, sometimes lurid narrative, put together in an episodic, slipshod manner and couched in a powerful but rough, undisciplined language, there emerges an anarchistic sympathy for the oppressed Indians among whom he lived, and a message of protest against colonial exploitation. But Cornelius Friebott would not have recognised the situation that Traven was writing about.

Also concerned with the question of *Lebensraum*, in a different spirit again, and also surrounded by the political pressures of the 1920s, is Réné Schickele's trilogy *Das Erbe am Rhein* (1925–8). Schickele's 'heritage' is his native Alsace, the cultural and political dichotomy of which is mirrored in the situation of this German-born writer who had French as his mother tongue and used German as his almost exclusive language of expression.

A socialist and a pacifist, he was editor during the war of the expressionistically-inclined *Die weissen Blätter* in Berlin and a leading figure in the radical political wing of the expressionist movement, a particular friend of Kasimir Edschmid and Heinrich Mann. That Alsace should be kicked to and fro between France and Germany like a football represented for him the kind of international politics that treated people like animals, and his protests issued in an uncompromising assertion of personal identity and dignity, a demand to be free to make one's own decisions. Schickele wanted an 'open' Alsace, whose people would move naturally in a European context and find their true role in their contribution to this context. The trouble was, as he wrote in 1931, that

today I could not name 20 Alsatians as thoroughly permeated by both French and German culture—which is what an Alsatian should ideally be—as Frenchmen like Romain Rolland, Jean Giraudoux and Henri Lichtenberger . . . . or Germans like Heinrich and Thomas Mann, Albert Einstein, Alfred Kerr . . . . Ernst Robert Curtius, Bergsträsser and Theodor Wolff . . . to say nothing of the late Rainer Maria Rilke, born in Prague, and Walther Rathenau, both of whom not only spoke French impeccably but were able to think in French.[39]

Schickele's tone is that of the spirit of reconciliation and European synthesis found after the Great War in the later work of the theologian Ernst Troeltsch.

The achievement of this cosmopolitanism was a matter of attitude, a process of education; and in order to illustrate this development Schickele created in the three novels of *Das Erbe am Rhein—Maria Capponi*, (1925) *Blick auf die Vogesen* (1927) and *Wolf in der Hürde* (1931)—an aristocratic Alsatian family through whose successive generations he could portray a pattern of historical events and the family's response to them. 'In the Breuschheim family', he wrote in a letter,

I tried to incorporate the best and the worst of the Alsatian character, a kind of statement of Alsatian potentiality, with that freedom of access to the outside world without which, I confess, I cannot conceive of an Alsace in the European sense. Without such access it will become simple-minded, in both senses of the term, or just be swallowed up like some insignificant creature—as had already happened to many in the period before 1918.[40]

Schickele, like Hans Grimm, writes of a community facing the problem of identity in a situation of geographical and cultural loneliness. Both are idealists, both had shared the lives of their characters. But where the emotional Grimm looks to an imperialistic solution, expansive in one sense but defensive, inward-looking in another, Schickele, more equable and realistic, stands for an integrated, European view. Grimm sounds the trumpet of 'the destiny of the German people' and appeals more to irrationalism than to reason, while Schickele, a more deliberate and conscious artist, seeks quieter ways to convey his ideals.

'The destiny of the German people' was a catch-phrase used to great effect during the years when Germany was groping her way out of the double disaster of a lost war and an economic catastrophe. At one end of the spectrum it represented a challenge to the people's moral fibre, a way of restoring national self-respect and providing a confident supra-personal context for the employment of individual effort. At the other end it became the rallying-cry of those embittered groups, like the *Stahlhelm*, the National Socialists and those who, turning their eyes from the realities of military defeat and the Versailles Treaty, exploited an injured national pride as a means of conditioning people's minds to rearmament and national self-assertion.

An extreme presentation of such values is found in the religio-historical Paracelsus-trilogy (*Die Kindheit des Paracelsus*, 1917; *Das Gestirn des Paracelsus*, 1921; *Das Dritte Reich des Paracelsus*, 1925) by Erwin Guido Kolbenheyer. Mystical and devotional in spirit, both expressionist and humanist in manner and language, these slow-moving, whimsical novels present the destiny of the German nation in terms of a religious yearning that issues from the allegorical struggle between Christ and Wotan. In the Faustian character of Paracelsus there rages a struggle between, on the one hand, a Protestant attachment to the word and the responsibility of the individual conscience, and on the other, a Catholic adherence to undifferentiated spirit and the illumination that comes unbidden from nature. On another plane it expresses the tension between the decline of the medieval aristocracy and the rise of the middle classes. Through the stages of Paracelsus' development Kolbenheyer presents his picture of the evolution of the religious essence and consciousness of the German nation, erecting as his epitaph the inscription 'Ecce Ingenium Teutonicum'.

The intoxicating enthusiasm, the *Rausch*, of a sense of national community and fate had been unreservedly exploited during the war by the propagandists of national pride. But the reality of such an enthusiasm, and of its involvement in the workings of fate, was acknowledged equally by men of very different persuasions. The near-pacifist Hermann Hesse wrote in his novel *Demian* of the sense of brotherhood created by the fight for the honour of the fatherland:

I too found myself being embraced by men I had never seen before, and I understood the experience and joyfully returned to it. They did it in a moment of *Rausch*, not of a deliberate striving after destiny; but their *Rausch* was sacred, because it was the product of that one brief, disturbing glance that they had cast into the eyes of destiny.[41]

That there was such a thing as a 'German destiny', just as there was a 'German character', was a precept that had been preached with special ardour since the unification of Germany in 1871. And once the philosophical, almost metaphysical, principle had been conceded, it became all the easier to prove the logical necessity of taking practical steps to turn the principle into reality. The sociologist Max Scheler, who is certainly not to be reckoned among the militarists and warmongers, distinguished in the Prussian character a quality he called *Gesinnungsmilitarismus*, an ethical property of the Prussian psyche, which, with its companion values of service, discipline and correctness, was bound to seek expression in public life. National self-expression demanded the involvement of all these qualities, and the organic movement towards their fulfilment was synonymous with the pursuit of national destiny. One dare not overlook the force of such ideas when one considers the destructive coincidence of totalitarianism, *Realpolitik* and the worship of violence and success which was to become the lot of Germany under Hitler. Nor dare one forget that all the moderate parties lost more and more ground to the extremes of left and right in the last sets of elections under the Weimar Republic, until almost 12 million Germans (33 per cent) voted National Socialist two months *before* Hitler was made Chancellor, and over 17 million (almost 44 per cent) little more than a month afterwards.

Among contemporary pseudo-philosophical appeals to the force of

German destiny probably the most remarkable and most influential is Oswald Spengler's *Der Untergang des Abendlandes*. Much of this controversial work had already been written before the outbreak of the Great War, and the first volume had been published in 1918. But it attracted little attention. After all, Germany was still looking for victory and saw little relevance in a historian's prognostication of a 'collapse of the West' in which Germany would be swallowed up. By 1922, however, when the complete work appeared, a fatalistic gloom had settled over the country. People now found comfort in a message which claimed to demonstrate that the entire West, the victorious Allies as well as the defeated Fatherland, was advancing towards its doom, a doom as certain as that which had befallen civilisations of the past at a comparable stage in their history. His conclusions, wrote Spengler in his preface to the 1922 edition, formed part of something far greater, namely 'a philosophy of destiny—the first of its kind'. And looking back on his completed task, conscious of the national context from which it had arisen, he found to his mingled pride and surprise that what he had achieved was 'eine deutsche Philosophie', a monument to his two great masters, Goethe and Nietzsche.

At the root of this 'German philosophy' lies a faith in dynamic nature, in spiritual regeneration. 'The divine principle', said Goethe to Eckermann, 'is active in living things, not in dead things; it shows itself in what evolves and changes, not in what has become fixed and petrified' (13 February 1829). Like Herder, Spengler saw cultures as organic wholes, developing in response to the driving forces within them. Applying this to world-history, he produced his naturalistic, positivistic pattern of the birth, growth, florescence and decay of cultures, a cyclical pattern governed by the workings of inexorable inner impulses. History is thus made not by men but by movements. There are no lasting truths, and if one believes one has discovered, by analogy, the direction in which the current of one's own culture is flowing, one cannot properly do other than swim in that direction.

Spengler concluded from his comparative study of cultures that Western civilisation was relentlessly moving towards scientific specialisation, technology, organisational efficiency, and a pattern of ethical and spiritual values based on relativity and pragmatism, not on absolutes. Consequently he seeks to wean us from philosophy, art, the challenge of personal responsibility (ours is the age of 'organisation men') and the quest for eternal verities. 'If this book leads the younger generation to become technologists instead of poets, soldiers instead of painters, politicians instead of philosophers, it will have had its desired effect. I could wish for nothing better.'[42] Why oppose the workings of fate in the name of liberalism and humanity?

Such is the purpose—dangerous, vicious, false, evil: the choice of epithets is wide—behind Spengler's book. As Adorno put it, with Spengler's proclamation of the impending 'collapse of the West' the wish was father to the thought.[43] It was a thought whose significance did not escape the 1920s and 1930s, and it was eagerly invoked by anti-intellectual, anti-cultural power-seekers anxious that the human values of the West should indeed collapse, and as soon as possible. And coupled with the reassuring concept of doom, in a paradox few cared to resolve, was a positive message—the urgent questing of what Spengler called 'Faustian man', embodiment of the restless, expansionist urge of Western man to conquer new areas of knowledge and experience.

So the Germans found in the message of *Der Untergang des Abendlandes*, as well as in striking essays of Spengler's like *Preussentum und Sozialismus* and *Die politischen Pflichten der deutschen Jugend*, a consolation, a justification and a challenge. A consolation, because what was rotten in the state of Denmark had been shown to be a general European canker. A justification, because the accusations of warmongering levelled at Germany were now seen to be even more false than before, since national characteristics were organic and inborn, and would only express themselves in a destructive manner if misunderstood or provoked from without. And a challenge, because to pursue these national characteristics was to act in accordance with the predeterminations of fate, which it was senseless to oppose. '*Docunt fata volentem, nolentem trahunt*', runs the proverb with which Spengler ends his *magnum opus*: 'Destiny leads the willing but drags the reluctant.'

To reflect on the message preached by Oswald Spengler, and on the eagerness with which it was received in so many circles, may seem a strange prelude to those works of Germany's greatest twentieth-century novelist which appeared during this period. But Thomas Mann, who was five years Spengler's senior, wrote from within an awareness of his country's political and spiritual condition as intense as that of Spengler or anyone else. *Der Zauberberg*, published two years after the complete *Der Untergang des Abendlandes*, springs no less from the cultural climate of the time than do his various essays and lectures. It is to the contest of warring forces embodied in these works that his report on the moral and spiritual state of his country belongs—indeed, of the state of Western civilisation, for Mann himself called his *Zauberberg* a work that should offer 'a conspectus of the problems facing Europe since the turn of the century'.[44]

At the outbreak of the 1914–18 war Thomas Mann's voice was

joined with those of Werner Sombart, Max Scheler, Oswald Spengler and many other intellectuals in the chorus of German patriotism. The German character and the nature of national development, he maintained, had been misunderstood both at home and abroad, and a posture of self-assertion was needed. This was not to be taken as a political self-assertion in the name of a particular form of government or a particular pattern of society, but as a declaration of the unity produced by the historical fusion of religious, philosophical and general cultural forces.

Thomas Mann's *Betrachtungen eines Unpolitischen*, published a few months before the end of the war, mark the public climax of his ideological dispute with his radically-minded brother Heinrich. Here he wards off the processes of 'Politisierung, Literarisierung, Intellektualisierung und Radikalisierung', which threaten the primacy of the individual and frustrate, in the name of 'democratic progress', the development of the national character—one might even say, with Spengler, the national destiny.

'The German spirit is, always has been, and always will be, conservative—as long, that is, as it remains its true self and does not become "democratic", i.e. is not extinguished'.[45] In place of the impersonal catchword 'Demokratie', which he called 'alien and repulsive', Thomas Mann proposes 'Volksstaat', a homely term truer to the spirit of the *Bürgertum* which formed the core of the German nation. (A quarter of a century later, in the address *Deutschland und die Deutschen* (1945), he still doubted the Germans' power to evolve a political democracy out of the ruins of the Third Reich and the Second World War).

But by 1922, only a few years after the publication of the *Betrachtungen*, and in a very different political climate, his tone had changed. 'My aim', he said in his address *Von deutscher Republik*, 'and I say this openly, is to gain your support for the Republic (inasmuch as this is necessary) and for what is called democracy—which is what I call *Humanität*, because of my distaste for all the extraneous humbug that has collected round the word democracy.'[46] Like most political pronouncements in these Weimar years, Thomas Mann's *Von deutscher Republik* is addressed especially to the young, the generation born into the age of the decaying Wilhelmine empire for whose fall they could claim no credit but, equally, in whose responsibility for the war of 1914–18 they could feel no involvement. This was the generation for whose attention Hitler was to make so successful a bid.

The apparent change of political direction on Thomas Mann's part was received with suspicion, in some quarters even with hostility. *Das Gewissen*, a periodical published by the conservative group centred on Moeller van den Bruck, which Mann himself had singled out in 1918 as the best political journal of the day, turned on him with an article headed 'Mann über Bord', calling his *Humanität* a 'whore of long standing' and leaving its readers with the challenge: 'What do we care about the republic? Long live Germany!'[47] On the other side of the political fence the intellectuals of firm left-wing persuasion, like his brother Heinrich, Döblin, Toller, Brecht, the *Weltbühne* circle and numerous others, were similarly unimpressed by a vague appeal to 'humanistic' values with no clear political framework in which to set them.

To a large extent the controversy that surrounds the relationship between the *Betrachtungen eines Unpolitischen* on the one side and *Von deutscher Republik* and later utterances of the 1920s on the other is a matter of semantics. The 'Demokratie' of which Heinrich Mann and other radicals spoke had prescriptive, authoritarian, even totalitarian overtones which provoked the 'anti-democratic' sentiments of the *Betrachtungen eines Unpolitischen*. Using the word with a rather different set of connotations, however, Thomas Mann was able to appear in public as a defender of the young republic—'this weak creature born of defeat', as he called it many years later—'without having the slightest feeling that I had anything to abjure. It was the very anti-humanism of that period which made it clear to me that I had never done other, or wished to do other, than act in defence of *Humanität*.'[48] His voice was that of the liberal conservative pleading for the protection of humane values against the inroads of ruthless 'reforms', and for the acknowledgment in the conduct of national affairs of what the traditions, and therefore the living personality, of the German people required.

To acknowledge the reality of the irrational principle in life is one thing; to make a cult of irrationality is quite another. The Nazis' anti-intellectual worship of *Rausch* drew from Thomas Mann the statement of an unambiguously liberal-humanist position in his *Appell an die Vernunft* (1930), which, together with the self-analytical study *Kultur und Sozialismus* of the preceding year, leaves no doubt as to his allegiance to the democratic republic. In particular, he looked to the Social Democrats as the party with the major responsibility for preserving national morale and the integrity of public life.

It is this same question of the individual's discovery of the humane values by which life should be governed that stands in the centre of *Der Zauberberg* (1924). Hans Castorp, the young man whose mind is the real scene of the action in the novel, and whose *Bildung* gives it its direction, belongs to the expressionist generation of men like Trakl, Hasenclever and Unruh. At the beginning of the story he is about to take his first job in a Hamburg shipyard; at the end, after staying seven years in the sanatorium on the mountain, we see him trudging across a muddy, corpse-covered battlefield during the Great War, with Schubert's song 'Am Brunnen vor dem Tore' on his lips. Whether he survived the war, we do not know. 'Frankly, it is an open question and a matter of more-or-less complete indifference'—such is the sentiment with which Thomas Mann takes leave of his hero. If he had come back from the war, he would have found himself among the rootless young men who rejected the world into which they had been born, were suspicious of the political manoeuvrings and moral inadequacies of the republic, and were easily swayed by the demagogic appeals of extremists.

So the mind of Hans Castorp becomes the object for which rival philosophies fight. Or, put in terms of an active hero pursuing his *Bildung*, Hans Castorp seeks the truth about life from among the rival philosophies exemplified by the patients in the sanatorium. At the one extreme stands the short, ugly, angular-featured figure of Leo Naphta, Jewish by birth, Jesuit by conversion, spokesman for the values of irrationality and mysticism, for *Geist* rather than *Vernunft*, for passionate, dogmatic outburst rather than cool, rational judgement, for Romantic, anti-bourgeois egoism rather than compassion and social responsibility. 'All individualism', he declares, 'has its rightful home in the realm of the religious and the mystical, the so-called "world of the morally chaotic".'[49] Sickness, he continues, far from being something which man should be spared, or which one should try to banish from the world, is what makes man what he is, since knowledge of his own sickness is the most powerful educative force to which he can respond. 'In man's *Geist*, therefore, in sickness, lie his dignity and nobility . . . the more sick he is, the more he is a man, and the spirit of sickness is closer to man's nature than the spirit of health.'[50] A writer who chose to deny himself the experience of suffering, like Bernard Shaw, says Naphta, could never reach the depths of a Nietzsche, a Dostoevsky or a Strindberg.

At the other extreme stands the tall, suave, Italian child of the Enlightenment, Lodovico Settembrini, apostle of rationalist humanism, believer in human progress and the supremacy of *ratio* over inspiration, champion of clarity over mystery, health and optimism over sickness and fatalism, humane sympathy over authoritarianism. 'If the State is concerned with human betterment and not just with the use of force', he asserts, 'it cannot requite evil with evil'.[51] Having attacked the notion of guilt on deterministic grounds, he rejects the concept of punishment, so in his tragi-comic duel with Naphta he naturally refuses to shoot his adversary. But he bears no less responsibility for Naphta's suicide than if he had killed him himself, and in Naphta's scream of 'Coward!' lay the admission 'that it took more courage to shoot than to be shot at.'[52]

Settembrini, incidentally, makes his appearance very early in the novel and is never far away from the action, whereas Naphta is only introduced in the penultimate chapter, by which time Hans Castorp has already travelled far along the road to self-knowledge. In certain respects he represents the *Vernunftliterat* who had been Thomas Mann's special target of attack in the *Betrachtungen eines Unpolitischen*. To be sure, by the time *Der Zauberberg* was published, he had aligned himself with a changed set of political emphases, but the rival philosophies—one might almost call them Sermons on the Mount—that surround Hans Castorp in the sanatorium are still those of the wartime years when Mann was working out his position in the *Betrachtungen*. The Wagnerian Naphta, with his German-Romantic irrationalism and intensity, has that insight into the educative power of suffering and death shown already in the *Betrachtungen*, while the figure of Heinrich Mann, archetype of the scorned *Zivilisationsliterat*, still contributes to the radical-democratic humanism of the Mazzini-esque Settembrini.

At the spiritual climax of the book, Hans Castorp, as he lies in the snow in danger of being frozen to death, has a vision. He sees the Settembrini-Naphta antithesis of Life and Death, Mind and Nature resolved in a new, higher *Humanität*—new and higher, because it has looked death in the face before turning away and declaring its confidence in life: 'In the name of goodness and love let man not allow death to control his thoughts.'[53] The *Rausch*-governed Naphta is defeated. The Schopenhauerian pessimism and denial of life in *Buddenbrooks* has been overcome by a Nietzschean affirmation of life, but the latter is an extreme position no more acceptable than the former. It is not a question of a forced choice between *Geist* and *Leben*, as Schopenhauer and Nietzsche demanded, but of a reconciliation of these extremes in terms of man himself—the *Humanität* that leads, and led Thomas Mann, to Goethe. In his essay *Goethe und Tolstoi*, written in the same period as *Der Zauberberg*, Mann puts it thus: 'Effortless Nature (*Natur*) equals crudity; effortless Mind (*Geist*) equals absence of life-giving roots. The encounter of Nature and Mind, which have been yearning to feel their way towards each other, is what constitutes Man.'[54]

Joachim Ziemssen, the cousin whom Hans Castorp has come to the sanatorium to visit, dies shortly after Castorp's vision of the true philosophy of life. He too, in his own uncomplicated way, had longed for life and detested the Romanticism that made a cult of death.

Then, very late in the novel, the big, white-haired, voluble Dutch coffee-planter Mynher Pieter Peeperkorn arrives, philosopher of hedonism, competitor with Hans Castorp for the favours of Clawdia Chauchat, obsessed by the fear that his sickness will leave him impotent, who commits suicide when this fear overwhelms him. Both Ziemssen and Peeperkorn, together with Castorp's love-affair with Clawdia, contribute their part to his choice of life over death—although then, in the last of the numerous ironies with which the book is shot through, one has to call war, institutionalised killing, an affirmation of life. Or in Thomas Mann's own words in a letter to Josef Ponten (5 November 1925): 'Do you know of any other work in literature or in art that sets out *to make Death a comic figure?*' (Mann's italics) It is the spirit that led Goethe to describe his *Faust II* as 'diese sehr ernsten Scherze'.

Through such ironies, through the establishment of a cool distance between the observer and the observed, negative values are made to contribute to positive solutions, and paradoxical situations put to the achievement of clarity of purpose. It is a dialectical process. Properly, *Bildung* should accrue through the mediation of the true, the beautiful, the inspiring, but the progress of the pilgrim Hans Castorp lies through the world of sickness and decay. A sanatorium for sufferers from tuberculosis should have a clear, dry air, but more often than not the Berghof in Davos is shrouded in a clammy mist. A clinic could be expected to have some measure of success in treating its patients, but at the Berghof they spend their days waiting for death—even the visitor who comes for a three-week visit catches an infection and stays seven years. A period in hospital is usually endured as a temporary restriction on a full and normal life, but the Berghof offers a life complete and perfect in itself, catering for all the physical and mental pleasures enjoyed by the inhabitants of the *Flachland* below.

Thomas Mann described his *Zauberberg* as 'a story which, in a strange, ironical, almost parodistic manner, seeks to renew the old German *Bildungsroman* of the *Wilhelm Meister* pattern,' which, as a quester legend, is 'the sublimation and spiritualisation of the adventure-novel.'[55] But this 'strange, almost parodistic manner' only conceals a deep concern for the issues he has raised and the characters he has created. What Friedrich Schlegel said of Goethe's *Wilhelm Meisters Lehrjahre* could as well be said of Thomas Mann's *Der Zauberberg*: 'Let no-one be deceived into thinking that, because he seems to treat his characters and situations so casually and capriciously, hardly ever referring to his hero in other than an ironical tone, and smiling down on his masterpiece from the eminence of his intellect, the author is not in deadly earnest.'[56]

So when the young Castorp, a man whose very mediocrity gives him representative status, leaves his *Bürgertum* behind for the world of the magic mountain, he is embarking on the path of learning along which sickness, death and the other negative forces in the sanatorium were to lead him to a presentiment of the humane values that should govern life. The *Flachland* from which he had come could never have taught him this. And as he has to seek the mean between the extremes of the irrational Naphta and the humanistic Settembrini, so the way for Germany as a nation lies in the reconciliation, in the name of humanism, of the conflicting pressures from East and West. The political implication of this philosophy was made explicit by Thomas Mann in an address to the PEN Club in Warsaw in 1927:

It is this dream of *Humanität*, the idea of reconciliation and union, that prevents us Germans from over-hastily taking up a one-sided position in this historical conflict [between East and West]. Our centre touches both East and West, our spiritual life partakes of both spheres, and our liberty—a shield against militant extremism—is ultimately directed towards the achievement of a permanent humanism.[57]

A similar synthesis of extremes in a Goethean spirit is sought by Mann's older liberal contemporary, the historian Friedrich Meinecke, in his *Die Entstehung des Historismus* (1936).

In 1929 Thomas Mann received the Nobel Prize for Literature. But ironically—yes, again!—it was not for his recent *Zauberberg*—'a record of the spiritual condition of Europe and the intellectual problems facing us in the first 30 years of the twentieth century', as he called it—but for the *Buddenbrooks* of almost 30 years earlier, chronicle of 'the disintegration of a family' in which art and intellectualism assert themselves, as Schopenhauer said they would, at the expense of vitality and the will to live.

Fifteen years after *Der Zauberberg* was published, Thomas Mann, in the unhappy role of the most distinguished literary emigré from Nazi Germany, was invited to give a talk about his novel at Princeton University. It was the same appeal to the humanism that Hans Castorp had glimpsed in his vision in the snow, which he left with his audience: 'The Grail he [Castorp] seeks . . . is a concept of man, the vision of a humanism tempered in a profound experience of sickness and death. This Grail—this humanism—is a mystery. For Man himself is a mystery, and all humanism rests on a reverence for this mystery.'[58]

Hans Castorp belongs to the younger generation. *Von deutscher Republik* is addressed to that generation, as were the nationalistic appeals of Spengler, Max Hildebert Boehm, Wilhelm Stapel and many others, and it was in particular the allegiance of youth that the Nazis set out to capture. Expressionist drama—most strikingly from Hasenclever's *Der Sohn* (1914) onwards, but the situation and the manner are already foretold in Wedekind's *Frühlings Erwachen*—throve on the subject of the conflict between children and parents, a subject which did not owe its existence to the war but which nevertheless drew an added intensity from it. Thomas Mann had chronicled the relationship between the generations in *Buddenbrooks*, and two years after *Der Zauberberg* he returned to the theme in the touching little story *Unordnung und frühes Leid* (1926), not angrily setting the members of the Cornelius family at each other's throats but ironically and affectionately portraying their attitudes to each other.

The antagonism between the generations had reached its climax immediately after the war and became a widely-accepted inevitability of life. When the young Carl Zuckmayer left his family to go his own theatrical way in Berlin, he did so, he records with a certain surprise and satisfaction, without a passionate enactment of 'the father-son conflict that was expected of all decent young writers at this time'.[59] Franz Werfel's melodramatic story *Nicht der Mörder, der Ermordete ist schuldig*, published in the same year, with its self-pitying hero locked in a ceaseless war of hate against his father, the General—'I was born to be a whipping-boy,' he wails—is far from being the most extreme of such works.

This same conflict, worked into a complex detective-story that hinges on a miscarriage of justice, forms the climax of one of the most popular of all German novels of the 1920s, Jakob Wassermann's *Der Fall Maurizius* (1928). Wassermann's reputation had been laid many years before with *Die Juden von Zirndorf* (1897), *Caspar Hauser* (1908) and other novels, but in *Der Fall Maurizius*, and in the continuation of the story of its hero, *Etzel Andergast* (1931), his bewildering narrative skill and power are at their height.

As a storyteller Wassermann has few equals. Moreover, through his personal awareness, as a Jew, of the social dispositions and pressures within a divided, self-conscious, perilously unstable national community, he invests his characters with a psychological vividness to match the thrust of his narrative. The result, unhappily, is sometimes melodrama: the final confrontation between father and son in *Der Fall Maurizius* is such a moment. Etzel has finally proven the wrongfulness of Maurizius' conviction, which is the moral end towards which the book moves, and it is entirely plausible that he should be outraged by the cruel discovery that justice—what he seeks—and the law—what his father, as a judge, administers—are not the same, and never can be. But the demented outburst that follows, culminating in his attempt to commit suicide, recalls the worst excesses of expressionist drama. The scene may have a certain ideological and sociological interest, but as a moment of literature it can hardly be taken seriously.

There were times in the 1920s when Wassermann was ranked with Thomas Mann. The epic sweep, the panache, the earnestness, the psychological intensity—some even compared him with his idol Dostoevsky—still have the power to grip the attention. But, unlike Thomas Mann, the grip soon slackens, doubts arise over subtlety and taste, and although the memory of a certain excitement may persist, the marks on our critical consciousness soon become faint.

Some writers rejoiced in this conflict of generations, seeing in it, through the victory of the son, the means by which the younger generation would come into its own. Others, while unable to avoid the conflict, suffered under it until it hypnotised both their life and their work—the tragic moment enshrined in Franz Kafka's 'Brief an den Vater'.

Not the specific father-son relationship, rather the experience of youth as such is the subject of Hermann Hesse's novel *Demian* (written during the war and published in 1919), a semi-autobiographical *Bildungsroman* which spans roughly the same period as Thomas Mann's *Der Zauberberg*—though Emil Sinclair is a younger man than Hans Castorp—and ends, also like *Der Zauberberg*, in the Great War.

For Hesse, who had already left Germany and was living in Switzerland, the outbreak of war in 1914 was a moment of tragedy. 'It can now be seen', he wrote later, 'that our psychology was wrong, and that at the beginning of the war we said and did things that were the product, not of our true will but of hysteria.'[60] Though living in a voluntary exile that he never abandoned, he still saw Germany as his rightful spiritual homeland, but he could only absorb this feeling in a Goethean spirit of pantheistic humanism, as the part is absorbed in the whole. This humanism, with earnest pietistic, at times mystical, strands within it, is his message to the world.

Again it is a message addressed above all to German youth, the youth apostrophised in the parable *Zarathustras Wiederkehr*, published in the same year as *Demian*. When it becomes known that Nietzsche's Zarathustra, inflammatory prophet of an earlier generation, has returned to earth, the young men of a defeated and demoralised Germany rush to him as a saviour. But Zarathustra has no simple comfort to offer them, no ready-made solution to their problems. His word is blunt, almost brutal: 'Learn to live your lives! Learn to know your destiny! . . . . There is no God but the God within you.'[61] It is a repetition of the oracle's stern message: 'Know Thyself'.

The outbreak of war; the destruction of the world with which Hesse had hitherto lived in harmony (he was 34 in 1914); the total revaluation of the principles of his life and art which followed his initiation into psychoanalysis, in particular his experience of the work of C. G. Jung; and the position of existential humanism in which he now, and for the rest of his long life, found the moral and spiritual justification of life—this is the world of influences from which *Demian* emerges.

There is a framework of material facts in the novel, but as in most of Hesse's works, only a minimum of physical action is contained within this framework. The spiritual *Bildung* that Emil Sinclair undergoes through his relationship with his schoolfriend Demian is the quest for 'the God within you' enjoined upon the young men of *Zarathustras Wiederkehr*. In the preface to *Demian* the quest is defined thus: 'Each man's life is a journey to his own self.'[62] Sinclair's episodic journey, overlaid with a mass of psychological and symbolical meanings, and redolent of Nietzsche in thought and language, leads from the dichotomy of the 'two worlds' of the opening chapter, the one a world of darkness, the other a world of light, to the existential unity of his own personality. But the discovery of this unity brings isolation in its train and only for a brief moment, with his love for Frau Eva and his reunion with Demian in the war, is he permitted an experience of the bliss that attends this unity. 'He had loved and thereby found himself. Most people love in order to lose themselves'[63]—although the words refer to the hero of a *Märchen* told by Frau Eva, their real reference is to Sinclair. At the same time he muses on how he had come to know 'the community of spirit that is attainable among those who have experienced total isolation.'[64] But such moments cannot last, and he returns to the loneliness of his quest, though now with the strength, gained through Demian's guidance, to survive alone. The experience of isolation in the search for the meaning of life is for Emil Sinclair what the experience of sickness and death is for Hans Castorp. And both men live under the shadow of Schopenhauer and Nietzsche: 'Doing and suffering, which together make up our existence, are a single entity, are one and the same.'[65]

Siddhartha (1922) is different from Demian in timbre—the Indian setting alone would produce this—but it sounds the same note. Or, to retain the image, it is like the same piece scored for different instruments and marked at times with different dynamics. The substance of external 'reality', already the more remote for its exotic context, has dwindled still further, the poetic stylisation of landscape and characters has reached the point of abstraction, and the essential action, transmitted by psychological portraits, is concentrated in the mind. The goal, which the hero only recognises as such when he has reached it, is to think, feel, and become immersed in the concept of union, the one-ness of the world. Sinclair's search had ended with self-knowledge and thus had a quality of assertiveness about it, the establishment of an original, individual personality; Siddhartha seeks the absorption of his individualism into the all-embracing cosmos. For both, however, it is a quest to re-establish the unity, the sense of belonging to 'all that is', which the pressures of modern life have destroyed. Hesse ascribes visions of this goal to Prince Myshkin in Dostoevsky's *The Idiot*: 'The highest moment for him is that half-second of supreme sensitivity and insight which he has experienced several times, that magic ability just for one instant to be everything, to feel everything, to suffer everything, to understand and affirm everything that is in the world.'[66]

Hesse's idealisation of the East bears the familiar Romantic hues revealed when German poets look at Hindu religion and mythology through their rose-coloured spectacles. Since the time when Herder had effusively invoked the virtues of Oriental cultures to revive the failing ideals of the West, the East had held a special fascination for inspiration-seeking poets. The ideals they claimed to find in Sanskrit literature and Hindu philosophy usually had a meaning quite different from that which they chose to give them in an alien Western context, but it was the ideals as such that mattered, not their historical authenticity. There was, to be sure, a scholarly side to certain Romantics' enthusiasm for the East, represented by the philological work of Friedrich Schlegel, Wilhelm von Humboldt, Friedrich Majer and others. But for Wackenroder, Novalis, Hölderlin, Heine and the many other poets who, in their different ways, found in the notion of the 'Romantic East' a vision of the Golden Age, or even just an occasional symbol, the facts mattered less than the fantasies.

Hesse, who had visited the East in 1911, was not uncritical of the Hindu writings he knew. But he looked at them through the eyes of an unshakeable Westerner, seeking, no less than the Romantics of the nineteenth century, what he could abstract for his contemporary Western purposes. Paramount among these purposes was the de-monstration of how, above all through the intercession of love, man can achieve that union with the cosmos which brings him to his fulfilment. *Siddhartha* is no cry of 'Back to Brahma'. For as Siddhartha himself—whose name means 'he who has reached the goal'—can only find fulfilment when he has understood, and affirmed by love, that he must needs lose his son to the attractions of the world, so also he comes to see that each man must find his own salvation. He cannot spare his son, or even vicariously endure, the suffering which lies along his son's road to self-fulfilment. That one of the trials along the road is the rejection of the father by the son, as Siddhartha had once deserted his own father, completes the interaction of fates which is spread out like a fabric of interwoven contrapuntal strands, a unity embracing a diversity. Hence the central symbol in the book of the river—eternal change within eternal constancy, relentlessness of motion, a multiplicity of forms yet a singularity of substance, the absorption of time into an all-consuming present. The merging of the self in a higher unity, the inadequacy of the intellect alone, the heuristic power of love, an existential ethic, an idealised search for serenity, the Romantic lure of the East—a mere catalogue of motifs from *Siddhartha* can explain the enthusiastic reception of Hesse by the youth of a strained, conflict-ridden Europe in recent years.

Living in the bourgeois placidity of his Swiss retreat, Hesse did not experience the turmoil of the post-war years of inflation, the desperate search for political respectability in the years that followed, or the social realities that lay beneath the re-emergence of nationalist extremism and the eventual take-over by National Socialism. Perhaps it is appropriate that his novels, together with his many occasional essays, move in philosophical realms and are devoted in the last analysis to the question of man in the universe, and in particular to the cultivation of what he called the 'magic' in life, by which man comes to realise the essential unity of all things. This 'magical thinking' shows man how to restore the lost harmony of life, and is brought into play at the end of both *Demian* and *Siddhartha*. It is also embodied in the 'Magic Theatre' of *Der Steppenwolf* (1927), a novel as frankly autobiographical as its two predecessors—autobiographical, that is, in the sense of a chronicle of the spirit, the only meaning that Hesse attached to the concept of biography. He once referred to his novels as prolegomena to a 'Seelengeschichte',[67] and it is this virtual substitution of spiritual action for physical action that led Thomas Mann to claim for *Der Steppenwolf* no less striking a degree of bold experimentation than had been accorded to James Joyce's *Ulysses* and André Gide's *Les faux-monnayeurs*.[68]

Like Hesse himself when he wrote the book, the hero of *Der Steppenwolf*, Harry Haller, is a 48-year-old intellectual who works his way from a position of utter despair over the world to a position of ironic humour from which he can make life tolerable. In a story whose substance and structure both owe a great deal to music—from the early novel *Gertrude* (1909) to *Das Glasperlenspiel* (1943) music and musicians occupy a central place in Hesse's work—Haller makes his way towards the realisation that the central value of the spiritual kingdom is eternity, in which the contingent features of the individual personality are transcended.

The 'magical thinking' required of Haller if he is to move towards this transcendence involves the union of the pole of life and nature with the pole of the eternal spirit. Pablo the jazz musician and Mozart symbolise the two poles in *Der Steppenwolf*, as do the eponymous heroes of *Narziss und Goldmund* (1930), and the Goethean reconciliation of the polarities brings the metaphysical unity in which alone true meaning is to be found. The journey of discovery is hard. Rare in twentieth-century fiction is that serene, idyllic passage from childhood to manhood described by Hans Carossa in *Eine Kindheit* (1922) and *Verwandlungen einer Jugend* (1928), autobiographical sketches set in a firmly delineated world to which it is each man's task to contribute according to his nature and gifts, and in which, as Carossa's *Rumänisches Tagebuch* also propounds, there is an equally firm moral order.

Der Steppenwolf, with its spiritualisation of the action, is an innovatory work, but Hesse never attached importance to novelty as far as his own works were concerned, defining himself rather as a 'traditionalist'.[69] Also traditionalist, at the outset, in its character as fable and in its organisation as novel of extension, is the trilogy *Die Schlafwandler* (1931–2) by Hermann Broch, whose *Der Tod des Vergil*, written in his American exile over a decade later, was to be as innovatory, in its own spiritualising way, as *Der Steppenwolf*.

The subject of *Die Schlafwandler* is the decay of an age and the sense of spiritual abandonment felt by the individual living in that age. Broch was Viennese, a Jewish businessman who knew from his own economic experience in the 1920s what decline meant. He was 45 when the first part of the trilogy, *1888: Pasenow oder die Romantik*—his first novel—appeared. The disintegration of the Austro-Hungarian empire fills the background of his late essay *Hofmannsthal und seine Zeit* (1951) but *Die Schlafwandler* is set in the Germany of the same period, and in areas, moreover, of which in part he had no personal knowledge. The decay which is his framework, however, was a European phenomenon, and the personal insecurity and spiritual deprivation which are his central theme were common European properties. As with Kafka, whatever regional significance one might find and choose to pursue appears insignificant in the face of the universal meaning that the modern reader can recognise and to which he can relate his own situation.

1888 was the year that Wilhelm II succeeded to the throne of Prussia, and represents, like the dates in the titles of the other two parts of the trilogy, one of what Broch called 'final stages in the old European pattern of values.'[70] The young Junker officer Joachim von Pasenow finds himself in a world in which the military code of discipline and honour seems to offer the only security against the *laissez-faire* of contemporary civilian ways. To try to hold on to these old-fashioned values is what his temperamental friend and opposite, the practical, rationalistic businessman Bertrand, calls 'romantic'; in the event, it is only by marrying a woman from his own social class, a woman, however, he does not love, that Pasenow preserves himself—for a while—from the decay of values represented by Bertrand and civilian life in general. The setting of the story and, at the beginning, its manner, recall Fontane, but physical actions increasingly give way to thoughts about actions and to interior monologues. Given the terms in which Broch viewed his own work, one may legitimately recall that Nietzsche was writing *Also sprach Zarathustra* through the 1880s, and that in 1888 itself he finished the 'revaluation of all values' that constitutes the unfinished work posthumously published as *Der Wille zur Macht*.

By the time of the next 'final stage in the old European pattern of values' in the second novel, *1903: Esch oder die Anarchie*, German society has disintegrated further. To match this the comparatively unproblematical narrative style of the first novel gives way to a more deliberately allusive symbolical technique. Esch the book-keeper is concerned with financial order and propriety, as Joachim had been with the requirements of class and military discipline. But in the absence of a cohesive social framework, and since it undermines a book-keeper's philosophy to be unable to enter every human being on either the credit or the debit side of the world's moral reckoning, Esch searches for some resolution of this 'anarchy' of human conditions. He finds it in the religious concept of redemption, which can only be conveyed by imagery and symbolism.

The last part of *Die Schlafwandler* has the title *1918: Huguenau oder die Sachlichkeit*. Its hero, emerging from the national chaos of defeat, lives by an 'objective', calculating rationalism which derives from a total amorality and lack of social commitment. There are no standards of conduct left in Huguenau's world, no value-judgments that involve observing one's actions from without as part of a social context. Having prised from Esch's control the provincial Alsatian newspaper that the latter has been running, Huguenau finally murders him, concerned only with the efficiency of his own activity and the strength of his own position. His ruthless logic, as Broch puts it, is entirely 'without ornamentation . . . But bound up with this freedom from ornamentation are Nothingness and Death, and behind it lies concealed the monster of a decay to which the whole age has succumbed.'[71]

In such a world 'anarchy' and 'rationalism'—or 'objective realism', as Huguenau would call it—are synonymous. And synonymous with both—such is the completeness of the decay—is the 'irrationality' which underlies Huguenau's actions, but of which he inevitably remains ignorant. The last chapter of the book gradually loses sight of the man himself as the author delivers his final philosophical reflections on the nature of human society. Here the *coincidentia oppositorum* in his terminology assumes striking forms. Of revolution he writes:

Revolutions are insurrections of evil against evil, insurrections of the irrational against the rational, insurrections of the irrational masquerading as strict logical reasoning against rational institutions complacently defending themselves by an appeal to irrational sentiment. Revolutions are struggles between unreality and unreality, between tyranny and tyranny, and they are inevitable, once the release of the ultra-rational has led to the release of the irrational, once the disintegration of values has advanced to its last integral unit, the individual. For the individual, isolated and autonomous, stripped of all prejudice, is defenceless before the invasion of the irrational.[72]

The accelerating disintegration of values of which *Die Schlafwandler* tells is reflected in the increasing heterogeneity of Broch's technique. The continuative realistic narrative style in which *Pasenow oder die Romantik* opens has by some way through *Huguenau oder die Sachlichkeit* given place to an episodic, associative, almost psychoanalytic manner, in which there are sections of epigrams, of dramatic dialogue (partly in verse), of philosophical reflections, and the serial story-within-a-story of the Salvation Army girl. Broch saw his task, not as the unfurling of a plot like a story-teller but as the employment of literature as a mode of understanding, and thus as the pursuit of an ethical aim through the manipulation of the techniques of his literary craft. One can, and should, therefore read his essays—*Der Zerfall der Werte, Logik einer zerfallenden Welt, Einheit wissenschaftlicher und dichterischer Erkenntnis* and others—alongside his novels, for what 'romanticism', 'anarchy' and 'objectivity' mean in Broch's diagnosis of the *Zeitgeist* and its manifestations is as open to discussion in philosophical, conceptual terms as it is in the specific human situations of his fiction.

This makes his novels very different in intention and style from those of his compatriot Josef Roth, whose *Radetzkymarsch* (1932) and

Die Kapuzinergruft (1938) are concerned with the decline and fall of the Austro-Hungarian monarchy. Roth's purpose is directly histori- cal, in the sense that here is a unique moment in history whose unique nature he sets out to uncover through the lives of characters caught up in that moment. The time *in* which he writes is very different from the time *of* which he writes, and these two novels have a reminiscential quality about them which is partly analytical, partly nostalgic. Broch, on the other hand, like Musil, makes a philosophical statement of an all-embracing nature, a statement about the *Zeitgeist* and the moral dilemmas that it poses; the specific becomes the representative, a demonstration of the general law, the physical event becomes a ripple on the surface of a deeper reality. Hence the symbolic function of Broch's three 'sleepwalkers', men unaware of what they are really doing: Pasenow cannot awake to the true values of contemporary life; Esch lives in a confusion which he can only resolve in otherworldly terms; and Huguenau has abandoned all moral commitment. 'Romanticism', 'anarchy' and 'objectivity' alike stand condemned.

An inability to cope with everyday reality is likewise the generating force behind a remarkable novel, ignored at the time it was written but now often spoken of in the same breath as Joyce's *Ulysses* and the works of Broch—Elias Canetti's *Die Blendung* (1935), Calmly, soberly, ruthlessly the gradual disintegration of the mind of the greatest Orientalist of the day is portrayed against a background of bizarre commonplaces and the life of the city underworld until his alienation from the outside world leads to total madness. He sets fire to his magnificent private library, mounts the steps of a ladder in the middle of the room and is burned to death together with his books—the only 'realities' he has ever known. 'When the flames finally reached him' ends the novel, 'he laughed more loudly than he had ever laughed in his life.'

Through the behaviour of Peter Kien in *Die Blendung* there runs a broad strand of repressed sexuality. An all-dominant creed of sex, however, floods Hans Henny Jahnn's *Peruddja* (1929), a heavily expressionist *Entwicklungsroman* whose hero, cast in the pagan Nordic mould which for Jahnn held the true promise of human fulfilment, turns hither and thither in his search for sensual satisfaction in the company of men, of animals and of nature. A distasteful air of Romantic barbarism and excess hangs over most of Jahnn's novels and dramas, but they have their symptomatic interest in the context of pseudo-utopian responses to the contemporary social realities which many found hard to bear and even harder to exploit.

A different kind of unbearable reality revealed by the eruption of psychological stress in the sexual realm is the subject of Schnitzler's short stories *Fräulein Else* (1924), and *Traumnovelle* (1926). These are late works by an Austrian who came of an older generation than Broch and whose real social material had been the decaying Austro-Hungarian monarchy of pre-war days, but who, in these psychoanalytical studies of grotesque erotic situations, captures the frenetic abandon and moral insecurity characteristic of the 1920s. So, in their own way, do the novels and short stories of Stefan Zweig, a long-suffering Jew who, much like Wasserman, put his faith in the ideal of an integrated European culture.

Zweig's short story *Amok* (1922) is a kind of modern *Die Marquise von O.* Kleist was a writer with whom he felt a particular affinity, and his essays on Kleist, Hölderlin and Nietzsche in *Der Kampf mit dem Dämon* (1925) are rich in psychological insights. *Amok* exudes an atmosphere of sexual strain similar to that of Schnitzler's *Fräulein Else* and *Traumnovelle*, and contains one of those portraits of the female psyche (the Novelle *Brief einer Unbekannten* [1922] is another) for which Zweig is especially famed. A close friend of Freud, Zweig the storyteller has sensitivity without penetration; a certain sentimentality hangs over his works, as over those of his hero Romain Rolland, and this puts him in the company of Werfel and Wassermann, but sets him apart from Schnitzler. He was an introspective, melancholy man, immensely successful as an author but increasingly depressed at the state of the world that acclaimed him. Although his works were burned by the Nazis in 1933, his libretto for Richard Strauss's opera *Die schweigsame Frau*, first produced in 1936, survived, chiefly through Strauss' loyalty; he escaped from Austria in 1938, first to England, then to the United States and finally to Brazil, where he committed suicide in 1942. His last book, a set of memoirs called *Die Welt von Gestern* (1942), belongs with works like Zuckmayer's *Als wär's ein Stück von mir*, Bruno Walter's *Theme and Variations*, Fritz Kortner's *Aller Tage Abend*, Ernst von Salomon's *Der Fragebogen*, Oskar Maria Graf's *Gelächter von aussen* and other works of reminiscence, to the fascinating raw material from which much of the social history of the 1920s and 1930s can be written.

Of the same generation as Broch, also a native of Vienna, and a writer whose work is set in the period of the decay of traditional values after the collapse of the Austro-Hungarian monarchy and the Kaiser's Germany, and whose concern, like Broch's, is to diagnose the metaphysical character of an entire age, is Robert Musil, whose *Der Mann ohne Eigenschaften* (1930–42) is one of the major novels of the twentieth century. Musil, professionally equipped as mathematician, engineer, psychologist and philosopher, had had a considerable success with his story *Die Verwirrungen des Zöglings Törless* (1906) and a handful of other works, and had devoted himself to literature from his mid-twenties onwards. He and Broch both left Austria after the Nazi invasion of 1938. Broch, who was in prison for some time, escaped to England and then to the United States, where he died in 1951, an honoured academic; Musil, who had spent the early 1930s in Berlin, went into voluntary exile in Switzerland and died in Zürich in 1942, an almost forgotten figure.

The long work that was eventually to be called *Der Mann ohne Eigenschaften*—it had a number of earlier provisional titles—occupied Musil's mind from the war of 1914–18 to his death. It was planned to appear in two volumes, each with two parts: Volume One was published complete in 1930, the first part of Volume Two in 1932. The remainder of the manuscript—Musil did not complete the book—has been posthumously published by a number of different editors; indeed, the editing of Musil's papers became something of an industry in the 1960s.

Although there are obvious things to say about this massive, epic novel, it is difficult to know where to start—and when to stop. As with Broch, the contemporary social and historical aspects are probably the most tangible and most readily revealing of that ironical detachment which leavens much of the book. On this plane lies the action that derives from the celebrations being planned in 1913 to mark what would have been the seventieth anniversary, in 1918, of Franz Joseph's accession to the Austrian throne (he died in 1916); the same year, ironically, would mark the thirtieth anniversary of the rule of Kaiser Wilhelm II, and the Austrians are anxious that their festivities shall outshine those of the Germans. So a committee called 'Vaterländische Aktion' is charged with the special planning of the celebration, and the activities of this committee and its individual members—behind some of whom are identifiable personalities, such as Walter Rathenau (cuttingly and often unjustly portrayed in the Jewish industrialist and intellectual Dr. Paul Arnheim) and the philosopher Ludwig Klages (concealed behind the 'prophet' Meingast)—hold the events of the novel together, particularly in the first volume. Interwoven with the ironical *Parallelaktion* of the anniversary celebrations is the theme of the maniac Moosbrugger, through whom Musil treats the subject of the responsibility of the individual before the law in a society that has lost its standards of moral judgement.

Ulrich, the hero of the book, deals with these and other characters in his search for 'Eigenschaften'—for with the passing of old values modern man has lost his identity and needs to acquire new 'qualities' in order to establish a new identity. Ulrich—we do not learn his family name—is not an individual but an archetype, and Musil's subject is no less than Man in the Twentieth Century, just as the 'grotesque Austria', as he called it, in which his novel is set, 'is no more than a particularly obvious microcosm of the modern world.'[73]

Hence the profusion of philosophical excursions interposed in the narrative, for Musil, like Broch, was concerned to establish a critical intellectual position satisfactory in its own right, as well as to allow his creative imagination free rein to explore the world in its own terms. The synthesis that Ulrich seeks is the product of just this blend of the irrational—the world of the spirit—and the rationally predictable—the world of the scientific intellect—for it is the discrepancy between man's huge intellectual skill and his inadequate moral consciousness, between what he can do and what he really understands, that produces Ulrich's 'lack of qualities'.

Moreover, since Ulrich is an intellectual, a man whose education has given him a privileged chance to find the answers to the questions posed by modern man, his lack of qualities is archetypal at the highest level. He is no proverbial 'man on the Clapham omnibus' but a 'hero of the age', as Musil called him, a man who faces his existential problem by unceasing reflection on the 'facts' of life, by a constant battle with 'reality'. That this reality exists simultaneously on different planes makes both for the incredibility of a simple chronological sequence in Ulrich's life and for the impossibility of a single-stratum narrative style in Musil's novel. 'The story unfolds in a timeless manner; everything is more or less present at the same time', he wrote.[74]

By the same token the real-life problems of Ulrich the man coincide with the stylistic and technical problems of Musil the story-teller. The shapeless reality which so dissatisfies Ulrich is conveyed in section-headings like 'Eine Art Anfang' and 'Seinesgleichen geschieht', and the search to overcome this shapelessness is what constitutes Ulrich's *Bildung*: 'It is so easy to be energetic, and so difficult to find something worth being energetic about.'[75] Similarly man's lower order of 'Wirklichkeitssinn' gives way before a new, vital 'Möglichkeitssinn', as Musil calls it,[76] a faith in a world beyond the world of appearances. The apprehension of this world demands a blend of rationality and mysticism, the two antithetical modes of experience that dominate the modern world. The former is the direct reflection of Ulrich's—and Musil's—nature and training; the latter is the principal source of his utopian visions, even of 'Möglichkeitssinn' itself, for thoughts transcend actions and the given conventionalities of life, and can overcome the irony that threatens the power of utopianism.

Musil's pervasive irony is a constituent of his 'Möglichkeitssinn' and a reflection of his attitude towards merely contingent realities—'God Himself probably prefers to speak of His world in the *conjunctivus potentialis* . . . . . for He made this world, knowing all the time that it could just as well have been different.'[77] Complementarily—and a significant strength in the structure and style of the novel—there is something of everybody in everybody else, something right in something wrong, something beautiful in something ugly. As Musil puts it in *Der Mann ohne Eigenschaften*: 'Irony is to give a portrait of a priest which is also a portrait of a Bolshevik, or to draw the character of an idiot in such a way that the author suddenly thinks "Ah, that's just like a part of myself!" '[78]

Characters in the novel often complement each other in this way through relationships of varying duration, predominant among them that between Ulrich and his sister Agatha, in which the antithesis of rationality and mysticism, *vita activa* and *vita contemplativa*, reaches its climax. These relationships, like the numerous intercalated philosophical discourses and reflections, have a remarkable richness and subtlety.

There is a timelessness, a sense of universal validity, about Musil's thought. Yet he also belongs unmistakably to an historical moment that sees the passing of one age and the birth of another. He rejected the modern cult of the expert and the urge to ever greater specialisation; at the same time he would only deal, like the modern age, in limited answers to limited questions. For him the basis of any possible solutions to the problems facing modern society could only be provided by a fusion of natural science, psychoanalysis and sociology, a fusion as inevitable as—to him—it was natural. In thoughts such as these, as in his principle of the inseparability of the ethical and the aesthetic in art, lies the importance of Musil the novelist as of Musil the thinker.

Although neither *Der Mann ohne Eigenschaften* nor the much earlier *Die Verwirrungen des Zöglings Törless* is autobiographical in the strict sense, there is much of Musil the man in the former, as there is of Musil the schoolboy in the latter. The centre of this autobiographical substance lies in the realm of the psychological: there is of necessity a social framework—Musil was a thoroughly traditional novelist whose greatest admiration was for Balzac, Tolstoi and Dostoevsky—but the passing of observations on the workings of society *per se* was for him an oblique, not a direct concern.

Among the lesser works more directly revelatory of life in the schoolboy world of Musil's *Törless* are Ernst Glaeser's *Jahrgang 1902* and Franz Werfel's *Der Abituriententag*, both published in 1928, and

Friedrich Torberg's *Der Schüler Gerber hat absolviert* (1930).

The aesthetic quality of Glaeser's once popular and often reprinted semi-autobiographical story of a group of adolescents in a South German school in 1914 is virtually nil, and the crudity of the central theme of youthful sexuality, treated in a Wedekind-like manner which suggests that little has changed since the days of *Frühlings Erwachen*, is painfully embarrassing at times. Yet it holds a social interest on two counts. On the one hand the tensions generated in these boys by different social backgrounds emerge with brutal clarity, in particular through contemporary attitudes towards the Jews. On the other hand we are given a picture of the war through the eyes, not of the men at the front, as in Remarque, Renn and Ernst Jünger, but of those left at home, the women and the children and the aged, trying to decide their attitude to the war and preserve the framework of civilian life while their menfolk were being killed at the front.

The strains on the minds of young people in the late 1920s showed themselves in a striking wave of suicides, and the subject became popular among writers concerned to probe the psychology of youth and the social pressures of the time. Friedrich Torberg, a precociously gifted Viennese writer who made a name for himself in the space of a few years, before mounting anti-Semitism forced him out of Austria in 1938, took this theme for his novel *Der Schüler Gerber hat absolviert*, in which an *Abiturient* who is afraid that he has failed his examination throws himself from the window of his classroom. The source of such powers of destruction—the same is true of Werfel's *Nicht der Mörder, der Ermordete ist schuldig* and Glaeser's *Jahrgang 1902*—lies not in the individual personality but in the society that spawns such evils. Torberg portrays the school as a microcosm of society at large, and the tensions and anxieties of school life as a reflection of the paradoxes of life outside. The cruellest of these paradoxes, in Torberg's story, is that Gerber's suicide is the product of a delusion: the examination committee decides that he has in fact passed his examination.

Werfel's *Der Abituriententag*, a more sensitive, more subtle work, plays on the contrast between the life of well-to-do schoolboys and that of their poorer *confrères*, exposing the sadism that runs through a schoolboy community in which material and intellectual inequalities prevail. When, 25 years on, 15 of the 27 boys who had graduated from the *Gymnasium* of Sankt Nikolaus in 1902 hold a reunion, the division into successes and failures is as harsh as ever. On the one side a handful of men at the top—an industrialist, a lawyer, an actor-manager, the judge through whose eyes the occasion and its sequel are related; on the other side those, the overwhelming majority, who had made little or no mark on life—'those who came off second best, cannon fodder, ekeing out a pitiful, hopeless existence'.[79] A guilt-complex, however, is not the prerogative of the poor. The privileged *Untersuchungsrichter*, protected son of a distinguished father, thinks he sees in the pitiful suspect before him a victimised former classmate of the same name, and his hysterical outburst shows the hidden pressure of a guilt that had never been fully purged. Between the flashbacks to those days in the *Gymnasium* lie the stages of the psychological study which is at the centre of Werfel's interest.

The portrayal of psychological stress also fills Werfel's novel *Verdi* (1924, later revised), a work in the genre of *Künstlerroman* so prominent in German fiction. From the age of Romanticism onwards—Wackenroder's Josef Berglinger, for example, or E.T.A. Hoffmann's Kapellmeister Kreisler—the artist had been portrayed as the antithesis of the conventional, middle-class *Bürger* whose values dominated the society of the time. Even the man who, though not a creator of works of art, has the soul of an artist, like Eichendorff's Taugenichts, or Anselmus in Hoffmann's *Der goldne Topf*, finds the modi of bourgeois society incompatible with the dictates of his artistic nature. At the turn of the century the sad little figure of Hanno Buddenbrook embodies both sociologically and spiritually Thomas Mann's reiteration of this incompatibility; Tonio Kröger and Gustav Aschenbach, in their different ways, live through the same tension, beset by the fascination and moral equivocation of art and beauty. Finally, in *Doktor Faustus*, Mann wrestles with the crisis of the artistic act itself, as Adrian Leverkühn, the artist in our time, brings together the polarities of life and *Geist*, community and art, in a synthesis of discord and destruction.

The Verdi of Werfel's story is captured in that period of despair when, a legendary figure with numerous successes behind him, he is struggling in vain to write an opera on Shakespeare's *King Lear*. For 15 years he scarcely writes a note, and has almost resigned himself to accepting that he has no more music left in him. He is in Venice. So too at this moment is Wagner. By coming to terms in his mind with the composer popularly seen as his rival, Verdi comes to terms with himself, and at the end of the story, a man now in his seventies, he is at work on *Otello*, one of the two great masterpieces with which his career came to its close.

The composition of the novel itself mirrored the hesitancy and the doubts with which its hero is plagued. Worried by the peculiar problems that attend the writing of historical fiction, with its demand for historical verisimilitude to be woven into the fabric of poetic imagination, Werfel hesitated for 12 years before carrying out his plan. The figure of Verdi himself, indeed, a man who shunned publicity, who called newspapers the bane of the age, and the posthumous publication of a man's letters simply wrong, seemed to resist being made the centre of attention. In the end, largely through the aggregation of sub-plots and numerous fictional episodes, Werfel overcame his difficulties by searching for what he called, in his preface to the novel, 'the purer, inner mystic truth, what is legendary about a person'.[80] The novel has most of the earnestly sentimental, endearingly honest traits characteristic of all Werfel's work and reveals more about its author than about its subject. Werfel was that kind of writer.

An incidental historical interest attaches to the publication of *Verdi* in 1924. Alma Schindler, widow of the composer Gustav Mahler, mistress of the painter Oskar Kokoschka, ex-wife of the architect Walter Gropius and married to Franz Werfel since 1929, tells in her memoirs of a meeting with a rich young Austrian called Paul von Zsolnay in 1923, to whom she complained with characteristic egotism that the inflation of the past year had ruined her royalties from the performances of Mahler's works. Knowing that Werfel was working on a new novel, Zsolnay, who saw an opportunity both to help Alma Werfel and to cast himself in the role of Maecenas, offered to found a new firm in order to publish the work, if she would bring him the manuscript. Werfel's current publisher, Kurt Wolff of Leipzig, was somehow appeased, and so the Paul Zsolnay Verlag, later to become one of Austria's leading publishing houses, came into existence—solely for the purpose of launching Werfel's *Verdi*.[81]

There is no work of art, be it in literature, painting, sculpture, architecture or music, but does not bear the marks of its age. Sometimes the *Zeitgeist* lies heavily upon it, giving it a quality of representativeness, a power to convey central truths about its age; or it may be crushed beneath the trivia of the times and claim little more than the passing attention either of its contemporaries or of later generations. On the other hand, by virtue of its substance, or of the personality of its creator, it may be more tenuously linked with the contemporary world and betray its historical setting rather through style and manner.

Although such a distinction may form part of one's characterisation of a given writer, or of a group of writers in a given age, it does not bring with it any criterion of quality. To be sure, greatness depends on the extent to which an artist lifts himself above the time-bound typicalities of his time and makes an individual utterance whose continued validity is acknowledged by later generations. Only in this way can we be moved by works of art from times and places remote from our own. But in company other than that of the supremely great—and on occasion perhaps even here also—the prominence or otherwise of here-and-now-ness is a feature absorbed into one's general characterisation of the work. Dickens and Scott, say, cannot be 'placed' by this criteria, let alone played off against each other. All we can observe is that some writers tell us more—socially, politically, historically, psychologically—about their age than others. Thomas Mann, Döblin, Remarque, Fallada, Broch, Musil, Werfel—all are time-bound in their different ways. So too is a writer to whom, on the one hand, time seems immaterial, so non-real are the settings and sequences of his stories, but who, on the other hand, has come to hold for the whole of the Western world a meaning inseparable from the circumstances of twentieth-century life, perhaps the most perplexing, most disturbing, most inescapable German author of his, and our, age—Franz Kafka.

Kafka's generation is that of the expressionist poets—Benn, Trakl, Loerke, Stadler, Heym, Klabund and numerous others—whose characteristic years *qua* expressionist poets lie between 1910 and the early 1920s. This is also the period in which Kafka's mature work falls. But there was little in the art of the expressionists for which he had any sympathy. The self-consciousness of their gestures, their high-pitched tone, their sensationalism only aroused his distaste. There was no need for the act of expression to be noisy and ostentatious. 'Der Lärm stört den Ausdruck', he is reported to have said to Gustav Janouch.[82] The poetry of his Prague friend Franz Werfel, with its often religious and moral overtones, was the only expressionist art for which he showed any admiration, and even this he found extravagant and unsettling.

An especially revealing contrast between Kafka and his contemporaries lies in their response to the conflict of generations. The message of Hasenclever's *Der Sohn*, of Bronnen's *Vatermord*, of Werfel's *Nicht der Mörder, der Ermordete ist schuldig* is a justification of the hatred which in the social circumstances of the time, a son may feel for his father, and it is a message shrieked from the housetops with an almost pathological intensity. Kafka's tragic relationship to his own father, an ambitious and dominating character with no understanding of his son's psychology or of the intellectual and literary concerns that filled his mind, overshadowed his entire life and work, and from it he extracted the emotional energy with which the works of the last 10 years of his life are charged. But he suffered in silence. Even in those works, such as *Das Urteil* and *Der Verschollene* (published as *Amerika*), in which the father-son relationship is crucial, he does not raise his voice above the flat, emotionless tone that characterises all his stories and gives them their shattering directness. He demanded from literature, his own as well as that of others, the truthful expression of an inner reality, and for him truth was not to be found in ranting emotional excesses or a desperate seeking after effect.

A situation of rootlessness, of not belonging, of living a life whose direction and meaning one is powerless to influence—if, indeed, it has any direction and meaning—was a reality to which the Europe of the 1920s readily responded. But the alienation of which Kafka wrote was in the first instance that of his own childhood and adolescence in the pre-war years. Prague belonged to the Austrian Empire, and it was German culture and the German language that dominated. The Kafka family, however, had come from a poor, Czech-speaking country district, and when, like all parents anxious that their family should climb the social ladder, Hermann Kafka sent his son to German schools in the city, then to the German university, he added to the Jew-Gentile tension the German-Slav antagonism which had smouldered throughout the nineteenth century and was to be savagely exploited during the Third Reich and its aftermath. The governing German minority looked on the Kafkas and their like as Jews (outsiders by birth and definition), the subject Czech majority looked on them as Germans (outsiders by cultural and social choice). How was Kafka to look on himself? He had even been deprived of a mother tongue, in the true sense, in which to express his deepest feelings and thoughts.

From the reality of this base-less, context-less biography emerged, in the years immediately preceding the outbreak of the Great War, the first of those fully characteristic statements about our base-less and context-less existence which have both unnerved and fascinated the Western world for the last 60 years. *Das Urteil, Die Verwandlung*, and most of *Amerika* were written in late 1912; *In der Strafkolonie* and most of *Der Prozess* in late 1914. This latter year marks the nadir of his personal depression and of his obsession with the father-dominated themes of guilt and punishment, an obsession intensified by his reading of Dostoevsky and Strindberg. Most of the stories and sketches published by Kurt Wolff in 1919 under the title *Ein Landarzt* were written during the war-years; the novel *Das Schloss* was one of works that occupied his last years, as were the pieces in *Ein Hungerkünstler*, the proofs of which he was reading at the time of his death in 1924. The works that he wrote for publication fill but a single, modest volume. All the rest, as his friend and literary executor Max Brod recorded – and this includes *Der Prozess* and *Das Schloss* – 'he did not mean to publish'.

Since the time when, against Kafka's instructions, Max Brod posthumously published *Der Prozess* (1925), *Das Schloss* (1926) and *Amerika* (1927)—all three left incomplete—the critical arena has been filled with rival interpretations of their meaning and their relevance. Indeed, so widely variant and incompatible have these interpretations become that one seems to be confronting a chameleonic *oeuvre* that adapts itself to the circumstances from which the reader approaches it, and becomes all things to all men. There is something remarkable at stake when *Das Schloss*, for example, can attract epithets as varied as Judaistic, existential, Christian, nihilistic, or 'a lovely, moving, memorable book', as a reviewer of the English translation called it. The modish appellation 'Kafka-esque', while embarrassingly superficial in usage, would not have acquired the currency it has but for an uncanny correspondence between Kafka's works and some of the more disturbing and destructive manifestations of modern life and modern society.

In senses that are sometimes more, sometimes less direct, the novels of the 1920s that have occupied our attention have generally had the life of the time, or some aspect of it, as the focus of interest, however far beyond this focal point the action may have moved. Where the subject is the Great War, for example—Remarque's *Im Westen nichts Neues*, Jünger's *In Stahlgewittern*, Carossa's *Rumänisches Tagebuch*—this is obvious. It is equally, though more subtly, true of the multi-strataed, panoramic works of Broch and Musil, with their philosophical, supratemporal concerns. On the one hand there are characters in these works who bear traits of contemporary historical personages; on the other it is through the spiritual realities of the age itself that such writers make their statements about the human condition at large.

But the realities of which Kafka writes—and they are no less real than those of men who choose to write of war, or revolution, or art, or the generation-gap—are in the first instance the realities of his own private spiritual existence, and it is in the world of his mind that one must begin one's search for the meaning—or one of the meanings—of his work. Much Kafka criticism, having launched itself on a level of cosmic interpretation, moves in a realm of more or less plausible allegorical fancy, which, though not without its attractions and its profits, is not properly the plane on which one should start. All writers write, in some sense or other, about themselves. But whereas with what one might call the object-centred writer one legitimately sets the created work, itself a tangible object, at the head of one's argument, with the 'private' writer, whose imaginative works are a kind of extension of the events of his personal world, one's approach resembles more that to a diary or a collection of letters. As, for instance, in discussing Novalis, one has to bring virtually everything he wrote—prose, verse, works finished, works unfinished, critical fragments, letters—to bear on the particular subject under scrutiny, so with Kafka the ensemble of known utterances, private and public, and in whatever form, make up a single, indivisible context.

True, all art claims its own objectivity, and only with the help of criteria generic to the context that the particular art-form has created in the course of its history can one arrive at valid characterisations or judgements. One cannot raise the stature of a work by appealing to its author's proven eminence in other works, or to his estimable qualities as a human being, nor can one invoke the general mediocrity of an artist's output, or the conventionality of his personal nature, in order to deny the originality that may reside in one isolated work. But in Kafka we are facing a narrative extension of the dark, yet frighteningly lucid world of fear, doubt, agony, resignation in which his mind lived. What he himself searched for is what his heroes—non-heroes, rather—search for. The despair and frustration of his own life, the reality of living in a private hell with its own intractable laws, administered by those closest to him, is what his characters are born into and learn to live with.

A primary document for the understanding of Kafka's spiritual biography, along with the many letters and diaries that have been published since his death, is the long, self-analytical *Brief an den Vater*, written in 1919, and given to his mother to be handed to his father. His father never saw it. Julie Kafka, having read the letter, gave it back to her son.

In his father's strength and self-confidence before the challenge of life, career and achievement lay the roots of the feelings of guilt and inadequacy that Kafka wrenched from himself in his letter. This was not simply a private matter of domestic psychology, but a situation that overflowed into all his personal relationships: 'I could not suddenly change when I was in the company of other people, but became aware of an even greater sense of guilt.'[83] Guilt means dependence, and it was in order both to break this dependence and to purge his guilt—in other words, to make a statement about his own true self, free of what he called 'the general pressure of anxiety, of weakness, of self-contempt'[84]—that he wrote his stories. 'It was *you* they were about', he said. 'And in writing them, I was slowly but surely freeing myself from you.'[85] It is idle to speculate whether Kafka would in fact have written anything at all had it not been for this need to 'free himself from his father', but it is from the pathological reality of this dominance, the central fact in his psychological history, that one must in the first instance approach his work. In his diaries, indeed, lie many patterns of thought, descriptive jottings, fragments of dreams and the like which were later to become published stories, and without the continuous process of self-analysis through diary and letter he could not have maintained the stamina to finish these stories.

This is not tantamount to saying that the key to the understanding of Kafka's stories is a judicious application of the concept of the Oedipus complex. A crude positivism of this kind has little place in literary criticism. But psychological realities cannot be exorcised from the creative mind, and the mind—Kafka's mind *a fortiori*—cannot be dissected into discrete areas defined as 'personal', 'social', 'artistic' and so on. The publication of Kafka's letters to Felice Bauer in 1967 led Elias Canetti to show again, by relating these letters to *Der Prozess*, how imperceptible is the frontier between the experience of art and the experience of life in the world of Franz Kafka.[86]

Two further vital characteristics of Kafka's claustrophobic world derive from this, both of them subjective realities which have acquired for his readers the status of representative utterances about the nature of the modern world. One is the crippling effect of self-doubt and indecision on the capacity for action, and the self-consciousness that attends the moment of action itself. A powerful presence seems either to pre-empt the individual capacity for choice or to stigmatise those who resist this pre-emption with the curse of moral uncertainty and isolation, thus fanning still further the flames of guilt. But the guilt *is* the situation: there is no question of escaping from it. The legitimacy of the arrest of Josef K. at the opening of *Der Prozess* cannot be disputed, and the court that tries him has never yet conceded a person's innocence. The datum is the individual's existential reality, from which the agony of choice is inseparable and for which the insistence on consequential action is inescapable. Terms like these show how willing, and how explicable, has been the response to Kafka in the context of the various existentialist *Weltanschauungen*, both Christian and materialist, that have been so influential in European culture since the end of World War II. They also recall the presence of Nietzsche, Dostoevsky and Kierkegaard in the background of Kafka's thought.

The other characteristic, related to this, is the self-containedness, the absoluteness of the personal world that Kafka inhabits. There *is* no other world for him, no reality other than the agony which gives his world its meaning, no common set of conventions or external values to which to conform or by which to be judged. The only world that K. knows, in *Das Schloss*, the world to which he seeks desperately and hopelessly to belong, is the hermetically sealed world of the Castle itself. The episode 'Vor dem Gesetz' in *Der Prozess* presents the same closed situation, as does the whole context of 'justice' in the novel.

As Kafka sought, guiltily and therefore compulsively, to be

accepted by his father for the different person he was, and not for a figure created in his father's image, so K. spends his life trying to be accepted by the Castle for what he claims to be. But he is an outsider, and outsiders are always wrong. K. is especially so, because the ruling powers with which he seeks to ingratiate himself are manifestly evil, so that he acknowledges evil as good while knowing that it is not, which only intensifies his feelings of guilt. As for those who live under the régime of the Castle—the villagers among whom K. finds himself and who represent, both for him and for the reader, the kind of society for which the Castle stands, their morality is that of Nietzsche's 'first stage' in his *Zur Genealogie der Moral*. To wit: what is and what should be are one and the same, a 'slave morality' of habit, sustained by the *vis inertiae*. When K. asks the Prügler, in *Der Prozess*, why he carries on with his inhuman job of flogging prisoners, he is told that all a man can do, if he is paid to flog, is to flog—it is simply his job. And K.'s agitation at seeing this treatment meted out to Franz and Wilhelm hardly even survives the further explanation that, if he had not complained about the two men's behaviour in the first place, they would not now be in the hands of the flogger. To the first plane of morality he no longer has access, since he has already passed beyond the slavery of habit; the other plane only leads him ineluctably back, through confrontation with the outside world, to the awareness of his inescapable guilt.

So Josef K. in *Der Prozess*, or K. in *Das Schloss*, or the Landarzt, or Gregor Samsa in *Die Verwandlung*, or Franz Kafka, or modern man—we may now call him what we will—is trapped in the logic of his own suffering and able to communicate his thoughts only about this suffering and about his estrangement from all else. Through his unemotional tone and the matter-of-factness of his manner—the 'Prager Deutsch' of his day has left its mark on his language—he shocks us into accepting the extraordinary as the everyday, the grotesque as the natural. The strongest epithet the officer can use to describe his machine of torture in *In der Strafkolonie* is 'peculiar'—*eigenartig*—and Gregor Samsa sees nothing unusual in having been turned into a beetle: he could not have prevented it, and after all, there is no known remedy for the condition. It is not a question of his *feeling* like a beetle: he *is* a beetle, and his reality is now a beetle-reality, beyond which there is nothing with which he can make contact. Man knows only the bounds of his own damnation. 'No people sing with such pure voices as those who live in the depths of hell; what we hear as the song of the angels is *their song*.'[87] This is the reality, the truth, that Kafka perceives and of which he writes.

NOTES

1. *The Modern Novel* (London, 1953), 8
2. 'Modern Fiction' (*Collected Essays* II, London, 1966, 106)
3. From an interview with Axel Eggebrecht in the Berlin literary weekly *Die literarische Welt*, 14 June 1929
4. *Essays* I (Stuttgart, 1960), 354–6
5. *Im Westen nichts Neues—eine Täuschung* (Idstein, 1929), 29
6. *Neues Deutschland*, 20 July 1961
7. *Der Krieg. Das erste Volksbuch vom grossen Krieg* (Berlin/Vienna/Zurich, 1929), 5
8. *Der Kampf als inneres Erlebnis* (Stuttgart, 1922), 37, 38,
9. *Essays I*, ed. cit. 53–4
10. *Essays* I, ed. cit. 13–14
11. *Das Wäldchen 125* (1925), 50
12. see J. Wulf, *Literatur und Dichtung im Dritten Reich* (Gütersloh, 1963), 39
13. *Der Waldgänger* (Essays I, ed. cit. 316)
14. see F. Baumer, *Ernst Jünger* (Berlin, 1967), 79
15. see J. Wulf, op. cit. '63
16. *Der Streit um den Sergeanten Grischa* (Potsdam, 1928), 110
17. ed. cit. 552
18. 'Der Roman lebt' (1955): in A. Zweig, *Ausgewählte Werke in Einzelausgaben* XV: *Essays* I (Berlin, 1959), 392
19. *rororo* edition (1964), 427
20. ed. cit. 348
21. *Kleiner Mann—grosser Mann, alles vertauscht* (Hamburg, 1959), 181
22. ed. cit. III, 824–5
23. *Kleiner Mann—was nun?* (Berlin, 1932), 353
24. Tucholsky called it 'ein Schritt in unbebautes Neuland, von bestem Instinkt geleitet' (ed. cit. III, 360). See also Walter Benjamin's essay of 1930, 'Politisierung der Intelligenz'
25. *Heute bei uns zu Haus* (Stuttgart, 1943), 33
26. 'Mein Buch Berlin Alexanderplatz' (*Berlin Alexanderplatz*, Olten, 1961), 505
27. 'Kunst, Dämon und Gesellschaft' (*Aufsätze zur Literatur*, Olten/Freiburg, 1963, 85)
28. 'Schriftstellerei und Dichtung' (*Aufsätze zur Literatur*, ed. cit. 94)
29. ed. cit. 90
30. 'Vom alten zum neuen Naturalismus' (*Aufsätze zur Literatur*, ed. cit. 145)
31. *Berlin Alexanderplatz*, ed. cit. 500
32. Döblin's 'Nachwort' to the 1955 re-issue of the novel (ed. cit. 508)
33. ed. cit. 339
34. Walter Muschg in his editorial 'Nachwort' to *Berlin Alexanderplatz*, ed. cit. 522
35. *Von der bürgerlichen Ehre und bürgerlichen Notwendigkeit* (Munich, 1932), 15; quoted in J. Wulf, op. cit. 337
36. *Deutsche Geschichte* (4 vols, Stuttgart, 1926–36, II, 485)
37. *Volk ohne Raum* (Munich, 1935), 10
38. see J. Wulf, op. cit. 337
39. *Werke in drei Bänden*, III (1959), 1154
40. loc. cit.
41. *Demian* (Frankfurt, 1960), 209
42. *Der Untergang des Abendlandes* I (Vienna/Leipzig, 1918), 41
43. T.W. Adorno, 'Spengler nach dem Untergang' (*Der Monat*, May, 1950, No 20, 122)

44. In a talk (1942) on his *Joseph und seine Brüder* (*Gesammelte Werke in zwölf Bänden*, Frankfurt, 1960, XI, 657)
45. *Betrachtungen eines Unpolitischen* (Stockholmer Gesamtausgabe, 1956), 576
46. *Gesammelte Werke in zwölf Bänden* (Frankfurt, 1960), XI, 819
47. *Das Gewissen*, 15 July 1928
48. 'Meine Zeit' (ed. cit. XI, 314)
49. *Der Zauberberg* (Frankfurt, 1964), 423
50. ed. cit. 425
51. ed. cit. 421
52. ed. cit. 648
53. ed. cit. 453
54. *Goethe und Tolstoi* (*Adel des Geistes*, 1945, 274)
55. *Der Zauberberg*, ed. cit. XIV
56. Friedrich Schlegel, *Kritische Schriften* (Munich, 1956), 270
57. *Gesammelte Werke* ed. cit. XI, 407
58. *Der Zauberberg*, ed. cit. XIV
59. *Als wär's ein Stück von mir* (Vienna, 1966), 324
60. 'Der Weg der Liebe', 1918 (*Krieg und Frieden*, Zurich, 1946, 93)
61. *Zarathustras Wiederkehr* (*Krieg und Frieden*, ed. cit. 115, 145)
62. ed. cit. 10
63. ed. cit. 194
64. *Gesammelte Dichtungen* III (Frankfurt, 1957), 236
65. *Zarathustras Wiederkehr* (ed. cit. VII, 212)
66. 'Gedanken zu Dostoiewskis "Idiot"' (ed. cit. VII, 182)
67. *Ein Stückchen Theologie* (1932: ed. cit. VII, 393)
68. 'Hermann Hesse Zum 70. Geburtstag' (*Gesammelte Werke* ed. cit. X, 519)
69. In a letter written in February 1949 (ed. cit. VII, 683)
70. Broch, *Briefe von 1929 bis 1951* (Zurich, 1957), 18
71. see R.H. Thomas, 'The Novels of Hermann Broch' (*The Cambridge Journal* VI, 1953, 596)
72. *Huguenau oder die Sachlichkeit* (*Die Schlafwandler*, Zurich, 1931/2, 673)
73. *Tagebücher, Aphorismen, Essays und Reden* (Reinbek, 1955), 226
74. Letter to G. (*Prosa, Dramen, späte Briefe*, Reinbek, 1957), 726
75. *Der Mann ohne Eigenschaften* (Reinbek, 1952), 757
76. Op. cit. 16
77. Op. cit. 19
78. Op. cit. 1645
79. *Der Abituriententag* (Zurich, 1928), 34
80. *Verdi* (Frankfurt, 1955), 6
81. Alma Mahler Werfel, *And the Bridge is Love* (London, 1959), 154f
82. G. Janouch, *Gespräche mit Kafka* (Frankfurt, 1951), 14
83. 'Brief an den Vater' (*Hochzeitsvorbereitungen auf dem Lande und andere Prosa aus dem Nachlass*, Frankfurt, 1953, 196)
84. *ibid.* 216
85. *ibid.* 203
86. E. Canetti, *Der andere Prozess: Kafkas Briefe an Felice Bauer* (Munich, 1969)
87. see E. Heller, *The Disinherited Mind* (Cambridge, 1952), 181

PART TWO

CHAPTER SIX

'Ein Volk, Ein Reich, Ein Führer': Society and Culture in Hitler's Germany 1933–1945

i. The Nazi takeover

FROM the beginning of his political life Hitler stood for war—war against the values of European civilisation. His transformation of values within Germany itself has been seen as tantamount to a revolution: Hermann Rauschning called it, in the title of a famous book published in 1939, a 'revolution of destruction'. But when did Hitler's revolution—or war—start?

His formal coronation as undisputed master of Germany took place on 30 January 1933, when the President of the Republic, the aged Field-Marshal Hindenburg, formally offered him the post of Chancellor. The days leading up to this moment of Hitler's triumph were filled with uncertainty and political intrigue, and until the support, or at least the tolerance, of the two most powerful conservative groups bent on destroying the republic was assured, viz., Hugenberg's Deutschnationale Volkspartei and the army, no one could tell which way the manoeuvring for power would go. Later the Nazis built into their propaganda an extravagant tale of how Hitler had been swept to power on an irresistible wave of popular demand, but the reality was very different. A large popular following he certainly had before 1933, but the Nazi party never came near to winning a majority in a free election. The forces that had desperately tried to save the Republic, like those—not necessarily the same—that now opposed Hitler, were hopelessly divided among themselves. Once the parties of the right agreed to admit him as a partner in government—for that is what they thought they were doing—his position became unassailable. The collapse of the Weimar Republic was a political inevitability. Hitler's coming to power was not.

In the broader sense, however, and especially for an understanding of the social history of the Third Reich, one needs to look back some three years from January 1933, to the aftermath of the Wall Street crash of October 1929. This, coinciding with the death of Stresemann that same month, finally shattered the brief prosperity of the Weimar Republic and led to the social conditions in which National Socialism thrived. Hitler's own political career, of course, goes back a further decade, but it is in the years 1930 to 1933 that one sees most clearly the aims of his war, or his revolution (in reality it was both), the methods by which he was to wage it, and the circumstances that so disastrously contributed to his success.

In the last days of October 1929 the New York stock market collapsed and panic selling swept across the United States. In a matter of months the effects of the depression hit Germany, as the Americans called in the short-term loans that had provided the foundation of Germany's short-lived economic recovery, and as world trade sharply contracted. The country faced bankruptcy, exactly as Stresemann said it would, if America were to find herself in an economic crisis. The so-called Great Depression was a world phenomenon, but it was bound to strike soonest and hardest at a country like Germany, so heavily dependent on foreign capital and with so closely integrated an economic system of employers' and workers' organisations within a state-controlled pattern of social progress and welfare.

Ironically it was these very features, the pillars of the post-inflation recovery, that through their centralised power and their rigidity now proved to be the country's heaviest liabilities. Spending power dried up, factories and businesses went bankrupt, possessions and property were sold in desperation. Above all unemployment began to rise alarmingly. The official figures of unemployed—that is, those registered as such, excluding those on part time, or unemployed but not registered—show a total of 1,320,000 for September 1929; a year later it was over 3 million, by September 1931 nearly $4\frac{1}{2}$ million, and in the first two months of 1932, over 6 million. This was the figure that Hitler inherited when he became Chancellor in January 1933.

What lay behind these cold statistics in social terms was experienced by Carl Zuckmayer, one of the many intellectuals and artists who either in contemporary accounts or later reminiscences recorded the life that surrounded them at this time:

In every district of Berlin through which one passed, but especially in the eastern and northern suburbs, one saw long queues of wretched men in rags, undernourished, unhealthy, their faces pallid and swollen. They were the 'dole merchants', more and more of them as time went on, becoming a more and more pitiful sight as they queued up in front of the labour exchanges for their unemployment benefit, a sum which was scraped together by the state by increasing taxation, reducing civil service salaries and various other unpopular measures, and which in any case was never quite sufficient for a man to live on, let alone a family. Summer and winter, in rain and cold, there they stood, the collars of their shabby jackets turned up and their numb hands plunged into their pockets.

They were a lamentable lot. They had lost their so-called Berlin sense of humour long ago, when the butter and the coal ran out, and they hardly had the strength to raise a rumpus or swear at the man behind the counter when he put up the shutters, or when the rumour went round that while they had been queuing for their hunger pay, the price of potatoes had gone up again. The situation in Berlin was repeated all over Germany, as rows of men lined up in front of labour exchanges, cooperative shops, derelict coal mines, and factories on part-time working. There were more than six million such men in Germany in the years between 1931 and 1933, men condemned to do nothing but wait in despair, full of resentment towards the world they lived in, towards the state that just about managed to keep them alive, towards themselves and their own patience.[1]

This sullenness had settled over large sections of the population. For the men in the dole queues were not just factory workers and labourers but also shop assistants—the caustically dubbed *Stehkragen-proletariat* so tellingly portrayed in Fallada's novel *Kleiner Mann, was nun?*—clerks, the white collar middle class as a whole, those who had suffered most in the inflation of a mere handful of years ago. And although those higher up the social ladder were cushioned against the worst economic effects of the depression, the loss of business confidence, together with a now even stronger sense of disillusionment with democratic republicanism, produced a strange solidarity of resentment across almost the whole social scale. There was no dearth of things, or individuals, to receive the blame: the Treaty of Versailles and the vindictive allies; the ineffectiveness of government and the corruption of political parties; the ruthless self-centredness of industrialists and landowners; the Communists, preaching the class war and aggravating the divisions in an already divided society; and, of course, the Jews.

Here, among the economically and intellectually depressed middle classes, lay the richest raw material which Hitler was to exploit. The 'little man', with his family pride, his sense of responsibility and his inward-looking attitudes, shrank from the violence of the Communists, who dangled one type of radical solution before his eyes, and could not be induced to join in the 'brotherhood of the proletariat'. The KPD, like the Communist Party in all non-communist countries, rested on heavy, yet far from total, working-class support at one end and a small but vigorous cadre of intellectuals at the other, with an empty middle ground between them. Anxious to emphasise their independence of the former, the lower middle classes had no access to the world of the latter, which in any case they regarded with suspicion. Add to this petty bourgeoisie the considerable number of disaffected social democrats, the non-communist working class, and above all the entire range, from proletariat to intelligentsia, of those for whom the unity and prosperity of the nation was the only conceivable foundation for personal and social well-being, and one sees how suited the people were to a takeover by a nationalist ideology.

Ernst Toller knew that his people had not changed. 'Everywhere the same lunatic belief', he wrote in 1933 in *Eine Jugend in Deutschland*,

that a man, a leader, a Caesar, a Messiah will suddenly appear and work a miracle; will arise and take upon his shoulders all responsibility for the future; will master life, banish fear, abolish misery, create a new people, a new kingdom of splendour; will emerge with supernatural powers to transform the old Adam into a new man.[2]

This was the cue for Hitler's entry. From the beginning he drew the discontents of all sections of the population into a single national context in the spirit of his later slogan 'Ein Volk, ein Reich, ein Führer'. The need to capture the masses for any policy of political revolution was a conclusion he had already drawn from history in *Mein Kampf*. From this conclusion it followed that the proper scene of a popular movement was not parliament but the factory and the street.[3] 'The average German, who felt himself let down by everybody and everything, seemed to find in the Nazi leaders' insatiable appetite for violence and power some slight hope of better times to come', wrote Carl Zuckmayer.[4] It quickly became more than a 'slight hope'.

Hitler knew that the way to capture a man's allegiance lay through his group ties: the ties of family, profession, political party, religion, local community, nationality. Without such ties the individual is lost. Hitler therefore set about undermining them as quickly as possible. Having first induced a state of bewilderment and insecurity, he supplanted the group pattern he had destroyed with an entirely new structure. Traditional social groups lost their place to the agencies and organisations of the new Nazi state. For once the familiar ties had been broken, the individual was lost in uncertainties, his moral sense weakened, his personality put in question.

With the individual reduced to this state of confusion, partly by the tactics of violence, partly by those of infiltration, Hitler now suddenly presents himself as a Messiah with a new pattern of life—and the people rise to him. On the one hand they thus deliver themselves into the hands of the terrorism by which the Nazi régime keeps itself in power; on the other they have acquired a personal loyalty to the Führer who has led them out of the land of darkness.

To be sure, many traditional group ties had in any case weakened through the 1920s, and bodies with a firm, not to say authoritarian, hold on their members—the Roman Catholic Church, for instance—were harder to penetrate. More votes were cast for Hitler in Protestant than in Catholic areas. But it remains the achievement of Hitler's uncanny psychological genius to have played on the German people's inadequacies and fears with such diabolical skill that they stood and watched—some did more—while books were burned, intellectuals hounded, Jews beaten up, the processes of justice flouted, and all the other inhumanities committed in their name. 'Formerly,' said Franz Gürtner proudly, Hitler's longstanding comrade and Reich Minister of Justice, 'we used to ask: "Is this right or wrong?" Today we ask: "What would the Führer say?"'

So when 35 million Germans—about 83 per cent of the electorate—went to the polls on 24 September 1930, 6½ million of them voted for Hitler, making the National Socialists second only to the Social Democrats in the Reichstag. After the elections of 1928 the Nazis had held 12 seats against the Social Democrats' 153; now they held 107, to the Social Democrats' 143. The Communists increased their representation from 54 deputies in 1928 to 77 in 1930, and now became the third largest party. The parties of the extreme right and extreme left, both of which openly declared their intention to overthrow the republican régime, had thus gained ground dramatically at the expense of the middle-class parties of the centre. Especially significant, Hugenberg's Deutschnationale Volkspartei, hitherto the rallying-point for right-wing nationalist opinion, and which in all parliaments of the Weimar Republic, except the very first in 1919, had been second only to the Social Democrats in strength, lost wellnigh half the votes it had won in the elections of two years before, and now had a mere 41 deputies.

'A black day for Germany', wrote Count Herry Kessler in his diary on the day after the elections. 'National Socialism is a fever belonging to these dying days of the German petty bourgeoisie, but the virus can cause decades of misery. There is no salvation for this class. But in its death-throes it can bring untold suffering upon Europe.'[5]

Hugenberg's chain of newspapers had given Hitler's activities prominence throughout Germany, but now, for all his wealth and influence, this formidable power-seeker, a man over 20 years older than Hitler, found himself playing second fiddle to the figure whom old President Hindenburg called 'this Bohemian private'. With other industrialists, politicians, generals and former comrades, Hugenberg joined the long list of men who thought they could use Hitler for their own purposes, only to find that it was he who was using them. After 1933, Hugenberg even lost his throne as emperor of the German Press to Max Amann, a sergeant comrade of Hitler's from the Great War, whose control, spearheaded by the *Völkischer Beobachter*, covered 82 per cent of the German Press by 1942. The 1930 elections made Hitler a figure of international importance, and except for the adherents of the radical left, such few voices of doubt, let alone of condemnation, as were heard outside Germany at the time, carried little weight. Lord Rothermere and the Marquess of Londonderry were not the only public figures, or the last, to greet Hitler as a welcome ally in the fight against international communism.

That the discontented masses whose support Hitler courted should have been won over is now not difficult to understand. More so is the apparent absence of any concerted intellectual opposition, apart from that of the Communists, at a time early enough to affect the course of events. The Harzburg Front of 1931, an alliance of Hugenberg's Nationalists, the *Stahlhelm* and the Nazis, stung young trade unionists into joining with the socialist *Reichsbanner* organisation to form their rival 'Eiserne Front' later the same year, but as Zuckmayer, himself a member of the 'Eiserne Front', put it, it was a matter of too little and too late. The masses were more impressed by the free soup dispensed by the brown-shirted Storm Troopers than by talk of democratic freedom and the rule of law.

Before September 1930 intellectuals could hardly be persuaded to take Hitler seriously as a political force. How, they laughed, could such a ridiculous upstart, with his execrable German and his bombastic slogans, make any headway in a country that set such store by the values of education and learning? That he did, shows yet again that fatal gulf in German society between those who gave philosophies and ideals to the nation and those willing, and able, to convert these ideas into political reality. Hitler was only one of those who saw how to exploit this gulf, but because his grasp of crude popular realities and expectations was surer than that of his rivals, his success became that much more irresistible and more complete.

Besides this, as the conductor Bruno Walter recalled, 'there were wide circles in Germany that considered the party's cruel actions and outrageous utterances, even its anti-Semitism, symptoms of a short-lived youthful complaint affecting an inherently sound movement.'[6] As late as the spring of 1934 Baron Neurath nonchalantly said to Hermann Rauschning: 'Let it run its course. In five years nobody will remember it.'[7] And when Hitler gave his long foreign policy speech to the Reichstag on 21 May 1935—by which time, as Churchill later wrote in *The Gathering Storm* (London, 1948, 148), 'there was now little hope of averting war or of postponing it by a trial of strength equivalent to war'—even Count Harry Kessler was able to write: 'This speech is a great feat of statesmanship, and its 13 points offer a foundation which, if developed with honourable intentions, could guarantee peace in Europe for decades to come.'[8]

Even after it had become abundantly clear what Nazi rule would amount to, influential men of culture, otherwise so outspoken in their disagreements, found nothing to say. Karl Kraus, whose sharp tongue spared nothing or nobody of whom he disapproved, had failed to see Hitler for what he was, and now that it was too late to check the infernal machine, he looked the other way and vented his spleen on the leading Berlin literary critic of the 1920s, Alfred Kerr—whose writings were burned by the Nazis in 1933. 'Zu Hitler fällt mir gar nichts ein', runs Kraus' well-known remark. It was not a joke—it was a tragedy.

But as well as capturing the attention of the malcontents who could readily be encouraged to vote for the liquidation of the republic, Hitler also produced a motley collection of optimistic principles and promises which appealed to those, intellectuals and artists among them, who looked for some kind of positive programme for the nation's recovery. One needs to recall that figures like Hans and Sophie Scholl, for instance, who later died for their organisation of anti-Hitler activity among students in Munich, were at first carried along by his movement. Lack of experience in the working of democratic political institutions, and a hasty rejection of their value when this lack of experience led to their initial ineffectuality, left a fertile soil for the growth of anti-democratic alternatives. When the alternative was decked out with appeals to national loyalty, to the singleminded revival of a truly 'German' ethic of personal and corporate life, and to an unconditional, almost mystic faith in Hitler's vocation to restore the German *Volk* to its destined greatness, people were in little doubt that they had found what they wanted.

After military defeat, the collapse of the November 1918 re-volution, and the failure of republican government to hold the nation together, let alone lead it forwards—and all this in the space of 12 years—a slogan like 'Das Dritte Reich' could not but stir imag-ination. Here lay the promise of a return—not a novelty, be it noted, but the restoration of a reality of German history—to the conceptions of the First German Empire of Charlemagne and the Second German Empire of Bismarck. Who would not respond to the challenge to take his place in this line of succession?

Two weeks after the elections of September 1930 the new Reichstag met. 'Throughout the afternoon and evening', wrote Count Harry Kessler in his diary for that day,

there were massive demonstrations by the Nazis rampaging down the Leipziger Strasse and smashing the windows of the Jewish department stores like Wertheim's and Grünfeld's. In the evening they gathered in the Potsdamer Platz, shouting 'Deutschland erwache!', 'Juda verrecke!', 'Heil, Heil!' and so forth, while the police, in trucks and on horseback, kept breaking them up. At half-past eleven I went down the Leipziger Strasse as far as the Friedrichstrasse and stood in front of the Fürstenhof Hotel for three-quarters-of-an-hour. Most of the Nazis demonstrating there were teenage rowdies who howled and ran for dear life the moment the police advanced with their batons. Never have I seen so many out-and-out riff-raff in this part of the city. In front of the Fürstenhof I noticed one or two of them carrying out a regular patrol—evidently unemployed youths paid to do so. One marched backwards and forwards between the Prinz-Albrecht-Strasse and the Potsdamer Platz like a regular sentry. Every now and then a band of youths, pursued by policemen, would rush past in confusion—poor devils who had been paid two or three marks from Thyssen's coffers to demonstrate their patriotic loyalty.[9]

In these Reichstag elections of 1930 the National Socialists won 18 per cent of the votes cast. In July 1932 they doubled this to 37 per cent, which gave them 230 seats in the Reichstag, almost twice as many as their only serious remaining rivals, the Social Democrats. That the Communists, as in 1930, also increased their representation, thus emphasising once more the inclination of the electorate towards extreme solutions to the problem of national recovery, now mattered little in parliamentary terms. Indeed, the Catholic Centre Party also gained ground between 1930 and 1932 during the chancellorship of their leader Brüning—a development of not the slightest political consequence.

Brüning had increased government control over industry and the business world in order to give a centralised impulse to the nation's economic revival, but he had also presided over an increase in the number of unemployed from $2\frac{1}{4}$ million to 6 million. When, for reasons still not fully understood, he was dismissed by President Hindenburg in May 1932, the debonair Franz von Papen, also from the Centre Party, became Chancellor with the weight of the landowners, the industrialists and many Reichswehr officers behind him. Papen was to unwittingly make Hitler's task all the easier by adopting almost grotesquely reactionary policies, like the abolition of the social security scheme, and by branding the Social Democrats, the Zentrum and any other party with the slightest vestige of liberalism as 'anti-patriotic' and 'morally corrupting'. He was also to join Hugenberg and the generals in being forced to realise that, far from bending Hitler to their own purposes, they were forced into the subordinate roles which, with the masses at his back, he was prepared to concede to them.

During the weeks that led up to the Reichstag elections of July 1932, it became ever clearer what Hitler had meant when he said, after his success in the 1930 elections, that Parliament was only a means to an end—the end being 'the liberation of the German people'—and that the National Socialists 'were not a parliamentary party on principle . . . [but] under constraint, by compulsion, a compulsion that is the constitution'.[10] That his aim was to destroy democracy in Germany became doubly plain in his election campaign of 1932.[11] In *Mein Kampf*, barely 10 years earlier, he had written: 'Present-day Western democracy is the forerunner of Marxism, which latter is inconceivable without the former. It is democracy that provides this world-wide disease with the soil from which it spreads like a canker.'[12] The terror tactics, the street battles, the persecutions and the murders which now became an even more prominent part of the Nazi stock-in-trade, represented the fulfilment of a proud electoral promise. Hitler's success has often been called that of a mere opportunist, capitalising on the blindness, indifference and faint-heartedness of others. But some of the more hateful aspects of his policies have a hideous consistency.

The Nazi ideology, moreover, like the National Socialist programme—the creation of the Grossdeutsches Reich, the persecution of the Jews and so on—was an open book, there for all to read, there for millions to give their assent to and to vote for. It was no bland façade, concealing unstated purposes and devious designs, but a brutally explicit statement of intent, a blue print for action, the action of an iron fist in an iron glove.

The veneer of tactical legality with which Hitler scrupulously covered the political activities of the Nazis right down to the moment when Hindenburg offered him the chancellorship on 30 January 1933, was a valuable possession. The failure of his attempted *Putsch* in 1923 had taught him one valuable lesson, viz., that to try to seize power through revolution would only end in another disaster. There were, however, those within the ranks of his party who had nothing in their heads but the overthrow of the republic by violence, the most powerful of these being the S.A., (*Sturmabteilungen*), the brown-shirted private army formed by the Nazis in 1921 under the leadership of Ernst Röhm. To the S.A., radical adherents of the principle that actions speak louder than words, control of the state meant not control of parliament but control of the streets, and the gang warfare that became a feature of life in Berlin and other cities between 1930 and 1933 reflected the S.A.'s way of doing things. When one Horst Wessel, an S.A. roughneck and pimp, was murdered in a prostitute's flat, Goebbels' propaganda machine built him up into a martyr who had died in the name of the Fatherland. The Bülow-Platz in front of the Volksbühne in Berlin was rechristened the Horst-Wessel-Platz (today it is the Rosa-Luxemburg-Platz), and some miserable verses he had written were converted into the Horst-Wessel-Lied, a marching song which became almost a second German national anthem in the Third Reich. Such were the saints in the Nazi calendar.

At the same time Hitler needed to win over the army, whose relations with the S.A. were far from cordial, and this required him to play down the theme of revolution and reiterate that of the legal transfer of power. That he succeeded in uniting behind his leadership these and other potentially dissident groups, like Himmler's black-shirted S.S., while also persuading big business to put more and more money into the party coffers, must regrettably be recorded as the reward of remarkable political skill. As a result of this balancing act he was able after 1933 to launch his 'national revolution' from a postion of (nominally) legally acquired authority. The 'revolu-tionaries' then came into their own; for those worried about 'legality' it was now too late to do anything.

After political manoeuvring had produced a vote of no-confidence in Papen's government only a few weeks after it had taken office, another general election in November 1932 virtually reproduced the results of four months earlier. The National Socialists did lose 34 seats but they remained far and away the biggest party, and the temporary gains made by the Communists at the one extreme and Hugenberg's Deutschnationale Volkspartei at the other had little consequence other than an intensification of the political in-fighting that preceded the appointment of General Kurt von Schleicher as Chancellor at the beginning of December. Schleicher had a vision of an alliance between the army and the Left—the Left even to include the more socialist of the National Socialists. How realistic Schleicher's vision was, became clear when, less than two months later, Hitler emerged from an audience with President Hindenburg as legally appointed Chancellor of the German Reich.

It was not long before Germany, and the world, saw what Hitler in power would set out to do. The Reichstag elections of March 1933 brought the National Socialists 43.9 per cent of the votes, the Social Democrats 18.3 per cent, the Communists 12.3 per cent and the Catholic Centre Party 11.7 per cent. Hugenberg's Nationalists fell to 8 per cent, and the remaining parties dropped out of the reckoning. This, the last free election in Germany until 1949, still left the Nazis short of an absolute majority. But with the support of the Nationalists, and since, being branded as responsible for the Reichstag fire of a few weeks earlier, the Communists were prevented from taking their seats, the Nazis knew that their power to govern was assured.

Much of German big business had been supporting Hitler for some time, and now, out of self-interest, employers' organisations as a whole put their weight behind him. More significantly, workers began to desert their trade unions and join the Nazi party, and the unions themselves anxiously declared their loyalty to the new Führer. Then, the day after the great May Day rally in Berlin, summoned by the Nazis with eager union support, union offices all over the country

were broken into by troops of the S.A. and S.S., union funds were
confiscated, union leaders arrested and beaten up, and a new German
Labour Front proclaimed, under the direct control of the party and
the state. The Reichstag fire of February 27, engineered by Goering
and Goebbels, had provided Hitler with the 'evidence' to discredit
the Communists. It also enabled him to have the President sign, the
day after the fire, an emergency decree which, nominally 'for the
protection of the People and the State', suspended many of the
personal liberties guaranteed by the Weimar Constitution and gave
him the power to deal as he liked with any protesters or querulants.[13]
By the summer, six months after coming to power, Hitler had
virtually achieved his revolutionary goal of destroying the constitutional state.

In political terms he did this through his 'Gesetz zur Behebung der
Not von Volk und Reich', the so-called Enabling Law, passed by the
Reichstag on 23 March 1933, which gave him power to govern by
decree (these were the precise terms also used in the Enabling Act
passed by the Reichstag in 1923 at the time of the inflation). The
result that Goering, President of the Reichstag, announced at the end
of the debate was 441 votes for the bill (the combined votes of Nazis,
Nationalists, the Catholic Centre Party and a few smaller groups),
and 94 against (the Social Democrats). Hitherto only the President,
under the famous Article 48 of the Weimar constitution, had had the
power to issue emergency decrees at the instance of the Chancellor.
Now, by their vote, the Reichstag handed Hitler the legal power to
rule by means of such decrees himself, independent both of President
and Reichstag. Article 48 had been conceived as a protection of the
constitution against those who, in the immediate post-war years,
made no secret of their desire to overthrow the Republic and could
not be contained by the democratic processes of parliament. The
administration of this Article now passed, through the will of
parliament—the cruellest irony of all—to the man who had devoted
his entire political career to the destruction of parliamentary
government.

Throughout the 12 years that Hitler's 'Tausendjähriges Reich'
lasted, the state of emergency declared after the Reichstag fire
remained in force, and the Enabling Law provided the only legal
framework necessary for Nazi rule. The Weimar constitution was
never formally abrogated, new laws being simply created as and
when Hitler chose. The Germans' respect for continuity, and for
doing things 'in the proper way', was greatly reassured by the
provision of this legal basis. Although many of those with senior
postions in public service may, given the patent evidence of Nazi

methods, have been apprehensive about the measures that would follow, they had already resigned themselves to the inevitability of the Nazi revolution and were disposed, with German conscientiousness, to contribute their mite to its administrative efficiency.

Count Hermann Keyserling, author of *Das Reisetagebuch eines Philosophen*, was shattered by the state of Germany during the revolutionary months following Hitler's appointment as Chancellor. At a meeting with Count Harry Kessler in Paris in May Keyserling said that.

notwithstanding his experiences in the Russian Revolution, the past three months had been the hardest in his life. To compare the Russian Revolution with the German Revolution was like comparing an elephant with a flea. The National Socialist coup, he said, was total revolution, the reduction of everyone to a common level, the virtual elimination of class-distinction. The Bolsheviks had replaced the old ruling class by a new one, the proletariat, whereas the Nazis were doing away with all classes . . . A petty bourgeois mentality prevailed, the dictatorship of anti-intellectualism. The intellectual, the artist, the writer all counted for nothing. This was precisely what the philistines had always wished for, and they found it an ideal situation. That was the reason why 70 per cent of the German people were so enthusiastic about Hitler and stood solidly behind him. This régime would therefore *remain*.[14]

Unhappily, but irresistibly, Keyserling was right. There are moments—an unwelcome but palpable historical truth—when a form of totalitarianism does provide a solution to the desperate problems of a society in crisis. The people may even greet such a solution with enthusiasm, grateful for its purposiveness and its restoration of stability, mindless of its implications and its aftermath. The eve of the National Socialist nightmare in Germany was such a moment.

ii. Volk and Führer

From the time when, in the last decades of the eighteenth century, the politico-cultural entity of modern Germany began to crystallise, two forces had been in conflict: liberalism and nationalism. The former, building on Enlightenment ideals of a rationally ordered society and the pursuit of humane values, was borne by men like Lessing, Herder, Goethe, Schiller, Wilhelm von Humboldt and other apostles of the individual and corporate ideal of *Humanität*. The latter, stemming from Herder's concept of the *Volk* as the source of all true culture, as the organic unit that is both point of departure and point of return for those that it embraces, was carried into the nineteenth century by the Romantics, and given ever more urgent political expression from the Wars of Liberation down to the unification of Germany in 1871.

But well before 1871 it became clear that victory in the struggle between these two forces had gone to nationalism. It may be a matter for debate whether a powerful urge towards national unity can in any developing situation retain the values of personal freedom and political liberalism. Liberalism is by its nature centrifugal, whereas nationalism demands the canalisation of effort towards a single overriding end. The half-century of German history from the Congress of Vienna to the establishment of the Second Reich tells a plain story of the ineluctable erosion of liberal-democratic influence under the coalescent pressure of the drive towards nationhood. The Wars of Liberation may have liberated the German princes from the domination of Napoleon, but they did not liberate the German people from anything perceptible. Indeed, the Metternich-dominated restoration era which followed 1815 induced an even greater subjection of ruled to ruler than before. Germany was still basically an agricultural country, without substantial coal production or large-scale industry, without a *Bürgertum*, and without an intellectual life that reached beyond the restricted circle of thinkers and artists communicating with fellow-thinkers and artists and with the members of the aristocratic milieu that offered them patronage. Moreover, when belated industrialisation did set in, it was seen in many quarters as a dubious blessing, a threat to the romantic vision of a *Volk* united by a mystic bond of *Geist* and chthonic values.

Thus when the new progressive ideas associated with the *Burschenschaften*, and spectacularly demonstrated at the Hambacher Fest in 1832, came to circulate, few outside the ranks of university students, together with a handful of progressive professors, were either equipped or disposed to assess them. The National Assembly that met in the Paulskirche in Frankfurt in 1848, led by some of the most distinguished minds of the time—Uhland, Anastasius Grün, Jakob Grimm, Gervinus—was, for all its reformatory zeal, predominantly monarchist. It quickly exhausted the patience of the voluble radicals who called for actions rather than words, but nor could it hold the allegiance of a constitutionally-minded liberal majority. Its ideals were noble, its paper programmes unexceptionable, but to expect it to know how to put its ideas into practice, or where to find men to do so, was to ask the impossible. 'It had to teach dancing to a pupil who could not even stand.'[15] By the time Bismarck became the German dancing-master, the pupils were being made to stand for rather different things.

Once given explicit political form, national unity became an almost sacred principle in the individual German's philosophy of life, cherished equally, however divergent the reasons, by peasant and intellectual, Junker and shopkeeper. As such it absorbed many of the conflicting interests which, in a context where a unified national political structure was a long-established reality, would have attracted their own separate followings. And as in any community that has just given public expression, through a declaration, a constitution, a bill of rights or some similar gesture, to its new-found conviction of togetherness, the primary need was felt to be to emphasise what united, not what divided. Only thus could the skeleton of the new corporate entity be given its covering of flesh and blood, and the new creature prove its individual identity in the company of its foreign fellows.

The preoccupation with wholeness, with unity in diversity, with the reconciliation of opposites, recurs time and again in German culture in the nineteenth and twentieth centuries. Goethe's concept of *Polarität* within the individual one-ness of nature; the Romantics' vision of a transcendental 'chaos' embracing the divergent forces of the universe and breaking down the artificial barriers between life, art, philosophy and religion; the final term, synthesis, in the dialectical thought-pattern of Hegel, later of Karl Marx; the fusion of values sought, in their different ways, by poets from Hölderlin to Rilke, and the restoration of the unity of *Geist* and *Leben*, mind and nature—these accompany the social and political movements that lead to the unification of Germany under Prussia in 1871. And the unification, once achieved, in turn helps to perpetuate the modes of thought and feeling that had brought it about, nourishing the confidence, even elation, with which the nation went to war in 1914.

Even the events of the war itself did little to sap this confidence. The agencies that stood for national unity, such as the army, industrialists, the financiers, politicians of conservative-nationalist outlook, leave alone rabble-rousing demagogues like the Nazis, found willing listeners after 1918 to a message of opposition to the new régime of social democracy. Party politics meant divisiveness, and a national parliament of party representatives was a forum for the public display of disagreements. Moreover from the National Assembly of 1919 onwards government was only possible by coalition, with the bargaining and the compromising that this involved—and preparedness to compromise had never been a striking feature of German public life. Compromise was branded as a betrayal of principles, and democratic government therefore as undesirable and un-German.

As the depression of the early 1930s followed the disillusionments of the 1920s, the republic was seen to be dying from inner dissension. The need of the moment could be plausibly presented as the restoration of strong control from the centre: this would not only bring the return of the consolidated greatness of the nation but also revive the confidence of the individual in his own future and in the destiny of the *Volk*.

Volk, völkisch, Volksgemeinschaft—the words had a hallowed ring. Their meaning lies within the field described by Richard Wagner: 'The *Volk* is the embodiment of all those who feel a common need.'[16] Excluded from this community in Wagner's terms—and Wagner was one of Hitler's great heroes, as much as a writer and pseudo-philosopher as a composer of 'Germanic' works of art—are those, like the rich (Hitler added the intellectuals), who choose to emphasise their independent interests and their exclusiveness, and those, like the Jews, whose dissipated and therefore inferior culture denies them access to the national heritage.

As an inspirational abstraction, the concept of *Volk* was probably the most effective weapon available to Hitler in his crusades for solidarity and loyalty during the Nazi era. The nature of the weapon, and the use he intended to make of it, were no secret. Pages of *Mein Kampf* are filled with descriptions of the racially pure 'völkischer Staat' of his dreams which 'reflects the innermost will of Nature' and must inspire any nation that has pretensions to a role as *Herrenvolk*.[17] Through this inner necessity, furthermore, a cadre of experts will emerge, natural agents of authority, a Darwinian *Führerauslese* not subject to the ill-informed, irresponsible pressure of democratic opinion. Authority is central and indivisible, and the realisation of the full powers of the *Volk* derives from the abandonment of parliamentary processes, with their talk of votes and majorities, for the exercise of singleminded, unquestioned leadership.

'A movement which, at a time of majority rule, is completely and utterly committed to the *Führergedanke* and the responsibility that this entails, will with mathematical certainty overcome the conditions of the past and emerge victorious.'[18] Thus Hitler in 1924, visualising the future role of the National Socialist movement. *Volk* and *Führergedanke* were inseparable, and, as many both before and after Hitler firmly believed, Germany could only be her true self as long as she was great. What, therefore, could be more natural, more in keeping with the true interests of the nation, than that the parliamentary bill giving Hitler *carte blanche* to restore this greatness should have explicitly invoked in its title the need to 'overcome the crisis in *Volk* and *Reich*'? The 'crisis', of course, was alleged to be the work of enemies of the state', who had to be disposed of. We shall only gain our freedom, said Hitler, when the enemies of freedom have been destroyed. In other words, a tyranny must be created in order to prevent a tyranny from arising. It is a syndrome that did not die with the Third Reich.

One of Hitler's most assiduously cultivated methods of drawing people's minds inwards and forcing them to see their activities as part of a central concerted effort was his elevation of physical work to the level of an almost sacred principle. The first formal expression of this principle in the organisation of the National Socialist state was the formation of the *Reichsarbeitsfront*, on the day after the Nazi-manipulated May Day rally in Berlin in 1933, when the trade unions were crushed at a single blow. Other manifestations were to be the Strength Through Joy tourist scheme, offering cheap mass holidays for the workers, and the conscription of young men and women into the *Arbeitsdienst* for compulsory work in factories or on the land. The *Hitlerjugend* and the *Bund Deutscher Mädel* also had the worship of work built into their constitution.

From the beginning the cult of physical labour made great play with studied informalities which could be interpreted as proof of the régime's 'common touch'. Hitler moved freely among the workers at their factory benches in a way no Brüning or Papen or Schleicher would have done, and shipyard workers shared the ceremonial platform with him when he launched a new ship. *Arbeit macht frei* and *Arbeit adelt* ran the Nazi slogans. The workers were wooed with public declarations that their labours were equal to the skills of the white-collar bourgeoisie or the achievements of the intelligentsia, so that 'socialism' could be seen to have obliterated false distinctions of class and status in the name of a 'national'philosophy. Indeed, upward social mobility did increase strikingly in the Nazi era compared with the years of the Weimar Republic.[19] In the same breath, however, one has to record that these upward paths, above all within the areas of production and service controlled by the state, were only accessible to those who had proven their loyalty to the régime by at least becoming members of the NSDAP or one of its affiliated groups.

This is one of the many two-edged situations characteristic of the National Socialist state. On the one hand people saw order being brought into the country's economic life and found themselves offered a plan for the nation's political advancement. Through large public works programmes, (the most famous among them the plan for 7,000 miles of *Autobahn*,) through tax concessions and investment incentives for industries that contributed to national defence, and other measures contained in the Unemployment Act of June 1933, unemployment dropped from 6 million in January 1933 to 3.7 million in September of the same year. To be sure, the Papen government had already introduced plans to stimulate the economy, and by the time Hitler became Chancellor, the worst effects of the depression had begun to wear off, but without the Nazis' radical four-year plan of

June 1933 and the financial measures inspired by the legendary Dr Hjalmar Schacht, the national economy could not have recovered as it did. The Nazis were in fact far more successful in dealing with the unemployment problem than, for example, Britain and America, and the success could be seen by every German. 'Erst kommt das Fressen, dann kommt die Moral', sang Brecht in *Die Dreigroschenoper*. Hitler too knew that conversion was easier if he first filled the bellies of his potential converts.

On the other hand there was a price to be paid for this economic progress, a price paid in the currency of personal liberty and freedom of political expression. Membership of the Nazi party, 'voluntary' work for one or other of the party agencies, subjection of personal morality to the norms decreed by party headquarters, acceptance for oneself and one's family of the cultural and educational ideals distilled from the Nazi ideology—these were the conditions on which the livelihood of more and more people came to depend, as the grip of the state on the body and mind of each individual citizen grew tighter. Hitler's policy of *Gleichschaltung*—obedience to the demands of the state, conformity to the Nazi *Weltanschauung* on the part of all political, social, cultural and religious organs—ran on through the 1930s like a juggernaut. Either one fled while it was still possible, like many artists and left-wing intellectuals, many of them Jewish; or one was crushed beneath it as a voluntary or involuntary outsider, like the Jews who could not, and a handful of Churchmen who would not, flee. Or, with the 90 per cent that were left, one took one's appointed place on the juggernaut as it careered along its destructive path, savagely purposeful when it started, utterly out of control at the end.

'I find the letters I receive from supporters of Hitler's Reich in Germany most extraordinary,' wrote Hesse to Thomas Mann in July 1933.

They all seem to have been written at a temperature of 100 degrees. . . There is an air of persecution and war, or happiness and heavy intoxication; they are the sounds of 1914 but without the naiveté which was then still possible. It will cost blood and other things besides—the whole thing has a thoroughly evil odour.[20]

The cult of *Volk* und *Reich* was inseparable from the cult of the Führer himself. Torchlight processions, parades, massed bands, mammoth open-air meetings, para-military displays—all the paraphernalia of National Socialist rallies was employed for the worship of Hitler the man. As events like the foundation of the NSDAP and the annual party rally at Nuremberg were added to the calendar of public holidays as the equals of Easter and Christmas, so too were Hitler's birthday and the day of his appointment as Chancellor.

Hitler's personality, his public image as a man remote from the prosaic life of the ordinary citizen yet understanding of humble human problems and solicitous for the well-being of all his people, especially the children, lent itself in a sinister way to the cultivation of the myth of a modern popular hero, the twentieth-century counterpart of the mighty figures of national history from Arminius and Dietrich von Bern to Charlemagne, Frederick the Great and Bismarck. He was a vegetarian, a teetotaller and a non-smoker; he had no family life; he was asexual and without human love. To this persona of monastic asceticism were added a legendary devotion to work and public service, a hazy but never entirely absent memory of the corporal who had been temporarily blinded in the Great War, and above all his uncanny intuition, an almost mystical insight into the psyche of his people, into what they wanted to hear and what would capture their devotion. His vehicle was not the written argument but the spoken—or rather, shouted—word, and the masses, spellbound by his charismatic appeal, placed their confidence in him whose shoulders would bear the cares of the nation: 'Der Hitler, der sorgt für uns!'

There are many eye-witness accounts of Hitler's demagogic power—too many for its menacing reality to be doubted or glossed over. Even those who maintained a defiant anti-Nazi stance, like the heroine of F.C. Weiskopf's novel *Lissy oder Die Versuchung*, could feel his sinister attraction and its effect on the multitude when he rose to address them:

With amazement Lissy watched the faces of the people around her change. They were the faces of dissatisfied people, of people used to being bullied, of unsuccessful people—people with narrow lips and dull, lifeless eyes, their faces wrinkled with bitterness and envy. But here a glow of anticipation came over them: in a moment the man down there would reveal to them how to become strong, happy and successful at a stroke.

She looked at Klaus. He was standing there, erect and radiant. Noticing that she was looking at him, he smiled at her, leaned across and whispered: 'Isn't it wonderful to become one with the community like this? Don't you feel yourself forced to get rid of all your selfish thoughts? Don't you find yourself forced to believe?'

She did not know what he meant, but she saw how happy and relaxed he was, and something of his happiness and the general excitement was sparked off in her too. She had the same sort of feeling as she had had many years ago when she was taken to the theatre for the first time: she felt elated and full of awesome anticipation.

The ultimate symbol of the identification of *Volk* with *Führer* was the now compulsory 'Heil Hitler!', styled by the Nazis, with breathless impudence, the 'German greeting'. Incredible as it now seems, the phrase itself, and the ritual arm movements that accompanied it, were adopted almost everywhere within a few months of Hitler's coming to power. Many must have been torn between conformity to the practice and their innermost hatred of all that the new régime stood for, but few dared to rebel, and those who did were quickly denounced and punished. By the same bizarre token, officials who were dealing, whether personally or by correspondence, with a social offender or other inferior member of the community, like a Jew or a gipsy, were at liberty to withhold their 'Heil Hitler', since the recipient was unworthy to share the national sentiments it symbolised. Mortal yet seemingly immortal, real yet seemingly mythical, the voice of one man yet seemingly the voice of the nation, the embodiment both of ideal and of action—small wonder that this demonic personality should hypnotise the masses and command the awe, the reverence, the fanatic devotion proper to a religious leader.

iii. The Nazi state

By the summer of 1933 virtually the whole structure of constitutional government in Germany had been dismantled. Political parties, the governments of the individual federal states, trade unions, industry—all had been subverted, banned, bribed or coerced into cooperation in the first stages of *Gleichschaltung*, the subsumption of all aspects of organised national life under the central directives of the National Socialist Party.

Even the churches failed to close their ranks. Some sections of the Protestant Church thought it might be possible to agree with the Nazis on the formation of a German State Church, and Bishop Otto Dibelius, for one, made compromising statements about Hitler as a great national leader even before he took office as Chancellor.[21] In the concordat it concluded with the National Socialists in the summer of 1933, the Vatican, for its part, gave formal recognition to the Nazi régime. Only a few weeks earlier the Catholic Centre Party had been forced to disband under the pressure of events—this, the party from which four of the 12 Chancellors of the Weimar Republic had come and which had consistently polled some 4 million votes throughout the 1920s.

Not that there were not individuals of all denominations who spoke out against brutality and tyranny. But unhappily there were more, both leaders and led, who followed the Nazi line on anti-Semitism, the persecution of Communists, the praise of national values and of military achievements like the occupation of the Rhineland in 1936, in return for permission to retain a modicum of control over their domestic ecclesiastical matters.

By a decree of 14 July 1933 all political parties in Germany were formally dissolved except the NSDAP. Actually there was nothing left to dissolve, for over the preceding weeks Hitler had driven the other parties one by one to the wall. The Social Democrats had had their entire funds and property confiscated, including the party newspaper *Vorwärts*. The leaders of the Bavarian People's Party had been arrested and the party had dissolved itself; its ally, the Centre Party, followed the next day. The Democrats (DDP), party of Max Weber and Friedrich Naumann, and the People's Party (DVP), once led by Stresemann, were now finally disbanded in the face of dwindling support. Most striking of all, Hugenberg's Nationalists (DNVP), for all their financial power and despite their support of Hitler in the coalition government, suffered the fate of all Nazi supporters whose usefulness Hitler considered had outlived itself, and were forced into liquidation. At the Reichstag elections of 12 November 1933 there was only one party to vote for, and almost 40 million voted for it—little short of 90 per cent of the electorate.

To show one's opposition, one could either deliberately spoil the ballot-paper or not vote at all: some 6 per cent did the former, between 4 and 5 per cent did the latter. Ten years ago Hitler had been in jail and the Nazis were a joke. Five years ago, they had gathered only 2.6 per cent of the votes. Three years ago it was still only 18.3 per cent, and the intelligentsia were still writing Hitler off as a fringe lunatic with no hope of popular support. In January 1933 Hitler became Chancellor; in July Germany became a one-party state; and by November 40 million people said 'Yes' to the man and his party. Political parties, the trade unions, the Churches—the very bases of communal organisation—had either capitulated or come to terms, their hold on people's loyalty exposed as a sham. Later the Germans—indeed, the whole world—could only look back on the years 1930–33 as an unbelievable nightmare, something of which one asks 'Did it really happen?'

As well as disposing of all the rival political parties, Hitler had to eliminate certain troublesome elements within his own party. The *Stahlhelm*, for example, which had been a useful agent of violence in the old days but had since become something of an embarrassment, was absorbed into the S.A., and the old *Freikorps* units were honourably disbanded with great ceremony. Street violence remained Hitler's basic method of impressing on the people the extent of his power, but the violence now needed to be centrally controlled.

Besides the thugs of the S.A. under Röhm, he had at his side the Gestapo, and in March 1933 Himmler, *Reichsführer SS* and subsequently chief of the Gestapo, ordered the first concentration camp to be built, at Dachau, for 'undesirable' elements in the population. The civil authorities, including the police, either refrained from taking action against violence or were intimidated into not doing so. The campaign against the Jews was intensified. And in all this the charismatic figure of Hitler carried the masses with him, firing the imagination of all who would see Germany restored to greatness, and offering a vision of power and success if the people would stand united behind him.

But violence feeds on violence, and when Hitler made it plain in the late summer of 1933 that the National Socialist revolution was over, and that its results must now be consolidated, the storm troops became disgruntled, feeling themselves deprived of their rightful spoils. For a whole year the struggle seethed, Röhm and his comrades looking for a second revolution, largely socialist, anti-capitalist in character, to supersede the first, Hitler trying to make sure that, if it came to the point, the Reichswehr would stand by him in defence of his 'legally' established régime. In any case, although the adjective 'socialist' belonged to the title of his party, and although there were men in the party from the early days, like Otto Strasser, to whom the anti-capitalist aspect was vital, Hitler himself was never a socialist. In the context of the NSDAP, 'socialism' stood for a form of loyalty to the state and submission to discipline akin to the socialism which Spengler equated with Prussian virtues in his *Preussentum und Sozialismus*.

The moment of truth came with the blood-bath of 29 June to 1 July 1934, when Röhm and the other leaders of the S.A., together with others considered a threat to Hitler's rule, were shot. The total number killed could have been as high as 400: most were executed by firing squad, some were assassinated in their own homes, others were reported by Goebbels to have 'committed suicide'. In one single moment of butchery Hitler had both removed that threat of any challenge to his leadership and made his position safe *vis-à-vis* the army. For now, by liquidating the S.A. while the army stood and watched, he could pose as the man who demonstrated that the army and its generals were the only legitimate military force in the land, a force with a right to its own autonomy and traditions. On 2 August 1934, the day old Hindenburg died, Hitler merged the two offices of Chancellor and President into one, and announced that he was now also Supreme Commander of the Armed Forces. The same day the army took a personal oath of loyalty to Hitler, not only as their new commander-in-chief but as 'Führer des deutschen Reiches und des deutschen Volkes'.

The revolution was over. Hitler was now the unchallengeable dictator of the country. 'The German people were simply not ready for parliamentary democracy', wrote the historian Friedrich Meinecke in 1933, as an epitaph to the Weimar Republic.[22] Moreover, if some had hesitated to believe it before, nobody could now doubt that Germany would be ruled not by law but by terrorism as long as Hitler's 'thousand-year Reich' remained.

Meinecke tells a wartime anecdote on this subject. Hitler was shown a little book which was to be distributed among the troops, urging them on in their fight against the Russians by reminding them of their 'German faith in God'. 'Religion? God?' retorted Hitler. 'Terror is the best God. You can see that from the Russians. Without terror they would not fight as they do.'[23]

As the power of the Gestapo grew, so the S.S. under Himmler was to acquire a military strength that undermined step by step the position of the generals. Everyone could see that the cloak of the 'legal revolution' had been thrown away. Yet through the mixture of threats, slogans and sophistries with which Goebbels' propaganda machine seduced the national conscience, and through political ignorance, social and political disillusionment, and a collective susceptibility to ideals often less noble than they sounded, the transition from social democratic constitutionality to Nazi dictatorship had been accepted with a remarkable *sang-froid*.

Whatever truth there may have been in the self-comforting phrase, heard in England in the 1930s and 1940s, 'It could never happen here', other countries were as deceived by Hitler's professions of peaceful intent as the Germans themselves. All politics is power politics, and many leaders besides Hitler had admired the techniques of *Realpolitik* described in Machiavelli's *The Prince*. But we are still left with the uncomfortable thoughts expressed by Meinecke at the end of World War II in *Die deutsche Katastrophe*, that classic work of national analysis which sees Nazism and the world-tragedy to which it led as a long-heralded outcome of the destructive cohabitation of unreconciled rational and irrational extremes within the German psyche:

It may well be true that in Hitlerism we have produced, not the only form of mass Machiavellian thinking but certainly the most dangerous. It is a question that will repeatedly exercise our minds, for we cannot but be shocked, time and again, by our sudden plunge from the heights of the Age of Goethe to the sordid depths of the Age of Hitler ... Bismarck's foundation of the Second Reich was a great historical achievement ... but we must admit today that the glory of that achievement has been allowed to conceal those points of weakness which became the source of later disaster, ... making Germany the more exposed to the dangers of *Realpolitik*.[24]

In themselves these events of 1933 and 1934 are of specific interest to the student of internal German politics or of the techniques by which a dictator can subvert the constitutional state and terrorise his way to power. But the reception of these events by the German people also reveals a great deal about the social and intellectual climate of the 1930s, which is to say, about the circumstances surrounding the writers and other artists of the time. The relationship between writer and public rests on a basis of reciprocity, like that between actor and audience, or preacher and congregation. This reciprocity takes a multitude of forms, each of which is a variable. The 12 years of Hitler's 'Tausendjähriges Reich' were a time of spiritual polarisation, of the barely credible coexistence of bewilderment and brutality, self-concern and hero-worship, resignation and aggressiveness, and above all life hung the iron hand of the state, controlling, 'co-ordinating', punishing. Many who could, left the country. Others chose to stay. And for them, as for their public, there was a scene of inescapable social realities against which life had to go on.

How far these events of 1933 and 1934, and the full nature of the social realities that accompanied them, were known outside Germany at the time is still a matter for debate. The foreign policy of other European powers cannot concern us here. But when one recalls the statement by Anthony Eden in the House of Commons in March 1936, after German troops had marched into the Rhineland: 'There is no reason to believe that the present German action implies a threat of hostilities'; and when one reviews the unhappy policy of appeasement, symbolised by Neville Chamberlain, that followed: then it is not hard to argue that the Allies bear a measure of responsibility for Hitler's continued domination, and that thoughts of resistance within Germany could not but fade in the face of the knowledge that little help could be expected from outside.

The political landmarks in the internal and external history of the Third Reich down to the beginning of the war in 1939 are familiar enough—the activities of the Gestapo and the building of more concentration camps; the intensification of the anti-Semitic campaign, with the Nuremberg Laws of 1935 which deprived Jews of their citizenship and forbade sexual relations between Jews and Aryans; the reintroduction of conscription, also in 1935, and the reoccupation of the Rhineland the following year; the Jewish pogroms; the annexation of Austria in March 1938, of the Sudetenland six months later, then of the 'rump' of Czechoslovakia a further six months afterwards; the Hitler-Stalin pact of August 1939, the German invasion of Poland a week later, and the outbreak of World War II.

It is a melancholy chronicle. To what extent there was within pre-war Germany, if not what could be graced with the description of an organised opposition of action, then at least a measure of expressed disapproval or uneasiness, is hard to assess. Individual writers of whose influence the Nazis were suspicious had their works banned, and the few surviving pockets of political resistance, like the circle round Ernst Niekisch and his national-revolutionary journal *Der Widerstand*—to which Ernst Jünger and his brother Friedrich Georg both subscribed articles—were one by one eliminated (Niekisch was arrested in 1937 and sentenced to life imprisonment). Rudolf Pechel continued to edit the *Deutsche Rundschau* until he was sent to a concentration camp in 1942 and the journal banned. Pechel survived the war and took over the *Deutsche Rundschau* again in 1946. His book *Deutscher Widerstand*, published in 1947, surveys the whole subject of resistance in the Third Reich, and stands alongside Fabian von Schlabrendorff's *Offiziere gegen Hitler* (1946) and other similar personal accounts on which later writers have based their investigations.

We know, for example, of a conspiracy in 1938 by a group of men, including General Ludwig Beck—a leader of the bomb plot against Hitler on 20 July 1944—and Dr Hjalmar Schacht, who had been Minister of Economics until the previous year, to capture Hitler after he had given the order to attack Czechoslovakia, and to bring him before a People's Court. We also know of plans for an army *coup* the following year, involving General Franz Halder, Chief of Staff, and his second-in-command General Heinrich von Stülpnagel (later prominent in the 1944 plot in Paris). Hitler himself made great capital out of his escape from what he claimed—after the failure of the attempted assassination of 20 July 1944—had been no fewer than seven attempts on his life, and posed as a man who led a charmed life so that he could carry out the will of Providence.

Such moments of contemplated rebellion, however, were mere drops in the ocean. Declarations of opposition by individual priests and pastors grew in number as time went on, and hundreds of Catholic and Protestant clergy died in concentration camps. Yet almost alone among the organised confessions before the war the small Bekenntniskirche of Martin Niemöller and Dietrich Bonhoeffer took an unyielding stand against anti-Semitism, the cult of *Volkstum* and the other principles of Nazi rule. Especially during the war a number of brave Catholic and Protestant bishops made outspoken condemnations of what the National Socialist state stood for, but when in 1945 representatives of the Protestant Church met with their fellows from western European countries and the United States, they spoke for all the German Churches in admitting that their opposition had been too late and too little, and that to this extent they must share in the German war-guilt.[25]

Members of religious bodies would sometimes find themselves in unexpected alliance with clandestine cells of resistance sustained by the KPD. Known Communists had been among the first to be imprisoned when the Nazis took power, and the destruction of a coherent central organisation within the country left the only possible initiative with individual local branches, contact between which became increasingly difficult and dangerous. In towns where their influence had always been considerable, like Berlin and Hamburg, and in the coal-mining areas of the Saar and the Ruhr, Communists were prominent among the instigators of absenteeism and various covert forms of go-slow among their fellow-workers, in an attempt to undermine armaments production and the war effort in general. But circumstances left little scope for effective central action.

Diplomatic records for the year 1940 show that at that time, before the German invasion of Denmark, Norway, the Low Countries and France, the British foreign office knew of the activities of a few anti-Nazi figures in Germany—Ulrich von Hassell, formerly ambassador in Rome, Carl Goerdeler, one-time Oberbürgermeister of Leipzig—and also had contact in Switzerland with a handful of prominent emigrés—the former German chancellor Josef Wirth, Prince Max von Hohenlohe, the industrialist Fritz Thyssen—who had plans for a new Germany. But the information gained from these contacts gave no reason to think that there was, or could be, any significant concerted opposition to Hitler within Germany.

The army would no doubt have been the sole institution with the power to overthrow Hitler, but here too the will to opposition lay only with a handful of officers. 'Opposition' is in any case a many-facetted term, and whether the values with which the generals would have replaced Nazism would have united the anti-Hitler elements in the country either before or during the war, is more than dubious. There could have been no question of an order from the commander-in-chief to revolt against Hitler. The commander-in-chief at the time was General Walter von Brauchitsch. When asked after the war about his connection with the anti-Hitler plots of 1938 and 1939, Brauchitsch made the revealing reply: 'For God's sake, why should I, of all people, have taken any action against Hitler? The German people had elected him and were extremely satisfied with his political successes.'[26]

This was it—from the mouth of a man whom Hitler made the scapegoat for the disastrous Russian campaign of 1941–2, and who might have been tempted after the war to claim at least a modest degree of laudable connivance at the subversive activities of his officers. Political success in foreign policy, economic success at home, forecasts of further success in store for the people that put their trust in him—how many can be expected to revolt against this? And the commander-in-chief, a servant of the state, still could not evade the constitutional truth that Hitler was the people's elected leader, for better or for worse, and at the same time his own superior officer.

The totalitarian state of which Hitler was dictator was a one-party state, and through that party had come the revolution out of which the totalitarian state was born. Before the Nazis' eyes stood the shining example of Mussolini's fascist Italy, with the police-state methods, the labour front, the youth organisations, the mass demonstrations—even the salute—which the Nazi state could import for its own revolution. *Der Führer* modelled himself on *Il Duce*, and although, as time went on, Italy became more and more the junior partner in the Axis, the two dictators retained close personal links to the end.

But the state as such mattered little to Hitler. From the time of *Mein Kampf* onwards he did not disguise that he saw the state merely as a means to an end, the end being the advancement of a *Volk* under the inspiration of a charismatic *Führer*. 'The state is not our master; we are the masters of the state.'[27] This is also the doctrine of the Nazi ideologist Alfred Rosenberg, from whose work *Der Mythus des 20. Jahrhunderts*, first published in 1930, many of the crassest racialist, pseudo-intellectual Nazi catch-phrases were taken. And the 'we' in Hitler's statement—in so far as it is not simply a euphemism for 'I'—stands for the Nazi party. Now that the revolution was officially declared complete, and troublesome elements like the S.A. had been eliminated, the tentacles of the party and its agencies, from the S.S. to the Hitler Youth, spread into all corners of public, and indeed private, life.

At the height of Hitler's 'Grossdeutsches Reich', with a total population of 80 million, the Nazi Party had 8 million members. Expressed in terms of the adult population, this meant about one in five. Distribution by occupation did not remain constant between 1930 and 1939, but the workers had always formed the solid core of membership, with white-collar employees the second largest group, the two together making up over 50 per cent. In terms of age the greatest support came, not surprisingly, from those in their twenties, while those of 40 and over contributed little. At the same time regional differences, which could stem from considerations of religion or of economics, or depend on such matters as the relative importance of agriculture and industry, could be considerable. Yet there was hardly any group, whether identified by age, sex, occupation or region, that did not offer some measure of support. Even some familiar names in the *Almanach de Gotha*, the Who's Who of aristocrats, starting with Prince August Wilhelm von Hohenzollern, son of Kaiser Wilhelm II, were to be found in lists of party members. What now are scorned as illogicalities and crude contradictions in Nazi doctrine could then be turned to advantage, for people read into such contradictions a meaning favourable to themselves, and all thought that they were right.

But statistics mean little, if one is trying to gauge the extent which German life was penetrated by Nazism, for membership of the party was not coterminous with support for the régime. For one thing, certain positions, particularly in the civil service, carried with them an obligation to belong to the party or to one of its agencies. A man in such a job would run the risk of losing it if he failed to join, but joining was an act of self-defence, not a declaration of faith. For another, it suited the régime to leave some of its supporters, especially among the intelligentsia, outside the party membership. This, they argued, would show the world the tolerance of the régime, and demonstrate that it also had support from outside the party. At the same time, it left them with some channels of access to those, both inside and outside Germany, who held aloof from the careerists and petty functionaries of the party. In fact, except for the minority in Goebbels' Ministry of Propaganda, most Party officials came from both socially and educationally inferior circumstances, and the Nazi hierarchy has been characterised as resting on an inverse ratio of power to education.[28] One might also characterise it as resting on a direct ratio of power to corruption, with Reichsmarschall Hermann Goering at the summit of power—but with the ascetic figure of Hitler himself apparently beyond reproach.

As ingrained in the Nazi way of doing things as corruption was the practice of turning informer. One way in which a police state preserves its hold over the people is by fomenting distrust, making each man suspect his neighbour's reliability and encouraging him to denounce any remarks or actions that might be interpreted as hostile to the régime. Criticism of an official's behaviour, buying from a Jewish store or consorting with Jews in any way, letting slip a word that might be interpreted as implying disapproval of party policy, listening in wartime to foreign broadcasts—reports of such behaviour, true or false, were welcomed. Children were told to report anything said or done by their parents that might seem to contradict party teaching, and not even the unity of the family could always withstand these denunciations. By undermining all loyalties other than that of the individual to the State or its official agencies, and so breaking up private allegiances, the Nazis created a classic example of the principle of 'divide and rule'.

At the same time—but solely for economic, ultimately military reasons—the Nazis pretended to attach great value to the family. The war, the following inflation and the depression of the early 1930s had combined to cause an alarming fall in the birth-rate, and it was an urgent priority to check this fall. For was the country not facing the need to fill the *Lebensraum* which, with expansionist persistence, Nazi foreign policy was always demanding? A system of marriage loans to newly-weds was introduced and special subsidies were given to large families; to have only one or two children was regarded as anti-social, while to have none at all amounted almost to a crime against the state. Fertility became a fetish, and if it could not be achieved within a marriage, then extra-marital excursions were encouraged, both for the husbands of barren wives and the wives of impotent or lethargic husbands. The grotesque culmination of this fertility cult was Himmler's *Lebensborn*, an institution in which prime physical specimens of the S.S. served as stud-bulls for the procreation of children by unmarried mothers who had declared their determination to 'present a child to the Führer'.

Once again the insidiousness of Nazi methods reveals itself. A policy is launched on a high moral level with well-nigh irresistible appeals to the national interest: the country needs strong leadership, the country needs a spirit of service, the country must look to its inner strength and foster the healthy growth of the family as the foundation of that strength, and so forth. Goebbels, master of the stick-and-carrot technique, knew exactly how high, or how low, to pitch the tone of the propaganda behind each such cause so as to induce that blend of pride in fulfilment, and shame—or worse—in disobedience, with which he held the nation together. Soon it becomes evident that acceptance of leadership means submitting to the caprices of minor *aparatchiks*; that service of the nation means impersonality and unrewarded effort; and that what is said to be in the public interest always seems to show itself in the form of increased restrictions on personal freedom. But by this time it is too late. And an outburst of resentment under stress, an unguarded moment of criticism, may find its way to the local office of the Gestapo.

The Gestapo, originally the Prussian Secret Police, had been founded by Goering. In 1934 its leadership passed to Heinrich Himmler, chief of the Bavarian police as well as Reichsführer of the black-shirted S.S., one of the most feared men in the country. Gestapo, S.S. and concentration camp were the weapons of Hitler's administration of terrorism, and they almost completely replaced the constitutional agencies of law and justice. The courts became more and more a part of the administrative bureaucracy, and the independence of the legal profession became more and more of a mockery. The power of the public prosecutor encroached ever further on the territory of the judge, giving him the authority not only to by-pass the lower courts in bringing a case before the Supreme Court but even to decide the final sentence.

In the penal code of the Weimar Republic there had been three categories of crime punishable by death. Between 1933 and 1943 the number grew to 43. On what basis? Because Hitler said so. Nothing was left of the principle *Nulla poena sine lege, nullum crimen sine lege*. In its place stood the arbitrary will of the Führer, as was made un-disguisedly clear by Hans Frank, later Governor General of Poland: 'All the political power of the German *Volk* is united in the Führer; it rests in his hand. All law therefore derives from him'.[29] Justice, in other words, is what Hitler says it is, and the task of everyone in the legal profession is to ensure that the Führer's commands are carried out. Certain favoured groups in the party machine, like the S.S., even had their own private courts which shielded them from the jurisdiction applicable to others.[30] A *de jure* puritan ethic for the masses and a *de facto* promiscuity among the ruling élite. It is a familiar pattern.

Totalitarian régimes always set the indoctrination of youth high on their list of priorities, and the *Hitlerjugend*, which, together with its complementary organisations, the *Bund Deutscher Mädel*, the *Jungvolk* and *Glaube und Schönheit*, was directly controlled by the party, allowed no-one to slip through its net. Like many other bodies in the Nazi state, the Hitler Youth sought to capture the masses by combining two things—a challenge to idealism and a public display of resolutely joyful unity. Bonfires, torchlight processions, camps and open-air activities, mass demonstrations, huge set-pieces of physical cul-ture like those that accompanied the annual *Parteitag* in Nuremberg—these were to appeal to the senses and stir the blood. They were also used to demonstrate how democratic the whole Nazi movement was, for had not all false distinctions of class and education been obliterated, as the youth of the country marched singlemindedly behind the *HJ*-banner to the strains of the *Horst-Wessel-Lied*? To this was added instruction in first-aid, formation drill, self-defence, target practice and other para-military activities that could be given a veneer of peaceful application, together with the mandatory learning by rote of the shibboleths of the Nazi catechism. Although there were irreverent and sometimes bitter jokes at the expense of the *Hitler-Jugend*, the *Bund Deutscher Mädel* and the rest, an atmosphere of frightening earnestness hung over all these activities, including those that one would normally designate as games and relaxation. Once more the Nazis had recognised a peculiarly German characteristic which could so readily be harnessed to their purpose.

This 'democratic' unification of the energies of young people from all social classes both reflected, and later contributed to, the reconciliation of divisive differences within the population at large. The elitist appeal of the S.S., which worked strongly on the adherents of traditional values and of a social and intellectual apartheid, shared the same context of ideals as the public egalitarianism of the *Arbeitsfront*, a form of *Gleichschaltung* that raised the self-esteem of the humblest and least privileged in society. In the same way the conscription of the young of all classes and backgrounds into the ranks of national organisations demonstrated the reality of the new unity in diversity. The old class structures crumbled, and with them the meaning of old class questions about the relative importance of industrialists and intellectuals, farmers and civil servants, factory workers and shopkeepers. What mattered now were the prescribed values of *Volksgemeinschaft*.

Although in all these contexts of indoctrination the individual is made to feel that it was on his own personal conversion and conviction that the future of the Fatherland depended, both the intention and the technique rest on the principle of impersonality. Mass support is what a dictatorship needs. The thinking, such as it is, can be left to the ruling élite, and the masses can then be taught, or told—they are the same—to think the same things. Hence the vital importance to the Nazis of central control over the media of communication and education.

The former was rapidly achieved. With the disappearance of all political parties except the NSDAP opposition journals folded up. The Nazi party's own paper, *Der völkische Beobachter*, published *the* truth, and through his central censorship Goebbels controlled all radio programmes, all published books and periodicals, all films and all cultural activities.

In schools, as in the Hitler Youth, indoctrination had a captive audience on whose shoulders the future of the Nazi state would eventually come to lie. Teachers were particularly exposed to denunciation by their pupils, so that if, for example, a teacher were to penalise a boy who had padded out an essay with material copied word for word from some Nazi pamphlet, the boy could complain to his headmaster that the teacher had questioned the tenets of the party. But this cannot in itself explain why so high a percentage of schoolteachers joined the party during the early years of the régime.

As minor intellectuals affectionately lingering over resentful me-
mories of a lost war, an unkind peace treaty and an ineffectual
republic, many became willing allies of any nationalistic creed and
found it but a short step to membership of the *Nationalsozialistischer
Lehrerbund*. Furthermore a high proportion of teachers had experienced the communal life of cadet camps or other para-military
institutions, and this drew them closer to their pupils in a context of
mass impersonality, giving a perversely convincing twist to the
hallowed ideal of *mens sana in corpore sano*.

The Nazification of school curricula followed the events of 1933
and 1934 as a matter of course. Religious instruction was quickly
banned. Other subjects, however, gained in importance. Biology
became the vehicle for teaching Nazi principles of race and heredity,
and there was even a Nazi physics, based by the Nobel prizewinner
Professor Philipp Lenard (*Deutsche Physik*, 1935) on the equation
'German = Aryan, natural, strong, i.e. true, truth-giving', as opposed
to the rootless and thus irrelevant 'Jewish physics' typified by Einstein
and the insidious, unacceptable concept of relativity.

Manipulation of the past being an easy matter, history lent itself
readily to the propagation of attitudes which portrayed the Third
Reich as the summit towards which all modern German history had
been aspiring. In the more distant past the figures of Charlemagne
and the pagan Saxon king Widukind were decked out in romantic
colours and presented as forerunners of the Führer, while from a still
more remote age the over-life-size heroes of Germanic mythology
were held up as embodiments of German honour and virtue.

Above all the school subject of German, which shaded into the new
Nazi history at many points, was used to inculcate the doctrines of
pride in the Fatherland, faith in the Reich and its Führer, and service
of the *Volk*. Through the choice of subjects for study, through a
nationalistic interpretation of historical and geographical facts,
through the selective perversion of the meaning of the literature of the
past, through the adoption of the frightening phraseology, and hence
of the thought-patterns, of official Nazi publications—in such ways,
some crude, some insidious, the study of German *Volkskunde* was made
to instil in children the principles of the Nazi state.

German studies in universities followed a similar pattern.
Germanistik was born in the heady days of nineteenth-century
Romanticism and had never lost its identification with the study of
the ideal of the German *Geist*, so that ready-made patterns of thought
and language were freely available for any movement or faction
whose appeal rested on a noumenal, almost religious concept of *Volk*
and *Das Völkische*. Esteemed Germanists like Heinz Kindermann and

Karl Vïetor made the interests of the *Volk* their supreme canon of judgement in the 1930s, using in their literary criticism a language often indistinguishable from that of Party dogmatists. And again, of course, the virtues of the national spirit were defined by reference to its 'enemies': liberalism, internationalism, democracy, intellectualism—and the Jews.

The *Gleichschaltung* of the universities as a whole was less straightforward than that of the schools—but not because there was a greater reluctance among university professors than among schoolteachers to align themselves with Nazi pronouncements. From the time of the Great War nationalist sentiment among academics had run high, and by no means only among those of extreme right-wing views. Conservative views, at their best, on the nature and function of the university, such as those given by Max Weber in *Wissenschaft als Beruf* (1919), embodied an orthodoxy which was bound to have a strong national content. The same is true of the moderate reformatory opinions expressed by Ernst Troeltsch in *Die Revolution der Wissenschaft* (1921) and by Erich von Kahler in *Der Beruf der Wissenschaft* (1920).

With enlightened works such as these to support them, and sustained by the ivory-tower inaction that accompanied the necessity to preserve the autonomy of scholarship, German professors did not provide the stuff of revolution or rebellion. Only a handful had supported the republic, and the hostility-cum-indifference of the vast majority was simply the obverse of their belief in the resurgence of a strong, purposeful nation. Hence the manifesto, signed by 300 professors, urging the people to vote for the Nazis in the Reichstag elections of March 1933, and the *Bekenntnis der Professoren an den deutschen Universitäten und Hochschulen zu Adolf Hitler und dem national-sozialistischen Staat* in November of the same year.[31] In the following years membership of the *Nationalsozialistischer Dozentenbund*, responsible for seeing that university policy and pedagogical aims conformed to party principles, became virtually compulsory for anyone who did not want to lose his job. Here again the identification of party philosophy with national well-being was presented as the way to overcome the socially divisive pattern of classical education in nineteenth- and twentieth-century Germany. 'In future,' said Professor Ernst Krieck at his installation as Rektor of the University of Frankfurt in 1933, 'we shall recognise no spiritual values, no culture, no education that does not promote the self-fulfilment of the German *Volk* and does not receive its whole purpose from this ideal.'[32]

After the Nazis had ridden the faculties of Jews, Social Democrats, liberals and other undesirables, there was an unpleasant eagerness on the part of various public figures to adopt the new cant and profit from their colleagues' misfortune. Professor Hans Naumann, speaking at the *auto-da-fé* in Bonn, where, as in all German university towns, the books of Jewish and other 'un-German' authors were publicly burned in May, 1933, emphasised in Nazi jargon the unanimity of the academic profession and the *Nationalsozialistischer Deutscher Studentenbund*: they were all determined, he said proudly, to root out those sources of infection that threatened the health of the pure German spirit. Even New Testament theology, in the person of Professor Gerhard Kittel of the University of Tübingen, joined in bringing intellectual respectability to anti-Semitism. Professor Franz Koch 'demonstrated' that Herder and Goethe were in reality forerunners of the Nazis in the field of racial doctrine,[33] while the philosopher Martin Heidegger made no secret of his loyalty in his inaugural address as Rector of the University of Freiburg. There could hardly be a greater contrast, in this regard, than that between the Nazi-tainted existentialist Heidegger and the unyieldingly humanist existentialist Karl Jaspers, who, dismissed from his Chair at the University of Heidelberg in 1937, preserved an uncompromised aloofness throughout the Nazi years and emerged from the war without moral stigma.

A particularly pathetic case of intellectual wavering is that of the literary historian Ernst Bertram, friend of Thomas Mann and Friedrich Gundolf. Bertram was expected to attend the ceremonial burning of the books in the University of Cologne, but that the works of Thomas Mann and Gundolf were to be among them filled him with dismay. Having managed to persuade the authorities not to throw Mann's and Gundolf's books on to the fire with the others, he said, with relief, in a letter to his friend Ernst Glöckner: 'I now feel able to attend the solemn *auto-da-fé*.'[34]

How different from the attitude of Oskar Maria Graf! Graf's books, except one, were deliberately spared from the flames in the hope that he could eventually be induced to serve the interests of the régime. Instead he joined the voluntary exiles, and in an article headed 'Verbrennt mich!', published in the Saarbrücken newspaper *Die Volksstimme* in May 1933, he challenged the Nazis to throw the rest of his books on the fire as well, and thus free him in the eyes of the world from any suspicion of dishonour. The Nazis' reply was to deprive him of his citizenship. As for the temporary reprieve of Thomas Mann, the University of Bonn reasserted the will of the National Socialists three years later by withdrawing the honorary doctorate it had awarded him in 1919.

But while scorning intellectuals and intellectual values, the Nazis were fully aware of the value to the state of men who had had an academic training. Later, therefore, they introduced schemes for the admission of unqualified school-leavers to university, hoping both to break the upper- and middle-class monopoly of higher education—only some four per cent of students came from working-class families, a proportion that hardly changed between 1919 and 1939—and to secure the supply of trained man-power the country needed. In fact, however, the anti-intellectual faction prevailed through the peace-time years of the Third Reich, and the number of university students fell from 118,000 in 1932 to 51,000 in 1939, increasing again only in wartime, when *numerus clausus* entry restrictions were relaxed and admission qualifications lowered.

iv. Nazism and culture

In the control of the instruments of public education and the media of culture—literature, art, music, the theatre, the cinema, newspapers, radio—lies the power of a totalitarian state over the minds of its citizens. The physical threat of beatings and concentration camps was in itself often sufficient to convert people to the approved ways of thinking, but these ways also needed to be made explicit through the regulation of the cultural material available for public consumption.

To this end Hitler charged Goebbels in September 1933 with the formation of a *Reichskulturkammer*. This consisted of seven branches individually responsible for literature, the press, radio, theatre, film, music and the pictorial arts. The activities of these *Kammern* were defined by statue and reported to Goebbels as Reichsminister für Volksaufklärung und Propaganda.

The censorship of literature expressed itself in two ways: firstly by the banning of the works of Jews, Communist and other left-wing authors, and any others whose thoughts were held to offend against the national interest; and secondly by a demand from the remaining writers of a sign of loyalty to the régime, in the form of joining the party, contributing to the corpus of approved party writings, or in some other way. Those who refused to submit to these conditions, or whose racial origins or political views now excluded them from taking any further part in the life of their country, faced a simple choice: to stay in Germany and await certain arrest, or to emigrate. Between 1933 and 1939 over 2,000 writers, among them almost all the most famous, sought refuge in other European countries or further afield. Thousands of actors, musicians, artists, scientists and scholars took the same path.

The purge started at the top, and at the earliest possible moment. In February 1933 Heinrich Mann, whose liberal-democratic views had long made him a thorn in the Nazis' flesh, was forced to give up his position as President of the Preussische Akademie der Künste. In March the members of the academy each received a confidential letter from their new President, the composer Max von Schillings:

In view of the changed historical situation, are you prepared to put yourself at the disposal of the Preussische Akademie der Künste? An answer in the affirmative precludes any political activity against the government and commits you to cooperate loyally in the national cultural programme which the Academy is by its new statutes obligated to carry out.

Answer *Yes* or *No*.

Thomas Mann, Alfred Döblin and Ricarda Huch said *No* and resigned. Käthe Kollwitz had resigned along with Heinrich Mann the previous month. Fourteen of the remaining members were expelled for the incompatibility of their personalities with 'the new principles governing the activities of official cultural bodies in Prussia': among them were Franz Werfel, Georg Kaiser, Alfred Mombert, René Schickele, Fritz von Unruh and Jakob Wassermann. At the burning of the books in May, the works of these writers were thrown into the flames with the rest. As Heine had written a hundred years earlier: 'Those who start by burning books end by burning men.'

Stefan George, whose imperious cult of the principle of leadership and discipleship laid itself open to Nazi perversion, left Germany for Switzerland in 1933 and rejected Goebbels' invitation to return as President of the Preussische Akademie der Künste. A newly-constituted Deutsche Akademie der Dichtung received as its president the one-time expressionist poet and dramatist Hanns Johst, whose nationalist bias, worship of heroic virtue and advocacy of violence made him the perfect candidate for the honour. Around Johst were grouped older authors—Wilhelm von Scholz, Ina Seidel, Erwin Guido Kolbenheyer, Hans Grimm, Hermann Stehr—whose earlier works played on aspects of German life and the German character which the Nazis found it convenient to extol, or who after 1933 were prepared to assent at least in part to the cultural policies of the régime.

Of the *causes célèbres* involving writers who voluntarily and publicly rallied to the Nazi cause in 1933 the best-known is probably that of Gottfried Benn. With appeals both to national political solidarity and to economic-cum-eugenic 'principles', Benn put his considerable reputation at the disposal of the Nazis. There was no pressure on him to do so, and although it is still difficult to be sure of his motives, and although some years later he retracted these views, one can hardly fail to see his action as at best a lapse into barbarism, at worst a preparedness to jettison humanity and morality for (temporary) personal advantage, or in response to (temporary) ideological conviction. Ironically Benn's expressionist past caught up with him a few years later—perhaps, indeed, it never left him. For in 1938 he was expelled from the Reichsschrifttumskammer for the 'decadent' nature of his poetry, and forbidden to write.

The aged Gerhart Hauptmann, who had excitedly exclaimed: 'I vote Yes!' in the plebiscite of August 1933 to approve Hitler's accession as Führer and Reichskanzler, was alternately approved and disapproved of by the authorities. Goebbels ordered that special performances of his plays should be given in 1942 to celebrate the 80th birthday of the Grand Old Man of German letters, but he proved of little use to the régime. By 1938 he was reported to have lost his illusions about Hitler: 'This miserable Austrian house-painter's mate has been the ruin of Germany.' And asked why, if he now thought thus, he had not emigrated or protested, he cried: 'Because I'm a coward! Do you understand? Because I'm a coward!'[36]

Open resistance to Hitler after 1933 was almost as impossible in the field of literature as it was in the field of political action. A limited number of works by Jews, published in special presses and with the racial origins of the authors prominently stated, were permitted up till 1938, and a handful of churchmen, both Catholic and Protestant, published occasional sermons and reflections on issues of conscience—with predictable results. Ernst Niekisch's national-revolutionary paper *Der Widerstand* survived for a few years, and socialist views found their way into German-language periodicals published abroad, like the *Zeitschrift für Sozialismus*. There were even a number of *Tarnschriften*, like that disguised under the title *Mass und Gewicht aller Staaten* which contained reports on the Spanish Civil War from the Republican standpoint, that managed to circulate. But the influence of such writings was infinitesimal.

The long arm of the Reichsschrifttumskammer, together with the influence of the party 'philosopher' Alfred Rosenberg and that of the *Parteiamtliche Prüfungskommission* under Reichsleiter Philipp Bouhler, reached not only authors themselves but also publishers, booksellers and libraries. As writers could be expelled from the Kammer, like Werner Bergengruen and Jochen Klepper, forbidden to write or lecture, like Benn, Kasimir Edschmid, Hermann Kasack and Rudolf Alexander Schröder, or simply arrested, like Leo Weismantel and

Ernst Wiechert, so publishers were told what they were allowed to print, and booksellers and libraries what they were allowed to distribute. Black lists of banned works were circulated, and premises raided to confiscate any stocks of such books. Translations of foreign works were frowned upon as hindering the development of indigenous talent, except where such works—Steinbeck's *Grapes of Wrath*, for example, or Cronin's *The Stars Look Down*—contained criticism of social conditions in the countries from which they came, criticism which the Nazis could add to their own xenophobic outbursts.

The cult of the *arteigen* also had its linguistic aspect, in the drive to ban 'foreign' words from the vocabulary in favour of words of Germanic origin. Such attempts to 'purify' the language have always reached their height at moments of national self-assertion—after the Thirty Years War, in the aftermath of Napoleon, after 1871 and at the outbreak of the Great War. Even before Hitler came to power, the journal *Muttersprache*, organ of the Deutscher Sprachverein, was mounting a campaign against *Fremdwörter*, and Nazi indifference to the question in the early 1930s met with disappointed criticism. The argument was, and always has been, carried on at a variety of levels—philological, stylistic, social, political—with great rational and irrational fervour, and each surge of cathartic zeal has left its detritus of lost causes. Thus as the *Sprachgesellschaften* of the seventeenth century proposed to substitute *Tageleuchter* for *Fenster*, *Zeugemutter* for *Natur* and *lustwandeln* for *spazieren*, so the nationalists of *Muttersprache* tried to make people call 'intellectual' activity *verstand-sam*, the process of 'industrialisation', *Gewerbsamung*, and university vice-chancellors, *Hochschulführer*.

But these antics irritated the authorities. It was not the place of 'linguistic acrobats', said Goebbels to the Reichskulturkammer in 1937, to try and base the German-ness of the language on intellectual sophistries, for the essence of *Deutschheit* lay in the *Volk*, not in a set of learned theories. The final word come from Hitler, who in 1940 declared that he wished to see an end to these '*gewaltsame Eindeutschungen*', which were 'foreign to the spirit of the German language and generally conveyed only very imperfectly the meaning of the *Fremdwörter* they aimed to replace'.[37] The servants must have felt rather hurt at their masters' ingratitude.

As the Reichsschrifttumskammer controlled the written, so the Reichstheaterkammer controlled the spoken, literary word. The theatre was now not merely a centre of entertainment, answerable only to commercial profit and the achievement of a passing popularity, but a medium of national education. A *Reichsdramaturg* was appointed in Goebbels' Ministry of Propaganda to ensure, as the decree put it, 'the application of National-Socialist cultural principles to the activities of the German theatre',[38] above all the national principles of idealism and heroism.

Inevitably the Nazis' anti-Semitic crusades made deep inroads into the world of the theatre, where Jewish actors and directors had always been prominent. Max Reinhardt, Fritz Kortner, Albert Bassermann, Alexander Moissi, Max Pallenberg, Fritzi Massary and Elisabeth Bergner were among their prominent victims. Jewish actors, it was maintained, had enjoyed a disproportionate share of the theatrical limelight, and it was high time they made room for 'real' Germans. 'Jews cannot be interpreters of German *Volkstum*', said Goebbels to a conference of theatrical producers in 1933, 'and it is only right and proper that they should in the future be pushed into the background.'[39] When a vacancy occurred in the cast of a play, preference among the applicants had to be given to a party member or a man who had fought at the front during the Great War.

Cheap anti-Semitic plays found ready sponsors. More despicable, however, was the perversion of classical dramas for anti-Jewish propaganda. Marlowe's *Jew of Malta*, for instance, was re-written by one Otto C.A. zur Nedden in order to bring out more strongly the 'inhuman' racial characteristics of the Jewish race.[40] An even more welcome work was Shakespeare's *The Merchant of Venice*, with Shylock the perfect figure for caricaturing those features through which the Jewish character could be made to appear distasteful. On Shakespeare's plays in general the party view was divided: at one moment his characters were praised for their 'Nordic' heroism, at the next he was branded as one of the false gods to whom German dramatists had turned in their search for a national style.

The *Blut-und-Boden* values, partly crudely nationalistic, partly primitively sentimental, that the Nazis cultivated in literature found their predictable way into the theatre. Since the 200 or so municipal theatres in Germany were subsidised from public funds, local and central, and since control of cultural policy lay in the hands of the Reichstheaterkammer, *Gleichschaltung* of the theatre throughout the whole country was as easy and as complete as that of radio and the press. Announcing the foundation in 1938 of an Academy of Dramatic Art for the whole of the Grossdeutsches Reich, Goebbels said:

We have ceaselessly proclaimed it as our demand and our goal to create a German National Theatre. This is no mere revolutionary phrase. For we were, and are, convinced that Germany is the cradle of world drama, and it is our political and cultural duty to ensure that Germany retains this awareness of her theatrical mission.[41]

Scarcely to be rated as drama, but part of the invocation of *Volksgemeinschaft* in dramatic form, are the extraordinary events christened by the Nazis *Thingspiele*—open-air displays, part military revue, part circus, part communal display of national solidarity, with charades, patriotic speeches by characters in costume, and community singing led by massed bands and a cast of hundreds. In effect the *Thingspiel* was a dramatised political demonstration, and to accommodate the thousands for whom the performances were mounted, grandiose plans were made for hundreds of special *Thingstätten* in open country, especially near places associated in folklore with pagan cults and the celebration of Germanic rites. Few of these ludicrous establishments, however, were ever completed.

The censorship of films by the Reichsfilmkammer followed the same principles as the censorship of plays. All films had to be submitted for approval, and sequences held to be contrary to the interests of the régime were cut. Certain films were banned altogether, not only those based on works by Jewish authors or with Jewish actors, but those which were held to offend against Nazi canons of morality or to give the world at large a false picture of true German values. *Das Hohe Lied*, based on a novel by Hermann Sudermann and starring Marlene Dietrich, was banned in 1934 for portraying upper-class life in Wilhelminian Germany as thoroughly immoral and reprehensible. A French film based on Zola's *Nana* met with disapproval in the same year because it dared to link a soldier, noble defender of the state, with the career of a prostitute.

Films sponsored by the régime followed predictable paths: war films glorifying the German soldiery, *Blut-und-Boden* works, pseudo-historical films embodying the *Führerprinzip*, sentimental escapist love films. A particularly famous blend of approved qualities, dominated by the figure of Hitler himself, makes up the pseudo-documentaries *Triumph des Willens*, a portrait of the Nuremberg Party Rally of 1934, and the two films of the 1936 Olympic Games, *Fest der Völker* and *Fest des Glaubens*, by Leni Riefenstahl. However strenuously Leni Riefenstahl protested her innocence of any intention to glorify Hitler and the Third Reich, the impression these films leave—and this is even truer of *Sieg des Glaubens* (1933)—is hardly one of professional exercises by an uncommitted technician. When she went to America in 1938 to try and sell her films, Hollywood, with the exception of Walt Disney, would have nothing to do with her.

Of the anti-Semitic films by far the most famous in *Jud Süss*. A version of Lion Feuchtwanger's novel had already been made in 1933 with Conrad Veidt in the title-part. (Veidt, together with Marlene Dietrich, Peter Lorre, Oskar Homolka and the directors G.W. Pabst, Fritz Lang and Josef von Sternberg, left Germany later the same year.) In 1940 the Nazis made their own film of the novel, directed by Veit Harlan, with Ferdinand Marian and Werner Krauss—neither of them, of course, Jewish—in the main parts. In fact, apart from the role of Süss Oppenheimer himself, taken by Marian, Krauss played all the Jewish parts in the film which, with *Die Rothschilds* and *Der ewige Jude,* made up a trilogy of vicious anti-Semitic films released in 1940 to prepare people for the 'final solution' of the Jewish question. Krauss, who also played Shylock at the Vienna Burgtheater at a time when anti-Semitism was at its height there, had a lot to live down after the war.

Such is the power of the written and spoken word that a dictatorship is bound to suppress any literature, not necessarily directly political in nature, that stands for contrary values. The visual arts present less of a threat since, although the spirit of opposition in them may be no less strong, they reach a smaller audience. Fewer people go to art galleries and concerts than read books and periodicals, and the broad mass of the population is barely touched by the activity of painters, sculptors and composers.

But Nazism is not a doctrine of censorship. Nor is it a form of government, or even a way of life. It is a *Weltanschauung,* and makes the total demands of a *Weltanschauung.* So painting and sculpture, no less than literature—and the directives bore the personal authority of Hitler the artist—were to deal only with the optimistic, the constructive, the practical, and the manner was to be 'realistic', 'normal'. The portrayal of suffering, despair or any form of physical ugliness, or of disturbing intellectual or emotional tension, was not to be tolerated, since the spiritual health of the country depended on a sense of positive purpose and 'co-ordinated' unity.

Thus the artists of expressionism, for example, from the painters of *Die Brücke* and *Der blaue Reiter* down to Kokoschka, Beckmann, Nolde, Käthe Kollwitz, Barlach and the other leaders of art in the 1920s, were banished at a stroke. To portray the misery of the poor, or to caricature the self-indulgence of the rich, is socially divisive, and therefore degenerate. To paint horses blue, and trees red, is abnormal and an offence against nature, therefore also degenerate. The human body has to be shown as strong and beautiful, its features heroic and aggressive, its values those of the earth, not of the sky. 'The German people in this twentieth century', announced Hitler to the Reichskammer der deutschen Künste in Munich, 'have newly awakened to an affirmation of life and are swept along by their worship of what is powerful and beautiful, and therefore healthy and life-giving. To this end the art of the people must continue to be based on a firm, dependable foundation which is able to sustain men of real genius. For genius is not madness.'[42] Madness—*Wahnsinn*—is an appropriate word in the context. But the Third Reich produced no geniuses, except in the arts of murder and destruction.

In music *Gleichschaltung* was characterised by the same heavy-handedness, the same cult of moral uplift, crude optimism and personal and national nobility as the other arts. The works of Mendelssohn, Meyerbeer, Mahler, Schoenberg and other Jewish composers were excised from the concert repertoire, and the master-pieces of German classical music 'reinterpreted' for the benefit of the general public.

One of the most acrobatic exercises of this interpretative energy was carried out on Beethoven's opera *Fidelio*. That tyranny was defeated, that treating prisoners like animals was publicly exposed as inhuman and immoral, that the oppressor Pizarro was arrested by the representative of a legally constituted government—all this was glossed over (theatrical production can, of course, do such things). Instead attention was focused on the sub-title of the opera, *Die eheliche Liebe*, and the work put out as a paean of praise for the institution of (German) marriage and the unshakeable loyalty of a devoted (German) wife. That *Fidelio* is set in Seville, and Florestan and Leonore belong to the Spanish nobility, is not allowed to interfere with the interpretation. If one is determined to give a work a particular meaning, one will not worry unduly if the facts tend to obstruct that meaning.

This determination produced other bizarre results. Seeking ways to demonstrate the 'Jewishness' of Jewish music as a foreign body in the corpus of European music, one Dr Helmuth Sommerfeld quoted Bach's *St John Passion*. In the chorales, we are told, especially in those put into the mouths of the Jews (such as 'Wir haben ein Gesetz'), Bach gives us a kind of rudimentary musical characterisation of the Jews by using syncopation and jerky rhythms to convey the agitated, unstable nature of the Jewish personality.[43] It was also questioned whether one could accept without hesitation the use of passages from the Old Testament in works such as Handel's oratorio *Judas Maccabeus* and Brahms' *German Requiem*.

All such perversity stemmed from the determination to prove how different in every respect Jewish modes of feeling, thought and expression were from those of the 'Aryan' Germans, and how essential it was to prevent the true values of German culture from being contaminated by contact with this foreign poison. Richard Wagner's

Das Judentum in der Musik, written in 1850, still leaves a nasty taste in the mouth when one reads it today, but it is as honey compared with Karl Blessinger's *Judentum und Musik* (1944), Richard Eichenauer's *Musik und Rasse* (1937) and other Nazi writings on the subject.

As the Nazi aesthetic banned the paintings and sculptures of the expressionists and other 'unnatural' artists, so the music of deliberate dissonance, at its head that of the twelve-tone composers descended from Schoenberg—'musical Bolshevism', as the authorities called it—fell an immediate victim to the new cultural decrees. Schoenberg himself was accused of pursuing 'an abstract and un-German style fundamentally anti-melodic in character',[44] and was forced to resign his teaching post at the Preussische Akademie der Künste in Berlin as early as May 1933. Alban Berg, Kurt Weill, Anton Webern, Hindemith, Stravinsky, Ravel and Milhaud were among the composers of European stature whose works were sacrificed to the principles of Nazi musical culture. But Bartók and Honegger—such was the fickleness of these so-called principles—somehow escaped proscription. Jazz was reviled from the beginning as the pseudo-music of an inferior negro culture, but it showed remarkable powers of survival, for its elemental rhythmic appeal to the young was too strong to be entirely eradicated.

Hitler's great musical hero was Wagner—and for reasons not only musical. The concept of the German *Volk* dominated Wagner's outlook on art and on its role in the community. The Jews, being a rootless, disintegrated people, were excluded from this, or any other, national community and therefore condemned to artistic inferiority. *Der Ring des Nibelungen* Wagner described as 'a large composite work . . . which, I am bold enough to maintain, will do honour to the German spirit',[45] and with *Die Meistersinger von Nürnberg* came the glorification of the German Middle Ages and 'holy German art'. Winifred Wagner, wife of Wagner's son Siegfried, was an early supporter of Hitler and sent supplies of paper, pens, ink and other materials into Landsberg jail so that he could write *Mein Kampf*. The marriage of Eva, Wagner's daughter, to the racist Germanophile Houston Stewart Chamberlain, whose *Grundzüge des neunzehnten Jahrhunderts* was one of the main sources of the cult of Aryanism, drew the Wagner family still further into the Nazi net, and honour was only restored by the anti-Nazi Friedelind, the composer's granddaughter. Hitler regularly attended the Bayreuth Festival and made it clear that he regarded these performances as the climax of each year's music in Germany. When Hitler came to power, records an article in the official Bayreuth Festival programme for 1936, the country acquired for the first time a leader 'who recognised to the full the greatness of Wagner's mission, and with it the significance of the Bayreuth Festival for the German people'.[46]

As Hitler, the painter, gave his personal authority to the fiats of the Reichskammer der bildenden Künste, so on occasion his commands came through to the Reichsmusikkammer also. An especially weighty pronouncement came on February 15, 1939:

> The Führer has decided that the German National Anthem, a hymn of praise, is to be played at the speed $\bf\int = M\ 80$.
> The Horst Wessel Song, on the other hand, a revolutionary marching song, is to be played faster.[47]

v. From Grossdeutsches Reich to collapse

In October 1933, with a characteristic blend of defiance and crocodile tears, Hitler announced that Germany was resigning from the League of Nations. The crocodile tears sprang from the regret which, for the benefit of the other nations in the League, Hitler claimed that Germany felt at being still dishonoured and humiliated 15 years after the end of the war; herself forbidden to rearm, she was surrounded by powers busily taking advantage of the situation while paying lip-service to disarmament, and German self-respect could no longer tolerate this situation. The defiance was partly a first trial of strength in foreign affairs, a successful gamble on the willingness of other countries to take his assurances of peaceful intentions at their face value, and partly a rallying cry to his own people to assert themselves at long last in a manner that befitted a nation of 65 million citizens. Who can wonder that in the plebiscite on Hitler's decision to withdraw from the League of Nations, 95 per cent gave him their support?

So German rearmament started in ideal circumstances for Hitler, both at home and abroad. The non-aggression pact with Poland in 1934 seemed to the outside world further proof of his desire for peace, and on this foundation he wrung one concession after another from Britain and France right down until 1939. It is one of the most uncannily successful sequences of deceit and bluff in the history of European politics.

From the earliest days of his political awareness Hitler used the word German to embrace all German-speaking people, whatever the nation to which they happened to belong. The opening pages of *Mein Kampf* discuss what he calls 'dynamic nationalism' and 'der Kampf ums Deutschtum' as the foundation of his politics, and the collapse of the ethnically heterogeneous Habsburg empire into which he had been born gave him the chance to put his ideas into practice in Austria—an area he called by the old, tradition-laden name of 'die Ostmark'. He could even invoke in his support President Wilson's Fourteen Points, according to which the peace settlement after World War I should respect the unity of nationalities and allow peoples the right of political self-determination. After all, was he not planning a plebiscite on whether Austria wished to join the Reich?

As a result of Hitler's successes in Germany between 1930 and 1933, and with the Austrian economy, like the German, at the mercy of the depression, the Austrian National Socialist Party had greatly increased its influence, and was waiting only for the day when Austria and Germany should become one. For years before the *Anschluss* itself, Nazi party funds had been sent from Munich to finance the Austrian Nazis' campaigns of terror and intimidation, and Pan-German sentiment was as rife in Austrian right-wing political circles as in their German counterparts. Dollfuss, whose dictatorship rested on the support of Mussolini, was a man of—to Hitler—satisfyingly anti-Semitic and anti-Marxist views, and in a speech given shortly after he had dissolved all political parties and imposed the *Christlicher Ständestaat* in Austria, he made his position clear: 'We are the representatives of the Christian-German people of Austria, called upon to inaugurate the rebuilding of our state in the spirit of a Christian-German *Weltanschauung*.'[48]

Dollfuss was murdered by the Austrian Nazis in 1934, but Hitler, despite the failure of the Nazi *Putsch* itself and a temporarily strained relationship with Mussolini, lost little of his personal standing. The new chancellor, Kurt von Schuschnigg, was as much a 'greater German' as his predecessor, and his July Agreement with Hitler in 1936, reiterating that Austria was a German state, provided for the inclusion of several Nazis in the cabinet. There were, to be sure, elements in the country, both on the right and on the left, that thought in terms of Austrian independence. But those on the right, from the moment of their emergence after the Great War, laboured under the handicap of being associated in one way or another with the authoritarianism of the monarchy, while those on the left put their socialism first, whether national or international. When one adds to these confusions the influence of Italian fascism, transmitted above all through the para-military movement which also claimed to speak with a national voice, one sees how powerless the country was against German pressure.

'There was a very strange atmosphere in Vienna at this time', recalls Carl Zuckmayer:

On the surface it was rather like a carnival, because the Nazi party had been instructed by their cunning bosses in Germany to get all the children out on to the streets but leave their parents at home. So during these last few days of Schuschnigg's Austria, with German troops already massing at the border, the streets of Vienna were filled with more and more children of all ages carrying swastikas, shouting 'Heil Hitler!' and obstructing the traffic in all the main thoroughfares. . . . Some were fighting in the gutter, rolling over and over as they clutched their swastikas—a real credit to their parents and teachers. Otherwise nothing happened. Children wandered around shouting while grown-ups stood and watched in silence, some of them amused, others resentful or sneering as they waited to see what would happen.'[49]

They did not have long to wait. On 13 March 1938, Austria was declared part of the German Reich. The following day Hitler arrived in Vienna to a tumultuous welcome from those who 25 years earlier had found no use for him. For the next seven years the history of Austria was the history of Hitler's Germany.

Vienna was the metropole of European Jewry. An average of 170,000 Jews lived there between 1930 and the *Anschluss*, about eight per cent of the population of the city. But because, from the beginning of the century, a higher proportion of Jews than of the population at large went to university, and thus came to occupy prominent positions in public life, anti-Semitism, a traditional outlet for envy and inferiority complexes, ran correspondingly high. It is only necessary to recall names like Schnitzler, Hofmannsthal, Werfel and Stefan Zweig, Mahler, Schoenberg and Egon Wellesz, Freud and Alfred Adler, and to know that Jewish representation in key professions such as medicine, law and journalism, including publishing, was proportionately far greater than the number of Jews *in toto* would lead one to suspect, in order to gauge their power. Against a background like this a totally non-existent 'Jewish question' was easily conjured up as a spectre haunting the life of Vienna and the whole country, and when in 1938 the laws of Germany also became the laws of Austria, Hitler's anti-Semitic measures received almost greater support from the new citizens of the Reich than they had from the old.

In Germany during the years of the Weimar Republic the Jews made up rather less than one per cent of the total population, and although thousands were poor, or worked in lower middle-class jobs, the Jewish share of the legal profession was 16 per cent, of the medical and dental professions 10 per cent, and of the financial world 17 per cent, in addition to their dominance of the clothing business, departmental stores and other branches of retail trade.[50] Official Nazi boycotts of Jewish shops and Jewish professional men began as early as April 1933, yet because so many citizens depended on the services offered by the Jews, they were not all ousted from their positions as quickly as one might have expected. If a Jew could be dismissed and immediately replaced by an 'Aryan', well and good; if his removal would cause difficulties in the community as a whole, he was tolerated for a while longer.

But after the Nuremberg Laws of 1935, depriving Jews of their German citizenship and forbidding marriages between Germans and Jews, the persecution grew more and more savage. 'Aryan' racial origin was now a condition for all official appointments—the civil service, public hospitals, schools, universities, local government and so on—and the *Anschluss* brought hundreds of thousands more under the same laws. On November 9 the same year came the nationwide pogrom known as the *Reichs-Kristallnacht*, when the windows of Jewish shops, offices and houses were smashed, synagogues set on fire and hundreds of Jews arrested. Little more than a month earlier Chamberlain and Daladier had acquiesced in the partition of Czechoslovakia. As a result Hitler's *Grossdeutsches Reich* acquired, by means of the gentlemanly negotiations through which he had always got his expansionist way, a further three-and-a-half million Germans from the Sudetenland, 'liberating' them from the racially inferior Slavs—*Untermenschen*, as he called them—under whose yoke they had suffered since 1920.

Some of the German public reacted to the events of the *Kristallnacht* with something close to approval, as they did the expulsion of Jewish children from schools, the confiscation of Jewish property, the compulsory wearing of the yellow star, the deportations and the other measures. Some even joined the S.S. men looting the shops and offices. The majority just stood and watched.

The entire exercise, like the anti-Jewish campaign as a whole, was conducted with a maximum of publicity, so that no-one could pretend he did not know what was going on—unlike the wartime extermination camps such as Auschwitz and Belsen, whose real function was certainly not known to more than a handful of people. And although the great silent majority of the German people must have found the shouts of '*Juda verrecke!*' distasteful, and the physical spectacle of beatings, lootings and savage arrests unpalatable, a kind of abstract anti-Semitism had lain in their minds at least since the defeat of 1918, turning them into indifferent spectators of one of the most horrifying displays of genocide—and this in peace-time—that the world has seen. In 1933 there were about 500,000 Jews in Germany. By 1939 almost half of them had gone into exile; of the rest only a few thousand survived to see the destruction of Hitler and his Germany.

'Every Jew active in Europe', cried Baldur von Schirach, leader of the Hitler Youth and Gauleiter of Vienna, 'represents a danger to European culture. If I were accused of having transported tens of thousands of Jews from this city, once the European capital of Jewry, to ghettos in the east, I would reply that I regarded my action as a positive contribution to European culture.'[51] With declarations like this in one's ears, one is tempted to regard the sentence of 20 years' imprisonment passed on Schirach at the Nuremberg Trials in 1945 as an act of clemency.

The Germany that Hitler took to war in 1939 was formidably strong. Unemployment had disappeared—indeed, there was more work to do than workers to do it. Workers were offered attractions unheard-of in the past, like lavish sports facilities, factory concerts by the nation's leading artists, subsidised vacations through the *Kraft durch Freude* scheme, and the promise of a Volkswagen car for 999 marks (£50 at 1939 values) paid in advance (no cars were ever delivered). Industry was flourishing, public works programmes multiplied, and Germany had the best road system in Europe. The rearmament programme, started as long ago as 1934, had restored the power and prestige of the army, whose support for the régime had not always been as wholehearted as Hitler would have liked. Above all there was Hitler's fantastic personal success in foreign policy, the formation of the *Grossdeutsches Reich*, the creation of *Lebensraum*, the final oblite-ration of the ignominies of the Treaty of Versailles—all achieved in diplomatic negotiations with Germany's one-time conquerors, and without a drop of German blood being spilled in battle.

But perhaps more important than this material power was the psychological strength that it generated. The birth-rate—usually a fair index of people's confidence, or lack of it, in the future—rose dramatically during the six peacetime years of the Third Reich (14.7 per 1000 of the adult population in 1933; 20.4 per 1000 in 1939, which equals almost one-and-a-half million children). To be sure, the increase of the 'Aryan' population was one of the Nazis' prime concerns, and social benefits of various kinds were introduced as inducements to marriage and procreation, but these inducements served in their turn to reinforce both confidence in the future and the satisfaction that personal desires should coincide with what was socially beneficial. With the memory of the depression still fresh, people were far better off than in 1930, and knew that they were. Again the psychological strengthened the physical, and again the collective profit accrued to Hitler.

So when on 1 September 1939 German troops marched into Poland to create new *Lebensraum*, and were joined at Brest-Litovsk by the Russian armies that had invaded from the east following the Russo-German non-aggression pact of a few weeks earlier, the mass of the German people saw yet another achievement for which to thank their Führer. As for Hitler, who had chosen for the first time to resort to war, the success of the Polish *Blitzkrieg*, together with what he regarded as the newly-acquired security of his eastern frontier, convinced him even more of his infallibility.

1940 saw the fall, first of Denmark and Norway, then of Belgium, Holland and Luxemburg, and finally of France, by which time Italy had entered the war on Germany's side. By the summer of 1941 Hitler concluded that Britain, the only country now left in the west, was as good as defeated. This belief revived the covetous policies for gaining territory in the east that he had already put out in *Mein Kampf*—at that time he had imagined Germany and England marching together against the Soviet Union—and on 22 June 1941, 129 years to the day after Napoleon, the Germans invaded Russia. Operation Barbarossa, as it was called, started with all the spectacular success that Hitler and the German people had come to expect, and by October, when the German armies had reached the gates of Leningrad and were advancing on Moscow and into the Ukraine, the Nazi empire stretched for 2,000 miles from the Channel Islands almost to the Caucasus, and for 2,500 miles from northern Norway to the Aegean Sea.

In 1942, despite the terrible losses sustained by the German armies unprepared for the Russian winter, Hitler's grip on occupied Europe and on his own civilian population became even stronger. Collaborators in the occupied countries were not difficult to find, and resistance movements had to contend with the large body of patriotic but inactive citizens who, like their counterparts in the Reich itself, had no wish to fall foul of the Gestapo. Men and women in these countries were made to work for the German war effort, and their agricultural produce was shipped back for the German civilian population. Hitler now preached a gospel of a New Europe led by a New Germany in which all the old privileges and class distinctions would be swept away and a new homogeneous national community created. The prosperity of this new community would in practice have been based on plundering the occupied territories and using their inhabitants as slave labour, but such technical details were not made public. 'Whether nations live in prosperity or starve to death interests me only in so far as we need them as slaves for our own Kultur', said Himmler to his S.S. generals in 1942.[52] At a meeting of

Nazi party leaders in 1943, Goebbels records, Hitler himself made the nature of his new European order plain: 'All the trash of small states that still exist in Europe must be liquidated as quickly as possible. The aim of our struggle must be to create a unified Europe: only the Germans can really organise Europe.'[53]

1942 also marked the launching of the 'final solution' to the Jewish question—the eradication of all the Jews in Europe. The S.S.—less than half of whom, incidentally, were *Reichsdeutsche*, the majority being made up of ethnic Germans (*Volksdeutsche*) and Aryan types from other races—had the responsibility of organising the extermination camps in which the 'final solution' was to be carried out. Indeed, as Camp Commandant Rudolf Hoess later testified, extermination camps were already in existence in Poland when he received his orders to establish extermination facilities in Auschwitz in June 1941. In November 1944 the crematoria at Auschwitz were blown up. Three months earlier a certain Adolf Eichmann, one of Himmler's assistants, calculated that by that time some 6 million Jews had been killed by the S.S. *Totenkopfverbände* in the various camps—Auschwitz, Treblinka, Wolzek, Mauthausen and the rest—or elsewhere.

It was all in *Mein Kampf*—for those, both inside and outside Germany, who troubled to read it. Whatever else in that book seemed too preposterous to be given a moment's thought, the events of the 1930s could have left no doubt that on this subject the policy was being put into terrible practice. But again the majority chose to look the other way.

Moreover, it was the war itself that created the circumstances which made it possible to announce, and almost to achieve, the 'final solution'. In the Reich itself very few Jews were left by September 1939, and the deportations from Pomerania, Baden, the Saar and other areas in 1940 reduced their numbers still more. The Jewish 'problem' now referred mainly to the millions in the territories that Germany had overrun since the beginning of the war. Having been conditioned to live with the persecution of the Jews in their own midst, the Germans would hardly make an issue of the extension of this persecution to countries of which most of them were entirely ignorant. In any case, war is not the time to raise doubts on matters of domestic policy which have been a central part of everyone's experience for years.

The military turning-point in the war came in November 1942, the month that decided the fate of the German divisions at Stalingrad and brought the defeat of Rommel's army at El Alamein. It also marks an important stage in the deteriorating relationship between

Hitler and his generals. The idea of retreat had always been anathema to Hitler, and all advice on 'tactical withdrawal' and 'regrouping' from his military leaders, who were desperately seeking strategies to deal with the nightmare of war on two fronts, was angrily brushed aside. How, he demanded, could such *Untermenschen* as the Russians thwart the advance of the *Herrenvolk*? When Field Marshall Ehrhardt von Milch visited him on the day after the final defeat at Stalingrad and told him that the war was lost, he cried: 'I must attack!'[54] Among the plans and half-plans for the assassination of Hitler only the officers' conspiracy of 20 July 1944 came anywhere near to success.

Whatever may have appeared inevitable about the outcome of the war to a handful of generals, some churchmen and a few others in 1943, and notwithstanding the shattered morale of the troops on the eastern front, the propaganda-drugged German public at home continued to look doggedly to the Führer for their salvation. In its milder way their attitude matches that of the thousands of S.S. troops who butchered men, women and children in the line of duty, defending their actions on the grounds that they were obeying orders. Like the flogger whose cruelty so upsets Joseph K. in Kafka's *Der Prozess*, but who assures K. that flogging is like any other job, and that someone has to do it, personal answerability to a moral code has disappeared. One does what one is told.

So long as success followed success, the rightness of the cause was self-evident; if things went wrong, there was the comforting thought of national solidarity to fall back on. There were also the much-trumpeted, and repeatedly delayed, secret weapons, the V-1 and V-2 rocket bombs, to look forward to. And in the last analysis one always had the Führer: 'Der Hitler, der sorgt für uns.'

Perverse as it seems, despite the ever-widening gulf between his speeches and orders and the realities of the situation, and although his generals and close party colleagues could see how irrational and irrelevant his behaviour had become, Hitler alone was still in charge of the country's destiny. Martin Bormann, Hitler's secretary from 1943 and ultimately his deputy, came to wield great power, particularly at the expense of Himmler and Goering, both of whom he ordered to be expelled from the party for trying to negotiate with the Allies in the last weeks of the war. But all three, like Ribbentrop, Ley, Seyss-Inquart, Frank and all the others who had risen to eminence in the régime, depended utterly for their positions on Hitler himself. Alone they counted for nothing, and the desperate situation only bound them the more tightly to Hitler's fanatical will. To admit, with Berlin, Hamburg, Cologne, the industrial centres of the Ruhr and a score of other towns in ruins, that the cause was lost and the *Tausendjähriges Reich* at an end, was treason. Germany had to be dragged down with him—for was he himself not Germany? 'Those who remain after the battle are of little value', he wrote to Speer, 'for the good have fallen.'[55]

Sitting in the underground bunker of the Chancellery in Berlin in April 1945, Hitler had passages from Carlyle's *History of Frederick the Great* read aloud to him, still casting himself in the role of the Prussian king's successor, the man chosen by fate to exemplify that historical greatness in which Carlyle too believed. Russian troops were working their way towards the centre of the city, and by 29 April they had occupied the Tiergarten and reached the Potsdamer Platz, only a few hundred yards from the Chancellery. On that day Hitler wrote his final address to the German people, reviewing his life of service to the nation, blaming international Jewry for a war that neither he nor Germany had wanted, accusing disloyal elements, above all the officers of the General Staff, of bringing about her defeat, and announcing that he 'preferred suicide to cowardly abdiction, let alone capitulation'.[56]

The following day, 30 April, he shot himself. His body, together with that of Eva Braun, with whom he had been living during the last weeks in the bunker and whom he had married the previous day, was burned in the garden of the Chancellery while Russian shells were destroying the buildings all around. On 7 May, just a week later, General Alfred Jodl and Admiral Hans von Friedeburg signed the unconditional surrender of all the German forces to Britain, France, Russia and the United States.

The Churchillian 'unconditional surrender' on which the allies insisted to the very end has sometimes been made out, usually by Germans themselves, to have had a share in keeping the people obedient to Hitler to the last. Had the Allies recognised in the course of the war, so the argument runs, that there were forces of resistance in Germany only waiting to be approached, and prepared to rally popular support behind them, thousands of lives could have been saved and the massive anti-German bitterness of the post-war years avoided, or at least softened.

There were, certainly, instances of such resistance, above all in army circles and among churchmen. The *Bekenntniskirche*, represented by Dietrich Bonhoeffer, Bishop Theophil Wurm and Martin Niemöller, has already been mentioned. Of the various wartime acts of resistance coordinated by army officers the best-known, because most nearly successful, was the attempt to assassinate Hitler at his military headquarters in Rastenburg on 20 July 1944. This action brought together a great number of very dissimilar men: from the military there were General Ludwig Beck, a former Chief of Staff, Field-Marshal Erwin von Witzleben, Count Klaus von Stauffenberg, Admiral Canaris, head of counter-intelligence (the *Abwehr*); there was the Prussian Finance Minister, Johannes Popitz; and the former German ambassador in Rome, Ulrich von Hassell, whose opposition had cost him his diplomatic career as early as 1937; there was Carl Goerdeler, former Oberbürgermeister of Leipzig and the man designated for the position of Chancellor after Hitler had been killed; and Otto John, legal adviser to the German airline *Lufthansa*, who was later to become a controversial figure as one-time head of the *Bundesamt für Verfassungsschutz* in the Federal German government. John escaped to Spain; all the others, together with many lesser-known figures, were executed. Implicated in the officers' coup in Paris on the same day as the attempted assassination of Hitler were Generals Speidel and Stülpnagel and Field-Marshal Rommel. Stülpnagel was executed a few weeks later; Rommel chose suicide.

There was also the remarkably resilient figure of Albert Speer, first Hitler's chief architect, then, from 1942 onwards, Minister of Armaments Production. Speer saw that Hitler would rather ruin Germany than admit defeat, and he planned to kill him by blowing poison gas into the ventilation system of the Führer's bunker, but technical problems prevented him from carrying his plan through.

Yet these and other, smaller attempts at opposition hardly constituted a united resistance. The only thing that united those who resisted the pressure of Nazism, in thought or in deed, was the recognition that Hitler must be got rid of. On who, or what, was to take his place, there was no agreement, and could not be, since the various factions never met and never discussed either ends or means. Those in the plot of 20 July sought a violent and radical solution; the leader of the so-called Kreisau Circle, Count Helmuth von Moltke, who was executed in 1945, took a religious pacifist line and regarded his group as 'poles apart from the Goerdeler faction and its sordid aftermath'.[54] The membership of these groups, moreover, was continually changing, so that the leaders never knew for certain on how much support they could count. Hitler's total war could only be met with total surrender, and there was no substitute to be found in the scattered activities of what H.R. Trevor-Roper unkindly, but uncomfortably realistically, described as 'a few highminded aristocrats, a few disappointed officials and dismayed parsons'.[58] The Third Reich was destroyed from without, not from within.

In his farewell address to the Officer Corps Grand-Admiral Doenitz, unexpected custodian of the Reich for the seven days between Hitler's suicide and the final surrender of the German armed forces, wrote as follows:

The most important thing is that we must keep a zealous watch over the greatest boon that has been given us by National Socialism—our unity. Despite today's complete military breakdown, our people are unlike the Germany of 1918. We have not yet been split asunder. Whether we want to create another form of National Socialism, or whether we conform to the life imposed upon us by the enemy, we should make sure that the unity given to us by National Socialism is maintained under all circumstances.[59]

These are the words of an officer, meant for the ears of fellow-officers. Doenitz was no Nazi. But in his appeal for unity, in his expression of gratitude to the Führer for having forged this unity, and with a hint that this is not the only possession of value that the people owe to Hitler, Doenitz reflects an attitude shared by a great number of German civilians. Honest, politically unsophisticated citizens by the thousand talked of Hitler after 1945 as a man who had admittedly made some grave 'mistakes', like embarking on war, and had at times 'gone too far', as in his persecution of the Jews, but who at the same time had 'done a great deal' for the country at a moment when the much-vaunted processes of parliamentary democracy had produced nothing but social and economic collapse. What has come to be known as 'die Bewältigung der Vergangenheit' became the task of another generation.

NOTES

1. Zuckmayer, *Als wär's ein Stück von mir* (Vienna, 1966), 445–6
2. Toller, *Eine Jugend in Deutschland* (*Prosa, Briefe, Dramen, Gedichte*, Reinbek, 1961, 28)
3. *Mein Kampf* (Zentralverlag der NSDAP, Munich, 1940), 118
4. Zuckmayer, op. cit. 449
5. Harry Graf Kessler, *Tagebücher 1918–1937* (Frankfurt, 1961), 641
6. Bruno Walter, *Theme and Variations* (London, 1947), 327
7. Hermann Rauschning, *Hitler Speaks* (London, 1939), 152
8. Harry Graf Kessler, op. cit. 734
9. Harry Graf Kessler, op. cit. 646
10. see *The Speeches of Adolf Hitler 1922–1939* ed. N. H. Baynes (Oxford, 1942),I, 188, 189
11. see *Hitler's Words* ed. G.W. Prange (Washington, 1944), 42
12. *Mein Kampf* ed. cit. 85
13. see *Documents presented in evidence before the International Military Tribunal, Nuremberg 1945–1946*, 1390-PS

14. Harry Graf Kessler, op. cit. 718
15. Monty Jacobs, 'The Year 1848' (*In Tyrannos* ed. H.J. Rehfisch, London, 1944, 193)
16. *Sämtliche Schriften und Dichtungen* ed. W. Golther (Berlin/Leipzig/Vienna/Stuttagart, n.d.) III, 50
17. *Mein Kampf*, ed. cit. 422
18. *Mein Kampf* ed. cit. 661–2
19. see. K.M. Bolter, *Sozialer Aufstieg und Abstieg* (Stuttgart, 1959), 139
20. *Hermann Hesse—Thomas Mann. Briefwechsel* (Frankfurt, 1968), 34
21. see D. Bronder, *Bevor Hitler kam* (Hannover, 1964), 276
22. *Ausgewählter Briefwechsel* ed. L. Dehio and P. Classen (Frankfurt, 1962), 138
23. F. Meinecke, *Die deutsche Katastrophe* (Wiesbaden, 1946), 129
24. op. cit. 82, 85–6
25. see M. Knappen, *And Call it Peace* (Chicago, 1947), 119f.
26. O. John, *Twice through the Lines* (London, 1972), 33
27. Hitler in *Der völkische Beobachter*, September 8, 1934; see F. Neumann, *Behemoth* (London, 1942), 59
28. D. Lerner, I. de Sola Pool and G.K. Schüeller, 'The Nazi Elite' (in *World Revolutionary Elites*, Cambridge, Mass., 1965)
29. *Zeitschrift der Akademie für deutsches Recht*, 1936; see F. Neumann, op. cit. 365
30. F. Neumann, op. cit. 372
31. see Hans Maier, 'Nationalsozialistische Hochschulpolitik' and the other contributions to *Die deutsche Universität im Dritten Reich* (Munich, 1966)
32. see A. Flitner, 'Wissenschaft und Volksbildung' in (ed.) Flitner, *Deutsches Geistesleben und Nationalsozialismus* (Tübingen, 1965), 231
33. F. Koch, *Geschichte deutscher Dichtung* (Hamburg, 1937), 176
34. *Thomas Mann an Ernst Bertram—Briefe aus den Jahren 1910–1955* (Pfullingen, 1960), 277
35. see J. Wulf, *Literatur und Dichtung im Dritten Reich* (Gütersloh, 1966), 23
36. see J. Wulf, op. cit. 154–5
37. see P. von Polenz, 'Sprachpurismus and Nationalsozialismus' in *Germanistik—eine deutsche Wissenschaft* (Frankfurt, 1967), 135, 137–8
38. J. Wulf, *Theater und Film im Dritten Reich* (Gütersloch, 1966), 39
39. J. Wulf, *ibid.* 255
40. J. Wulf, *ibid.* 279
41. J. Wulf, *ibid.* 51
42. *Mitteilungsblatt der Reichskammer der bildenden Künste*, 1 August 1938; see also J. Wulf, *ibid.* 379
43. J. Wulf, *Musik im Dritten Reich* (Gütersloh, 1963), 392
44. J. Wulf, *ibid.* 44
45. in a letter to the publisher Schott, 17 October 1861
46. L. Reichwein, 'Sechs Jahrzehnte Bayreuther Bühnen-Festspiele' (*Bayreuther Festspielführer* 1936, 28)
47. see J. Wulf, *Musik im Dritten Reich* (Gütersloh, 1963), 128
48. see K.R. Stadler, *Austria* (London, 1971), 143
49. Zuckmayer, *Als wär's ein Stück von mir* (Vienna, 1966), 65–6
50. see E.B. Natan, 'Die demographische und wirtschaftliche Struktur der Juden' (in W. E. Mosse, (ed.) *Entscheidungsjahr 1932* (Tübingen, 1965), 87–131
51. see J. Wulf, *Theater und Film im Dritten Reich* (Gütersloh, 1966), 7
52. *The Trials of the Major War Criminals before the International Military Tribunal (Nuremberg, 1947–9)*, Vol. XXIX, 123

53. *The Goebbels Diaries* ed. L.P. Lochner (London, 1949), 279
54. *The Trials of the Major War Criminals* (ed. cit.), Milch Case, Vol. II, 668
55. see H.R. Trevor-Roper, *The Last Days of Hitler* (2nd. ed., London, 1950), 82
56. for the full texts of Hitler's political testament and personal will, both drawn up on April 29, 1945, see *Documents presented in evidence before the International Military Tribunal, Nuremberg 1945–1946*, Vol. 3, 369-PS
57. *A German of the Resistance: The Last Letters of Count Helmuth James von Moltke* (London, 1946), 21
58. H.R. Trevor-Roper, op. cit. 260
59. see J.W. Wheeler-Bennett, *The Nemesis of Power* (London, 1956), 699

CHAPTER SEVEN

The Nazi Canon of Literature

i. The perversion of the past

THE year 1933 marks a tragic dividing line in the development of German culture. Political dates that brand themselves on the life of a country—1776 in the United States of America, 1789 in France, 1917 in Russia, 1914 and 1939 in the whole of Europe—cannot leave cultural life untouched. They may also, like the events of 1789 and 1917, penetrate deeply into the political life of other countries. Rarely, however, except under totalitarian pressure of one kind or another, do such dates mark a radical change of direction in the cultural realm comparable with that in the political or social. There *are* revolutionary moments in art—Beethoven's String Quartet Op. 127 in 1823, Monet's 'Sunrise' in 1874, James Joyce's *Ulysses* in 1922, Schoenberg's Serenade Op. 24 in 1923. But they are the products of minds under the stresses of art itself, which is to say, of life itself—moments of discovery that lead a painter, a composer, a writer into regions where new creations are made to grow. And while the revolutionary political moment may well find echoes in art, this is quite different from the incidence of changes that stem from the inner development of art itself.

But 1933, the year when personal and political freedom disappeared in Germany and the rule of totalitarian terror set in, cut as deeply into cultural life as into political history. Culture was made to serve the political machine, artists were issued with directives to which to work, the élite of the nation's writers were forced for racial or political reasons into exile, and history rewritten to exemplify a primitive new ideology of racialism, persecution, national aggression and the worship of violence. State control was absolute and ruthless, and *Gleichschaltung* both demanded and received conformity of public utterance to the principles of the régime.

At no time during its reign did the party, or any of its collaborators in academic circles, produce what could be graced with the name of a National Socialist aesthetic. Instead, as part of their transformation of values, they hastily erected an emotive ideal of public service—'Dienst am Volksganzen', as they hideously called it—and required all artists to bow down before it. Whoever failed to worship the idol was stigmatised as a traitor, on the principle of 'he who is not with us, is against us.' Together with the other arts and with the

236

media of mass communication, literature was a tool to secure the intellectual basis of the political revolution, and the task was to be accomplished in the name of the *Volk*. The Reichskulturkammer functioned as the agency of cultural pressure within Goebbels' Ministry of Propaganda, ensuring that the raciocultural 'purity' of the German *Volk* was maintained. Central control is vital to a dictatorship, and Hitler announced to the Reichstag as early as 23 March 1933 that the cultural autonomy enjoyed by the individual states in the Reich up to that point (an autonomy restored after the war to the constituent *Länder* of the Federal German Republic) was to be abolished.

One of the first duties of the Reichsschrifttumskammer—the section of the Reichskulturkammer with responsibility for the written word—was to establish a canon of precepts and an approved list of authors for the guidance of the public. Young people above all needed this guidance, for in their hands would lie the consolidation of Hitler's revolution. They must be shown literature that expresses what National Socialism stands for, and the national heritage must be interpreted in order to reveal how the values of National Socialism have in fact been latent in German culture for centuries. The task, in other words, was to re-write history and create a new literary pantheon. Control of what was published, sold in bookstores and lent by libraries then completed the circle of *Gleichschaltung*.

So there appeared a rash of popular books with titles that tell their own story—Adolf Bartels, *Einführung in das deutsche Schrifttum für deutsche Menschen* (1933), Ernst Adolf Dreyer, *Deutsche Kultur im Neuen Reich* (1934), Hans-Friedrich Geist, *Die Wiedergeburt des Künstlerischem aus dem Volke* (1934). Joseph Nadler's four-volume *Literaturgeschichte der deutschen Stämme und Landschaften*, first published between 1912 and 1928, was rechristened *Literaturgeschichte des deutschen Volkes* in 1933, while in 1934 the famous literary journal *Euphorion* was metamorphosed into *Dichtung und Volkstum*: the name 'Euphorion', explained an editorial note, had reflected 'the excessive dependence of German culture on humanistic learning'.

One of the most influential of such works was Hellmuth Langenbucher's survey of modern literature, *Volkhafte Dichtung der Zeit*, first published in 1937 and reissued many times thereafter. Langenbucher's Preface to the fifth edition makes the spirit of his work explicit: 'I launch this new edition of my book in the hope that it will be destined to contribute, like its predecessors, to the achievement of those great and noble goals that confront us all in our National Socialist Germany.'[1] The contemporary writers in Langenbucher's hierarchy—Kolbenheyer, Stehr, Ina Seidel, Paul Ernst, Binding,

Hans Grimm, Johst—are those respected by all critics in the Nazi establishment as exemplars of true German virtues, while of those who had left Germany after 1933—Heinrich and Thomas Mann, Brecht, Döblin, Werfel, Broch, Musil and the others—not a word, of course, is breathed.

One of the most insidious of Langenbucher's 'interpretations by inference', as they might be called, and an object-lesson in the methods of Nazi critics, is his chapter on Stefan George. For the greater part of George's work, from the early *Hymnen* through *Der siebente Ring* to *Der Stern des Bundes*, Langenbucher has little sympathy, seeing it as of merely historical interest. In *Das Neue Reich*, however, he finds material that lends itself to Nazi purposes, such as the final lines of the poem 'der dichter in zeiten der wirren':

> . . . *er [sc. der Dichter] heftet*
> *das wahre sinnbild auf das völkische banner*
> *er führt durch sturm und grausige signale*
> *des frührots seiner treuen schar zum werk*
> *des wachen tags und pflanzt das Neue Reich.*

(He [the poet] nails the true emblem to the people's banner, he leads his faithful band through tempest and terrible fanfares of the dawn to the tasks of waking day and plants the New Kingdom)

The crusading spirit and the vocabulary ('völkisch', 'führen', 'schar', 'das Neue Reich') are all that a Langenbucher could desire.

But we must not, Langenbucher then warns, take George's 'Neues Reich' to be the same as Hitler's, for George is writing of a poetic, not a political, kingdom. Yet—and here lurks the sly association—'the sentiments and attitudes that George invokes in this poem correspond to the demands for a new pattern of life for the German people in the political realm. He has reached a point where the gulf between his poetic nature and the destiny of the age no longer exists'. And what enabled him to reach this point? 'It was ultimately his racial origin, the blood in his veins, that gave him the power to resist the temptations latent in his early poetry, the temptations which confronted a mind that tended to isolationism and a spirit that tended to aloofness.[2] From beneath a pretence of critical discernment and reserve Langenbucher thus implies that one of the most original poets of recent times, intellectually withdrawn from the life of the day, somehow presaged the coming of the 'neues Reich' of National Socialism, and that this vision was a product of his 'Aryan' blood.

Germanic society of the distant past readily lent itself to exploitation in *völkisch* terms, and literary historians found little difficulty in presenting German culture down to the end of the Middle Ages as expressive of a national unity sustained by mythology, folk-song, folk-tales, folk-drama and the other manifestations of a popular creative will. From the mid-sixteenth century, however—so the thesis ran—foreign intellectual elements began to undermine this national culture, setting up intellectual 'European' values that reached their apogee in eighteenth-century Enlightenment. The individualistic prevailed over the corporate, reason over faith, men were encouraged to pursue what separated them from each other rather than what united them, and to challenge traditional assumptions rather than build upon them. By the mid-eighteenth century a return to 'normality' was emerging: Klopstock, followed by Herder and the *Stürmer und Dränger*, is the new hero of the *Volkstumsgedanke*—Klopstock the author of the *Bardiete* and the patriotic odes, not, of course, of the *Messias*.

Herder, coiner of the word *Volkslied*, herald of the cognitive power of the emotions, occupied a central position in the National Socialist canon of literature. But like so many apparent allies, he had to be treated selectively. The Herder of *Von deutscher Art und Kunst*, *Über den Ursprung der Sprache*, the *Volkslieder* and *Auch eine Philosophie* was welcomed with open arms. The Herder of the *Humanitätsbriefe* and the *Indeen zur Philosophie der Geschichte der Menschheit*, on the other hand, had to be portrayed as a senile character gambolling through his second childhood in the playground of the discredited humanitarian ideals of the Enlightenment; he also held regrettably cosmopolitan ideals and was altogether too tolerant towards the Jews and other inferior races. Had he had the fortune to live a century and a half later, we are made to feel, National Socialism would have weaned him from these unfortunate aberrations.

The Romantics, as Herder's spiritual heirs, also offered rich treasures for the literary historians of the Third Reich to plunder. The cult of irrationalism and surrender to emotion in Novalis and G.H. Schubert; the national political sentiment in Fichte, in Kleist and in Hölderlin; the *Volk* values uncovered by the researches of the Grimm brothers and invoked by the rhetoric of Ernst Moritz Arndt and 'Turnvater' Jahn; *Des Knaben Wunderhorn* and the pursuit of folk-poetry: here were riches indeed. There were, to be sure, Romantic writers—Wackenroder and Friedrich Schlegel, for example, or E.T.A. Hoffmann—who could not be readily assimilated. But they could be ignored. The historian's task, after all, was to prove the existence of a tradition, not to draw attention to what lay outside it.

Lessing proved difficult to accommodate to Nazi double-think, and the dogma about him was not uniform. The venerable anti-Jewish literary historian Adolf Bartels passed one form of condescending judgement: 'For the Jews, whose cause he has greatly benefited by his *Nathan*, he represents "Truth", but we others have known for a long while that from his feud with Gottsched down to his polemic against Goeze there was a great deal about him that was not as it should have been.' So Bartels concludes, quoting Hebbel and Grillparzer in his support: 'Lessing has for us today nothing but historical value.'[3] On the other hand *Minna von Barnhelm, Laokoon* and the *Hamburgische Dramaturgie* met with general approval, and a total rejection of Lessing on the basis of his rationalism and tolerance would be too primitive, as one critic put it, 'to enable one to claim that one had thereby penetrated the heart of the National Socialist *Weltanschauung*'.[4]

Less intractable then Lessing was Schiller. The passionate crusading spirit of *Die Räuber*, the grand military and historical sweep of *Wallenstein*, the power of faith in *Die Jungfrau von Orleans*, the assertion of the popular will in *Wilhelm Tell*—all this was grist to the National Socialist mill. In 1934 a book called *Schiller als Kampfgenosse Hitlers: Nationalsozialismus in Schillers Dramen* was published by one Hans Fabricius, at that time leader of the party caucus in the Reichstag. Treating each major play under a suitably tendentious slogan—'Sozialismus and Führertum' (*Die Räuber*), 'Volksstaat und Führerehrgeiz' (*Fiesko*), 'Soldatentum und Politik' (*Wallenstein*), 'Glaubenskraft und Volkserlösung' (*Die Jungfrau von Orleans*), 'Volksnot und Freiheitswille' (*Wilhelm Tell*)—Fabricius claims Schiller for the National Socialist movement, which draws, as he puts it, 'on the same sources of everlasting German strength' as Schiller:

Our battalions march inexorably onwards. Our comrades who laid down their lives in battle 'march in spirit at our side'[5] together with the dead from the wars of German history. At their head, in front of the banner with its shining swastika and side by side with the leaders of today, stride the great spirits of the past whose bodies now lie beneath the earth. Towering above them, proud and erect, goes the radiant figure of Friedrich Schiller.[6]

There is an ironical postscript to the story of Schiller and the Nazis. *Wilhelm Tell* abounds in lines which have become familiar quotations. But some of these embody thoughts none too congenial to the Nazi mentality, or liable to set the mind working in undesirable directions—'Dem Friedlichen gewährt mangern den Frieden', for example; or: 'Unbilliges erträgt kein edles Herz'; or: 'Was Hände bauen, können Hände stürzen.' Having had this drawn to his attention, the administrative head of the Reich chancellery sent a directive to the Reichsminister für Wissenschaft, Erziehung und Volksbildung in 1941:

It is the Führer's wish that the play *Wilhelm Tell* shall no longer be used as a school text. On technical grounds the Führer does not consider it feasible, or even necessary, to excise from readers and history books at present in use or in bookstores those poems and basic quotations that have been taken from the play. However, new school books, and new editions of earlier school books, may no longer contain such poems and quotations.[7]

Goethe offered far more resistance to Nazi assimilation than Schiller. In his 600-page survey of German literature, *Einführung in das deutsche Schrifttum für deutsche Menschen*, Adolf Bartels performs the remarkable feat of devoting a mere six pages to Goethe, over half of them consisting simply of a catalogue of Goethe's works. Again it was a question of selection—or selective misrepresentation. Goethe the 'pagan' hedonist, worshipper of Nature, could be pressed into service in the attack on Christianity and other-worldly ideals. The notion of 'Volksgemeinschaft' in Act V of *Faust II* and in *Wilhelm Meisters Wanderjahre* is held up as proof that Goethe believed in what Franz Koch called 'the fulfilment of the personality within the framework of a supra-personal order'.[8] Similarly Goethe's scientific conception of organic growth, development according to in-dwelling, hence exclusive, forces, is taken to imply a belief in the *Volk* and in its right to self-expression. Another classic of National Socialist literary history, Walter Linden's *Geschichte der deutschen Literatur von den Anfängen bis zur Gegenwart* (1937),[9] draws approving attention to assorted remarks of Goethe's with an anti-Semitic flavour, such as those in which he expressed his satisfaction that no modern Jewish state had yet come into existence, and in which he considered the diaspora to be of general benefit.[10] One book even maintained that the figure of Mephistopheles was intended to represent a Jew.[11]

On the commemoration in 1939 of the 190th anniversary of Goethe's birth the Ministry of Propaganda issued a directive listing the headings—social, racial, economic, educational, scientific—under which Goethe's achievements were to be praised. The slanted use of quotations from his works, and their absorption into a Nazi phraseology, are an object lesson in the art of propaganda. Of Goethe's general character we read: 'It is wrong to see him solely as a man of composure and an harmonious artist. He was, in fact, for ever a fighter.' Under the heading 'Social' attention is drawn to Goethe's dislike of smoking and heavy drinking (a subtle parallel with Hitler here). The height of bizarrerie is reached with a section headed 'Sport', based on what is called 'Goethe's fight against over-education (*Überbildung*) in theoretical and intellectual subjects'. The complete document makes astonishing reading, and for the Nazi mind or the ignorant outsider it must at the time have seemed frighteningly credible.[12]

Hitler liked to compare himself with Napoleon—to the latter's disadvantage—and even after the defeat of the German armies in Russia in 1943 he held forth to Mussolini and others on how *he* would not make the same military errors as the Frenchman. So the most appropriate last word on the subject of Goethe and the Nazis—appropriate for us, that is, not for them—comes from Goethe himself, proud member of the *Légion d'honneur* and unswerving admirer of Napoleon:

> *Verflucht sei, wer nach falschem Rat,*
> *Mit überfrechem Mut,*
> *Das, was der Korse-Franke tat,*
> *Nun als ein Deutscher tut!*
> *Er fühle spät, er fühle früh:*
> *Es sei ein dauernd Recht;*
> *Ihm geh es, trotz Gewalt und Müh,*
> *Ihm und den Seinen schlecht!*

(Cursed be the misguided man who, as a German, insolently tries to do what the Corsican did. Whether it be sooner or later that he realises there is absolute justice, I wish him and his ilk, for all their might and power, a miserable end!)

(*Des Epimenides Erwachen,* final stanza)

The 'Bohemian private', as Hindenburg called him, was Austrian, not German. But a century later Goethe's curse struck home.

Other nineteenth-century writers, in so far as they were not unmentionable, like Heine and Börne, were pillaged in the same way. That Hebbel's *Judith* and *Maria Magdalene* were on Jewish subjects was discreetly ignored, since his *Nibelungen* trilogy showed that at bottom, as Langenbucher put it, 'he derived his whole vital strength from the fount of our national ethos (*volkhafter Wesensgrund*)'.[13] Hölderlin, too, presented a Janus-like aspect. As the poet of 'Heidelberg', 'Gesang des Deutschen' and 'Der Rhein', he could be held up as a great national figure. At the same time Nazi critics could not conceal that his values lay in an ideal, 'foreign' past, and that when Hyperion returns from Greece to Germany, he finds not only a house divided against itself but a country bereft of 'total' human beings, men in whom mind and heart, action and contemplation, the personal and the communal are bound in a proud unity.

Kleist, on the other hand, perhaps even more fully than Schiller, was held to embody the heroism and sense of national glory that could inspire a true patriotism. *Die Hermannsschlacht*, naturally, dominates the scene; 'It is a drama that has great contemporary significance', wrote Adolf Bartels, 'and should be read in every German household.'[14] *Der Prinz von Homburg* was also held to have great didactic value in its portrayal of Prussian virtues, while pieces such as *Was gilt es in diesem Kriege* and the *Katechismus der Deutschen* could be exploited in the pursuit of ruthlessness, xenophobia and other principles on which the Nazi régime depended.

Nietzsche, of course, was a very special ally. In his violent radicalism, his scorn of culture, his 'will to power', his anti-Christianity, his notion of the 'dangerous life', and his inflammatory, intemperate manner, Nazi apologists found much to praise. About his Europeanism, however, and about the 'Umwertung aller Werte' of *Jenseits von Gut und Böse* and other works, they have nothing to say, and that he despised nationalism, anti-Semitism and any form of *Volk* veneration is something they conceal. At the same time Nietzsche did believe that a higher race could and must be bred, and was prepared to see the slaughter of millions to that end. So the Nazis gleefully perverted Nietzsche's Superman to their own vision of the *Herrenvolk* and extracted from his vulnerable profusion of often contradictory, always brilliantly-turned aphorisms the items that served their purpose. Even a simple phrase like 'the will to power' could be exploited to frightening effect. One needs to distinguish Nietzsche from Nietzscheanism, and even more from Nazism, yet there remain areas in Nietzsche's thought that are directly linked with, and responsible for, later movements of destruction that invoke his name. 'Nietzsche's Superman', wrote Thomas Mann in 1947, 'is nothing but the idealisation of a Fascist dictator.'[15] The punishment of men like Nietzsche, in the words of Léon Brunschvicg, 'is that their antithesis still resembles them'.[16]

Amongst modern classics the case of Gerhart Hauptmann presents a curious picture in the 1930s. Hauptmann's important, naturalist plays belong to the 1890s. Imperial Germany did not welcome him; in the years of the Weimar Republic he shared literary pre-eminence with Thomas Mann but, unlike Mann, wrote little of significance. In January 1933 he made a public display of his support for Hitler, though this lip-service brought him no reward: he was criticised for having a Jewish publisher (Samuel Fischer, founder of the S. Fischer Verlag and publisher of Thomas Mann, Hesse, Schnitzler, Döblin, Wassermann and a host of others, including Ibsen and Shaw in translation) and written off as a non-*volkhaft* author tainted with Social Democratic republican praise. Yet in 1937 Goebbels suddenly ordered celebrations to commemorate Hauptmann's seventy-fifth birthday, and his plays remained in the repertory throughout the war. The pendulum swung back again when Alfred Rosenberg, second in the Nazi party only to Hitler in ideological matters, expressed disapproval even of this degree of tolerance, and eightieth-birthday tributes in 1942 were not to include any association of his name, a party directive stated, with the philosophies of National Socialism.

As for Thomas Mann, who left Germany in 1933 and did not set foot in the country again until the Goethe bicentennial in 1949, the literary historians of National Socialism make him the perfect representative of everything un-German, the living denial of a healthy, vital *Volkstum*. 'Everyone knows', sneered Bartels, 'the part he played in the German republic.' Biographically, too, Mann is easily disposed of: 'Like Dehmel he once worked in a fire insurance office, then attended two terms of lectures at Munich University, went to Rome, became editor of that infamous journal *Simplicissimus* and married a Jewess.' In sum: 'He is vastly overrated . . . . . I doubt whether anything of his will last.'[17] Mann's incompatibility with what the Nazi régime expected of its authors was made clear by Paul Fechter:

Remote from life, entangled in his own world of unreality, he was out of touch with the new reality in Germany, and rejecting his birthright, he left the country. That he was then deprived of his German citizenship merely crowned a fate which in literary terms had long been sealed. Since he went abroad, his speeches and essays have had nothing in common with the real Germany and its spiritual life.[18]

The 'real Germany'? At the time it was certainly real enough to millions, both inside the country and outside. Was the 'real' Germany the Germany of Bach, of Kant, of Goethe, of Beethoven? Or of Frederick the Great, Bismarck—and Hitler? How does one set a people of religious and idealist tendency, steeped in nature worship, sentimental yet intense, 'a land of poets and thinkers', against a people that put national self-assertion before individual and social freedom, that said 'Yes' to Hitler, and that watched the persecution of millions for belonging to the wrong race?

However improbable, unhappy, disastrous the paradoxes, the reality that one confronts at the end must be one Germany, not two. German history and intellectual development since the time of Luther has moved by violent swings from the introspective to the aggressive, from the rational to the irrational, from idealism to *Realpolitik*, from the spiritual to the materialistic, from the sublime to the depraved. But these oscillations lie within a single set of extremes.

> *Natur hat weder*
> *Kern noch Schale,*
> *Alles ist sie*
> *Mit einem Male*

(Nature has not got a heart and a shell but is all of a piece.)

—run Goethe's lines. The psychology of the German people shares the same indivisibility and has to accommodate its polarities in its own way.

ii. Personae Gratae

The dead make good allies. They cannot protest if their name is called in vain, or explain what they really meant if their successors are determined to prove that they meant something different. And if one suspects that they are not allies at all, one can condemn them to an irrevocable limbo of silence. *De mortuis nihil nisi utile.*

But a totalitarian state also looks for support among the intelligentsia of the day—both established writers whose works appear to buttress what the régime stands for, and younger artists prepared to make the philosophies of the régime the *raison d'être* of their career. The author is no longer a 'freischaffender Künstler' but, in the hideous word coined by the bureaucrats of the Reichsschrifttumskammer, a *Kulturschaffender* bound in service to the state, a feudal dependant with his prescribed role in society. 'Our state rests on National Socialism', wrote Karl-Friedrich Schrieber, legal attaché to the Kulturkammer. 'The people must therefore be educated accordingly, and this education is primarily the task of those whose creative work determines the nation's intellectual image. They will therefore only discharge their function if they set out to achieve the goals for which the new state is striving.'[19] Those writers who accepted their appointment as latter-day *praeceptores Germaniae* naturally came to enjoy the profits of official approval, and the status of a willing *Schrifttumsschaffender* equalled that of a senior executive in the party machine.

The *Nationalsozialistische Bibliographie* of Erich Unger, published in 1934, lists the following authors as approved antecedents of the National Socialist *Weltanschauung*: Houston Stewart Chamberlain, Fichte, Gobineau, Heidegger, Jahn, Paul de Lagarde, Julius Langbehn (author of *Rembrandt als Erzieher*), Theodor Litt, Hermann Löns, Josef Nadler, Nietzsche, Eduard Spranger, Adolf Stöcker, Hermann Wirth, Max Wundt.[20] It is an extraordinary, yet at the same time shrewdly-selected group, an example of the eclecticism in which the Nazis excelled. There was no such thing as a National Socialist philosophy, merely a rag-bag of prejudices, peremptory dicta and irrational appeals, a rag-bag from which one could pick whatever item seemed most useful for the occasion. Chauvinism, racialism, irrationalism, mysticism, the cult of violence, anti-liberalism—all these can be found in the authors that Unger lists. But the meaning of their work as a whole is brushed aside in favour of a policy of selective plundering.

Among the established men of letters who in one way or another consented—to put it no higher—to the association of their names with the policies of the National Socialists, there are a few whom one encounters time and again in discussions of *arteigene Literatur*. A glance at three of these 'authorities' will show what principles sustain this literature: Hans Grimm, Erwin Guido Kolbenheyer and Hanns Johst.

Hans Grimm is remembered today solely as the author of *Volk ohne Raum*, a novel of interminable turgidity which acquired in the 1930s the status of a received text. Grimm was one of the first group of writers to be appointed to the reconstituted Akademie der Dichtung in May 1933, three days after the expulsion of Werfel, Kaiser, Schickele, Unruh and others. In his own small way the hero of *Volk ohne Raum* had embodied the fate of the German nation through his life in the colonial territories of southwest Africa, his imprisonment by the British, his return home and his murder as he addresses a political meeting. The German national inferiority complex, fed by the belatedness of her political unification, of her expansionist colonial urge and of her evolution into a modern social and industrial society, is the psychological reality behind the events of the novel. What the German achieves by his proverbial industriousness—a quality proper to the 'Nordic' races, according to Grimm—becomes a source of envy and hatred to his loose-living rivals, who take advantage of his idealism and lack of practical experience; so after the Great War what few colonial possessions Germany had acquired were spitefully taken away, together with parts even of the homeland itself. 'Hans Grimms *Volk ohne Raum*', concluded Langenbucher, 'is one of those works in our literature that will live on through the ages, and in which distant generations, trembling before the greatness of their country's solemn destiny, will perceive the spirit of their nation, its profound and everlasting strength, the voice of its true ancestry.'[21]

However, apart from the use made of *Volk ohne Raum* and his other stories of colonial Africa—*Das deutsche Südwesterbuch* (1928), *Der Richter in der Karu und andere Geschichten* (1930), *Lüderitzland. Sieben Begebenheiten* (1934) etc.—Grimm himself was a far from unwilling ally in the Nazi cause. In a book called *Von der bürgerlichen Ehre und bürgerlichen Notwendigkeit*, published in 1932, he made his position plain: 'Together with a number of others I regard National Socialism as the *first* and *only real* democratic movement there has been in the

German nation' (Grimm's italics)[22]. The political commitment of the writer is to him a matter of course, and the occasional pieces collected in *Der Schriftsteller und die Zeit* (1931) preach that the day of literature as art is past but the age of literature as a means to a political end is about to dawn. In essays and speeches of the 1930s he makes explicit the racial arguments, already illustrated in the tensions between the white and black races in *Volk ohne Raum*, in favour of the supremacy of the Nordic races and against any degree of bastardisation. Indeed, there is in these writings hardly a word that could not have been written by Hitler himself.

No less chauvinist-racialist, but in an imagistic, mystical, cocoon-shrouded manner very different from the directness of Grimm, are the works of Erwin Guido Kolbenheyer. Both share that worship of man's elemental, primitive impulses which is so destructively powerful in German thought in the 1920s and 1930s, from Spengler to Gottfried Benn, from Ernst and Friedrich Georg Jünger to Hitler and the crudest exhortations of Nazi propaganda. But where Grimm is blunt, practical and exhortatory, Kolbenheyer unravels in his fictional and theoretical works an elaborate metaphysical picture, based on the analogy of organic biological evolution, of man in the throes of an immense upheaval. In response to these biological pressures, man, in his ethnic reality, asserts himself in all forms of his society, and the individual who comes, as he must, to see himself as but a cell in the organic structure of his community, has grasped the necessity of subordinating himself to the forces of history, and thereby of serving the society to which he belongs. By recognising the irresistibility of these 'biological laws', man will recognise what Kolbenheyer calls 'der rassenbiologische Sinn des Nationalismus unserer Zeit'.[23]

All this is murkily expounded in his principal philosophical work *Die Bauhütte* (1925) and in the collected articles of *Die Stimme* (1931), *Unser Befreiungskampf und die deutsche Dichtkunst* (1932) and other compendia. Kolbenheyer joined the Nazi-style Akademie der Dichtung in 1933, welcomed the National Socialist revolution as a force that shook the German people out of their listlessness and lack of purpose, and accepted many important literary awards from the hands of the authorities. In 1948 his record led to a conviction for complicity in the rise of Nazism, although the large-scale historical novels and dramas which form the basis of his literary reputation, and mostly belong to earlier periods, would in themselves hardly have provoked a denazification trial (*Amor Dei*, 1908, built on the antithesis of Spinoza and Rembrandt; the *Paracelsus*-trilogy [1917, 1921, 1925]; *Heroische Leidenschaften* [1928], a drama on Giordano Bruno; *Gregor und Heinrich* [1934], a drama on Pope Gregory VII and King

Henry IV). However, the poem, steeped in Nazi vocabulary, that he subscribed in 1941 to the anthology *Dem Führer. Worte deutscher Dichter*, leaves no doubt about where he stood:

> *Es lebt ein Dank, mein Führer, den die Jugend*
> *Dir nicht zu bringen weiss und Deiner Grossmut:*
> *Dank reifer Herzen, denen deutsches Schicksal*
> *Das eigne war in Spannung, Not und Sturz . . . .*
> *Denn Deine Tat rief den gelähmten Willen,*
> *Und der Geweckte, wissentlich geballt*
> *In klare Zucht, wuchs auf zur Lebensmacht,*
> *Macht, die für alle Zeit gebrochen schien*
> *Nun aber selbsterlöst die Welt befreit.*[24]

(There is a gratitude, my Führer, that the young do not know how to express to you and your magnanimity—the gratitude of mature hearts that shared the fate of Germany in times of stress, of affliction, of defeat . . . For your action awakened our feeble wills, which, once roused and held in the conscious tension of pure breeding, grew in strength, attaining a power over life which had once seemed broken for all time but now, having itself found salvation, will redeem the world.)

The third member of this doleful trinity, Hanns Johst, can lay claim to being the lynchpin of the National Socialist literary establishment—a role acknowledged in 1949 by the denazification court that sentenced him to three years in a labour camp, the confiscation of half his property and a 10-year publication ban. He was President of the Reichsschrifttumskammer, President of the Akademie der Dichtung, Preussischer Staatsrat and Reichskultursenator, positions that gave him the official rank of SS-Brigadeführer and led to personal friendships with Himmler, Bormann, Darré, Hitler's adjutant Karl Wolff and other figures in the inter ring of power. His essays and speeches from this period exude a fawning anxiety to be associated with the military, racial, party-political, cultural and other aspects of National Socialist policy.[25] From 1933 onwards he virtually ceased to be a literary figure at all, devoting himself instead to writing propaganda copy for Goebbels' publicity machine and panegyrics in honour of the Nazi leaders.

Johst had first appeared on the literary scene in his twenties with a number of lurid expressionist plays depicting in violent action, and even more violent language, characters in a state of rebellion against the constrictions of their environment. *Der Einsame* (1917) has as its hero the dramatist Grabbe, whom the expressionists saw as one of their precursors, while *Propheten* (1922) portrays the struggles of Martin Luther, less in terms of the individual religious consciousness than of the awakening of that sense of national German unity which was as urgently needed now as it had been 400 years ago. It was

Luther's role to urge the people on towards this unity, and the same ideal of service sustains the novel *Kreuzweg*, published the same year.

From this point onwards the chauvinist purpose of Johst's work became clearer and clearer. The drama *Thomas Paine* (1927) is not really about the American War of Independence, of which Paine is shown to be the servant, but about the German people's struggle for freedom, an emotional call to the nation to cast off the shackles of foreign interference and of self-seeking, 'un-German' forces in the country itself. 'The true work of art must become completely absorbed by the people to whom it belongs. True drama is the augur of freedom.'[26] Johst's language and manner have in *Thomas Paine* the expressionist shrillness they had never lost, an intemperateness that is the appropriate concomitant of the anti-intellectualism and irrationality of his appeal.

1933 saw the first performance of the work which his name will always bring first to mind, the work given that pride of place by the Nazis which *Hamlet* or *King Lear* or *Othello* occupies in the civilised world—the play *Schlageter*. Leo Schlageter, an unprincipled thug who joined the terrorist 'Organisation Heinz' after the First World War and became a member of the National Socialist party in 1922, was shot by the French for his acts of sabotage during the occupation of the Rhineland in 1923. Hitler glorified him as a martyr in *Mein Kampf*, and like the pimp Horst Wessel, murdered in 1930, he became a folk-hero of the Nazi movement. The première of Johst's crude, hysterical, boring play was given on Hitler's birthday, 20 April 1933, with distinguished names like Albert Bassermann, Paul Bildt and Veit Harlan in the cast. Its dedication runs: 'Für Adolf Hitler in liebender Verehrung und unwandelbarer Treue.' It is, incidentally, one of a considerable number of dramas and novels from those year—*Die endlose Strasse* (1930) by Sigmund Graff and C.E. Hintze; Graff's *Die vier Musketiere* (1932) and *Die Heimkehr des Matthias Bruck* (1933); Friedrich Bethge's *Reims* (1934); Richard Euringer's *Deutsche Passion* (1933); Ernst von Salomon's *Die Geächteten* (1930); Dwinger's trilogy *Die Armee hinter Stacheldraht* (1929), *Zwischen weiss und rot* (1930) and *Wir rufen Deutschland* (1932)—that return to the Great War and its aftermath for their subject-matter.

From the self-centred drama of expressionism, with its generation conflicts and its juvenile outbursts, Johst has advanced to the drama of self-sacrifice and total collectivisation, with the same conflicts and the same outbursts, but now in the name of National Socialism. Not only Schlageter himself stands for the regimentation of the individual: his comrades too are committed to violence as a way of achieving their aim, the aim being the establishment of a 'völkisch'

German state. 'Those of us lads who stick by Schlageter,' says the revolutionary son of the Regierungspräsident, making the generation gap plain, 'don't do so because he's the last soldier from the Great War but because he's the first soldier of the Third Reich!'[27]

As one who from his expressionist beginnings had put emotionalism before reason, force before morality, Johst was a not unsurprising convert to the Nazi cause. His plays, novels and poems, still more so his political and 'philosophical' essays, lie in an oblivion for which one must be earnestly grateful. Yet the career of an expressionist writer who was a pacifist in World War I, looked suspiciously at democracy in the early days of the Weimar Republic, and finally embraced a militant nationalism as a faithful servant of the Führer, cannot but have its representatively bizarre significance.

On the base of the statue of an unknown prisoner that stands in the former concentration camp of Dachau are engraved the words: 'Den Toten zur Ehr, Den Lebenden zur Mahnung'. Hanns Johst and his fellows bear their own share of guilt for this episode in German history.

In literary as in political terms National Socialism stands, not as an erratic block in the landscape of German history and culture but as a destructive fusion of ideas and practices individually identifiable in the German past. The year 1933 marks an end, not a beginning—a culmination of firmly-rooted, often mutually contradictory tendencies that had been working their way through the German consciousness since the dawn of the vision of cultural and political nationalism in the late eighteenth century. The phenomenon of National Socialism may have been unique, but its rise was not unprepared, nor were its manifestations unforeseeable. It cannot be excised from the body of German culture as though it were a growth without roots. The debate on whether it was a peculiarly and inevitably German phenomenon will continue: the fact remains that for the twentieth century, as six million Jews, nine million Allied soldiers and countless masses of European civilians testified with their lives, it *was* German. And scattered through German literature and thought in the nineteenth century lie the elements, sometimes pernicious, sometimes grotesque, but often also natural and respectable, even noble and distinguished, that combined to produce an orgy of devastation which almost destroyed the Western world.

The areas from which the Nazis drew the strands of their syncretist *Weltanschauung*, as it showed itself in the *arteigene Literatur* that they prescribed, can be grouped under four headings. Firstly, an area of pseudo-mystical, pseudo-metaphysical irrationalism dominated by a vapid, emotional idealism; secondly, the cult of the soil, of the local and the domestic, based on the ideology of *Blut und Boden*; thirdly, the power of nationalism, associated with militarism and the anti-Social Democratic pressures of the so-called conservative revolution; and finally, the areas of the contemporary scene—political rallying-points, the meaning of the Nazi cause, the cult of power, the figure of the Führer—in terms of which the demands of the Third Reich could be made explicit. The last of these is made up of purpose-bound trivia that arose, and died, with the Tausendjähriges Reich; the other three have their roots in nineteenth-century Romanticism, source of so much beauty, so much glory and so much misery in the national life of modern Germany.

German Romanticism grew from a heterogeneous assemblage of impulses and interests ranging from philosophical idealism and aesthetic subjectivism to folk-lore and political nationalism, from exotica and medievalism to the pursuit of irrationality and the metaphysics of music. It was never a 'school of thought', with a single, unchanging message, but a complex of divergent, often contradictory beliefs and activities linked by little more than a faith in the validity and the heuristic power of subjective experience and expression. Accompanying this faith were a scorn of bourgeois society, a cult of the inscrutable, the equivocal and the vague, and an appeal to passion, instinct and the life of the spirit.

Towards the end of the nineteenth century, above all in the figure of Nietzsche, this Romanticism, in one sense or another, reasserted its influence through Stefan George and his circle, in Richard Beer-Hoffmann, Schnitzler and the early Hofmannsthal, in philosophers like Wilhelm Dilthey and Georg Simmel, and in Freud. In the wake of this neo-Romanticism, held in a spell of idealism and *Rausch*, followed Hermann Stehr, Erwin Guido Kolbenheyer, Börries von Münchhausen, Ina Seidel, Wilhelm von Scholz, Josef Weinheber and the other *epigoni*, many of them founder-members of the new Akademie der Dichtung, whose names became linked with the Nazi cause.

The appeal to irrationalism and Romantic mysticism took a variety of forms, each calculated to stimulate a particular area of the imagination, each vague, evocative part merging with the others to form a vague, evocative whole. The call to experience by feeling rather than by thought, and the invocation of mysterious, chthonic forces felt through surrender to the emotions, prepares the ground. Hans Friedrich Blunck, writer of provincial, historico-mythological tales, and President of the Reichsschrifttumskammer from 1933 to 1935, explained the situation thus:

I believe that it is good for the poet . . . . to be on the side of those concerned for their national identity. Revelling in the struggle, he should strive to set feeling above cold, calculating reason, which always seeks to reassert itself. He should immerse himself in those mysterious, primeval currents on which man, earth and sky are carried along. He should give himself over to a sense of reverence for the spirit of life and its foundations.[28]

The search for the 'spirit of life' and what Heinz Kindermann called 'the mystic rebirth of the German soul'[29] fills the work of the man who received perhaps more veneration than any other from the high priests of National Socialist culture—Hermann Stehr, a native of Silesia. Langenbucher introduces him in words that must be savoured in the fulsome original: 'Im dichterischen Werk Hermann Stehrs findet der Kampf um die göttlichen Rechte der menschlichen Seele eine grossartige, aufwühlende, in alle Tiefen des menschlichen Seins hinunterspürende, in alle Höhen des menschlichen Strebens hinaufreichende Darstellung.'[30]

Not only did Stehr's literary career, like that of most of the writers pressed into National Socialist service, reach back well into the early years of the century—it was already virtually over. Blunck, Hans Grimm, Kolbenheyer, Dwinger, even the Gabriel of Nazi literature, Hanns Johst—all, like Stehr, had reached by 1933 a state of almost complete literary silence, as though stricken by a merciful blight. Stehr's characters, in novels and *Novellen* published between 1898 and 1931, search for their true soul, the soul of Silesian mysticism, in struggles between sensuous and spiritual reality, and this all-powerful soul, source of both the highest bliss and the profoundest suffering, is equated with fate and ultimate knowledge. When man penetrates the depths of his own soul, writes Stehr, he experiences

all life, the whole cosmos, God in His entirety, with all His secrets, for our foundation is also God's foundation. The man who knows this will cease his lamentation, and his mortal self will melt away from his immortality. Rejoice! For here lie peace, happiness, light, beauty, which no man can take from you.[31]

A natural corollary to this search for the soul is the denigration of the intellect. The imposition of the Nazi ideology depended on suffocating the critical faculty in a fog of mockery and abuse. The intellectuals are identified as enemies of the people, traitors to the true cause of the *Volk*, while the masses lose their sense of inferiority and are made to feel that it is they that constitute the nation and control its movement towards its true destiny. 'The new state has been born in opposition to the intellectuals', cried Gottfried Benn, in a broadcast talk in April 1933 which he never lived down. 'All those who counted themselves among the intellectuals these past 10 years opposed the birth of this new state.'[32] By intellectuals Benn meant liberals, social democrats, Jews, Marxists, pacifists and others, many of them no longer in Germany, who would have taken his remark as a compliment. Reason was nothing, feeling was everything. And since everyone had feelings, while the exercise of rational control was the dubious prerogative of a few, the new ethic could be based on spontaneity and an undefined sense of the 'real' meaning of things. The plethora of poems and novels on mythological subjects from the gloomy, blood-stained Germanic past helped to create the impression of an historical tradition rich in the mystical, instinctive, anti-rational values by which the present rulers of Germany governed, and which they adduced in order to identify the noble 'Nordic' racial strain that ensured the preservation of 'true' German qualities.

Clamped on to this pattern of mysticism, worship of elemental forces and submission to the commands of national destiny was the iron grip of authoritarianism, of the will to power. On one side this led to the literature of hero-worship—eulogies of the Führer and affirmations of blind obedience to his charismatic will; on the other it merged with the political nationalism and racial blood-cult to produce the literature of the Herrenvolk.

So irresistible, supra-human, almost mystical a figure had Hitler become, the demi-God to whom, whatever one's hardships of the moment or misgivings for the future, one could always appeal for intercession and salvation, that poems addressed to him have the aura of hymns. Such is Hermann Claudius' wartime Deutscher Spruch, beginning:

> Herrgott, steh dem Führer bei,
> Dass sein Werk das deine sei . . . .[33]

(O Lord, support the Führer, that his works may be Thine)

But the worship of power too has its immutable character. For in all history there are those chosen by fate to rule, and those, the mass, chosen by fate to be ruled. Standing by an emperor's tomb, the Austrian poet Josef Weinheber muses on the distinction in a Sapphic stanza:

> Düstrer Sarg zu Särgen: und trägst doch, starrer
> Schädel noch die Krone? Ja, Staub, er wird zu
> Staub. Doch Fürst bleibt Fürst. Nur die Bettler sterben
> ganz mit dem Fleische.[34]

(Sombre coffin among coffins; yet, staring skull, dost thou still wear the crown? Dust—yea, thou dost turn to dust. But a prince is always a prince—only beggars die utterly with the flesh.)

('Kaisergruft', 1936)

Weinheber is the only tragic figure, and almost the only real poet, among the writers who were seduced into collaborating with the régime. He belonged to the younger generation of authors born in the last decade or so of the nineteenth century but only became well-known in the 1930s, first with the poems collected as *Adel und Untergang* (1934), then with the collections *Späte Krone* (1936) and *O Mensch, gib acht* (1937). At his best he had a sombre power of language made the more impressive by the classical forms—Sapphic and Asclepiadean strophes, Alcaic ode, and variants thereof—in which it is cast. In return for the patronage of the invaders of his country he contributed didactic poems on the virtues of honest toil, on obedience, on loyalty, on selflessness, on the noble character of the Führer and so on, to boost the morale of the people during the war years. In 1945, less than a month before the end of the war in Europe, he committed suicide in a mood of remorse and depression. Two years before his death he characterised the substance of his poetry as 'Einsamkeit, Urangst, Frömmigkeit.'

Many may choose not to forget Weinheber's involvement with the affairs of the National Socialists. But above all the poems of *Adel und Untergang* and *Kammermusik* (1939), in the classical tradition of Klopstock and Hölderlin, and full of striking language and formal artistry, have a grave beauty that has too often been swamped in the sycophantic raving and ranting that passed for literature in the Third Reich. The appeal of his poetry is crystallised in the last lines of W.H. Auden's poem, written in 1965 to commemorate the twentieth anniversary of Weinheber's death:

> For even my English ear
> Gets in your German
> The workmanship and the note
> Of one who was graced
> To hear the viols playing
> On the impaled green,
> Committed thereafter *den*
> *Abgrund zu nennen*.[35]

To give the romanticising mysticism of Stehr, Kolbenheyer, Blunck and the others a private, homely context, the custodians of the Reichsschrifttumskammer eagerly diverted the already well-established pursuit of provincial *Heimatdichtung* into the paths of family sentimentality, the cult of the noble peasant, and what has become known in general as the literature of *Blut und Boden*.

The Nazis' magic password in these regions was Nature. The honest tiller of the soil, the peasant at one with his simple, health-giving surroundings, received a romantically stylised image, and a mystical link was declared to exist between Man and Mother Earth. The stories of the Mecklenburger Friedrich Griese, of Richard Billinger from Upper Austria (who later fell foul of the Nazis) and Karl Heinrich Waggerl from the Hohe Tauern struck the desired tone of sentimentality and local pride, as the poetry of Heinrich Lersch and the tales of Anton Dörfler idealised the toil of the worker and the craftsman, and the novels of Martin Luserke, in the wake of Gorch Fock's famous *Seefahrt ist not!*, glorified life at sea. But it was above all the life of the peasant that embodied the ideal of nature, an ideal that was to draw men away from the false gods of modern civilisation, the gods of a rational and responsible social ethic, of a faith in the human mind and human progress. In programmatic terms:

It is our Reichskanzler Adolf Hitler's historical achievement to have evolved a new approach to these matters and to have made it accessible to all responsible sections of the German people. Only a new mode of thought, regional in scope and tied to life on the land, can free us from the dazzling but specious dogmas thrust upon us in the name of a so-called belief in progress.[36]

There is a kind of specious 'Back to Nature' air about these primitive calls to abandon the intellectual challenge of civilisation and revert to a worship of elemental forces, manual labour and direct involvement in the fortunes of the nation:

> *Nicht in Parlamenten and Regierungspalästen wird Deutschland.*
> *Nicht bei schönen Reden und lärmenden Festen wird Deutschland.*
> *Weit uber Strassen und Plätze und Mauern,*
> *Bei Ackersknechten, bei Säern und Bauern,*
> *Wo die braune Erde die Frucht gebiert,*
> *Wo die Hand des Herrn die Zügel führt, wird Deutschland.*
> *Wo Hämmer Eisen schmieden, wo Maschinen drönen, wird Deutschland.*
> *Wo Kolonnen marschieren und Schlachtrufe tönen, wird Deutschland . . .* etc.

(Germany will not be born in national assemblies or government mansions. Germany will not be born in fine speeches and noisy celebrations. Far away from streets and squares and walls, with ploughboys, sowers and farmers, where the brown earth brings forth her harvest, where the master's hand guides the bridle—that is where Germany will be born. Where hammers forge the iron, where machines hum—that is where Germany will be born. Where columns march and battle-cries ring out—that is where Germany will be born.)

(Kurt Eggers, *Deutsche Gedichte*, München, 1934, 8)[37]

Heinrich Lersch, the best-known of the 'Arbeiterdichter' of the 1920s, also allowed himself to be drawn into this context and exhibited as a model of the living culture of the common people.

This is the *Boden*, the call of Mother Earth, whose voice is that of unchallengeable destiny. Equally immutable, equally determinative in its power, is the mystic entity of *Blut*. Heredity guarantees tradition, and purity of heredity guarantees the purity of the tradition—which is to say, the fulfilment of personal and national destiny. *Boden* is the physical reality, the known and understood, the practical context of our lives; *Blut* is the mystical substratum, real but mysterious, the biological yet at the same time spiritual governing force of our existence. And all but a few families, as the champions of this line of thinking insistently pointed out, came ultimately from peasant stock:

To recognise this is to recognise the significance of the German peasantry for our cultural life, for it is one of the basic principles of the National Socialist *Weltanschauung* that the creative urges of a people are determined by blood, source of all national characteristics. If therefore the peasants are the healthiest and most prolific section of the community, and thus the most vital factor in the perpetual regeneration of the people, the creative powers of the people must needs be continually refreshed, directly or indirectly, by infusions from the same source.[38]

Poems, novels and short stories too numerous to mention, both by writers whose names are remembered—Emil Strauss, Ina Seidel, Griese and the others quoted above—and by a mass of forgotten hacks, undertook the task of ensuring that this 'refreshment' was forthcoming.

The values of *Blut und Boden* also helped sustain the third area in which literature expressive of National Socialist aspirations found a rallying point—the area of national pride. Since the unification of the Second Reich under Bismarck in 1871 a great deal of energy had been channelled into cultivating the qualities that would preserve the political cohesion so painfully and belatedly won. A certain self-conscious aggressiveness is inseparable from such moments, inasmuch as the new identity has to be defined, on the one hand by looking inwards at what holds the young community together, and on the other hand by emphasising, for the benefit of both the domestic and the foreign public, the indigenous qualities that set it apart from the communities around it.

This conservative, consolidatory nature of a young political entity is of particular relevance here, because in political as in literary matters it has often been too readily assumed that the forces of nationalism in Germany, above all from 1914 onwards, represent a form of reactionary conservatism which merges with virtually no transition into National Socialism. A belief in authority, whether in personal, communal or national affairs, does not make a man a Fascist or a Nazi: no political group in Germany laid greater stress on discipline and conformity in the 1920s than the Communists. Conversely, that so many were prepared to invoke the principle of total obedience in order to underpin the Nazi ideology does not invalidate the concepts of authority and obedience *per se*. By whatever subtle argumentation Max Scheler, Spengler, Moeller van den Bruck, Hans Delbrück and others may be burdened with an intellectual responsibility for the rise of Hitler, they were not Nazis. Nor, accused of standing for values of a different but no less destructive kind, was Ernst Jünger. Even novelists like Ernst von Salomon and Edwin Erich Dwinger, literary spokesmen for the so-called 'conservative revolution' of the late 1920s and early 1930s, are entitled to be seen, at least in part, as men engaged in the not dishonourable task of salvaging a national self-respect from the failures of an inglorious republican régime, not as rabble-rousers in the service of National Socialism.

Undoubtedly the political naiveté of the people—also a character-istic feature of the early life of a new political system—enabled this combination of conservatism and national self-assertion to make the impression it did. Defeat in war, together with the dictated peace that followed, were realities fresh in the mind, and by borrowing from the concepts and vocabulary of Romanticism, nationally-minded con-servatives found it easy to capture support for patriotic programmes. The great strength of their appeal lay precisely in this blend of the realistic and the familiar with the spiritual and the irrational, for while the imagination could be stirred by the concept alone, the reality of the concept could also be demonstrated by reference to history. This appeal is particularly strong, for example, in Ernst Jünger. For him the physical reality of the *Fronterlebnis* experienced by so many fuses with a challenge to the nation to rise to the spiritual values which this personal commitment embodies.

As Hans Grimm invoked the need for national unity in terms of Germany's lost colonies in *Volk ohne Raum*, so Ernst von Salomon in *Die Geächteten* (1930) and Edwin Erich Dwinger in the trilogy *Die deutsche Passion* (1929–32) did so against the background of a lost war, a futile revolution and a lost peace. Johst's play *Schlageter* preaches the same message of self-sacrifice in the name of national self-respect, and numerous poems take as their starting-point the God-given unity of the country:

> *Wir haben nichts als dies im Sinn: das Reich,*
> *Reich aller Brüder, im erkor'nen Raum,*
> *Den Gott uns zugewiesen. Und kein Fremder*
> *Dürft' unserer Freiheit rühren Rain und Saum.*

(We have nothing in our minds but one thing—the *Reich*, that kingdom of all our brethren, in the chosen realm assigned to us by God. Let no foreigner lay a finger on even the fringe of our freedom.)

      (Blunck, 'Das Reich als Ernst', in *Balladen und Gedichte*, Hamburg, 1937)

Poems in praise of those who gave their lives in defence of national honour, like Baldur von Schirach's 'Der Tote' and Heinz Steguweit's 'Feldherrnhalle', both induce an appropriate reverence for the cause and remind the people of the qualities of obedience and discipline demanded of them.[39] War becomes, in Heraclitus' words, 'the father of all things'—not merely a holy crusade to preserve all that is worth living for but the noblest mode of life open to man. Ernst Jünger's brother Friedrich Georg lauds the power of war in a classical elegy called simply 'Der Krieg':

> *Unter Himmeln von Eisen umarmt sich die sterbende Jugend.*
> *Furchtlos naht sie dem Tod, der mit Gesang sie begrüsst.*
> *Falle, was mag! Verwelkst du schon, Rose? Mit Hämmern zermalmet*
> *Morschender Zeiten Gebild. Nimmer beklag' ich dich, Tod.*[40]

(Dying youth embraces beneath skies of iron, fearlessly approaching death, which welcomes them with song. Perish what may! Dost thou wilt, O rose? Smash with hammers the image of a decaying age! Never shall I mourn thee, O death.)

Support for the appeal to national solidarity came also from historical and mythological novels devoted to figures from the Germanic tradition who had struggled to achieve what the Germany of the present day was struggling to regain. Hans Blunck's trilogies *Urväter-Saga* (1928–33) and *Werdendes Volk* (1934: the parts had been published individually in the 1920s) belong here, as do the ballads of Börries von Münchhausen and the numerous modern versions of medieval romances and lyrics by Will Vesper. Similarly favoured by the literary establishment of the 1930s was Wilhelm Schäfer, a prolific author of novels, short stories and anecdotes, whose career started back in the last decade of the nineteenth century and who found his material in every conceivable period of German history, from Gothic times (*Theodorich, König des Abendlandes*, 1939) through the sixteenth century (*Huldreich Zwingli*, 1926) and the eighteenth and nineteenth centuries (*Winckelmanns Ende*, 1925; *Hölderlins Einkehr*, 1925) down to the twentieth century (*Der Hauptmann von Köpenick*, 1930—a novel on the same subject as Zuckmayer's well-known play).

From the cultivation of a belligerent nationalism to the exaltation of the day-to-day activities, ideals and popular heroes of the National Socialist state—the substance of the fourth and final thematic category—is a small step. In ideological terms it represents the transition from the authoritarianism by which the Nazis forced their will on the German people during the early years of the régime to the totalitarianism of the monolithic Nazi state. Once the power of the party had been consolidated and its domination of the country made absolute, Hitler could embark on his policies of European aggression, knowing that his *Volk* would identify itself with his achievements—indeed, that these achievements could be presented as manifestations of the real will of the people. Hitler *was* Germany. What Hitler achieved, Germany achieved. And the demonstrable success of Hitler's conduct of affairs from 1933 until at least 1941 made it all the easier for Goebbels' propaganda machine to proclaim both the rightness of the Führer's cause and the material and moral benefit that consequently accrued to his *Volk*.

Little of what was written in this spirit can be graced with the description 'literature'. Mob violence, *Gleichschaltung* and racial persecution are not values conducive to the creation of great art. The tone is high-pitched, reminiscent of expressionism, with an abundance of hyperboles, fiery challenges and rhetorical appeals. Among the most popular subjects, inevitably, was the Führer himself, object of ostentatious praise and fauning veneration both to party hack-writers and, unhappily, to others.

In 1941 August Friedrich Velmede edited a collection of poems under the title *Dem Führer. Worte deutscher Dichter*. Most of the items were either pretentiously pompous, their authors trying desperately to show their skill in classical metres and original strophic forms, or depressingly banal in the manner of Will Vesper's 'Dem Führer', which begins:

> So gelte denn wieder
> Urväter Sitte:
> Es steigt der Führer
> aus Volkes Mitte.[41]

(The customs of our ancestors shall prevail again as the Führer rises from amid the people.)

But alongside Vesper, a minor chauvinist novelist and poet who probably wrote more poems in honour of Hitler than any of his contemporaries, we find in this anthology more substantial figures—Kolbenheyer, Carossa, Weinheber—who were not above contributing to the general adulation. Four years earlier, in 1937, Kolbenheyer had already sung the Führer's praises:

> *Im Schicksalssturm der Völker wächst der Mann,*
> *Der seinem Volk die Bresche bricht zum Licht.*
> *Er trägt Verlangen nach der starken Stunde,*
> *Die blanke Waffen führt und keinem Munde*
> *Das überflüssge Wort vergeben kann.*
> *Er sucht die Tat. Die Tat nur hat Gewicht.*[42]

(As the peoples surge towards their destiny, there arises the man who will clear his people's path to the light. He cherishes a yearning for the moment of strength which comes with shining weapons and can never forgive the lips that utter a needless word. He seeks action. Only action carries weight.)

Strict control was exercised over the publication of pseudo-documentary biographies of Hitler which purported to reveal aspects of his life in the days before he came to power. The Parteiamtliche Prüfungskommission under Philipp Bouhler saw to it that attention remained focused on Hitler's achievements in office, and only Hitler's court photographer Heinrich Hoffmann was allowed to publish glimpses of his private life in albums such as *Hitler, wie ihn keiner kennt* and *Das Antlitz des Führers*. These books of Hoffmann's, issued by Franz Eher, publisher of *Mein Kampf*, and including titles like *Hitler in seinen Bergen*, *Hitler baut Grossdeutschland* and *Mit Hitler in Polen*, sold in their millions.

Of the figures in the Nazi hall of fame who were made the subject of literary works, the unsavoury character Horst Wessel, poet of the SA's marching song 'Die Fahne hoch', holds pride of place. Hanns Heinz Ewers' novel *Horst Wessel—ein deutsches Schicksal* (1932) presents this martyr to the Nazi cause as a freedom fighter comparable to Theodor Körner, although Ewers' emphasis of the erotic side of the story—which would have come as no surprise to those acquainted with Ewers' novels and poems from the early decades of the century—met with disapproval.[43] A flood of dramas on Wessel followed, though here too many dwelt on the sordid side of the story and were banned by Staatskommissar Hans Hinkel as unworthy of the noble hero and—a touching afterthought—as likely to cause distress to his mother and sister. The numerous lyric effusions, on the other hand, were unequivocal to the point of emptiness, witness the poem by the prolific poetaster and leader of the Hitler Youth, Baldur von Schirach:

> *Kaum einer von uns, der dich gekannt,*
> *Und doch auch keiner, der dich nicht kennt!*

Dein Name brennt
Wie ein Feuer dem Vaterland!

Kameraden alle: ihr braune Schar,
Die Fahne pflanzt auf der Türme Knauf!
Das Wort macht wahr:
Horst Wessel fiel, und Deutschland steht auf![44]

(Scarcely any of us that knew you, yet none that does not know you. Your name burns like a fire for the Fatherland! Comrades all, you brown cohorts—set the flag on the pinnacle of the spires! Make the slogan come true that Horst Wessel fell and Germany is arising!)

At the Nuremberg Rally of 1934 the Hitler Youth sang:

Nicht Christus folgen wir, sondern Horst Wessel,
Fort mit Weihrauch und Weihwasserkessel![45]

(It is not Christ we follow but Horst Wessel. Away with the incense and the holy water bottle!)

A nation gets not only the politicians, but also the saints, it deserves.

NOTES

1. H. Langenbucher, *Volkhafte Dichtung der Zeit* (5th. ed., Berlin, 1940), 24
2. *ibid.* 549–550
3. A. Bartels, *Einführung in das deutsche Schrifttum für deutsche Menschen* (Leipzig, 1933), 111
4. H. Fechner, *Nationalsozialistische Erziehung* (Munich, 1935), 321
5. a quotation from the *Horst Wessel Lied*
6. H. Fabricius, *Schiller als Kampfgenosse Hitlers* (Berlin, 1934), 128
7. see J. Wulf, *Theater und Film im Dritten Reich* (Gütersloh, 1966), 207
8. F. Koch, *Geschichte deutscher Dichtung* (Hamburg, 1937), 162
9. p. 318
10. such as Goethe's remarks to Friedrich von Müller on December 14, 1808, and to Wilhelm von Humboldt in a letter of November 17/18 of the same year.
11. A. Raabe, *Goethes Sendung im Dritten Reich* (Bonn, 1934), 52
12. V. Mathieu, 'A Nazi Propaganda Directive on Goethe' (*Publications of the English Goethe Society* XXII, 1952–3, 129ff)
13. *Deutsche Dichtung in Vergangenheit und Gegenwart* (Berlin, 1937), 188
14. A. Bartels, op. cit. 211
15. *Nietzsches Philosophie im Lichte unserer Erfahrung* (*Gesammelte Werke in zwölf Bänden*, Frankfurt, 1960, IX, 701)
16. L. Brunschvicg, *Le progrès de la conscience dans la philosophie occidentale* (Paris, 1927), 431
17. A. Bartels, op. cit. 541–2

18. P. Fechter, *Geschichte der deutschen Literatur vom Naturalismus bis zur Literatur des Unwirklichen* (Leipzig, 1935), 379

19. Karl-Friedrich Schrieber, *Die Reichskulturkammer* (Berlin, 1936), 10; see D. Strothmann, *Nationalsozialistische Literaturpolitik* (Bonn, 1960), 82

20. see Strothmann, op. cit. 323

21. H. Langenbucher, op. cit. 463

22. see J. Wulf, *Literatur und Dichtung im Dritten Reich* (Gütersloh, 1966), 337. Oskar Loerke, who was a reluctant member of the Academy in 1933, regarded Grimm, strangely enough, as not to be classified with the Kolbenheyers, the Beumelburgs and the rest, but as 'ein Mensch, ein Dichter' who wanted to get out of the Academy as quickly as possible (O. Loerke, *Tagebücher 1903–1939*, Heidelberg, 1955, 276, 278)

23. see E. Loewy, *Literatur unterm Hakenkreuz* (Frankfurt, 1969), 76

24. E. Loewy, op. cit. 259–60

25. *Ich glaube! Bekenntnisse* (Munich, 1928); *Standpunkt und Fortschritt* (Oldenburg, 1933)

26. H. Johst, *Ich glaube! Bekenntnisse* (Munich, 1928), 18

27. *Schlageter* (Munich, 1933), 85

28. H.F. Blunck, 'Volkstum und Dichtung' (*Des deutschen Dichters Sendung in der Gegenwart*, ed. H. Kindermann, Leipzig, 1933, 199)

29. H. Kindermann, *Die deutsche Gegenwartsdichtung im Aufbau der Nation* (Berlin, 1935), 7

30. H. Langenbucher, op. cit. 118

31. quoted in Langenbucher, op. cit. 129

32. Benn, *Der neue Staat und die Intellektuellen* (*Gesammelte Werke*, Wiesbaden, 1961, I, 440)

33. see E. Loewy, op. cit. 262

34. Weinheber, *Sämtliche Werke* (Salzburg, 1954), II, 211

35. W.H. Auden, *City without Walls and other poems* (London, 1969), 20. The German of the last lines is a quotation from Weinheber's poem 'Kammermusik (Eine Variation)'.

36. H. Langenbucher in *Deutsche Landschaft und Bauerntum* (Berlin, 1935); see J. Wulf, *Literatur und Dichtung im Dritten Reich* (Gütersloh, 1966), 353

37. see J. Wulf, op. cit. 328

38. F.K. Moraller, 'Bauerntum, Volkstum und Kultur' (*W.z.R.-Dienst-Im Auftrag des Kulturkreises der SA*, 1. Dezemberfolge 1938); see J. Wulf, op. cit. 355–6

39. see E. Loewy, op. cit. 204

40. F.G. Jünger, *Gedichte* (Berlin, 1934), 42

41. see E. Loewy, op. cit. 256

42. Kolbenheyer, *Gesammelte Werke* (Munich, 1940), VI, 672

43. Ewers' novel was subsequently banned, partly, it seems, because of his obvious delight in the erotic aspects of a subject in which the Nazis wished to see only heroism and self-sacrifice, but partly also because of Ewers' less than complete commitment to National Socialism before 1932. A film of the novel made in 1933 led to a comical series of events. At a private showing arranged by Goebbels it was enthusiastically received, but a few weeks later Goebbels banned it without explanation. Then, again after a few weeks, he announced that the film could be shown, provided it avoided direct reference to Horst Wessel and were given a different title. So it was adapted, rechristened—not too flatteringly—*Hans Westmar: Einer von vielen*, and released as a general portrayal of the life of a Nazi patriot. Its final frames depict the symbolic victory of Nazism, as a man with

features uncomfortably like those of Stalin, right arm raised in the gesture of Communist solidarity, slowly opens his clenched fist and stretches out his arm until it is held erect in the Nazi salute.

44. J. Wulf, op. cit. 347
45. J. Wulf, op. cit. 344

CHAPTER EIGHT

'Whether 'tis nobler in the mind . . . .': Those Who Stayed

ANY survey of themes and attitudes in the officially approved literature of the Nazi period finds itself chained, inevitably and with only rare exceptions, to the work of inferior authors who showed themselves willing, whether with hesitation or with a fanfare of trumpets, to write what would ingratiate them with the régime. The political situation of these writers is usually as clear-cut as their work is forgettable.

The writings of their political opposites, the handful of men and women who declared, however guardedly, an attitude of opposition, will concern us shortly. Between the two extremes stand a number of writers of divided allegiance, men who either welcomed Hitler at the beginning and then recanted when it was too late, or who tried to steer a survival course between submission and protest, seeking to avoid public confrontation in the hope of preserving their independence of mind.

Some were just ignored, whether because it was considered not worth the effort to try and force them into line, or because the Nazis found it advantageous to preserve a handful of men who had neither joined the party nor been treated as outcasts for not having done so. Marieluise Fleisser, for example, was one who, though *persona non grata* by virtue of her socially critical short stories and her Wedekindian social drama, highly praised by Brecht, *Die Pioniere von Ingolstadt* (1927; revised 1968), withdrew from the scene and was allowed to survive, even though her works were burned in 1933 and she was forbidden to publish after 1935. Hans Fallada, on the other hand, though the Nazis were constantly peering over his shoulder, continued to publish social novels about life in the Weimar Republic (*Wer einmal aus dem Blechnapf frisst*, 1934; *Wolf unter Wölfen*, 1937). *Der eiserne Gustav* (1938), a novel of bitter family conflict and decay, reveals the sort of concessions to Nazi ideology that Fallada thought it necessary to make in order to be allowed to go on writing.

Others were prepared, not without misgivings, to allow their names to be used in propaganda exercises in return for a measure of tolerance which at least assured their safety and their permission to continue writing.

To assign all these writers to a single category, whether one calls it *innere Emigration* or anything else, would misleadingly imply a unity

264

among them and disguise the individual character and fate of each man who inhabits the no-man's-land of 'neither-nor'. A glance of some of these authors will show what was at stake.

One is Rudolf G. Binding, whose Novelle *Der Opfergang* enjoyed an extraordinary popularity from the moment it was published in 1911, and was still selling in its thousands in 1938. A conservative, humanistic, slightly aloof figure, whose short stories recall Theodor Storm in their blend of realism and muted sentimentality, and who, also like Storm, had a special gift for the portrayal of tragic love relationships and the psychology of women, Binding was drawn in 1933 to declare his support for Hitler's 'new' Germany. Discipline, a sense of duty, an acceptance of obligation to the community, a belief in national pride and therefore in a nation united, not torn apart by political bickering and the pursuit of sectional interests—Hitler seemed more likely than anyone else to restore these virtues. Life made harsh demands on men, in peace and in war, and Binding scorned evasion. His poems and addresses on the fallen youth of the Great War—*Stolz und Trauer* (1922), *Deutsche Jugend vor den Toten des Krieges* (1924)—found favour with the Nazis, but one must repeat: conservatism, patriotism and praise of heroism are not to be equated with Nazism, the vulgarity of which belongs in a different world from the clean, aristocratic tone of Binding's poems and stories.

In May 1933 Romain Rolland wrote a letter to the *Kölnische Zeitung* denouncing Hitler and prophesying ruin for the Germany that had forsaken her true destiny and delivered herself into the hands of barbarians. Binding, together with Kolbenheyer, Wilhelm von Scholz and others, contributed a defence of Hitler's Germany to a symposium, *Sechs Bekenntnisse zum neuen Deutschland*, published a few months later. In this he gave it as his view that violence, racial persecution, *Gleichschaltung* and other Nazi principles were nothing but 'peripheral phenomena which do not affect the essence or the truth of this great movement.'[1]

Yet in October of the same year he withdrew his name from the list of 88 members of the Reichsverband deutscher Schriftsteller (later absorbed by the Reichsschrifttumskammer) who declared a personal oath of loyalty to Hitler.[2] He wrote letters opposing the persecution of the Jews (his own wife was Jewish, and unlike many others married to Jews, he did not abandon her) and kept his personal ties with Jewish writers and publishers. In 1937, in another *volte-face*, he wrote to Baldur von Schirach, reaffirming his loyalty to the state and recalling the early support he had given it in his riposte to Romain Rolland.[3] These contradictions cannot be resolved, even if they are understandable in terms of Binding's nature on one hand and professional position on the other—though as a popular author now in his seventies, he could hardly have feared physical reprisals. He died in 1938. Perhaps he would have been glad that the party was not officially represented at his funeral.

The career of Hans Carossa, a writer often included among those of the so-called *innere Emigration*, is similarly flawed. 'Inner emigration' was a term coined by the novelist Frank Thiess to define the attitude of mind of those intellectuals who, unwilling or unable to emigrate from Germany in the 1930s, deliberately sought to estrange themselves from events in the world around them and thus rescue something of their spiritual integrity. At the end of the war Thiess assumed the role of spokesman for these intellectuals, accusing those who had gone into exile, at their head Thomas Mann, of deserting their people and forfeiting any right to speak in their name.

Thiess himself, despite his cryptically anti-Nazi novel *Das Reich der Dämonen* (1941), managed to survive without harm. In 1933, however, he had been prepared to compromise himself in a new preface to his novel *Der Leibhaftige,* originally published in 1924, by adding approving references to Hitler and to the need to defend the Third Reich against threats from within and without. For a writer true 'inner emigration'—which is not the same thing as resistance—would entail complete silence. But how can one demand this from a man whose livelihood depends upon communication? Escapism, a choice of subject matter as remote as possible from the issues of contemporary life, is one answer. Fallada, for example, retreated from Berlin to Mecklenburg and left the social novel for children's stories and autobiographical musings; Erich Kästner abandoned the satirical social portraiture of *Fabian, die Geschichte eines Moralisten* (1932) for the juvenile world of *Emil* and *Drei Männer im Schnee* (1934)—indeed, in 1933 the Nazis suppressed all his earlier works except *Emil und die Detektive* (1929). But complete innocence is a rare state.

Carossa, basically a composed, humanistic, unpolitical figure whose literary ideals descended from Goethe and Stifter, allowed himself to be elected to the refashioned Nazi Akademie der Dichtung in 1933. Two more volumes, *Geheimnisse des schönen Lebens* (1936) and *Das Jahr der schönen Täuschungen* (1941), in his series of autobiographical novels that had started in 1922 with *Eine Kindheit* and included *Der Arzt Gion* (1931), were published with the approval of the Nazis, who found in them qualities, like faith in the youth of the country and commitment to the service of society, from which they could draw satisfaction. He also accepted the presidency of the Europäische Schriftstellervereinigung, a body created by Goebbels in

1941 as a prestige organisation of writers from all countries under German control.

At the same time he also wrote in the course of the war a handful of clouded, imagistic poems in which the hour of Nazism is symbolically portrayed as an hour of darkness out of which the Germans must emerge into the light:

> *Aus Träumen steigt einmal ein Segentag,*
> *Wo wir das Licht nicht mehr verhehlen müssen*
> *Und wieder frei mit Urgewalten spielen.*[4]

(A day of blessing will one day emerge out of dreams, when we shall no longer have to conceal the light but freely play once more with primeval forces.)

('Abendländische Elegie', 1943)

Carossa repeatedly returned to the antithesis of light and darkness in the same spirit as Goethe, trusting in the regenerative power of nature and in the organic wholeness of life.

This polarisation, an almost idealised presentation of the terms of opposition, characterises much of what is accounted the poetry of 'inner emigration'. The sonnets of Rudolf Hagelstange, for example, in his *Venezianisches Credo* of 1944 show the same tendency, for all that Hagelstange, who was over 30 years Carossa's junior, strikes far more pronounced attitudes of opposition. It is the human evil and ignominy that have issued in National Socialism, rather than the evil and ignominy of National Socialism itself, that fill these poets. Many move from the particular to the general, from the contingent to the essential, writing poetry that is properly seen as philosophical and spiritual rather than political. The urge is to promote understanding of a situation and to induce the modes of thought that will overcome that situation, not to incite suicidal revolution against what is only a passing reflection of deep, basic, recurrent realities.

Such generalities also make up the atmosphere surrounding the novels and short stories of Ernst Wiechert, whose erratic course leads from the pessimism of his novels of the mid-1920s to the *Blut und Boden* determinism of *Die kleine Passion* (1929), its anti-war sequel *Jedermann* (1931) and the kind of Christian agnosticism that emerges from *Die Majorin* (1935), *Das einfache Leben* (1939) and his novels written after 1945. In 1933 and 1935 Wiechert expressed his misgivings at the rise of Nazism in two lectures given at the University of Munich. *Der Dichter und die Jugend* warns against the self-perpetuating euphoria that followed the events of early 1933, events which placed in the hands of youth a power it had never before possessed. Two years later, with the same Christian overtones, he spoke on *Der Dichter und seine*

Zeit, counselling his young audience against the submergence of the individual personality beneath a common mediocrity, and against the hubristic claim that it is man, not God, who rules the earth. The Nazis are not mentioned by name, but no one could fail to understand what, and who, was in Wiechert's mind.

In 1938 he was sent, first to the concentration camp at Oranienburg, then to Buchenwald, where he spent five months. *Der Totenwald* (1945), written as a third-person narrative, tells of his experiences there, not so much in physical as in spiritual terms. On his release he was personally warned by Goebbels that any further criticism of the régime would result in his execution, and what he wrote from then on until 1945 he hid and published when the war was over. The ties of blood and nature matter a great deal to him, and to tread a lonely path that seems to lead now to Christianity, now to an agnostic humanism represents for him the moral challenge of life, but there is a curious diffuseness and flaccidity about his work. Like that of Bergengruen, his style is steeped in the language and imagery of the Bible, and one of his best known tales, the *Hirtennovelle* (1935), is a retelling in the setting of his native East Prussia of the story of David. Unlike Bergengruen, however, the strength and directness of the biblical message have not found their way into either his thought or his manner.

Perhaps the best-known names among the company of writers who stayed in Germany throughout the Nazi era are those of two men, very different from each other, round whom persistent controversy has collected over the last 50 years—Gottfried Benn and Ernst Jünger. Both men served in World War I, lived through the inflation, the brief prosperity and the final disarray of the Weimar Republic, watched the rise of Hitler and the establishment of National Socialism, put on uniform again in World War II and survived to see the defeat of one Germany and the rise of another. Benn died in 1956, a few weeks before Brecht; Jünger, now 85, lives in the country near Lake Constance.

Both men had an established reputation long before Hitler came to power, Benn above all as the poet who had erupted on the literary scene in 1912 with the expressionist *Morgue und andere Gedichte*, Jünger as diarist and cultural essayist, author of *In Stahlgewittern*, *Der Kampf als inneres Erlebnis* and *Die totale Mobilmachung*. Neither man contemplated leaving the country after Hitler's accession as Chancellor in January 1933 or the overwhelming National Socialist victory in the Reichstag elections a few weeks later. Quite the reverse.

On 20 April, Hitler's birthday, Benn attended the first performance of Johst's anti-culture play *Schlageter* as the personal guest of Bernhard Rust, former Gauleiter, now Prussian Kultusminister and shortly afterwards Reichsminister für Wissenschaft, Erziehung und Volksbildung. Four days after this occasion, of his own initiative and under no political pressure, he delivered on the Berlin radio an address called *Der neue Staat und die Intellektuellen*, in which he called for the ranks to be closed in support of the new régime and declared national solidarity to be the overriding need of the moment.

Ernst Jünger was less importunate. After months of hesitation he declined nomination to the Akademie der Dichtung. But he pledged at the same time his 'firm determination to cooperate fully with the new State',[5] and this in spite of having had his Berlin apartment searched by the police because of his association with the 'National Bolshevik' Ernst Niekisch. (Friedrich Georg Jünger, whose sympathies were very like those of his elder brother, and whose essay *Die Perfektion der Technik* [1939] is a kind of counterpart to Ernst's *Der Arbeiter*, was also close to Niekisch, and both brothers wrote articles for Niekisch's journal *Der Widerstand*.) In 1945 Ernst Jünger made the characteristically dismissive gesture of refusing to fill in the questionnaire by which a man's political record in the Third Reich was judged, but the ban that was then put on publishing his works was soon lifted. Benn, for whom the Nazis had quickly decided they had little use, spent the immediate post-war years clearing his name and was allowed to publish again in Germany in 1949.

Jünger and Benn met only once—in 1952, in the house in Berlin where Benn had his medical practice. Their natures were very different, but their experience had linked them over the past 40 years, and they seem to have had a considerable respect for each other. Today Jünger appears as a figure of the past, as his trench-warfare of 1914–18 belongs to the past, and although the values for which he stands will always provoke opposition, the controversy that once surrounded them has been superseded by other controversies. Benn, on the other hand, was at the height of his fame between 1949 and his death, a fame based not only on the memory of his early expressionist verse but also on his living influence on post-war German poetry.

Benn published his *Gesammelte Gedichte* in 1927. The climax of his poetry composed during the latter years of the Weimar Republic came with the oratorio text *Das Unaufhörliche* (1931), set to music by Hindemith. His essays of this period, some aesthetic, some medico-sociological in focus, showed an undiminished desire to explore the nature of the human psyche in its personal, social and creative constitution. Yet in the years 1931 to 1933 his letters show him dejected, weary, disgusted with the political state of the republic and 'less inclined than ever', as he wrote to Thea Sternheim in August 1931, 'to commit myself to any human association'.[6] Disintegration beset his personal life and the life of the community, and like so many other intellectuals, he searched desperately for a means of restoring the lost unity. He was not, however, the man to question the here and now, to look for the decisive errors of the past that had led to an undesirable present. Things were as they were, and history was 'das elementare, das stossartige, das unausweichliche Phänomen'.[7] The energy of his essays of the 1920s was the energy of nihilism, generated both by the forces within his own personality and by his Nietzschean view of history and the state of society. His search in these essays for an autonomy of art, an aesthetic absolute, as a unifying principle by which to overcome his nihilism, is one manifestation of his desire to recognise a central authority. The welcome he gave to Nazism in 1933, conveyed chiefly in *Der neue Staat und die Intellektuellen* and *Antwort an die literarischen Emigranten*, is another.

The essay *Züchtung* of the same year, in which Benn lends his medical authority to the Nazi programme of eugenics for breeding the characteristics of an Aryan *Herrenvolk*, also makes quite specific the source of the Nazi appeal for him: 'This immense historical revolution can be called in its initial form that of "the total state". This "total state", as opposed to the pluralistic state of the previous era, ... asserts the complete identity of power (*Macht*) and mind (*Geist*), of individualism and collectivism, of freedom and necessity.'[8] The merging of what Benn had formerly characterised, and was later to characterise again, as irreconcilable demands brought with it the subjection of the individual to the collective—on the one hand a sacrifice to the larger entity, on the other a guarantee of protection through service, a kind of feudal relationship. The inspired authority of the charismatic leader held everything together, and a romantic irrational abandonment to *Rausch*, in the tradition of Nietzsche and Stefan George—a concept equally valued, albeit in different contexts, by Ernst Jünger—became the governing force in men's lives. The state was all, the individual was nothing. Or, in the imperious challenge at the beginning of *Der neue Staat und die Intellektuellen*: 'When history speaks, let the individual keep silent.'[9] It is the sort of phrase that provoked Döblin's description of Benn as 'a sworn nihilist in the wake of Nietzsche, pathologically weak and an inveterate worshipper of power.'[10]

The unqualified welcome that Benn gave to Hitler's 'new state', reiterated in further essays written even after the burning of the books—including those of Heinrich Mann, whom he much admired—and the first official steps in the systematic persecution of the Jews, had a shattering effect on the German intelligentsia, especially the young. For this was no faceless, run-of-the mill, *passé* expressionist poet talking, but one of the leading German poets of the day. 'How could you bring yourself', wrote Klaus Mann to him from France in May 1933, 'you, whose name signifies for us the epitome of excellence, to become a servant of those who stand for the basest values ever seen in the history of Europe and whose immorality makes the whole world shrink in repulsion?'[11]

Step by step Benn retracted his views of 1933–4: an essay of 1940, for example (*Züchtung II*), recants the nightmarish eugenic policies advanced in the earlier *Züchtung* essay. But even the much later autobiographical work *Doppelleben* (1950) still retains an air of self-justification. He shows a willingness to concede an 'error of judgement'—as though support for persecution of the Jews, for policies of world domination and for the breeding of a 'Master Race' came into the category of errors of judgement—but sees no cause to reflect that his action might have betrayed those who looked up to him.

Ironically, Benn's efforts on behalf of the Nazis brought him no reward. Johst, Kolbenheyer, Hans Grimm, Stehr, Beumelburg and many other literary pygmies received the accolade of official patronage and status, while Benn, a giant in such company, was ignored. The Nationalsozialistischer Ärztebund agitated against him, and by 1934 he saw that he had no future in civilian life either as a doctor or as a writer. The following year he rejoined the army as a medical officer, still distrusted by the Nazis and, worse, spurned by the friends he had lost through his pro-Nazi articles and speeches. Oskar Loerke, whose own expressionist poems had linked his name with Benn's 20 years before and who had recently used his influence with Berlin publishers to get some of Benn's essays printed in cultural journals, noted in his diary after Benn joined up: 'He has left a bad image; people are saying it was high time he withdrew. He has taken refuge in the army.'[12] For this forced move Benn himself coined the bitter phrase: 'The army is the aristocratic form of emigration.' What is aristocratic about joining the army, except in so far as it removes one from the day-to-day concerns of the common people, the concerns on which the real life of the community depends, Benn never explained. Neither the exiles from Hitler's Germany nor the writers of the 'inner emigration' could have explained it either.

But Benn's degradation was still not complete. His *Ausgewählte Gedichte 1911–1936* was censored because of the inclusion of 'degenerate' poems like 'Mann und Frau gehn durch die Krebsbaracke',

'D-Zug' and 'Untergrundbahn', and a second edition, omitting these offensive items, had to be prepared. In 1938 he received the news that he had been expelled from the Reichsschrifttumskammer and banned from writing. The essays and poems he wrote secretly after this time have strong overtones of despair and show a hatred of Nazi barbarism as consuming as had been his enthusiasm for the National Socialist brave new world 10 years before. One of the most savage of these poems is 'Monolog', from *Zweiundzwanzig Gedichte 1936–1943*, a collection printed privately in 1943 and circulated clandestinely among his friends. All the roughness and calculated crudity characteristic of Benn the anti-bourgeois expressionist surges to the surface again at the thought of Hitler and his subject peoples:

> *Den Darm mit Rotz genährt, das Hirn mit Lügen-*
> *erwählte Völker Narren eines Clowns,*
> *in Spässe, Sternelesen, Vogelzug*
> *den eignen Unrat deutend! . . . . .*[13]

(Feeding their gut on snot, their brain on lies—chosen peoples the fools of a clown, seeing their own filth as jokes, horoscopes, flights of birds . . . .)

To the same year as this poem belongs the powerful essay *Kunst und Drittes Reich*, in which Benn scornfully contrasts the cultural tradition that culminated in the nineteenth century with the despicable modern commodity defined as culture by the National Socialists—'das teutonische Kollektiv auf der Grundlage krimineller Sozietät', as he witheringly called them.[14] Like Ernst Jünger in his essay *Der Friede*, Benn sees a future when some vague, unified 'Europe of the mind' will arise, from which Germany will learn and to which she will contribute. Benn's poetry was always rich in classical allusions and in imagery drawn from classical mythology, and now, looking for a set of values to put against the crude nationalism of the Nazis, he returns to the organic unity of Western civilization based on Greece and Rome. The essay *Pallas* (1943) invokes the Greek goddess as the symbol of that sphere of the creative artistic imagination, lying between the historical world and the nihilistic world, which he calls the 'Ausdruckswelt', while *Franzosen* (1941) returns to the praise of the Romance realm as the custodian of the Latin legacy.

Yet Benn still possesses, notably in the essay *Zum Thema Geschichte* (1943), a significant sense of continuity within an apparent oscillation from one extreme to the other, by putting forward a diagnosis of Nazism, not as a single, inexplicable, demented outburst but as an expression of forces embedded in the German national character. Nihilism and disintegration, sometimes cold, sometimes passionate, rest on one side of the balance; desperate yearning for unity, and the embrace of anything that promises it, rests on the other side. It is the old antithesis of subjective and objective, of the centrifugal and the centripetal, the old romantic dilemma, the old spectre of the nineteenth century. Benn is a creature of these polarised forces, an exemplar of that continuity of often contradictory and tragically destructive urges which runs through modern German history and culture.

Of Benn's career during the dark age of Nazism Dieter Wellershoff, editor of Benn's collected works, wrote:

There was no necessity for Benn to act as he did. He could have decided differently. He had sufficient cause to expect that political events would force him to abandon his ideological prejudices in favour of a clearer appreciation of the situation. One must regard it as a moral failing on his part that this did not come about—or more precisely, that it came about so late, and then, in part or even in whole, only because of the way the rulers of Germany had used their power against him.[15]

In the 10 years or so that he lived after the end of the war, Benn's nihilism brought him the approval of those, especially the young, for whom resentment and a philosophy of *ohne mich* appeared the only acceptable political stance. But in 1945 officialdom still disapproved of him. In the Soviet zone of occupied Germany the Kulturbund zur demokratischen Erneuerung Deutschlands, presided over by Johannes R. Becher, had his name put on the black list of 'undesirable' authors. Alfred Döblin, like Benn, a writer of influence in the expressionism of 20 and 30 years earlier, and who now, after 12 years in exile, was cultural adviser in the French occupation zone, also refused to sanction publication of his work. 'When for 15 years', Benn wrote to the editor of *Merkur* in 1948, 'as I have, one has been publicly called a skunk by the Nazis, an idiot by the Communists, an intellectual prostitute by the democrats, a traitor by the emigrés and a pathological nihilist by the religious-minded, one is not too keen on appearing before the public again.'[16] Maybe. Were the Nazis, the Communists, the democrats, the emigrés and the religious-minded all wrong? And if they were, who, apart from Benn himself, was right?

Whereas the events of 1933 caused Benn to veer and tack with the direction of the wind, Ernst Jünger, despite his declared decision 'to cooperate fully with the new state', barely changed the course by which he had always steered, a course of independence, aloofness and aristocratic discipline. In refusing appointment to the Deutsche Akademie der Dichtung, he pointed to the 'essentially military character' of his work, 'which I do not wish to prejudice by accepting any official commitments.'[17] A letter to the *Völkischer Beobachter* in

June 1934 makes it clear that he had equally little desire to contribute to the organs of the National Socialist press.

In the 1930s, both before and after Hitler came to power, Jünger travelled widely, both within Europe and to North Africa and South America, and wrote colourful autobiographical accounts of his experiences (*Dalmatinischer Aufenthalt; Myrdun; Atlantische Fahrt* etc.). The most important work of this period, however, a systematic exposé of his ideas on the state of the times and the needs of the future, is the long essay *Der Arbeiter* (1932), significantly subtitled *Herrschaft und Gestalt*.

Starting from a diagnosis of nineteenth-century *Bürgertum* as a phenomenon that had run its course and now had to give way to some new social force, Jünger looks for the formation of a new hierarchy, an élite whose nature is already manifest in the soldier whose qualities have been tempered in war. This élite would be pledged to total commitment—one aspect of what Jünger called 'totale Mobilmachung—and sustained by a determination to serve life and hence realise the demands of history. To grasp this truth is to gain power over life: 'to rule and to serve are one and the same.'[19] And using the means that modern technological society offers, the more completely one commits one's faculties to this service, which is to say, to the will to power, the more perfect an 'Arbeiter' one becomes. In consequence the fuller becomes the 'Gestalt' produced by the assimilation of one's contingent physical realities to one's essential metaphysical nature.

The heady dangers of such a doctrine, set around, as it is, with a highly selective use of facts in its presentation of what made up nineteenth-century bourgeois capitalism, are plain. So too are the reasons why the Nazis, impressed by a vocabulary of service, sacrifice, power, courage and the virtues of soldiery, found it convenient to allow him the non-rebellious independence he demanded. *Der Arbeiter* is to a large extent an attempt to rationalise his appeal to *Rausch* as the inspiration behind the urge to war, the display of courage and the glory of heroic sacrifice, an appeal to which he had remained faithful since the time of *In Stahlgewittern* and *Der Kampf als inneres Erlebnis* in the 1920s. And as a rationalisation, the depiction of an idiosyncratic, nihilistic utopia, it will only persuade those who are already predisposed to believe what Jünger believes. It rests on a faith which is neither humanist nor democratic—he shed no tears over the demise of the Weimar Republic—and whose language does not know words like 'love', 'tolerance' and 'compassion'. He sees human destiny as tragic, and liberal institutions like democracy as no longer relevant: one chapter in *Der Arbeiter* is called 'Der Übergang von der liberalen

Demokratie zum Arbeitsstaat', another, 'Die Ablösung der Gesellschaftsverträge durch den Arbeitsplan.' Likewise the individual, in his proud uniqueness, counts for nothing in the face of the demands of 'total mobilisation'. As for the Gottfried Benn of this time, the individual is nothing, the state, all.

Jünger returned to his *Arbeiter* many times and has published a substantial volume of prolegomena to a continuation of what, together with his books from World War I, *Die totale Mobilmachung* and, in part, *Über den Schmerz*, he called his 'Old Testament'. 'In the second part I would describe how the dynamic principles were absorbed in a superior order of tranquillity. When the house has been equipped, the electricians and technicians will leave. But who will then be in charge of the place?'[20] This second part was never written.

In August 1939 Jünger rejoined the army, shortly before the publication of his novel *Auf den Marmorklippen*. On the political plane this striking work is an allegorical attack on the terror and the primitiveness of the National Socialist régime. It also has elements of a *roman à clef*: Jünger himself revealed that the savage Oberförster in the story, the despot whose rule of bloodshed sets the context of the narrative, was compounded of traits of Bismarck, Goering and Stalin. Over and above these two planes, however, *Auf den Marmorklippen* has a mythological, almost theological meaning as a study in the overthrow of peace, justice and order by the forces of tyranny. First the Oberförster uses propaganda and threats to undermine the morale of a peaceful community and corrupt its members; then he sends in his troops to destroy the community. The two heroes of the story defend themselves, but the hermitage in which they have been living a life of contemplation devoted to the study of nature is burned to the ground, and surrounded by ruins and by fleeing refugees, they leave to seek a new home elsewhere.

On one side Jünger presents a Nietzschean pattern of history as a cyclic progress of alternating creation and destruction, sustained by its own inner dynamism; nothing can check the onward march of the power-hungry Oberförster and his savage Mauretanian hordes, or impede the heroes' emergence from devastation into a new life of peace. On the other side lies the Christian concept of history as linear movement towards a goal, the goal of salvation, which is a fulfilment and therefore an end. The stages of the movement towards this goal are not predetermined, for since man is free—as in the Nietzschean vision of Eternal Recurrence he is not—to reject his destiny, his salvation, there can be retrogression as well as progression. The character of Pater Lampros, who becomes for the heroes a figure of inspiration, embodies this Christian view as one, in Otho's words, 'who, withdrawn behind his monastery walls like a dreamer, is perhaps the only one among us who lives in full reality'.[21]

Yet *Auf den Marmorklippen* depicts a situation in which, for the moment at least, history as salvation has yielded to history as inexorable necessity, a situation often presented through dream-like episodes which, like Hans Castorp's vision in the snow in Thomas Mann's *Der Zauberberg*, carry the expression of the deepest realities. From the irrationality of dream-sequences derives the richness of the symbolism in the book, above all the cluster of motifs centred on the serpent, a creature to which Jünger had already given prominence in *Das abenteuerliche Herz* and *Afrikanische Spiele*. It is these vipers that save the narrator of the novel—one of the two heroes—from being torn to pieces by the Oberförster's hounds, and thus give him, the Jüngerian seeker after danger and fulfilment in death, the opportunity to live out his own form of 'Stirb und werde'.

Jünger was already in the army when *Auf den Marmorklippen* was published. World War II, however, much of which he spent in high society as an officer in the German garrison in Paris, was an ironically calm interlude in his life. In Paris he had the good fortune to move in the company, first of General Speidel, a supporter of the officers' opposition to Hitler, then of Speidel's successor, General Heinrich von Stülpnagel, who was to be executed in 1944 for his part in the anti-Hitler plot of 20 July. Both these officers acted almost as patrons towards Jünger, and his essay *Der Friede*, written between 1941 and 1943, circulated privately among the Paris conspirators who were waiting to put their part of the July plot into operation. His experiences of the war years 1939 to 1945 are recorded in the diaries published in 1949 under the collective title *Strahlungen*.

Der Friede, in Jünger's words, is 'an appeal to European youth'.[22] The first part, called 'Die Saat', treats of war and suffering as the 'seed' that is to outgrow the menace of nihilism and particularism; the second part, with the title 'Die Frucht', adumbrates a form of European solution to the question of how peace, the 'fruit' of war, is to be secured. Jünger describes the arrival of that moment in the terms of his own earlier works: 'Peace is achieved when the creative forces that were devoted to total mobilisation are liberated. At the same time the heroic age of the Worker (*Arbeiter*—though in Jünger's usage the word reaches far beyond its normal associations), which is also the age of revolution, will reach its fulfilment.'[23]

Practical as his purpose appears to be, an air of metaphysical abstraction quickly settles over the argument. His presentation of the relationship between Germany and the certain war is at odds with his vague picture of a Europe, including Germany, that is to make the peace, and political realities sometimes seem far away. He still envisages (Section 8), for example, that some 'arrangement' could have been made between the West and Hitler in 1940—as Hess thought when he flew to Britain the following year. And even when facing the persecution of the Jews, he avoids any concern with a specifically German responsibility in favour of an often religiously coloured image of the common responsibility of a European community torn by internal strife, like France in 1789. Jünger's is not, and never has been, a rational, humanistic message: 'As always in such moments, [i.e. the Revolution in France] it was the dark, insistent forces that prevailed, not the voices of reason . . . We are in the grip of the power of destiny.'[24]

When, after a three-year ban at the end of the war, Jünger was allowed to resume writing, the same voice addresses us in *Der Waldgänger* (1951), in which the unity of his *oeuvre* and of the values by which he has lived is expressed in terms of three of his symbolic figures: 'We called the Worker and Unknown Soldier two of the great figures of our age; the 'Waldgänger' is a third, which is emerging ever more clearly'[25]—the 'Waldgang' being defined as 'in erster Linie Todesgang'.[26] Jünger's life may, as he himself claimed, be divided into two parts, but there are no contradictions between them, and it is the unity of his personality that he asks us to observe, quoting the words of Pascal: 'Every writer has a meaning which absorbs all his opposites—otherwise he has no meaning at all.'[27]

It is a principle characteristic both of Jünger's independence of mind and of the sometimes frightening demands, expressed in an incisive, brilliant, steely language, that he makes. The energies of sexual love have been diverted into the manly energies of adventure and war, and irrational faith, absolute in its claims, has taken the place of irrational emotion. In his essay on Jünger, Eugen Gottlob Winkler put it thus: 'One must believe without knowing the content of that belief.'[28] Adorno left a similar epigram: 'The only true thoughts are those that do not understand themselves.'[29] This is Jünger's world of unconditionals and imperatives, and a chapter in the history of the modern German mind could be written in terms of the polarisation of attitudes which his challenges provoke.

'Inner emigration', in its various nuances and forms of articulation, embraces a certain body of attitudes and values. Shading into it, but, at least in its most fully committed manifestations, distinguishable from it, is the literature of opposition, declared or concealed, a literature carried by authors in spiritual, and often also physical, torment.

With total centralised control of all media of communication, nothing openly critical of the principles and practices of the state could be published: indeed, no one but a determined martyr would even betray the existence of such a critical manuscript to other than his most trusted friends. Nevertheless there were writers who went further than, for example, Binding, Carossa or Thiess in their refusal to compromise themselves before the evils and the inhumanities of the régime. For some—Ernst Wiechert, Günther Weisenborn, Albrecht Haushofer, Dietrich Bonhoeffer—this refusal led to the concentration camp. While many suffered in the name of Communism, even more, perhaps, derived their moral strength from Christianity. Incompatible in their philosophies and points of reference, these two spiritual world-powers found themselves temporarily allied, under a yoke of tyranny and oppression, in a definition of human dignity and humane values. The humanism invoked by one faith has not always looked like the humanism invoked by other faiths over the centuries, but at this moment the claims are linked.

Among the Christian writers is Werner Bergengruen. From romantic, often whimsical or mysterious tales of the early 1920s, reminiscent of Jean Paul and E.T.A. Hoffmann, he turned to historical novels with a contemporary relevance—*Das Kaiserreich in Trümmern* (1927), *Herzog Karl der Kühne* (1930)—and from these in turn to the works, mainly of the 1930s, on which his reputation chiefly rests—the novels *Der Grosstyrann und das Gericht* (1935) and *Am Himmel wie auf Erden* (1940), the Novellen in the collection *Der Teufel im Winterpalais* (1933) and the collections of poems *Die Rose von Jericho* (1934) and *Die verborgene Frucht* (1938).

Two motifs, one negative, the other positive, dominate these works—a sense of impending catastrophe, and the hope of a revival of the unifying Christian, more particularly Catholic, consciousness. The allegorical *Grosstyrann und das Gericht* portrays the inability of men to preserve their integrity under the pressure of political authority. Yet it is not a simple world of black and white that Bergengruen presents, either in terms of the tyrant's despotic rule, or of the people's powerlessness to resist the temptations into which he leads them. For as the tyrant is humbled into penitence by the willingness of the simple dyer, Sperone, to confess to a crime he did not commit, so Sperone embodies the power of the common man to assert his goodness and his love of humanity. Catastrophe and destruction do not in the end descend on tyrant and people, but the threat of destruction jolts them into an awareness of where the values of true humanity lie, values whose presence is guaranteed by the Christian essence that infuses the world.

Being called to account, in a retributory sense, before some form of judgement seat has held a significant attraction for modern writers—Kafka's *Prozess*, various plays by Brecht (*Die Ausnahme und die Regel, Die Massnahme, Lebendes Galilei, Das Verhör des Lukullus, Der kaukasische Kreidekreis*), Dürrenmatt's *Es steht geschrieben, Besuch der alten Dame, Der Richter und sein Henker* and others, Heinar Kipphardt's *In der Sache J. Robert Oppenheimer*, Peter Weiss' *Die Ermittlung*—and in Bergengruen's *Grosstyrann und das Gericht* man is tried by God. When the test is over, and human frailties have been exposed and recognised, hope remains—hope that a new era of understanding will dawn in the tyrant's country, and confidence in the victory of God's hidden but ever-present and absolute truths. Like Novalis in *Die Christenheit oder Europa* Bergengruen envisages a re-establishment of the medieval *sacrum imperium* as the only durable answer to the political and social confusion of modern times. And like Jochen Klepper's *Der Vater*, a Christianised biography of Friedrich Wilhelm I, father of Frederick the Great (1937), Elisabeth Langgässer's *Das unauslöschliche Siegel* (1946), and Gertrud von Le Fort's *Der Papst aus dem Ghetto* (1930) and *Die Magdeburgische Hochzeit* (1938), Bergengruen's *Der Grosstyrann und das Gericht* and *Am Himmel wie auf Erden* show that all great political issues are at the same time religious issues. Contemporary relevance shades into the timeless realm of spiritual absolutes, the latter redeeming the ephemeral character of the former and also, as in the conditions of Nazi Germany, protecting it. Bergengruen's God is the God of history, and history, that is, present interlocked with past, is the progress towards the fulfilment of God's purpose. The indebtedness of Bergengruen's style and language to the Bible is the natural counterpart to this eschatology.

Bergengruen here represents a kind of literature of camouflaged opposition, a literature which, beneath a surface of allegory, parable or apparently harmless fancy, secretes a message of criticism or protest. The challenge to the writer's subtlety and skill is to convey one meaning to the censor and another to the real audience, and the variety of such 'real' meanings is as wide as the variety of the ideals and goals—personal, social, religious,political—of the writers themselves. Thus works otherwise so different from each other as *Der Grosstyrann und das Gericht*, Adam Kuckhoff's *Der Deutsche von Bayencourt*, Reinhold Schneider's *Las Casas vor Karl V*—three *romans a clef* all published in 1937—and Ernst Jünger's *Auf den Marmorklippen* (1939), together with the lyric verse of Oskar Loerke (*Magische Verse*, 1938), and the 70-year-old Ricarda Huch, all share at this moment a common context *vis-à-vis*, on the one side, the literature of National Socialism and on the other, literature that was being illegally written and circulated.

Der Grosstyrann und das Gericht has a fictitious medieval Italian setting which in itself distracted the censor's attention, and the book sold steadily through the late 1930s. In 1937 however, Bergengruen was expelled from the Reichsschrifttumskammer as 'unsuitable'—in the words of the official letter—'to participate in the task of developing our German culture.'[30] *Am Himmel wie auf Erden* (1940), a novel describing how fear can destroy the moral consciousness of the individual and thereby the cohesion of society, was banned shortly after its publication, as was the thinly disguised anti-Nazi collection of verse *Der ewige Kaiser* (1937), but despite the suspicion that surrounded him, Bergengruen survived the Third Reich without harm. Towards the end of the war he wrote a sequence of poems under the title *Dies irae*, which circulated illegally before being published in 1945. In these honest, often appealing poems of opposition to the forces represented by Hitler he returns to the question of human guilt posed in *Der Grosstyrann und das Gericht*, asking with sadness and embarrassing directness

> *Wer will die Reinen von den Schuldigen scheiden?*
> *Und welcher Reine hat sich nicht befleckt?*[31]

(Who is to distinguish the pure from the guilty? And where is the pure man who has not sullied himself?)

Ironically, this high moral tone, coming from one who had survived the 12 years of National Socialism with no apparent injury, caused considerable resentment after the war, for it seemed to shrug off the specifically German responsibility for the enslavement of Europe, the slaughter of the Jews and the other manifestations of Nazism, and to preach instead a haughty message of universal human guilt. Maybe the whole world *is* guilty. But as Max Frisch wrote of 'An die Völker der Erde', the last poem in *Dies irae*, a German in Bergengruen's position in 1945 had little right to such a pose. 'The truth does not lie in words alone', said Frisch, 'but in the relationship between words and the position from which they are spoken.'[32] The general does not absorb, still less absolve, the particular.

Nevertheless, the evidence of Bergengruen's work as a whole hardly allows one to suspect the sincerity of his convictions, and many, on both the political and the religio-moral plane, would share at least in part his belief in a common human responsibility for individual crimes and tragedies. Nor dare one forget how readily, albeit often unconsciously, one finds oneself in the stance of the outsider passing judgement from a position of safety on the conduct of men facing imprisonment or death for an imprudent word or action. 'Let him who is without sin among you cast the first stone', might have been Bergengruen's feeling towards a Max Frisch in Switzerland or a Thomas Mann in the United States. His works before, during and after the Nazi years ensure that we do not lose sight of these problems. But they were German problems before they became European and world problems.

Eleven years Bergengruen's junior, and one of his closest friends, was Reinhold Schneider, also a Catholic, also an historico-religious novelist and poet with a dual vision of contemporary political protest and ultimate moral issues. His historical novels—*Das Leiden des Camoes* (1930), *Die Hohenzollern* (1933—written, in Schneider's words, 'gegen die Vergötzung des Blutes') and *Las Casas vor Karl V* (1937)—were followed in 1939 by a collection of sonnets, but in 1941 his work was banned. Despite this he continued to write poetry and religious essays which a publisher in Colmar somehow managed to produce in small editions. Like Bergengruen, he avoided the Gestapo by the skin of his teeth and lived on to witness the rise of the Federal German Republic. *Verhüllter Tag* (1954) gives his own account of his career, and in the same year he co-edited *Du hast mich heimgesucht bei Nacht*, a moving collection of letters and poems written by men in prisons and concentration camps. Schneider's *Verhüllter Tag* and Bergengruen's *Schreibtischerinnerungen* (1961) together provide a moving commentary on the physical hazards and mental strains suffered by those whose bodies were in Hitler's Germany but whose spirits were in exile.[33]

The historical novel *Las Casas vor Karl V* has as its hero the Spanish bishop Bartolomé de las Casas, who interceded with the Emperor Charles V for the rights of the Indians in the Central American colonies. In Schneider's mind, however, as he wrote later, was a protest against the Nazi persecution of the Jews, 'and at the same time I was gripped by the old subject of the guilt of Europe, of Christendom, in the face of the world—the tragedy of expansionism.'[34] The vampire imagery of a poem on Hitler, starting—

> *Er kommt auf heissen Rädern hergeflogen,*
> *Den Wahn verbreitend und vom Wahn gefeit,*
> *Indes ihn aufgewühltes Volk umschreit,*
> *Aus dem er gierig seine Kraft gesogen.*[35]

(He flies towards us on wheels of fire, spreading delusion and protected by delusion; round him clamour the inflamed masses from whom he greedily sucked his strength.)
('Der Getriebene', 1937)

—is a striking contrast to the sycophancies of Kolbenheyer, Vesper, Weinheber and the rest.

But, again like Bergengruen, Schneider thinks less in the political terms of the moment than in the metaphysical terms of the struggle between good and evil, fought out both in the individual mind and between the nations of the world. The destruction of the present is to jolt man into abandoning the vanities of earth for the moral and spiritual beauties of heaven; he must expiate his guilt by turning to God and ridding himself of his evil dreams, and Schneider's wartime poems, clandestinely written and circulated, explore this theme in tones of mingled exhortation and worship. The lyric verse of Elisabeth Langgässer and Gertrud von Le Fort breathes a similar Catholic spirit of intensity and consolation. A more active Christian involvement, on the other hand, characterises the work of the Austrian Bernt von Heiseler, who in his poetry and dramas (the trilogy *Was des Kaisers ist*, 1939–48; *Cäsar, 1941* — a portrayal of the conflict between dictatorship and democratic republicanism following Brutus' murder of Julius Caesar) sought to project a religious ethic by which to overcome the shattered moral order of the age. After *Cäsar* he was banned by the Nazis from publishing, but this frustrated energy spawned a large number of works from the end of the war until his death in 1969.

An intimate friend of the Catholic Schneider was the tragic figure of Jochen Klepper, son of a Protestant pastor, who worked for a time as a journalist in the Evangelischer Pressverband in Berlin and Breslau. In 1931, at the age of 28, he married a Jewish widow 13 years his senior; two years later he was forced to give up his post with the Ullstein Verlag as being tainted with Jewish influence, and in 1937 he was expelled from the Reichsschrifttumskammer. Attempts to get exit permits for his wife and his Jewish stepdaughter failed, and in 1942 all three gassed themselves.

From 1932 until his death Klepper kept a harrowing diary of how a man tries to retain a Christian humanitarianism while his family waits for the extermination camp and his fellow-citizens are driven into moral ruin. These diaries were published posthumously (*Unter dem Schatten deiner Flügel*, 1956; *Überwindung*, 1958) but Klepper became known during his lifetime through, first, his attractive story of the boatmen on the Oder, *Der Kahn der fröhlichen Leute* (1933), then through his long novel *Der Vater: Der Roman des Soldatenkönigs* (1937), an historical romance on the life of King Friedrich Wilhelm I of Prussia, father of Frederick the Great. The hero is portrayed as the model of a Christian monarch, his idealised virtues emerging as very different from those that the arbiters of National Socialist culture deemed desirable in a Prussian leader, and Klepper's removal from the Reichsschrifttumskammer later the same year came as no surprise. *Der Vater* has its impressive moments, but like so many tortured souls in these years of suffering, Klepper finds his true voice in the realm of lyric poetry (his collected poems were published in 1962 under the title *Ziel der Zeit*).

To this context of religious verse belongs also the venerable Protestant figure of Rudolf Alexander Schröder, whose outlook, despite its different confessional environment, is very similar to Reinhold Schneider's in its call for the acknowledgement of human sinfulness and for man's need to throw himself on God's mercy. Some of Schröder's works—the beginnings of his literary career lie back in the Wilhelminian era—were suppressed during the Third Reich, others were not. The Nazis can hardly have found him a congenial figure but he did not stand for declared political opposition, and to have taken stronger action against him, certainly before the war, might have provoked a public resentment that outweighed the advantage of silencing his voice completely. The same is true of Ricarda Huch, who had resigned from the Reichsschrifttumskammer in 1933, when she was almost 70, yet whose pantheistic, humanistic poems of the Nazi years were tolerated. The intense, recondite mature poetry of Wilhelm Lehmann, represented above all by the collection *Antwort des Schweigens* (1935), similarly passed through the censor's hands without demur—also, one suspects, without comprehension. The one volume of verse that he published during the war, however (*Der grüne Gott*, 1942), was later suppressed. Karl Krolow, a younger 'inner emigrant' whose poetic career belongs in essence to the post-war period, came through the Nazi period in the wake of Lehmann's *Naturmagie*, and found, with Lehmann, Britting and a few other non-conformists an occasional outlet for 'poetry of withdrawal' in the national-liberal literary weekly *Das Reich*, which in 1940 took over the role of Fritz Klein's journal *Deutsche Zukunft*.

Whereas Schneider, Rudolf Alexander Schröder, Ricarda Huch and Wilhelm Lehmann, in their different ways, preach a positive message, the wartime poems of Georg Britting published in 1947 as *Begegnung*—again in sonnet form, like Rudolf Hagelstange's *Venezianisches Credo*, Reinhold Schneider's *Jetzt ist des Heiligen Zeit* (1943) and *Die Waffen des Lichts* (1944) and Albrecht Haushofer's *Moabiter Sonette* (1944–5)—have a Baroque concentration on human transience and death very different from his poems of the 1930s. Another opposition poet who passed from a light, lyrical mood to an obsession with the horrors of wartime life is Hans Leip, whose *Mitternachtsreigen* (1947) contains some of the most gruesome poetry written in Germany during the war years.[36]

These writers, from Bergengruen to Leip, survived the Third Reich without imprisonment; some knew their position from the beginning, others, like Haushofer, found it only during the war. There remains a handful of men and women who achieved the almost inconceivable feat of composing poetry and songs in prisons and concentration camps. Some of this verse circulated secretly among the prisoners or was read aloud, but for the most part it remained a private, intensely personal monologue in which intensity of experience prevailed over consciousness of form or other aesthetic demands. Little of it is of lasting quality, and often its preservation seems to rest only on one's awareness of the poignant conditions under which it was written.

At the same time it had, strangely, almost perversely, the quality of *Gebrauchslyrik* for those who composed it and those to whom it was first communicated. Survivors of Auschwitz, Theresienstadt and other camps have told how, on the one hand, it gave them thoughts and visions to hold on to in their agony, and on the other hand how the dedication of the mind to the supra-physical, supra-momentary meaning of their suffering enabled them to open a gap between subject and object, to distance themselves from the realities of the moment by looking back at that moment from an imagined point of detachment in the future. Hard as it may be to believe, there was even a concentration camp humour which found its way into some of this verse and helped to preserve the prisoners from total despair.

In the camp of Börgermoor three of the inmates composed the 'Lied der Moorsoldaten', with its refrain for the prisoners marching out to forced labour each day—

> *Es zieh'n die Moorsoldáten*
> *Immer mit dem Spaten*
> *Ins Moor.*

(Out go the swamp-soldiers as usual with their shovels, marching into the swamp.)

—and with the defiant hope of its final strophe and new refrain:

> *Doch für uns gibt es kein Klagen,*
> *Ewig kann's nicht Winter sein,*
> *Einmal werden froh wir sagen:*
> *Heimat, Du bist wieder mein!*
>
> *Dann zieh'n die Moorsoldaten*
> *Nicht mehr mit dem Spaten*
> *Ins Moor!*[37]

(Yet for us there is no lamentation; it cannot stay winter for ever. One day we shall say joyfully: 'Homeland, thou art *mine* again.'

Then the swamp-soldiers will no longer go out with their shovels, marching into the swamp.)

Much of this concentration camp poetry is Christian, or Christian-pantheist, sometimes like a monologue, sometimes addressed to the German people, sometimes a meditation on human cruelty and human survival, on retribution and forgiveness, on the state of the world and the future of mankind. The God of the Jews becomes the God of the Gentiles, sectional differences dissolve in the consciousness of a common humanity, a humanity of indistinguishable hope:

> *Wenn viele Hoffnungen auch längst zerschellten,*
> *Der Morgen graut. Die Totenfelder keimen,*
> *Der Himmel lacht. Der Untergang von Träumen*
> *Bedeutet nicht den Untergang von Welten.*
>
> *Noch sprudeln Quellen, Lebende zu laben.*
> *Die Blüten sonnen sich im Frühlingslichte.*
> *Es wurde nur ein kleines Stück Geschichte,*
> *Die älter ist als Gottes Bild, begraben.*
>
> *Gott lässt noch Licht zu Regenbogen brechen,*
> *Die Zeugnis sind. Die Welt geht nicht verloren.*
> *Ein kleines Stück Geschichte, leidgeboren,*
> *Alt wie die Erde, liess Er nur vernichten.*[38]

(Though many hopes have long since been shattered, morning dawns. The fields of dead are sprouting. The sky is smiling. That dreams perish does not mean that worlds perish.

Springs are still bubbling up to refresh the living. The blossoms are sunning themselves in the spring light. The only thing that was buried was a little bit of history, older than God's image.

God still causes light to be refracted into rainbows, which bear witness. The world is not going to come to an end. All God caused to be destroyed was a little bit of history, born in suffering and as old as the earth.)

Hermann Adler's earlier collection, *Gesänge aus der Stadt des Todes* (1945), describes in narrative hexameters and lyric stanzas the humiliations and agonies of the Jews in the Polish ghettos—the 'city of death' is Warsaw in 1943. 'Lest we forget' is the motto of these moving poems. Forgive—yes. Forget—never. The voice we hear is not that of Adler the Jew but Adler the man, and he is speaking to all mankind. An anthology edited by Manfred Schlösser in 1960 under the title *An den Wind geschrieben* covers the whole range of this poetry from the years 1933 to 1945.

Inevitably, perhaps, it is the themes of these poems from prisons and concentration camps, rather than the personalities of individual poets, that penetrate the mind most deeply. The world will not readily forget, however, the name of Dietrich Bonhoeffer, the young radical pastor of the Bekennende Kirche who was shot in the concentration camp of Flossenbürg in 1945. But long before this his outspoken opposition, political as well as moral, to the Nazi régime and to the war had made him a thorn in the side of the authorities, and his prison poetry, most of it posthumously collected in the volume *Auf dem Wege zur Freiheit* (1951), includes political verse as well as religious poems of prayer, of penitence and of comfort.

Alongside the religious poets stands a group of writers of the left, mostly Communists, among them Günther Weisenborn, remembered from pre-Hitler days for his anti-war drama *U-Boot S4* and for his collaboration with Brecht on the play *Die Mutter*. These and his other works were burned in 1933. He joined the underground organisation 'Die Rote Kapelle', whose members the Nazis tirelessly hounded, and spent the last three years of the war in jail. After the war he founded, with Karlheinz Martin, one of the great directors of the 1920s, the Hebbel-Theater in Berlin. In 1953 he edited a documentary volume on the political prisoners of the Third Reich, based partly on material from Ricarda Huch, under the title *Der lautlose Aufstand*, to which Martin Niemöller wrote an introduction. His experience in the resistance underlies the drama *Die Illegalen* (1946), which made a great impact at the time, and *Memorial* (1947), memoirs written, as he put it, 'behind bars, partly on the backs of paper bags'.

Another who found his way to the extreme left of the political spectrum, but from a starting-point on the extreme right, was the extraordinary Viennese character Arnolt Bronnen. From dramas of the 1920s, including that most ludicrous of expressionist effusions, *Vatermord*, he turned to writing film scripts for the UFA corporation in Berlin, where he became a friend of Brecht. National Socialism, however, quickly captured his loyalty, and he was one of the 88 writers—among them also Gottfried Benn, Otto Flake and Ina Seidel—whose names appeared on the *Treuegelöbnis* handed to Hitler in October 1933. (Some of the signatories to this document said later that their names had been used without their knowledge or consent, but the presence of Bronnen's name raised no eyebrows.) After publishing a novel called *Rossbach* (1930), celebrating Hitler's abortive *coup* of 1923, he persuaded Goebbels to put him in charge of radio drama production. When it became known that he was of 'non-Aryan' descent, he lost his position and was banned from writing; during the war he deserted from the German army and joined the Communist underground in Austria, was arrested in 1944 and released soon afterwards in circumstances that are still not entirely clear. Later he became installed in posts of cultural influence in Austria. In 1955 he moved to East Berlin, where he died in 1959.

His *arnolt bronnen gibt zu protokoll* (1954), which reads more like a novel than an autobiography, gives his own account of the bewildering to-ing and fro-ing of his career down to the end of the war—a remarkable picture of the professional, political and moral pressures under which, like many others, he virtually disintegrated. Even the form of the book reflects the schizophrenic situation. Each of the 50 chapters (Bronnen was 50 in 1945, where the book ends) opens with a specific indictment of his conduct throughout the successive stages of his life, put into the mouth of an interrogating judge; in the remainder of each chapter Bronnen defends himself against the charge by autobiographical testimony—hence the title of the book. He is fully aware of what the world will want to know about his Nazi past, and of his accountability for his actions; the value of his career as a whole, as his imaginary interrogator puts it, will depend on whether he has now grasped, in 1945, that 'only the man who truly loves his fellow-men has the right to contribute to culture.'[39] One wonders whether Bronnen did either of these things.

Also associated, like Weisenborn, with the 'Rote Kapelle' and with the conspirators of 20 July 1944 was Albrecht Haushofer, writer of political dramas (*Scipio*, 1934, *Sulla*, 1938, *Augustus*, 1939—a trilogy classical in setting but contemporary German in relevance) and of the *Moabiter Sonette*, which are among the best-known works of resistance literature.

Haushofer wrote these sonnets in jail in Moabit during the months before being taken out by a group of SS men in April 1945 and shot. They deal in part with the outward manifestation of Nazism. But to a far greater extent they are a free record of the experiences and thoughts of an intellectual as concerned to analyse the historical and political circumstances that attended National Socialism as to contribute to its downfall. The tone of the poems, which occasionally reminds one of Brecht, is not cool, but neither is it passionate or, like much religious opposition poetry of biblical inspiration, emotionally exhortatory in its appeal. Haushofer's earlier faith in the will of the German people to resist has by this time been whittled away, hence his turn from the outer to the inner world, as one reminiscing in a disjointed monologue or reading from a personal diary. Yet neither his loss of confidence in his people nor the imminence of his own death could deprive him of a final Christian vision which comes to him with the memory of Matthias Grünewald's Isenheim altar-piece:

> Jetzt fühl ich, dass nur eines gültig ist:
> Wie sich dem Meister Matthias Er gezeigt-
> doch nicht der Fahle, der zum Tod sich neigt-
> der Lichtumflossne: dieser ist der Christ.[40]

(Now I feel that only one thing is valid—how He revealed himself to Matthias the master. Yet not the pale figure slumped in death, but the figure bathed in light—*that* is Christ)

('Qui resurrexit')

Of the form of this poetry, as of all opposition verse, whether written in the misery of concentration camp and prison, among the dangers of the battlefront, or in moments of secret withdrawal from an existence inwardly detested but outwardly conformed to, there is little to say. It is at the best of times a pursuit of questionable value to isolate and seek to define the 'literary' content of literature, the more inescapably so when that literature is the product of such moments of human suffering and degradation. 'Wes das Herz voll ist, des gehet der Mund über', runs the phrase from Luther's Bible. The hearts of these men are heavy with anguish, and their cry goes from the heart to the heart. The form that the cry takes, the imagery at which it grasps, are scarcely objects of analysis, so faint and fragile are they.

Maybe, therefore, among the generally simple, conventional strophic patterns in which most of this poetry is cast, the particular attractiveness of the sonnet lies both in the reassurance that derives from tradition and in the specific formal challenge that faces the poet who chooses to contribute to this tradition. These are not the conditions that favour expansive verse in ingenious formal patterns, or the craft of extended, broad-scale narrative fiction, but the direct, almost sudden lyrical utterance. The sonnet, imposing on the poet the discipline of octet and sestet, and being of a length to demand more than a violent emotional outburst yet less than an argued statement of philosophical position, seems to have offered the degree of challenge to which poets in these circumstances could respond. Although there is no florid emotionalism or public beating of the breast in the Baroque manner, and although the language of this opposition poetry is usually as restrainedly intense as that of most Baroque poets is frenetically flamboyant, the association with the sonnet form of the themes of death, the transience of life and the culpability of man does recall Gryphius, Paul Fleming, Weckherlin and other poets of the seventeenth century.

Closer in circumstance to the sonnets of Haushofer, Britting, Hagelstange and Reinhold Schneider are the *Geharnischte Sonette* of Rückert. Here, against the background of the Napoleonic Wars, Rückert appeals to the patriotic conscience of his slumbering Fatherland, praising fallen heroes like Theodor Körner and lamenting the state of war-torn Europe. Likewise Platen, who spent the last nine years of his life in exile in Italy, wrote seething patriotic lyrics in sonnet form, while from the revolution of 1848 came Ludwig Pfau's cycle of 'Flüchtlingssonette 1849', one of many collections with similar titles which were published in Switzerland by political refugees of the time. The attraction of the sonnet to exiled poets contemporary with Haushofer, Britting and their companions in Germany is reflected in the work of authors as different as Johannes R. Becher (*Der Mann, der alles glaubte*, 1935 and other sequences), Paul Zech (*Argentinische Sonette*, 1939), Elisabeth Langgässer and Gertrud von Le Fort.

'The poems of this anthology', wrote Gunter Groll in 1947 in *De Profundis, Deutsche Lyrik in dieser Zeit*, a collection from the years 1933–45,

. . . convey suffering, despair, the sense of death—yet also hope and an indestructible sense of consolation . . . . If the reader is disturbed or repelled by being confronted again and again with devils, terrible visions, fires of destruction, dances of death, let him judge from this what spiritual conditions were like at this time, how these men of the 'other Germany' suffered, how they despaired, where their guilt lay—but at the same time, what they believed in and how they sought to transcend the present.'[41]

These poems may not be high literature. But they are human documents from an era whose genesis and whose nature we forget at our peril.

NOTES

1. see J. Wulf, *Literatur und Dichtung im Dritten Reich* (Gütersloh, 1966), 106
2. Binding's name was originally among the 88, but obviously without his knowledge. This is probably true of others also. According to Oskar Loerke and Otto Flake a number only signed in order to protect their publishers (see Wulf, op. cit. 112ff).As with many so-called factual documents of the Nazi period, one must beware of accepting this 'declaration of loyalty' at its face value
3. *Binding. Die Briefe* ed. L. F. Barthel (Hamburg, 1957), 361
4. Carossa, *Gesammelte Werke* (Wiesbaden, 1949), I, 93
5. see his letter to Beumelburg quoted in Wulf, op. cit. 38–9
6. *Ausgewählte Briefe* (Wiesbaden, 1957), 49
7. *Antwort an die literarischen Emigranten*, 1933 (*Gesammelte Werke* I, Wiesbaden, 1961, 241)
8. ed. cit. I, 214
9. ed. cit. I, 440
10. Döblin, *Aufsätze zur Literatur* (Olten/Freiburg, 1963), 192
11. published by Benn in his *Doppelleben* (Wiesbaden, 1950), 84ff.
12. O. Loerke, *Tagebücher 1903–1939* (Heidelberg, 1955), 313
13. ed. cit. III, 226
14. ed. cit. I, 316
15. D. Wellershoff, *Gottfried Benn, Phänotyp dieser Stunde* (Cologne/Berlin, 1958), 156
16. *Berliner Brief, Juli 1948* (ed. cit. I, 281)

17. J. Wulf, op. cit. 37
18. see A. Mohler, *Die Schleife. Dokumente zum Weg von Ernst Jünger* (Zurich, 1955), 88
19. *Der Arbeiter: Werke* (Stuttgart, 1960), VI, 20
20. *Das zweite Pariser Tagebuch (Strahlungen* II, 1949; *Werke* III, 24)
21. *Auf den Marmorklippen* (ed. cit. IX, 238)
22. Preface to *Strahlungen* (ed. cit. II, 18)
23. *Der Friede* (ed. cit. V, 230)
24. *ibid.* (ed. cit. V, 224, 219)
25. *Der Waldgang* (ed. cit. V, 316)
26. *ibid.* 342
27. Ernst Jünger, *Blätter und Steine* (Hamburg, 1934), 13
28. see H.E. Holthusen, 'Epitaph. Eugen Gottlob Winkler' (*Merkur* I, 3 1947, 431)
29. *Minima Moralia* (Frankfurt, 1971), 254
30. J. Wulf, op. cit. 518
31. *Dies irae* (Zurich, 1945), 26
32. M. Frisch, 'Stimmen eines anderen Deutschlands? Zu den Zeugnissen von Wiechert und Bergengruen' (*Neue Schweizer Rundschau* XIII, 1945–6, 546
33. An anthology of prose and verse by exiled German authors from Heine and Georg Herwegh to Brecht and Thomas Mann has been edited by O. Mohr under the title *Das Wort der Verfolgten* (Basel, 1945).
34. R. Schneider, *Verhüllter Tag* (Cologne/Olten, 1954), 146
35. *Sonette* (Leipzig, 1939), 85
36. Leip—an incongruous and quite irrelevant fact—is the author of the song 'Lilli Marlene', which he wrote as a young soldier in Berlin in 1915
37. W. Langhoff, *Die Moorsoldaten. 13 Monate Konzentrationslager* (1935; repr. Tübingen, 1973). The actor Wolfgang Langhoff was arrested in 1933. After his release from concentration camp in 1934 he went into exile in Switzerland and published his account of his experiences the following year. It made a deep impression and was quickly translated into other languages. Langhoff himself wrote the refrain of the song.
38. Hermann Adler, *Balladen der Gekreuzigten, Auferstandenen, Verachteten* (Zurich, 1946),50
39. *arnolt bronnen gibt zu protokoll* (Hamburg, 1954), 495
40. Haushofer, *Moabiter Sonette* (4th. ed., Berlin, 1954), 495
41. *De Profundis. Deutsche Lyrik in dieser Zeit* (Munich, 1947), 20

CHAPTER NINE

Those who left: Writers in exile

'You have brought with you everything of that Germany which we love and respect. You bring the spirit of Goethe and Beethoven, Lessing and Marx.'

Such were the words of welcome addressed by Romain Rolland to the authors and scientists, actors, painters and musicians, who escaped from Nazi Germany between 1933 and the beginning of the war and started a new life in a new country. Over 1,300 men of letters were of this company, ranging from those with established reputations—Brecht, Arnold Zweig, Thomas and Heinrich Mann, Stefan George, Döblin, Werfel, Zuckmayer, Stefan Zweig, Toller, Schickele, Georg Kaiser, Broch, Musil—to the mass of small-town journalists, critics and free-lance essayists, whose livelihood disappeared when freedom of expression died. History knows of many writers who have sought voluntary or involuntary exile from their homeland—Sappho, Dante, Comenius, Byron, Victor Hugo, Mickiewicz, Büchner, Heine, Boerne. Both the Septuagint and the Koran are the work of men in exile. But the mass exodus of thousands of intellectuals from Hitler's Germany has no parallel in the history of modern Europe.

In the beginning it was above all the political opponents of Hitler who left. The Reichstag fire of 27 February 1933, spectacular climax of the Nazi plan to demonstrate that the Communists were about to launch an attack on the state, became the pretext for rounding up left-wing intellectuals in Berlin. Carl von Ossietzky, editor of *Die Weltbühne*, was arrested during the night of the fire and tortured in the concentration camp of Papenburg-Esterwegen for three years. He died of his wounds in 1938. The radical poet Erich Mühsam was arrested at the same time and murdered the following year in the concentration camp of Oranienburg. Willy Bredel and Friedrich Wolf were imprisoned but later released and found exile in Russia, returning to East Germany after 1945, like Johannes R. Becher and Theodor Plievier. Paul Zech was arrested in 1933 but set free in error and eventually found refuge in South America, haven also of Erich Arendt, Republican fighter in the Spanish Civil War, most of whose poetry was published after his return to East Germany in 1948. Ernst Toller's name was also on the list but he had already fled the country. The 30-year-old Anna Seghers, who had at this time written only a few social-revolutionary stories, was arrested, escaped to France and eventually found her way, like Ludwig Renn, Bodo Uhse and Egon Erwin Kisch, to Mexico, returning in 1947 to become the *doyenne* of East German letters.

The meaning of these arrests was not lost on those of left-wing sympathies, both Communist and others, such as Döblin, Leonhard Frank, Klaus Mann, Hermann Kesten and Ludwig Marcuse, who had for the moment escaped the attention of the Gestapo. But when, in the course of the next few weeks, they packed their bags and left for France, Austria or some other neighbouring country, most of them felt sure that they would be back within a matter of months, if not weeks. The Nazi nightmare, they said, would pass as soon as the Germans came to their senses and realised the nature of the monster they had voted into power. Klaus Mann travelled to France 'just to be on the safe side',[1] and Döblin called his escape to Switzerland 'only an excursion', adding: 'We'll wait till the storm has passed.'[2] With each successive foreign adventure on Hitler's part, from the absorption of the Saar in 1935 to the invasion of Poland in 1939, a further wave of refugees, swelled by those who had stayed in countries now overrun, spread across Europe, eastwards to the Soviet Union, westwards to France, England and the United States. The storm was going to last longer than Döblin thought.

As Hitler consolidated his power, the number of Jewish and politically non-radical refugees, which in 1933 and immediately afterwards had been fairly small, rapidly grew. Initially Jews were permitted, even encouraged, to emigrate, albeit at a sacrifice of much of their money and possessions, but from 1937 onwards those still in the country were hounded ruthlessly towards the 'final solution' of the Jewish problem. Many of these had not taken steps to leave because, closing their minds to the intentions of which the Nazis had never made any secret, they too believed that the terror was temporary and represented a continuation of a basically political campaign against left-wing intellectuals, many of whom happened to be Jews. Also, the non-intellectual German Jew—the tailor, the small shopkeeper, the white-collar worker, even the prosperous owner of a departmental store—was loyally patriotic and found it impossible to believe, until it was too late, that his own and his country's interests were not one and the same.

The events of 1938, culminating in the *Reichskristallnacht* of 9 November, shattered the last illusions, and by the outbreak of war some 250,000 people, half the Jewish population, had fled. Franz Werfel, Stefan Zweig, Bruno Frank, Alfred Döblin, Lion Feuchtwanger, Max Brod, Alfred Kerr, Hermann Broch, Martin Buber, Else Lasker-Schüler among writers; Max Reinhardt, Fritz

Kortner, Otto Klemperer, Kurt Weill, Bruno Walter, Arnold Schoenberg from the world of music and the theatre; Sigmund Freud, Albert Einstein, Max Born; scholars like Erich Auerbach and Ernst Cassirer—the list is endless, and the effect of their flight on German cultural life immeasurable. Small wonder that Romain Rolland should have hailed the refugees, Jews and non-Jews together, as bringing with them 'everything of that Germany which we love and respect'.

Yet it was statements of this kind, true in one sense, mistaken in another, that helped to bring about the unhappy ideological polarisation of German literature written after 1933 into that written by the 'inner emigrants' at home and that written by the exiles abroad. Who, it was asked after 1945, had been the true custodians of the cultural tradition—those who had stayed or those who had left? Those who had submitted to humiliation, harassment, even imprisonment and death but tried to uphold their integrity without breaking the bond that held them to their fatherland? Or those who, knowing that freedom of expression was impossible as long as National Socialism ruled, had considered the continued expression of true cultural and moral values paramount both for Germany and for the world, and had chosen the foreign freedom that made this possible? What, indeed, did this 'literature of exile' constitute? For whom was it, or should it have been, written? What did it seek, or should it have sought, to achieve? Or should one be talking, not of 'the literature of exile' but simply of 'writings by Germans abroad', as Döblin maintained?[3]

Questions like these were thrust into the limelight when, shortly after the end of the war, the novelist Walter von Molo, writing from the physical and spiritual ruins of Germany, sent a letter to Thomas Mann in California, begging him to return and lend his authority to the task of restoring honour to the name of Germany. Von Molo's approach was followed by an article from Frank Thiess, who had also spent the Nazi years in Germany, in which he claimed for the *innere Emigration*— a term of his own coinage—a higher moral standing than the emigrés. These latter, Thiess concedes, could not in general have acted other than they did, but their absence had cut them off from their native culture and induced a dangerous remoteness from the German reality of the year 1945; rather than look back in sorrow or in anger, assuming that it was they rather than the von Molos and their like who had preserved the tradition of German culture, they should return and publicly re-establish the natural unity which the unnatural events of 1933 had destroyed.

Thomas Mann's answer to Walter von Molo bears the blunt title

Warum ich nicht nach Deutschland zurückgehe. Leaving aside the purely biographical aspects, one finds expressed in this lengthy *plaidoyer* the tragic duality of the situation of so many exiled writers. On the one hand they clung to their faith in the unity of German literature, wherever it was written and whatever threatened to tear it apart. On the other hand they feared that they would find the Germany of 1945 both changed and unchanged from the Germany of 1933—changed, because the years of National Socialism had cut too deeply into men's minds for anyone to return unhesitatingly to the moment before the reign of terror began; unchanged, because people would have learned little from the experiences of those 12 years, and many become so infected with what they had experienced that their minds could no longer be reached.

To be sure, Thomas Mann never wanted to be thought of as other than a German, and would have no truck with talk of the 'good' Germans who had emigrated and the 'bad' Germans who had stayed. As early as 1936, in an open letter to Eduard Korrodi, literary editor of the *Neue Zürcher Zeitung*, he had pleaded for a sense of unity and for an understanding on the part of those who had left for those who, for whatever reason, had not:

'Those living outside the borders of Germany,' he wrote, 'ought not, I think, to look down with indiscriminate contempt on those who chose, or were made, to stay at home, nor ought they to link their aesthetic value-judgments to the question of who left and who remained. They suffer. But there is also suffering among those inside Germany. Let them beware of self-righteousness, which is so often a product of suffering'[4]

Yet for all his humanism, all his tolerance, all his preparedness to accept the oppressive paradoxes of German history and the German character, Thomas Mann could not refrain, in his letter of 1945 to Walter von Molo, from branding all books published in Germany between 1933 and 1945 as 'worse than worthless. . . They smack of blood and dishonour and should be pulped'.[5] So he did not go back. On his first visit to Europe after the war, in 1947, he did not even set foot in Germany. It was not until the Goethe year of 1949 that he visited, first Frankfurt in the West, then Weimar in the East, where he received from the hands of Johannes R. Becher the 20,000-mark Goethe Prize. This money he immediately donated towards the restoration of Herder's Stadtkirche in the town.

Particularly in the immediate aftermath of Hitler's assumption of power there was considerable public discussion in emigré periodicals of what tasks the writers in exile should set themselves. An essay in

1934 by the Dutch critic Menno ter Braak in the Paris journal *Das Neue Tagebuch* demanded that they should define their identity by breaking absolutely with the past and pursuing a European line radically opposed to all that National Socialism represented. The Marxist emigrés talked in terms of a popular front but found themselves increasingly at odds with those of non-conformist mind. The *Neue Deutsche Blätter*, for instance, which began publication in Prague in September 1933 under the editorship of Oskar Maria Graf, Anna Seghers and Wieland Herzfelde (brother of John Heartfield), quickly grew critical of those, Thomas Mann, Alfred Döblin, René Schickele and Stefan Zweig among them, who retained a 'bourgeois' conception of the role of the artist in society.

Das Wort, published in Moscow between 1936 and the Stalin-Hitler pact in 1939, and edited by Brecht, Feuchtwanger and Willy Bredel, took the same line, and, with contributions from men as different as Brecht, Arnold Zweig, Max Herrmann-Neisse and Arthur Koestler, came increasingly to imply in its editorials that it alone merited the appellation 'opposition journal.' The other Moscow periodical, *Die internationale Literatur*, which had been founded in 1931 as an organ for the presentation of Soviet socio-literary policy, also broadened its basis by inviting contributions, at opportune moments, from bourgeois writers, but always reflected the prevailing political interests of the Soviet Union. It survived until 1945. *Die Neue Weltbühne*, successor to the *Weltbühne* of Jacobsohn, Ossietsky and Tucholsky, which had been an early victim of Nazi censorship, appeared successively in Vienna, Prague, Zurich and Paris, and demanded more and more insistently the formation of a 'Popular Front' of anti-fascist writers. The same message was carried by *Freies Deutschland*, the organ of the refugees in Mexico, led by Anna Seghers and Egon Erwin Kisch.

Others periodicals declined to accept an overriding need for the politicisation of all literature or for the establishment of a collective emigré image. In so far, however, as all these journals, few of which survived for more than a few years, were sustained by men and women driven into exile and deprived of their natural audience, bitterness and a polemical tone were often inescapable. A militant political line runs, for example, through Klaus Mann's *Die Sammlung*, the first of the emigré literary periodicals (Amsterdam, 1933–5), which also, however, included contributions from Aldous Huxley, André Gide, Ernest Hemingway, Carlo Sforza and other European writers. *Mass und Wert*, on the other hand, edited in Zurich from 1937 to 1940 by Thomas Mann and Konrad Falke, and containing material by Ernst Bloch, Walter Benjamin, Hesse, Döblin and René

Schickele, sought to emphasise the independence of literature from politics and to preserve the integrity of the German intellectual tradition. Its tendency, therefore, was not revolutionary but conservative, 'in that it seeks to preserve what has hitherto constituted the dignity of man—the concept of a set of standards and values which transcend the personal, the political and the national'.[6] The editorial of the first issue takes its stand on a quotation from Goethe: 'What matters today is what one weighs when one steps on to the scales of humanity. Everything else is mere vanity.'[7] Similar in tone to *Mass und Wert*, and also literary rather than political in accent, was *Deutsche Blätter*, published in Chile 1943–1946 under the motto 'For a European Germany, Against a German Europe', which carried essays and poems by Else Lasker-Schüler, Paul Zech, Albert Einstein, F.C. Weiskopf, Carl Zuckmayer and others. Of the journals addressed to the community of Jewish emigrés the most important was *Aufbau*, founded by Manfred George in New York in 1934 and still published there today.

Taking the place of the German publishers who were forbidden to handle the works of the emigré writers, foreign publishing houses quickly seized the opportunity to circulate these works in the free world. This was far from being merely the piece of commercial opportunism it might at first seem. First, the market outside Germany for German-language books was small, and became smaller with each Nazi invasion of a country that formed part of this market. More importantly, royalties paid by foreign publishers were often the only regular income that writers in exile received, and without men like Allert de Lange and Emanuel Querido in Holland, and Emil Oprecht in Zurich, who arranged systems of regular payments to their authors as long as they could, many emigrés would hardly have survived. From 1933 to 1938 Heinrich Mann, for instance, lived in France almost entirely on a monthly allowance of 250 guilders from Querido, and Döblin, Arnold Zweig and Anna Seghers too had little more than Querido's allowances to keep them alive during the first years of their exile.

Quite apart from the economic uncertainty that beset the majority of these writers in their new homelands—few had the international reputation, and the complementary financial reassurance, of a Brecht, a Stefan Zweig or a Thomas Mann—the very fact of having to find a role for themselves in a foreign environment induced a state of intense loneliness and depression. For although the Hitler régime was disliked in Europe, refugees from that régime were not always welcome guests. 'It is always somehow suspicious', said Golo Mann many years later, 'to be at odds with the authorities of one's country and to have no valid passport.'8 The writer, whose tool is his native language, must needs feel this isolation more intensely than, say, the scientist or the business-man, in whose realms there is an international currency of ideas and practices, and whose activities can to some extent insulate them from the political and spiritual reality outside. For the writer in exile has lost his natural public. His language, with the social conventions, the morality, the modes of life, the patterns of thought with which it was born and to which it is linked, is not that of his environment, and the pressure of being an outsider not only brings changes in his subject-matter but affects the very heart of his work and thought. To have stayed in Hitler's Germany—even, in the few cases where it might have been possible, as 'inner emigrants'—was unthinkable for them. But the price of salvation was high.

Some, like Zuckmayer and Alfred Kerr, urged their fellow-exiles not to cling nostalgically to the threads of their German past but to find a place for themselves in the culture of their new surroundings. Marxists and Jews, for different reasons, were prominent among those who, as Ernst Bloch put it in an address given in New York in 1939, 'really thought that Hitler was here for a thousand years, and, having been made bankrupt themselves, now wrote Germany off as a complete loss'.9 Others, however, Musil and Stefan Zweig among them, felt so insecure and helpless in their new surroundings that they sought all possible ways of preserving their spiritual links with the Austria they had left behind. Zweig's pessimism ended in suicide—an act which, like Ernst Toller's suicide three years earlier, evoked resentment at what was branded in some quarters as a betrayal of the emigrés' anti-Nazi calling. Others again, like Thomas Mann, came to feel an increasing sense of gratitude to the land that had given them refuge, while neither denying their national heritage nor wishing to see a wedge driven between the Germans of Hitler's Reich and the Germans in exile. And numerous calls were made for a determined optimism with which to face the years until the Nazi nightmare had passed.

Yet even when this moment came, the tragic plight of the exiled writers was not resolved. They had warned the world of the rule of terror and destruction that the rise of Hitler would bring. The world had not listened. What satisfaction was there, now that Europe lay in ruins, in being proved right? Resistance fighters in the occupied countries could now rejoice at the enemy's defeat, but for the German emigré, in the painful ambiguity of his situation, the freedom bell gave a cracked sound. With one half of his being he was on the side of the allied victors; with the other half he belonged to his disgraced and defeated fatherland. Of those who survived the war Heinrich Mann, Unruh, Feuchtwanger, Albert Ehrenstein, Werfel and Broch stayed in the United States, their chosen refuge, and died there; Thomas Mann and Zuckmayer returned to Europe but made their home in Switzerland, not in Germany, and Friedrich Torberg went back to Vienna; Erich Fried and Richard Friedenthal stayed in London; Paul Zech died in Buenos Aires, Wolfskehl in New Zealand. Anna Seghers, Brecht, Becher, Erich Weinert, F. C. Weiskopf (after a post-war career as a Czech diplomat) and Arnold Zweig eventually returned to Germany to serve the socialist cause in the East. Almost alone among the names familiar in literary circles before 1933, Alfred Döblin and Ferdinand Bruckner went back to West Germany.

i. Drama in exile: Brecht

In the course of the 1920s the drama had moved from a post-war 'expressionist' mood of personal passion and cynicism, extravagance and bitterness, to a hard realism of social content, whether in tragedy or comedy, and whether in the spirit of the detached observer or the didactic reformer. The comedies of Zuckmayer and Hasenclever, social panoramas like Walter Mehring's *Der Kaufmann von Berlin*, historico-analogical studies like Wolfgang Goetz's *Gneisenau* and the early one-act plays of Bernt von Heiseler, the agitprop school of Piscator in Berlin, the Wedekindian crisis-plays of Ferdinand Bruckner in Vienna—these and other works share the spirit of 'new objectivity' which held many writers in its sway from the mid-1920s onwards.

In one form or another this objectivity continues to dominate the drama of the 1930s and 1940s. Dramatists need theatres, and foreign-language drama is in any country, and at the best of times, hardly an economic proposition. The dramatist in exile, unless his works are immediately translated, suffers perhaps more from his isolation than the poet or novelist, who, though he may reach only a small public, has a more direct access to this public, without the need for the intermediacy of actors, producers and the whole apparatus of commercial theatre.

The disillusionment and pessimism of Ferdinand Bruckner's plays, for example—*Die Rassen* (1933), a protest against anti-Semitism; *Timon* (1932), a latter-day *Timon of Athens*; *Die Marquise von O.* (1935), a dramatisation of Kleist's story—border at times on the expressionist in their extravagance, and his comedies *Napoleon der Erste* (1936–7) and *Heroische Liebe* (1938) made little impact. More famous is Carl Zuckmayer's *Des Teufels General* (1942), written during his wartime years as a farmer in Vermont. Zuckmayer left Germany in 1933, lived in Austria until the *Anschluss* in 1938, then went to Switzerland and eventually, in 1940, to the United States. *Des Teufels General* has the panache and versatility that he shows in all his works, yet somehow without convincing us that he is doing much more than make display of a formidable skill, developing the theatrical potentialities, rather than the moral significance, of his theme. Later he himself seems to have had doubts about the 'message' he had given. He withdrew the work in the 1950s for a number of years, releasing it again in 1966 with a modified final scene in which the character of Oderbruch, the resistance fighter, is more firmly delineated.

Quieter in tone than the effervescent Zuckmayer is *Das heilige Experiment* (1943) by the Viennese dramatist Fritz Hochwälder, who, like Zuckmayer, emigrated to Switzerland after the *Anschluss*. An earnest, thoughtful play, it has a place alongside Reinhold Schneider's *Las Casas vor Karl V* as a drama, historical and religious in setting, on the subject of dictatorial power and the moral corruption to which it leads.

But none of these works can bear comparison with the plays of the most powerful playwright of this period, the one German dramatist of the inter-war years to acquire European stature and influence—Bertolt Brecht.

When the Reichstag building went up in flames on 27 February 1933, Brecht knew, like so many others, that the moment had come to leave Germany. Via Austria, Czechoslovakia, Switzerland and France—'changing countries more often than shoes', as he put it in his poem 'An die Nachgeborenen'—he settled in the autumn of 1933 in Denmark, where, apart from visits to Paris, New York and elsewhere to see productions of his plays, he stayed until shortly before the outbreak of war. In 1935 he paid his one visit to Moscow, and the following year he became co-editor, with Feuchtwanger and Willy Bredel, of the Marxist German-language periodical *Das Wort*, published in the Soviet capital. In 1939 he left Denmark for Sweden, and the following year left Sweden for Finland. There he applied for a United States visa, travelled the whole breadth of the Soviet Union to Vladivostok, without giving any hint that he might stay in that country, and sailed for the United States in a Swedish freighter. He reached California in July 1941, where he found Thomas and Heinrich Mann, the sociologist and musicologist Theodor Adorno, Ferdinand Bruckner, old collaborators of the 1920s like the composer Hanns Eisler and the actors Fritz Kortner, Oskar

Homolka and Peter Lorre, together with the film director Fritz Lang. Many long-established residents of the Los Angeles area, among them Charles Laughton, Aldous Huxley and Charlie Chaplin, soon became counted among his friends.

Brecht was to live in California for six years. When he left in 1947, the day after the Committee for Un-American Activities acquitted him of having spread Communist propaganda in the United States, he travelled first to Switzerland and lived near Zurich for a year. Finally, in 1949, he moved with his wife Helene Weigel to East Berlin, where he stayed until his death in 1956, though he never became a citizen of the German Democratic Republic. 'Ich benötige keinen Grabstein', runs the first line of a poem written a year before his death. But he left instructions for the manner of his interment—even down to prescribing a zinc coffin—and his gravestone stands among those of the cultural élite whose ashes rest in the Dorotheenstädtischer Friedhof, beneath the windows of his house in the Chausseestrasse.

By the time of the 'Lehrstücke' of 1929 and 1930 Brecht's Marxist position and didactic intent seemed fixed. The concept of epic theatre, initially derived from Piscator in both purpose and practice, was pressed into the service of his social and political message, and the technique of *Verfremdung*, he assumed, would induce the audience to see that the world needed to be changed accordingly. The early plays of his exile, like *Die Rundköpfe und die Spitzköpfe* (1931–4) and *Furcht und Elend des Dritten Reiches* (1935–8), still show the world that is— *realexistierend*, as Marxist literature uses the term—as being changeable.

There is no necessary link between a Marxist outlook and either epic theatre or *Verfremdung*, and there are familiar historical precedents for the presence in drama of narrative, epic techniques: there is the Japanese No-play, for instance, and the epic theatre of Sanskrit literature (for example, Kalidasa's *Sakuntala*, so admired by Herder), together with the Chorus of Greek tragedy, and of Shakespeare. Moreover Brecht is only one of a number of twentieth-century playwrights—Anouilh, Thornton Wilder and Dürrenmatt are others—who use epic moments to present a more variegated, more richly stratified reality than 'dramatic' drama—'Aristotelian drama', as Brecht calls it—could achieve alone. His theory of epic, 'non-Aristotelian' drama, which underwent considerable modification between the formula put out in 1931 in his notes to *Aufstieg und Fall der Stadt Mahagonny* and his *Kleines Organon für das Theater* of 1948, is, moreover, concerned rather with the redistribution of emphases than with the rigorous pursuit of antitheses. The contrast between traditional dramatic theatre, sustained by the spectator's self-identification with the events being enacted before his eyes, is deliberately overstated in the interests of detaching the spectator's feelings from the emotional turmoil of the play and inducing him to pass rational, 'objective' judgment—a frankly pre-determined and manipulated judgment, to be sure—on the scenes he witnesses.

But although epic theatre does not have to be Marxist, or Marxist drama epic, for Brecht it did. The environment in which his characters live is shown as basically the product of the social and economic pressures of capitalism; the spectator has first to be made aware of this in a spirit of scientific inquiry, and then to be made to see that such conditions must be changed. Hence Brecht's theory rejects dramatic theatre which 'allows the spectator to have feelings' in favour of epic theatre which 'demands decisions from him'; rejects experience and feeling in favour of *Weltanschauung* and reason; rejects the assumptions of growth and evolutionary inevitability in favour of sudden leaps and the techniques of montage.[10] The apparatus of *Verfremdung*—in the text of the play itself, in its production, in the style of acting and in all other aspects of the theatrical occasion—is for Brecht the means to a Marxist end, and one can as little separate the one from the other as one can separate Brecht the poet from Brecht the political animal.

The extent to which Brecht's dramatic practice, above all in his four major plays written in exile—*Mutter Courage und ihre Kinder* (1938–9) *Leben des Galilei* (1938–9, with later additions), *Der gute Mensch von Sezuan* (1938–41) and *Der kaukasische Kreidekreis* (1944–5)—conflicts with the demands of his theory, will concern us in a moment. We may also note that by the time of the *Kleines Organon für das Theater* the old, scorned notion of the theatre as entertainment has edged aside the conception, dominant in the period of his 'Lehrstücke', of the theatre as a moral institution. The greater the 'enjoyment' felt by the spectator, which means the greater the extent to which his heart and mind are carried along by the representation on the stage, the less the degree of detached observation he retains, and the weaker his will to reform becomes. One does not have to be a Marxist to accept the reality of social change, and to envisage, as Engels did, a perpetually changing world of matter both inde-structible and self-regenerating is to lose for the moment the vision of a classless society as the ultimate social reality.

Perhaps the most vital shortcoming in Brecht's aesthetic theories, however, whether from the 1920s or the 1940s, is their avoidance of the concept of human tragedy. His attitudes assume that ame-lioration of the human lot, in all places and at all times, is purely a matter of human decision, and that the catastrophes portrayed in

Greek tragedy or in Shakespeare should now be seen, not as inevitable but as avoidable. Society, the argument runs, can change itself if it so wishes, and both prevent a repetition of the mistakes of the past and see to it that people recognise the true nature, that is, the Marxist analysis, of the present. There is no room in Brecht's theory for the situation of a man faced with irrevocable disaster, whether caused by natural or by human agency, for in the modern 'scientific' age man is in a position to see that such disasters do not occur.

Once again it becomes clear how identification with the sufferings of the hero, in the manner associated with Aristotelian catharsis, is to be avoided. The spectator is made to look dispassionately at the dramatic situation from outside and ask himself what rational steps must be taken in order to prevent it arising again. In the year before his death Brecht reaffirmed this position:

In an age whose science is able to change nature to an extent that makes the world appear almost habitable, man can no longer be described as a mere victim, a victim of an unknown, unalterable environment . . . The world of today can be described to the human beings of today only as a world that can be changed.[11]

In practice the theatre of Bertolt Brecht has neither convinced the thousands who have seen his plays that the world can be changed, still less that it has to be changed in the way he says it must, nor has it demonstrated that his epic theatre is *the* form of theatre for advancing the cause of the class struggle. On the contrary, the Soviet Communist Party had decreed that the modes of production and style of acting proper for Marxist drama were those of Stanislavsky and the Moscow Art Theatre—the theatre of illusion and identification that represented what Brecht was out to destroy.

At the end, in the essay 'Die Dialektik auf dem Theater' and the shorter pieces published posthumously under this title, Brecht himself can be seen in the throes of withdrawing from his categorical 'epic drama' position, but without leaving much idea of what the new 'dialectical drama' would look like.

The gulf between Brecht's theatrical demands, or occasional statements of his own intent, and the effect on un-alienated audiences of the powerful plays he wrote during his years in exile, is strikingly apparent in the first of these plays, *Mutter Courage und ihre Kinder*. Brecht envisaged his seventeenth-century heroine as a negative and despicable character, a woman driven only by her determination to make a living by the war, too stupid to learn the lessons of experience and too obtuse to realise the baseness of her actions. That she sacrifices her three children to her profiteering greed is the price she pays for her immorality, but it is a price she does not find too high, and at the end she is still pulling her cart along in a desperate attempt to catch up with the army that is moving on ahead of her.

War is evil, says Brecht, and those who live by war are wicked. But audiences have never been able to completely withhold their sympathy from the shameful Mother Courage. Instead of being moved, as Brecht intended, to protest against war, they rise in pity at the sight of the poor woman with whom war has dealt so cruelly. Brecht subsequently made alterations in the play in order to emphasise more strongly the parasitic nature of her trade, but it made no difference. If there were a villain in the play, people continued to say, it could not be an impersonal thing like war but only the carriers of war, that is, the soldiers, whose acts of brutality are pitilessly displayed; certainly it could not be the poor woman who, after all the tragedies that had befallen her, struggled to her feet and somehow managed to drag herself along in the only mode of life she knew. Audiences have similarly let Brecht down by being unwilling to cast the landowner Puntila, in *Herr Puntila und sein Knecht Matti* (1940–1), as a thorough villain, and Matti as a noble worker.

That Brecht altered his original text in order to make his didactic purpose plainer, leaves little doubt about his own position. But even the performance of the revised version by the Berliner Ensemble after the war failed to change the audience's response. When it was suggested, however, that Mother Courage—one of Helene Weigel's star roles—might be given a speech at the end in which she made the message explicit, Brecht declined. To have stamped this message so crudely on the audience's consciousness would have amounted to an admission that he had failed to make the message clear in the action of the play itself; at the same time the artist in him refused to allow the play *qua* play to have its inner being destroyed. He was the victim—fortunately—of his poetic instinct, and especially in his later career one has to set this against what sometimes appear as his equivocal dealings with authority. Survival was what mattered.

Emphasising the immoral side of a character for whose behaviour one might otherwise develop too sympathetic an understanding also underlies the later revisions that Brecht made to *Das Leben des Galilei*. The negative aspects of Galileo's nature are patent: his self-indulgence, his swindling, his capitulation before an authority he despises. At the same time he is a genius, and the world needs geniuses; he is also a scientist, and the exercise of the human reason in the pursuit of knowledge cannot but be reckoned among the most laudable of activities. 'I wanted to portray Galileo's heroic fight for his conviction that the earth does move,' said Brecht in an interview for the Copenhagen *Berlingske Tidende* in 1939, shortly before finishing the first version of the play. So in this original version, written between 1938 and 1939 in Denmark, Galileo's retraction of his 'Eppur si muove' is justified as an act of cunning by which he could survive to complete his scientific work and smuggle his revolutionary treatise out of the country.

But in the 1945–6 American version Brecht motivated Galileo's recantation by cowardice—fear of being tortured—instead of by cunning, introducing an ethical dualism into the action and trying to make us aware of the criminal within the hero—criminal, because not only has Galileo betrayed the cause of science in the face of pressure from the state, but also, more vitally, because he has ignored the social responsibility of the scientist. The rationality and accountability of the scientific mind do not withstand the acquisitive urge for knowledge, knowledge at all costs and whatever the conditions, even those—as Brecht had in his mind when writing the final version (1953–5)—which require men to build atomic bombs. 'I maintain that the only aim of science is to ease the burdens of human existence,' says Galileo at the end. But he did not live up to this principle. Hence: 'I have betrayed my vocation. Any man who does what I have done cannot be tolerated in the ranks of science' (Scene 14).

'Both as a technical and as a social phenomenon,' Brecht wrote later, 'the atom bomb is the classical end-product of his [Galileo's] skill in science and his betrayal of society.'[12] We may now know more about science but we know less and less about who, and what, governs the world. As Galileo puts it: 'The movements of the heavenly bodies have become clearer, but people understand as little about the actions of their rulers as they did before.' (Scene 14) The productions of the Berliner Ensemble have from the beginning, when Ernst Busch took the title role, set out to minimize the danger that the audience would discover a human sympathy for Galileo's ambivalence. Yet as in all these late plays of Brecht's, it is the personal predicament of the hero that moves us, not—whatever Brecht himself subsequently claimed he intended—the presentation of a social problem.

Also morally flawed, half hero, half scoundrel, is the judge Azdak in Der kaukasische Kreidekreis, a character who, like Galileo, bears many character traits of Brecht himself. Here, as in Das Verhör des Lukullus (1939), the 'epic' nature of the drama itself is reinforced by the presence of a narrator on the stage, who, like the Chorus in Greek drama and in Shakespeare, introduces the action as an illustration of his message.

Through the extraordinary unpredictabilities and contradictions in the character of Azdak Brecht presents in its most entertaining form his recurrent conflict of emotion and instinct. Exalted by a series of preposterous events to the position of judge, Azdak is an insult to any legal profession, abusing his position, accepting bribes and dispensing a kind of Robin Hood justice based on the principle that the poor are innocent and the rich guilty ('Property is theft', as Proudhon put it). He is guided solely by instinct, heedless of other people's judgment on him, and ensures, precisely through his reliance on instinct, the almost certain failure of what he sets out to achieve.

In *Der kaukasische Kreidekreis* the summit of Brecht's humanity and poetical power is reached with the coincidence of the career of Azdak with that of the peasant girl Grusche. Grusche pays as little heed to the opinions of the world as does Azdak, and lives by the same lights of instinct: she is prepared to endure suspicion of her own character in order to protect the child she has rescued, and her honesty and her persistent courage and self-sacrifice make her the most unequivocally appealing figure in the whole of Brecht's work. So it is with a feeling that natural justice has been done that we hear the corrupt but 'right' judge Azdak declare that not the child's real mother, but Grusche, who has displayed true motherly virtue, shall be the custodian of the child. As we have come to know Grusche, no other solution would have been proper; as we have come to know Azdak, no other decision would have been in character. The *coincidentia oppositorum*—opposites sometimes within the individual character, as well as the external contrast between the two characters—has, for the moment, been resolved, and we find ourselves witnesses of what the 'epic' folk-singer-cum-narrator calls at the end 'a brief Golden Age of near-justice'.[13]

The only heroine to rival Grusche in gaining the audience's almost total sympathy is the 'good woman', the prostitute Shen Te, in *Der gute Mensch von Sezuan*. Shen Te is perhaps the most modern, most movingly convincing of all Brecht's characters in these last plays of his exile. As Mother Courage, Galileo, Azdak, Grusche and Shen Te have a fullness of personality, a realistic humanity foreign, for example, to the montage creature Galy Gay in *Mann ist Mann*, the lurid figure of Joan Dark in *Die heilige Johanna der Schlachthöfe* or the spokesmen for the theory and practice of pre-digested world revolution in the various 'Lehrstücke', so the more obtrusive 'epic' elements recede from the technique. And as the character of Shen Te shows, it could not be otherwise. For here is a woman torn between her natural goodness and the need for survival: the gods, both at the beginning and at the end of the play, declare her unique goodness, but her life between these two moments is sustained by the egoism, the deception and the ruthlessness which she finds to be the only means of staying alive. Her dichotomy is made the more unbearable by her knowledge that, while she loves the man who is the father of her unborn child, his only concern is to swindle her out of her money and then abandon her. Either she can perish with her naive goodness or survive on an unpleasant lie. 'Who would not be a good man!' asks Peachum rhetorically in the *Dreigroschenoper*. He, in his cynicism, knows that one cannot be good. Shen Te shows that one can—but one cannot live with, let alone by, one's goodness.

Such a character will always find her way into the hearts of an audience. To be sure, there is a sociological aspect of the play which presents the capitalist world in which such a dilemma arises as ripe for change, but Shen Te's agony is not just the product of social pressures, nor can it be healed merely by changing the social order. Shen Te embodies a modern existentialist problem, one which even the scornfully portrayed gods—'We are only observers', they say in pitiful self-justification—are powerless to solve. Nor has Brecht himself, in the epilogue to the play, any answer to propose. All he can do is encourage his audience to propose one:

> *Wir sind zerschmettert und nicht nur zum Scheine!*
> *Der einzige Ausweg wär aus diesem Ungemach:*
> *Sie selber dächten auf der Stelle nach*
> *Auf welche Weis dem guten Menschen man*
> *Zu einem guten Ende helfen kann.*[14]

(We are shattered, and not just apparently. The only way I can see out of this dilemma is for *you* to start thinking at once of some way to help this good woman arrive at a good outcome.)

In another version of this epilogue Brecht, while repeating that in places like Sezuan one cannot be good and at the same time survive, takes his leave with a couplet of rare optimistic benevolence:

> *Kein grösseres Glück gibt es auf Erden nun*
> *Als gut sein dürfen und Gutes tun.*[15]

(There is no greater happiness on earth than doing good and being permitted to do good.)

So—

> *Verehrtes Publikum, los, such dir selbst den Schluss:*
> *Es muss ein guter da sein, muss, muss, muss!*

(Away you go, good people, and look for your own ending! There must be a good one somewhere—there must, there must, there must!)

If the status of the 'sweeping ineffectiveness of a classic' which Max Frisch conferred on Brecht[16] be taken to refer to the failure of Brecht's didactic plays to rouse their audiences to political action, sending them out of the theatre with a burning zeal to change the system responsible for the ills of his heroes, then his plays are indeed models of ineffectiveness. But real, flesh-and-blood characters like Mother Courage, Galileo, Azdak and Shen Te—'round' characters, as E.M. Forster would have called them—have an effectiveness, a power to move, which is inseparable from the truly poetic presentation of scenes from the condition of contemporary man. Language and imagery join—Brecht would have said 'conspire'—to compel us to identify with the hero's predicament, and the infiltration of 'epic' acting or 'epic' production will change nothing.

Mounted on the wall of Brecht's study was a slogan that read 'Die Wahrheit ist konkret'. 'Exploitation', 'social change', 'society' itself, are concepts, abstractions. Concrete is the individual, his personal involvement in the process of social change, his personal struggles within his society, his personal fate. Slogans are no substitute for characters, and although a drama may induce in its audience an awareness of contemporary social conditions that need to be changed, it must be shown through the physical and mental travails of the characters on the stage that change is possible, what the nature of the change is, and that individuals can demonstrably act in ways to bring it about. Whatever we know from elsewhere about Brecht's beliefs is irrelevant, for conviction and feasibility must emerge from within the work of art itself. A play is not a party political broadcast.

Brecht's later statements on his dramatic theory, often, it seems, deliberately blurred and ambivalent, limp along behind the practice of his later plays, shedding bit by bit the claims and demands which 20 years earlier seemed inalienable. Indeed, throughout his career Brecht's theorisings have the quality of intellectual-biographical commentaries on, or *a posteriori* rationalisations of, circumstances, developments, changes of focus already manifest in poetic form in his plays. *Das Leben des Galilei*, an out-and-out 'Aristotelian' character drama, he described at the time of the first version (1939) as 'opportunistic'; a few weeks later he supplied an equally 'opportunistic' justification of it in ideological terms. 'After I read Marx's *Kapital*,' he wrote in 1926 (*Schriften zum Theater* I, 181), 'I understood my plays.' If he says so. Many think they can understand the plays he means—*Baal*, *Trommeln in der Nacht* and *Mann ist Mann* among them—without reading Marx's *Kapital*. After all, Brecht wrote them without having done so. The analytical is secondary—primary is the creative. The *poète malgré lui* has won.

ii. Lyric poetry

When one surveys a span of years with a view to characterising the
nature of society, the nature of literature, and the relationship
between the two, one is bound to observe that, while literature
undoubtedly responds in various ways to the quality and movement
of society, it also has its own momentum, the product of its own inner
laws and of the forces of its tradition. Sometimes it may reflect and
confirm elements of the society to which it belongs, sometimes it may
convey a rejection of them. Equally it may have the most tenuous of
links with society and be the expression of a fantasy world, which is
yet as real to the poet as is the world of verifiable data to society at
large. The novel, for instance, may in general be closer to this
objective reality than, say, lyric poetry, and therefore be more
directly susceptible to external impulses. In its turn drama, again in
response to its inner formal needs, may present in selective and
concentrated form the vital areas of conflict in the society of the
moment. All these interactions are held in a series of delicate and
ever-fluctuating relationships, as the writer comes to grips with the
substance, objective and subjective, from which he has to fashion his
work.

It is partly because of the nature of social life in Germany in the
1920s and early 1930s, but partly also because of in-dwelling aesthetic
forces, that the basic characteristics and relative significance of
literary genres during the era of the Weimar Republic should pass
with little change into the exile literature of the late 1930s and 1940s.
The Weimar years had produced only one great dramatist—Brecht;
he remained in exile the only great dramatist. They had favoured the
growth of the novel—social, historical, allegorical, artistic, utopian;
and the novel, far more than any other form, commanded the
attention of writers in exile and was the field of their greatest
achievements. The lyric had withered in the Weimar years: except
for Brecht, and an occasional moment in Werfel, Nelly Sachs,
Wolfskehl and a few others, it continued to hang its head through the
years of isolation from 1933 to 1945. Apart from Stefan George's *Das
neue Reich* and a handful of poems by Gottfried Benn, the last sustained
and substantial lyric poetry to be published had been Rilke's *Duineser
Elegien* and *Sonette an Orpheus*, both in 1923.

Perhaps the very isolation of the emigrés, new members of societies
to whose ways they had yet to adapt, added its own sad influence to
the inner history of lyric poetry in these years. Forced to learn new
obligations and new conventions, thinking in one language
and—except for the few in Switzerland—surrounded by another, the

poet turned in upon the traditions of his art. But the traditions had worn thin. The flourish of the expressionist lyric had passed, and *Neue Sachlichkeit* seemed to demand a set of values by which only a hard, *engagé* poetry could survive. The lyric muse was confined in the spirit in the way that most of these exiled poets were confined in the flesh, a confinement in which the deep personal relationships which are the stuff of lyric poetry become more strained, and harder to find.

For some, above all those sustained by a political commitment, the externalisation of inner convictions offered the occasion to continue in the pre-war mould, perhaps even with greater determination than before. Paramount in this company is Brecht, whose poetry of these years, the best of it of a power and a poetic conviction unrivalled in modern German literature, is permeated by the same forceful, sombre awareness of 'times out of joint' that fills his plays of the late 1930s and early 1940s. In his review of *Bert Brechts Hauspostille* in *Die Weltbühne* in 1928 Tucholsky suggested that, talented as Brecht was as a dramatist, his power as a poet was still greater. Much of this poetic power finds its way into the songs which, from *Mann ist Mann* onwards, became so characteristic a feature of Brecht's dramas. *Die Dreigroschenoper*, with its adaptations of Villon ballads set to the haunting emptiness of Weill's music, is the first that come to mind. But the late plays—'Das Herrenlied', 'Das Lied vom Fraternisieren' and others in *Mutter Courage*; the water-carrier's song and the 'Lied vom achten Elefanten' in *Der gute Mensch von Sezuan*; 'Das Lied von der Moldau', 'Das Lied vom Weib des Nazisoldaten' and Frau Kopecka's other songs in *Schweyk im Zweiten Weltkrieg*; 'Das Lied vom Chaos' in *Der kaukasische Kreidekreis*—all these are no less rich in such mordant verses.

But these years also see the publication of individual collections of lyric poems, most of them didactic or satirical in intent, and all of them, even those one might describe as reflective, aggressive in manner. The *Gedichte, Lieder, Chöre*, published in Paris in 1934 and set to music by Hanns Eisler, which also include choruses and songs from *Die Massnahme* and *Die Mutter*, are predominantly political in substance and of greater biographical interest than poetic quality. The 80 or so *Svendborger Gedichte*, on the other hand, written during Brecht's period in Denmark and published in London in 1939, contain a number of poems, some narrative, some lyrical, which have their deserved place alongside the big dramas of those years. Narrative poems like 'Der Schuh des Empedokles' and 'Gleichnis des Buddha vom Brennenden Haus', with their oblique autobiographical content, their merciless vitality and their abrasive intolerance of tone, are the true vindication of Tucholsky's judgment.

Most gripping, because most personal, of these late poems,

however, is the *apologia pro vita sua* called 'An die Nachgeborenen', the last of the *Svendborger Gedichte*. The mask of steely impersonality from behind which he usually speaks—but without being able to disguise his voice—is dropped, and for a moment we look him straight in the eye as he bequeathes his world to posterity, a cruel, guilt-ridden world in which an air of happiness signifies merely ignorance of the truth, an apparent serenity proves merely a lack of sensitivity, and in which good intentions lead to hell:

> *Auch der Hass gegen die Niedrigkeit*
> *Verzerrt die Züge.*
> *Auch der Zorn über das Unrecht*
> *Macht die Stimme heiser. Ach, wir*
> *Die wir den Boden bereiten wollten für Freundlichkeit*
> *Konnten selber nicht freundlich sein.*[17]

> (Yet we know that
> Even hatred of meanness
> Distorts one's features. Even anger at injustice
> Makes one's voice hoarse. For we
> Who sought to pave the way for sympathy, O we
> Were not able to be sympathetic ourselves.)

Such is the wretched legacy Brecht leaves to future generations. A decade or more earlier, in 'Vom Armen B.B.', he had already cynically characterised these generations:

> *Wir wissen, dass wir Vorläufige sind*
> *Und nach uns wird kommen: nichts Nennenswertes.*[18]

> (We know that we are temporary
> And that we shall be followed by—nothing worth mentioning.)

Der kaukasische Kreidekreis may show us an ideal moment of 'near-justice', but can those devoid of sympathy, with distorted features and hoarse voices, or those just 'not worth mentioning', profit from such a moment—or even recognise it? The price of survival is eternal scepticism.

A political comrade of Brecht's, an immensely productive and influential poet second only to him in the poetic hierarchy of the German Democratic Republic, is Johannes R. Becher. A Communist since 1917, he left Germany early in 1933, lived from 1935 to 1945 in Moscow and returned immediately after the war to East Berlin, where he died in 1958. For the last four years of his life he was Minister of Culture.

On the one hand Becher had a political faith, international as well as national in application, to sustain him, and the class struggle, the Spanish Civil War and the ideology of the Soviet Union gave him both strength and subject matter:

> *Tausend Jahre werden vergangen sein:*
> *Aber immer noch*
> *Wird einen Namen man nennen:*
> *Lenin!*

> *Tausend Jahre werden vergangen sein:*
> *Auf allen Türmen der Erde*
> *Wird die rote Fahne wehen*
> *Und nachts von unten her beleuchtet sein . . .*[19]

(A thousand years will have passed, yet one name will still be heard—Lenin! A thousand years will have passed, and from all the towers in the world the red flag will fly, lit up at night from below . . .)

('Der tausendjährige Lenin')[19]

Or the poem 'Dank an die Freunde in der Sowjetunion', which begins:

> *Ihr aber habt mich brüderlich empfangen,*
> *Und alles gabt ihr mir, dass mein Gedicht*
> *Soll weiterleben.*[20]

(You received me like a brother and gave me everything to enable my poetry to survive.)

Similar values sustain the voluminous output of the direct, albeit generally unsubtle political poems of Erich Weinert, himself a fighter with the International Brigade and, like Becher, an exile in Moscow during the war.

But Becher also retained a love of homeland, a sense of personal relationships, and an unshakeable awareness both of his responsibility to the German literary tradition and of the historical role in Europe which a socialist Germany should play after the war. At one moment he could be wistful and sentimental:

> *Die Apfelbäume blühn. Ein weicher Schimmer*
> *Liegt überm Land. Es blüht aus dir heraus.*
> *Still. Nur der Fluss, das Blühn . . . Ich wünsch mir: immer*
> *Möcht ich hier sein. Hier bin ich ganz zu Haus.*

> *O Nacht, belebt von Sternen, Mond und Wind—*
> *Ob ich dich, Neckar, jemals wiederfind?!*[21]

(The apple-trees are in blossom. A soft glow lies over the countryside. Blossoms spring from your midst. Silent. Only the river, the blossoming . . . I wish I could stay here for ever. Here I am completely at home. . . O night, alive with stars and moon and wind—shall I ever see you, Neckar, again?)

('Neckar bei Nürtingen',)

Then, submitting to a formal poetic discipline echoed in the sonnets of Rudolf Hagelstange, Albrecht Haushofer and other anti-Nazi poets of the 'inner emigration', Becher could turn his mind to ode, sonnet and elegy in a spirit of Renaissance revival. His collected sonnets of 1935 to 1938 were published in Moscow under the title *Gewissheit des Siegs und Sicht auf grosse Tage*, among them those of the collection *Der Mann, der alles glaubt* (1935), in which Heinrich Mann claimed to have found some of the finest sonnets written since classical times.

Becher's personal experiences of the 1920s and 1930s never weakened his patriotism or his identification with the German *Heimat*. In this attachment to the 'true' Germany from which they had been driven, writers in exile on the run, or in uneasy refuges, found perhaps their most faithful inspiration, whether in hope or despair, in sorrow or in fury. Max Herrmann-Neisse, for example, an often moving poet given to extremes of happiness and misery, was near desperation in his early months of banishment:

> *Lass mich das Leben noch schmecken,*
> *eh die Vernichtung uns trifft:*
> *Gaskrieg, Marter, Verrecken,*
> *Bombe, tückisches Gift.*

(Let me taste life before destruction strikes us—gas warfare, torture, going west, bomb, treacherous poison.)

('Rast auf der Flucht', 1933)[22]

Yet the thought of the homeland from which he had been expelled later stung him into defiance:

> *Wer mich zu entehren glaubte,*
> *wenn mit frevelndem Befehle*
> *er das Heimatrecht mir raubte,*
> *ahnt die ewig lenzbelaubte*
> *Heimat nicht in meiner Seele.*

(The man who thought he could dishonour me with a blasphemous command that deprived me of the right to live in my own homeland, has no idea how lush and eternally youthful is the homeland in my soul.)

('Ewige Heimat', 1935)[23]

Becher utters the very same thought:

> *Ich bin ein Deutscher. Mögen Narren mir*
> *Auch aberkennen meine Bürgerrechte,*
> *Ich weiss, dass ich sie darum nicht verlier.*

(I am a German. Though fools may deprive me of my citizenship, I know that will not make me lose it.)

('Ich bin ein Deutscher')[24]

Love of country, and with it a faith in the imperishability of the German spirit, fills the work of one of the most truly poetic among these writers in exile—a Jewish refugee, 64 years old in 1933, who saw that exile in France, Czechoslovakia, or even London (where Herrmann-Neisse spent the last years of his life) was only a half-measure, and therefore embarked for New Zealand: Karl Wolfskehl. A member of the George Circle, a man of great learning, an essayist, translator and poet whose collected works had been published as long ago as 1903, Wolfskehl was almost a spent force by the time Hitler came to power. Under the spell of a strange, new world, however, yet never renouncing his pride in being both German and Jew, he lived the last 10 years of his life, almost completely blind at the end, in a poetic Indian summer. 'Never look back', was his motto.

Wolfskehl's clearest declaration of unrepentant German-ness—and he was far from unhappy in his *ultima Thule* of Auckland—rings out from the fine poem 'An die Deutschen', published in 1947, the year before his death. Built round a series of unequal sections starting with parallel lines such as 'Euer Wandel war der meine', 'Eure Kaiser sind auch meine' and 'Eure Sprache ist auch meine', the poem lays out Wolfskehl's arguments for the historical and spiritual unity of German culture, a culture created and carried by every German, wherever he be. *Germanus sum: Germani nihil a me alienum puto* is the sum of his attitude. Or, as he puts it in 'An die Deutschen':

> *Wo ich bin ist deutscher Geist.*[25]

(Wherever I am, the German soul is there.)

The sorrow, bitterness, loneliness and other concomitants of banishment cannot but find their way into Wolfskehl's poetry, yet the broader, objective, almost cosmic reality drowns the small voice of self, the subjective insignificance, and by casting himself in the image of Job, he brings together the sufferings of all exiles, Jews and Gentiles, political and religious outcasts, in a single symbolical figure:

Du bist allein, entrückt, gemieden, sag es
Nur tiefer stets dir in den düstern Sinn.
Du wolltest dich, nur dich, Hiob, ertrag es,
Nun unter andern Sternen wirf dich hin.

Ins Ungewisse, das wie Mondlichtnähe,
Wie Mondlichtwolke farbig fahl dir droht,
Droht oder lockt.

(You are alone, displaced, shunned—make this clearer and clearer to your dulled mind. You wanted yourself, Job, only yourself—accept it. And now, under new stars, cast yourself down into that uncertainty which threatens you with colourless colours like hazy moonlight, like a moonlit cloud: threatens—or entices.)

('Hinfahrt': from *Sang aus dem Exil*, 1949)[26]

This humanist religious intensity sustained many besides Wolfskehl at this time, among them a number who had chosen to stay and suffer in silence in Germany—Ricarda Huch, Elisabeth Langgässer, Werner Bergengruen, Rudolf Alexander Schröder, Gertrud von Le Fort. The figure of the prophet Job stands also behind the poetess Nelly Sachs, who pondered the sufferings that befall the innocent and who, like the prophet, 'feared God and eschewed evil'. Nelly Sachs left Germany for Stockholm in 1940, and lived there till her death in 1970. So unbearable did she find the memory of her German past that in a volume of essays and poems published to celebrate her 75th birthday in 1966 she requested that the bibliography should omit all reference to what she had written before she went to Sweden. 'Death was my master', she once said. 'What else could I have written about, since my images are my wounds? This is the only way to understand my work.'[27] Titles such as *In den Wohnungen des Todes* (1947) and *Noch feiert Tod das Leben* (1965) tell their own story.

The nearness of death, yet death infused with the serenity of the divine will, also hangs over the last poems of Franz Werfel. No doubt it was during the 'expressionist decade' of 1910 to 1920 that Werfel had reached the height of his fame as a lyric poet, and the last years of his life, including those in exile in the United States, are more readily remembered as the period of his large-scale novels. But whether Werfel the novelist is Werfel at his deepest, his most authentic, may be questioned; perhaps Werfel the lyric poet speaks more clearly, more convincingly. Like Schumann and Mendelssohn as symphonists, who succeeded in acquiring the grand manner yet without becoming quite at their ease in it, Werfel has a directness and religious sincerity which finds a more natural expression in the lyric than in larger, more dramatic forms.

However justified a general scepticism may be at mechanistic biographical explanations of the processes of artistic creation, this sustained lyrical flow of Werfel's last years surely owes more than one will ever know to the remarkable personality of Alma Schindler, Mahler's widow, whom Werfel had married in 1929. Werfel was a man of uncertain health, given to bouts of depression and near-despair, and although he was financially among the more fortunate of the exiles, he would not have summoned the confidence and the energy to continue writing, had it not been for Alma Werfel's spiritual succour. Like so many, he clung until the last moment to the illusion that free Europe, as it was in 1938, when he left Austria, would be safe against the forces of Nazism and Fascism, and not until the end of 1940, when he and his wife sailed on the last ship to make the regular run from Lisbon to New York, could he force himself to leave. In America he found the same frightening unawareness of what the Nazi menace meant to the world as had characterized Europe in the 1930s. Like so many who had escaped, he might have replied to the question of how he felt in America with the words of the novelist Annette Kolb: 'Grateful—and unhappy.'

The basis of Werfel's philosophy of life, in these exile years as in the poetry of 20 years before, is man's submission to the omnipotence of God. Without God man's virtues have no meaning, man's achievements no weight, and only through Him does life make sense:

Du sollst Gott lieben

Frage: *Gott will unsre Liebe, so lautet die Lehre.*
         Doch was kann dem Schöpfer der Himmelsgestirne
         Die Lieb einer Laus, eines Wolfs, einer Dirne
         Und des ganzen Gewimmels bringen für Ehre?

Antwort: *Das ist wahr! Er könnte getrost verzichten*
         Und jauchzend in den Grund seines Daseins tauchen.
         Er braucht unsre brenzlichte Liebe mitnichten.
         Er will sie nur haben, weil wir sie brauchen.

('Thou shalt love God'

Question: God wants our love, we are taught. But of what benefit can the love of a louse, of a wolf, of a prostitute, of the common rabble be to the Creator of the firmament?

Answer: It is so—He could well dispense with it and plunge exultantly into the essence of His own Being. *He* has not the slightest need of our dubious love—he only wants it because *we* have need of it.)

(No. 3 of 'Fünf Sinngedichte', from Kunde vom irdischen Leben, 1943)[28]

Werfel's poetry became increasingly mystical towards the end of his life, resembling in spirit, as that of his expressionist years had more especially resembled in manner, that of the Baroque world of Angelus Silesius and other *dévots*. Sonnet, epigram, dialogue and other seventeenth-century poetic forms became frequent vehicles of these religious thoughts *sub specie mortis et aeternitatis*. The final poem in *Kunde vom irdischen Leben*, his last cycle, written in 1943 and published in Los Angeles the year after his death, expresses the situation of many of his fellow-exiles—men whose experience has in one sense set them at the head of their time, but who in another sense are aware that they have almost reached the end of the journey.

Auf den alten Stationen

Auf den kleinen alten Stationen,
Die mein eigner Zug schon längst verlassen,
Ahn ich das Gedränge von Personen,
Die am Bahntrakt auf die Abfahrt passen.

Und ich möchte fast mich überheben.
Über sie, die warten am Geleise,
Dass ich schon so weit auf meiner Reise
Vorgedrungen bin im Rüttel-Leben,

Dass ich kenne Brücken und Tunnelle,
Meer- und See- und Fels- und Stadtkulissen,
Dass mir gellen Aug und Ohr von Wissen,
Jenen unbekannt an ihrer Stelle,

Dass sie werden noch im Zeit-Zug sitzen,
Stumpf am Fenster schauend Funkenspiele
Und der tragischen Signale Blitzen,
Wenn ich ausgestiegen längst am Ziele.[29]

(At those little old stations which my own train left long ago I sense the crowds of people who are waiting on the platform for the train to leave.

And I almost begin to feel superior to those who are waiting by the tracks, because I have travelled so far along the line of my own restless life;

Because I know the bridges and tunnels, and all the corners of the sea and the lake and the rocks and the town; because my eyes and ears are ringing with knowledge of which the others are still ignorant;

Because they will still be sitting in their time-train, looking dully out of their window at the bright sparks and at the lightning flashes of the tragic signals—while I shall have long since got out at my destination.)

iii. The novel

For all the political and social upheaval that lies between the consolidation of the Weimar Republic in the mid-1920s and the defeat of Hitler in 1945, there is a remarkable continuity in the fate of literary genres. The drama of *Neue Sachlichkeit*, social in reference, realistic in language, was carried into exile by Brecht, Zuckmayer, Friedrich Wolf, Hasenclever and a few others. Since the expiry of expressionist utopianism and the death of Rilke, lyric poetry had been at odds with the spirit of the age, leaving individual moments of mastery like Brecht's *Hauspostille* and Stefan George's *Das neue Reich*, but feeling, with the humankind of Rilke's first Duino Elegy, 'not too reliably at home . . . in the world as interpreted'.

The novel, however, rooted in reality, whether historical or modern, and infinitely malleable both in substance and in form, offered the same endless opportunities to the writer in exile—or, for that matter, to the writer who stayed in Germany—as it had to the writer of the 1920s. Indeed, it is the same writers—Thomas and Heinrich Mann, Broch, Döblin, Werfel, Hesse—that dominate the scene. Not that the 'reality' on which one so readily calls in discussions of the novel is to be thought of as some uniform, unchanging commodity to which the writer simply helps himself, as and when he chooses. Each artist constructs his own reality, and his selection of 'facts' to include in this reality presents an ever-changing pattern. The novelist *may* intend to paint a portrait of the society he sees, in which case the social historian *may* be entitled to recognise in a novel evidence of the contemporary state of society and of social attitudes. But the evidence cannot be taken at its face value until the novelist's intention is known. For even after allowing for the idiosyncracies of personal viewpoint, one has to reckon with deliberate distortion, with irony, with parody and a host of similar interpretative or aesthetic ruses which act as a kind of filter through which the material reality is made to pass.

Yet however subtle may be the relationship between the elements of this reality and the transmuting power of the artist's mind, the novel and the short story, to a greater extent than the drama or the lyric, rest on a sequence of causally related events with a logical interest in their own right. This is no doubt the sense in which the novel is credited with being 'closer to reality' than poetry or drama. A looser format, a manner discursive rather than epitomic, free from the practical exigencies of performance and less trammelled by the traditions of form—such considerations also played their part in creating conditions especially favourable to the writing of prose fiction, and German writers in exile, even those with little immediate prospect of seeing their work published, carried forward through the 1930s and 1940s the narrative vigour that had characterised the years of the Weimar Republic.

Sometimes this vigour was devoted to the portrayal of an historical, religious, artistic or other theme not immediately derived from the life of the present. Sometimes, on the other hand, it found its way into novels set in contemporary reality, whether the reality of Nazi Germany or the reality of exile. Of the former one of the most popular is Anna Seghers' *Das siebte Kreuz* (1942), the story of an escape from a concentration camp by seven men, only one of whom survives, leaving his cross in the camp—the seventh cross—unclaimed.

Anna Seghers, whose commitment to Communism often emerges from her stories as emotional rather than intellectual, has an honoured place in the Socialist literary gallery. Before fleeing from Nazi Germany in 1933, she had made her mark with *Aufstand der Fischer von St Barbara*, a story of a Breton fishermen's revolt, which was awarded the Kleist Prize for 1928—the year Anna Seghers (her real name is Netty Reiling) joined the German Communist Party. The need to understand the true nature of Fascism, and to present a popular revolutionary front against it, already informs her novels of the 1930s (*Der Kopflohn*, Amsterdam 1933; *Die Rettung*, Amsterdam 1937), and the same demand, conveyed by characters in a variety of situations who are made to live out the inexorable consequences of the challenge, has continued to dominate her works written since her return to East Germany from Mexico in 1947.

Das siebte Kreuz was published first in English translation (New York), later the same year in German (Mexico), and made into a striking film a mere two years later (1944). Its heroes are held together by a common humanity that transcends, and often shames, the world of politics that drives men apart and forces them into war, and the story is less an exercise in socialist realism than a self-conscious, montage-like assemblage of episodes whose unity is human and aesthetic before it is ideological. Negative characters, such as the politically apathetic citizens, and even the agents of the Nazi régime, have as firm a plasticity as 'sympathetic' figures, and the human reality is as strong as the political reality.

It is not surprising that exile itself, with the conflict between the uprooted or persecuted individual and his environment, should become the subject of more-or-less autobiographical novels, and that writers should see in this situation a symbol of the wider struggle between brute force and the values of the mind, or between the demands of political commitment and the dictates of the artistic consciousness. Klaus Mann's *Der Vulkan* (published by Querido in Amsterdam, 1939), Hasenclever's *Die Rechtlosen* (written in 1940 but published posthumously in 1963) and Anna Seghers' *Transit* (published in Mexico, first in English [1944], then in German [1948]) are among the works that have the realities of life in exile at their core. Novels such as these complement the openly documentary and reminiscential accounts of these years by Döblin (*Schicksalsreise*, 1949), Feuchtwanger (*Unholdes Frankreich*, 1942), Heinrich Mann (*Ein Zeitalter wird besichtigt*, 1946) and others.

Some emigré writers saw it as their duty to unite behind an uncompromisingly anti-Nazi front and establish, partly for their own morale, partly for the benefit of the outside world, a clear political position. Others saw in any such conformism an infringement, even a contradiction, of their nature as artists, and refused to believe that it should be their prime task to work for the overthrow of the inhuman régime responsible for their misery.

A fascinating portrayal of these conflicting attitudes, and at the same time a panorama of life for an exile in France between 1933 and 1940, is given by Lion Feuchtwanger in his novel *Exil*, published in Amsterdam in 1940. Feuchtwanger had enjoyed great international popularity since his very first works of the 1920s, *Die hässliche Herzogin Margarete Maultasch* (1923) and *Jud Süss* (1925). These flamboyant historical novels expansive in manner, fortissimo in tone, and not free from a certain strident vulgarity and a threat of *Kitsch*, seek to uncover the motive forces of social history through an exploration of the apparently ineluctable conflict between *Macht* and *Erkenntnis*, the exercise of power and the possession of knowledge, the assertion of the ego and the pressures of the environment. The commercial success of these works abroad, especially in Britain and America, meant that Feuchtwanger enjoyed an economic independence rare among the emigrés, and subsequently this success spread to the Soviet Union, where an edition of his works in Russian translation was published as early as 1946.

When Klaus Mann returned from the International Writers' Congress in Moscow in 1934, he reported in glowing terms how literature in the Soviet Union had been given a real function in society, and how the writer could feel that he had his own part to play in building a brave new world (by the time of his autobiography *The Turning Point* [1942], Klaus Mann had become a good deal less starry-eyed). Three years later Feuchtwanger too visited Moscow, a visit which brought about profound changes in his attitude to the role of the artist in society. He became co-editor, with Brecht and Willy Bredel, of the Marxist emigré journal *Das Wort*, founded in Moscow in 1936, and in *Moskau 1937* he painted an even more inspiring picture of Soviet culture than Klaus Mann. It was the writer's duty, he declared, to serve the dictatorship of the proletariat and to realise that the new society could not be built on mere statements of good intent, let alone on the application of independent intellectual and aesthetic principles, but demanded the employment of force under central authoritarian leadership.

Yet Feuchtwanger, like Brecht, never joined the Communist Party. Unlike Bredel, Becher, Arnold Zweig and Weinert—but again like Brecht—he did not seem to want to spend longer in the Soviet Union than necessary, and he made no move to leave Hollywood, where he lived from 1940 till his death in 1958.

Exil, together with *Erfolg* (1930) and *Die Geschwister Oppermann* (1933), belongs to a trilogy called *Der Wartesaal*, which, in Feuchtwanger's words, was to portray 'events in Germany between the wars of 1914 and 1939 . . . a frightful period of transition, when the old was not yet dead and the new was not yet born . . . a miserable waiting-room'. Writing in the guise of an historian looking back from the year 2000, he shows in *Erfolg* a corrupt, contradictory society in Weimar Germany, threatened by the rise of fascism, but a society to be overthrown by reason, not by force.

By the time of *Exil* his view has changed. Sepp Trautwein, the man round whom the story is built, is himself an emigré, a writer on music who has come from Munich (Feuchtwanger's home town) to Paris and there finds himself confronted with the choice between withdrawing into the cocoon of his art and working for the political cause of his fellow exiles. He chooses the latter, for only by facing the political challenge of the time can the artist, like everyone else, discharge his social responsibility and thus earn the right, when the immediate political aim has been reached, to return to his natural métier. Trautwein and his friends arrive at a form of humanism in which art becomes a weapon in the fight for human dignity and justice—and fight they must, for reason has failed. Liberal democratic ideas are not enough: the figure of André Gide, both in *Exil* and elsewhere, embodied for Feuchtwanger the human liberal conscience that lacks the ruthless sense of purpose which alone can expect success in the fight against fascism. As Trautwein tells his son Hanns at the end of the book: 'A just social order cannot be established without force.' Only Soviet socialism, says Feuchtwanger, has this sense of purpose. That its methods—these are the days of Stalin—are as repressive and tyrannical as those of the fascism it seeks to destroy is accepted as inevitable, since the end, as Lenin said, justifies the means. Brecht took the same view: 'Civilisation, attacked with physical weapons, has for far too long been defended merely with intellectual weapons. For it is not only an intellectual entity but very specifically a physical entity, and must be defended with physical weapons.'[30]

Exil and the preceding two parts of the *Wartesaal*-trilogy, together with Feuchtwanger's further trilogy *Josephus* (1933, 1935, 1945: a free version of the life of the Jewish historian) and the best-known of his pre-exile works, are cast as historical novels, and it is no coincidence that a number of emigré authors found in this sub-genre a form peculiarly appropriate to the circumstances in which they were now forced to write. Feuchtwanger claimed that to treat a contemporary subject in historical guise was the best guarantee of avoiding the arbitrary subjectivity that threatened the portrayal of a contemporary situation, above all one so intensely felt as that of the racial and political refugee. Similarly the historical content, in his philosophy, was not there for its own sake but 'as a stylistic means of achieving the illusion of reality in the easiest manner'.[31] A similar symbolic presence of the past in the present, the present in the past characterises the religious historical novels of Gertrud von Le Fort (*Der römische Brunnen*, 1928, *Die magdeburgische Hochzeit*, 1938 and others).

The appeal of the historical novel was also felt by writers still in Germany at this time. That crude glorification of figures from the German past was highly valued by the Nazi arbiters of taste was to be expected. But for 'inner emigrants' too, like Gertrud von Le Fort and Walter von Molo (*Eugenie von Savoy*, 1936; *Geschichte einer Seele*, 1938: a novel on Heinrich von Kleist), spiritual companions of their countrymen in exile, an historical setting offered both a refuge and an inspiration.

Döblin, writing in *Das Wort* in 1936, noted a special value in the historical novel in that it offered the exiled writer, torn from the society to which he properly belonged, the chance to find in history parallels to the conditions of the present.[32] Far from representing a flight into the past, the historical novel illuminated the nature of the contemporary scene, and with it the scope of action open to the future. Over and above this concern with social and political realities and with the symbolic relevance of the past, the writer can vent his imagination on history in a spirit of 'what might have been', envisaging new combinations of personal and situational elements, with new motivations and new outcomes. 'The historical novel is, of course, not in itself a product of distressful circumstances, but it is a ready companion of writers in exile. Understandably so, for apart from their lack of a true present, these writers feel a desire to find historical analogues to locate and justify themselves in history; they feel a need to reflect, together with a tendency to console themselves and to take their revenge—at least in their imagination.'[33]

This is a creative writer's attitude to history—history as a source of raw material for his art, not history as a springboard for the advocacy of political action. Critics of emigré writers' 'flight into the historical novel' usually spoke from a committed political position and took a narrow sociological view of the novelist's task. George Lukács accepted the validity of the emigrés' interest in what he called 'anti-Fascist' historical subject matter but blamed them for looking to the history rather of other peoples than of the Germans.[34] Lukács expected the writer who took his subject from history to reinterpret the past in order to help explain the meaning—the meaning, that is, as the Marxist sees it—of the present. And since the present stood under the sign of Nazism, the task of the historical novelist should lie in the investigation of the psychological forces in German history that had led to the rise of Hitler and, in dialectical consequence, of the anti-fascist counter-forces.

Lukács' conception of the nineteenth-century novel, and in particular the exclusive definition of 'realism' which he derived from it, provoked a characteristically unyielding public controversy with Brecht, who sought a wider, more 'modern' meaning for the term 'realist'. But Lukács' description of the past, in *The Historical Novel*, as the concrete precondition of the present matches Brecht's aim in his uncompleted novel *Die Geschäfte des Herrn Julius Caesar* (1938; published posthumously in 1957) of presenting, through a pseudo-historical allegory, the rise of Hitler and the social conditions of the Nazi present as the product of a corrupt and violent capitalist system. As the figure of Frederick the Great had attracted writers at the time of the First World War, so now, for totally different reasons, the Caesar-theme presented itself to a number of novelists—Alfred Neumann (*Der neue Cäsar*, 1934), Feuchtwanger (*Der falsche Nero*, 1936), as well as Brecht—who related the dictatorship of imperial Rome to the tyranny of the Nazis and the Fascists.

Building on parallels between Caesar and Hitler as leaders brought to power by economic crisis, between the Roman Senate and the Reichstag, between the conspiracy of Catiline and the activities of the German Left, and above all between the position and behaviour of the Roman and the German middle classes, Brecht deploys a technique of parallel narratives and converging perspectives to depict the rise of Caesar—an irresistible rise, unlike that of Arturo Ui—in terms of the class struggle. The Roman republic over which Caesar became dictator is made, sometimes more, sometimes less plausibly, to resemble the Weimar Republic, and Caesar himself is reduced from the colossus of received history to a callous, albeit successful careerist. As in his *Dreigroschenroman* (1934) and, for that matter, in so many of his plays, Brecht's larger-than-life distortions of historical reality, however obvious their purpose and entertaining their effect, bring their attendant problems, especially in the context of narrative fiction. The reality that one scourges or parodies must be real, otherwise the scourge will not wound or the parody strike home. That Brecht, having written some two-thirds of the novel, could not see a convincing way of finishing what he had started, and left Caesar's Rome for Galileo's Padua, tells its own story.

Among the most accomplished historical novels of these years are Heinrich Mann's two works on King Henry IV of France—*Die Jugend des Königs Henri Quatre* (1935) and *Die Vollendung des Königs Henri Quatre* (1938). Like Feuchtwanger, Heinrich Mann left Germany in 1933 and was deprived of his German citizenship the same year; also like Feuchtwanger he lived in France until the early months of the war, then left Europe for the United States and spent the rest of his life in California, putting his faith in a radical-materialist, increasingly para-Communist solution to the problems of the world.

In the years before 1914 Heinrich Mann had found in the history of France, and above all in the French Revolution, a positive force to be set against the crumbling tradition of imperial Germany, and in his assertion of the case for rational revolution, embracing the identification of art and politics, lies the root of the fundamental difference of opinion with his brother which was not to be resolved until after the war. But with the failure of the German revolution of November 1918—through which he relived the failure of the revolution of 1848—came disillusionment with the ideal of a democratic renewal of Germany. This is the mood of his novel *Der Kopf* and of his essays from the Weimar years. Now, at the time of his exile in France, the last fully creative period of his life, he returns to his preoccupation with the duality of *Geist* and *Macht*, of idea and reality, expressing once more, through the career of his royal French hero and the dialectic processes that it embodies, his conviction of the ultimate victory of the rational over the irrational.

The historical reference of Heinrich Mann's *Henri Quatre* touches three ages: that of the sixteenth-century King Henry IV of France himself, leader of the French against the Habsburgs; that of Napoleon, as he rises from the revolution as Emperor and national leader against the Holy Alliance; and that of the Germany of Mann's own day, with Stalin in a Napoleonic role. 'It is neither transfigured history nor a comforting tale', he wrote in his autobiographical retrospect *Ein Zeitalter wird besichtigt*: '—simply a true parable'.[35] And as a parable, with a relevance that extends beyond the individual historical moment, past or present, *Henri Quatre* presents the development of European civilisation from irrationalism to rationalism since the sixteenth century, a development in which the French Revolution was the lynch-pin, fascism—and the attendant reality of exile—a mere passing paroxysm, and Stalinist Russia the logical culmination.

Heinrich Mann's world, like the world of Brecht in the 'Lehrstücke' and down to the later 1930s, is a black-and-white world, and once the goal has been set, all means to reach it are justified. He accepted, for example, that the Moscow trials under Stalin were a necessary accompaniment to the achievement of Communist ideals, and he came to believe that only rigid discipline, untrammelled by the 'support' of free-thinking liberals, would lead to the fully rational society. It was in this spirit that Lukács stigmatised the weaknesses of the historical picture in Feuchtwanger's *Der jüdische Krieg*—written before Feuchtwanger's visit to Moscow—as 'survivals of liberal ideology'. Such survivals, Lukács goes on to say, as the Heinrich Mann of the same period could also have said, 'are closely connected with the isolated position of progressive intellectuals in the great class struggles of late capitalism, a position which the best intellectuals . . . are overcoming from day to day with the help of the practical example of the popular front'.[36]

At the time of his *Henri Quatre*, however, Heinrich Mann was not yet committed to such a position, and the hero of his novel, though a didactically conceived apostle of humanity and reason, has attractive personal shortcomings and an undogmatic approach to the religious conflict between Catholic and Protestant, the conflict which poses the greatest challenge to his statesmanship. 'Was weiss ich?' becomes a *Leitmotif* in the novel, and in his first encounter with Montaigne Henri receives an indirect answer to the question—'Know thyself! Only self-knowledge is worthy of our attention.'[37] The stages of this self-knowledge in *Die Jugend des Henri Quatre* are chronicled in the French *moralités* which conclude each section of the novel.

In terms of the history of the novel, *Henri Quatre* shows a revival of the influence of Victor Hugo, on the one hand in the Romanticism of the monumentalised hero as the champion of an ideal, on the other, through its transitional position in a movement away from such idealisation, a movement towards the cultivation of rational values drawn from the situation of man in society. In terms of the intellectual development of Heinrich Mann himself, and in its presentation of his

basic dualistic theme of *Geist* against *Macht*, idealism against pragmatism, it stands at the threshold of a hardening of attitude towards
independent, that is, critical, declarations of liberal humanism.

An historical novel of a very different kind and purpose is Werfel's
Die vierzig Tage des Musa Dagh (1933), which has as its subject the
Turkish siege of the Armenian Christians on the mountain of Musa
Dagh, an episode in the massacre by the Turks in 1915 of all
Armenians on Turkish soil. The humanitarianism, usually with
religious, often mythical overtones, that fills Werfel's work—drama,
lyric poetry and novels alike—emerges here on three planes. In its
historical setting the story stands with the war-novels that are filled
with the horror and the meaninglessness of the events of
1914–18—Remarque's *Im Westen nichts Neues*, Renn's *Krieg*, Arnold
Zweig's *Der Streit um den Sergeanten Grischa*, Leonhard Frank's *Der
Mensch ist gut* and others. In its social and psychological aspect *Die
vierzig Tage des Musa Dagh* is concerned with the responsibility of the
individual to his community in times of stress. Personal salvation, like
patriotism, is not enough. *Gemeinnutz geht vor Eigennutz* runs the
German proverb: the plight of the beleaguered Armenians on the
mountain forces all men to realise, even the military commander
himself, that the meaning of life on earth—life symbolised by, even
embodied in the changing aspects of, the mountain itself—lies in the
recognition that we are all one of another.

Finally Werfel's novel presents, through this one historical moment, a parable of the history of the Jewish people in their fight for
survival. Each of the three books of the symmetrically and symbolically constructed novel (the 40 days; the seven villages whose
inhabitants fled to the mountain; the seven chapters of each of the
two outer books and the four chapters of the central book) is prefaced
with a quotation from the Book of Revelation, and the career of the
Armenian leader is made to resemble that of Moses. By thus setting
the action of his story under the constellation of the Old and New
Testaments, Werfel raises it to a symbolic level on which the meaning
becomes one of national self-assertion and ultimate deliverance from
the powers of oppression. He finished writing it in March 1933, within
two weeks of the Nazi victory in the Reichstag elections, and a few
days before the official launch of a policy that was to end with the
murder of six million European Jews.

The religious consciousness, whether Jewish or Roman
Catholic—the two poles of his own religious experience—dominated
Werfel's thought during his years in exile and brought him a strength
which showed itself in a greater fluency of writing than ever. For his
purpose as an author, he wrote in the preface to *Das Lied von Bernadette*

(1941), had always been 'to glorify the mystery of God and the holiness of man, heedless of the scorn, the rage, the apathy with which this age turns its back on these ultimate values in life.'[38]

Probably Werfel's best-known—though certainly not best—work, is *Das Lied von Bernadette*, written as an act of gratitude for the sanctuary he had found in Lourdes on his way across France to Lisbon and then to the United States. More relevantly, in the context of his literary career it is the last of a group of, in the broad sense, religious novels sustained by the character of a woman cast in the social role of a servant. *Barbara oder die Frömmigkeit* (1929) had portrayed a humble girl whose unquestioning religious faith is the sole motivation for her actions, a mystical faith so naive and so absolute that it takes account neither of human knowledge nor of the material realities of the human condition. Though a very different personality from the pious Barbara, the figure of the old servant Teta Linek in *Der veruntreute Himmel* (1939) also seeks to define her relationship to God. Teta acts out of self-interest, has the slenderest of human contacts with her fellow-men, and lives only for a guarantee that she will in the end be granted eternal bliss in Heaven, but she is made to see that salvation cannot be bought. While the warm, humane Barbara instinctively puts her faith to the service of humanity, the calculating Teta uses the agencies of society to further her claim to the favour of the Almighty: only when confronted with the deception that her nephew has perpetrated on her, and *pace* the embarrassing sentimentality of the final audience with the Pope and its consequences, does she realise that without love there is no admission to the realm of the blessed. The inseparability of love and divine grace creates a spiritual bond between Werfel, the exile, and writers, Catholic and Protestant alike, left in Germany who preserved the values of the spirit in religious novels, short stories, and in religious verse—writers like Bergengruen, Elisabeth Langgässer, Gertrud von Le Fort and Jochen Klepper.

The contemporary malaise which Werfel diagnoses, and which the career of the pathetic old Bohemian servant Teta Linek symbolises, is described in the epilogue to *Der veruntreute Himmel*, in which the author muses on the story he has just told. His thoughts express the *credo* that informs all his work, down to his last Utopian novel, *Stern der Ungeborenen*, finished two days before he died:

Wenn ich als junger Mensch durch die Strassen der Städte ging, da war mirs, als müsst ich all diese dahinhastenden Leute mit ihren stumpfen Gesichtern festhalten und ihnen zuschreien: So bleibt doch stehen und denkt einmal nach und kostet es aus, dieses ungeheure Woher—Wohin—Warum! Ich habe schon sehr früh erkannt, dass der Aufstand gegen die Metaphysik die Ursache unseres ganzen Elends ist. In den protestantischen Völkern ist er logischerweise zuerst ausgebrochen, der

Puritanismus hat ihn zum Sieg geführt, indem er Zeit—Arbeit—Geld an die Stelle der göttlichen Dreifaltigkeit erhob, und den tollsten Triumph dieses Aufruhrs erleben wir jetzt in unserer eigenen Heimat. Dabei ist der Aufruhr selbst noch weniger verabscheuenswert als die Gleichgültigkeit in seinem Gefolge, die kosmische Verdummung des Menschen. Ich sags noch enimal, sie ist der absolute Urgrund all unseres Elends . . . Unsere Seelen wollen nicht mehr an ihre Unzerstörbarkeit glauben und damit an ihre ewige Verantwortung. Der veruntreute Himmel ist der grösste Fehlbetrag unserer Zeit. Seinetwegen kann die Rechnung nicht in Ordnung kommen, weder in der Politik noch auch in der Wirtschaft, denn alles Menschliche entspringt derselben Quelle.[39]

(When, as a young man, I used to walk through the city streets, I felt as if I had to stop all those expressionless people hurrying past and shout: Stand still for a moment and think the mighty Why and Wherefore of life through to the end! I realised long ago that the cause of all our misery is the revolt against metaphysics. It started, logically, in Protestant countries; Puritanism led it to victory by substituting Time, Work and Money for the Holy Trinity, and it is celebrating its grandest triumph in our own country today.

Yet this revolt itself is less despicable than the apathy it brings in its train. A cosmic process of ignorance has set in. I repeat: this indifference is the root cause of all our misery . . . Our souls refuse to believe any longer in their indestructibility and hence in their accountability. The greatest discrepancy in the accounts of our present age results from our embezzlement of Heaven—which is why the account will not balance, either on the political or the economic side, since all human activity has a common source.)

Novels such as Feuchtwanger's *Exil*, Anna Seghers' *Transit* and Klaus Mann's *Der Vulkan* have the physical reality of exile set in the centre of the action, with strands of autobiography woven into the texture of the story. Many historical novels, like those of Feuchtwanger, or Heinrich Mann's *Henri Quatre*, seek to abstract from situations in the past values with which to heal—or at least to examine—the wounds of the present. But there are also emigré authors in whose work the experience of exile, whether in direct or allusive form, plays little or no part. Robert Musil, for example, finished *Der Mann ohne Eigenschaften* in Switzerland, but the subject of exile does not enter the story, even though, unlike Hermann Hesse, who had emigrated to Switzerland many years before, he never felt entirely at his ease away from his native Austria. Thomas Mann, to be sure, especially during the war, devoted himself in talks and articles to the problems of the emigré writers; on one plane his *Doktor Faustus* moves to the rise and fall of the Third Reich, while the Biblical story of banishment and return behind *Joseph und seine Brüder* has its parallel in the course of his own life after 1933. But none of his novels centres on the predicament of the emigré or the problem of exile *per se*.

Hermann Broch's great work *Der Tod des Vergil* (1945) presents a situation analogous to that of the exiled writer, in that Virgil went abroad in order to work on the final version of his *Aeneid* and now, as the novel opens, is returning to Italy, a dying man, his mind torn by the problem of the purpose of art in an age of social and spiritual crisis.

Yet it is the very timelessness of such a theme, as of the themes that dominate the work of Thomas Mann, Hesse, Musil and even, on occasion, Werfel, and the unremitting intellectual struggle to probe its essential nature, that sets the gulf between these writers and their contemporaries with narrower concerns and commitments. The realities of the present are the legitimate stuff of literature, but the writer, if his work is to outlive the moment, must sense a meaning of these realities that remains valid beyond the moment. Indeed, such realities, quite apart from the meanings invested in them, may themselves remain valid beyond the moment. The greatest works of these Nazi-dominated years, which may come from men as different as Thomas Mann and Brecht, and whether written inside Germany or in exile, are not those that centre on the inhumanities of the Nazis, the horrors of the concentration camps, the suffering and futility of the war, but those that treat of the ageless conflicts in man, the crises in the contemporary world at large, the spiritual and moral needs of the human race. The moments of formal revolution in modern art—moments marked by the names of Joyce, Picasso, T.S. Eliot, Schoenberg—likewise signify a concern with life and art in their unchanging essence, not in their contingent manifestations. The particular is contained within the general, the transient within the eternal.

With Thomas Mann, who had left Germany in 1933, and Hermann Hesse, who was already living in Switzerland before the outbreak of the Great War, Hermann Broch belongs to the great trio of novelists writing abroad during the years of the Third Reich. (If one excludes Musil from this company, it is only because most of *Der Mann ohne Eigenschaften*, still unfinished at his death, had been written before he left Austria, and because he spent his years in exile working only on this book.) Both racially and politically unacceptable to the Nazis, Broch was arrested in Austria immediately after the *Anschluss* in 1938, released shortly afterwards through the efforts of *inter alios* James Joyce and Willa and Edwin Muir, and came to Britain; later the same year he went to the United States, where he lived mainly on grants from research foundations until his death in 1951.

In his trilogy *Die Schlafwandler* Broch had chronicled a disintegration of values, a decay of moral and spiritual life that reached its nadir in the figure of the unscrupulous, 'realist' entrepreneur Huguenau in *Huguenau oder die Sachlichkeit*. The thought that obsesses the mind of Virgil during his dying hours is that of the role of art in life. As death approaches, he is haunted by the fear that in bowing to the dictates of the poetic mind, he has betrayed life and substituted a self-indulgent pursuit of beauty and aesthetic pleasure for a commitment to truth and morality. Hence he meditates in his final hours on whether it is not his duty to destroy the manuscript of the *Aeneid*, which he has brought back with him from Greece.

For Keats was wrong: truth is not beauty, nor beauty truth. Beauty may take on the outer semblance of truth but it is without ethical value, and cannot therefore be truth. The artist who succumbs to the cult of beauty stops short of ultimate reality and cannot claim to be its servant:

So must it have been with Orpheus and his song, for he was an artist, a poet, a charmer of the ear, poet and audience alike held in the spell, he and they captivated by the daemonic beauty, daemonic in spite of his divine gift, a bringer of intoxication, not of salvation—and this he should never be. For the true saviour has shed the language of beauty and penetrated beneath its cold surface, beneath the surface of poetry.[40]

Like the figure of Henry IV in Heinrich Mann's novel *Die Vollendung des Königs Henri Quatre*, Broch's Virgil comes to see that self-knowledge and the pursuit of truth constitute the true goal of the poet as of the man of action: 'He knew that the duty of all who follow the calling of art is to discover themselves in the course of discovering truth and expressing truth, and that this task is laid upon the artist in order that the soul, conscious of the great balance between the self and the cosmos, shall rediscover itself in the cosmos.'[41] And like Heine, Nietzsche and Thomas Mann, Broch brings an awareness of suffering and death into the world of experience from which knowledge and understanding are derived. The closer Virgil approaches to death, the more complete his understanding becomes, until, finding that his work does indeed embody the ethical values which his philosophy demands, he can finally contemplate death with the serenity of the man who has fought the good fight. 'The sense of life is determined by death', wrote Broch in a letter to Hans Sahl.[42]

Der Tod des Vergil has little physical action. Its scene changes merely from the ship to Virgil's journey to the palace and thence to the room in the palace where the dying poet is brought; the other characters are not flesh-and-blood figures but intellectual foils to the movement of Virgil's own thoughts. Broch described the work in one place as 'an interior monologue and thus a lyrical work',[43] in another as 'like a rolled-out lyric poem'.[44] Sinuous, swaying sentences, meandering over page after page, thought leading to thought, motif to motif, word to word, convey the poet's stream of consciousness during his last hours as he looks backwards to life, forwards to death, reflecting on the simultaneity of dream and reality, of spiritual intuition and rational analysis, drifting from symbol to symbol in free association, allowing new perspectives to open up through the unplanned discovery of new combinations of thoughts—all this held within the unity of the individual mind that seeks to embrace the meaning not simply of its own time but of the whole of existence.

As an 'interior monologue' *Der Tod des Vergil* is inevitably seen as standing in the shadow of James Joyce. Broch had read *Ulysses* in 1930, at the time he was working on *Die Schlafwandler*, and its influence especially on the third volume of the trilogy, *Huguenau oder die Sachlichkeit*, was quickly noted. Broch was delighted that *Die Schlafwandler* was accepted for publication by the firm that in 1929 had published the German translation of *Ulysses*, and in 1932 he wrote an essay, *James Joyce und die Gegenwart*—an interesting counterpart to Ernst Robert Curtius' pioneering essay *James Joyce und sein Ulysses*, published three years earlier—in which he expounds a theory of the 'polyhistorical' novel on the basis of Joyce's work. A letter of 1945 to Frau Daisy Brody, wife of his Swiss publisher, even goes so far as to claim *Der Tod des Vergil* as 'the only post-Joycean book worth considering'.[45] *Ulysses* spans one day, *Der Tod des Vergil*, 18 hours; *Der Tod des Vergil* and *Finnegans Wake*, both written in a lyrical semi-poetry, semi-prose, are each divided into four books, the last of which envisages a union, in cyclical style, of beginning and end. Such affinities tell their own story.

For Broch, who all his life felt the pull of the mathematical sciences and resisted any notion of poetic isolatedness, the creation of imaginative fiction and the investigation of theoretical principle went hand in hand. As the essay on Joyce, together with *Das Weltbild des Romans, Denkerische und dichterische Erkenntnis* and a few other essays, falls together, in compositional terms, with *Die Schlafwandler*, so in the same year as *Der Tod des Vergil* he published an essay in honour of Thomas Mann's seventieth birthday, with the title *Die mythische Erbschaft der Dichtung*. Here he both returns to Joyce and also lays out a philosophy of the timelessness and abstractness of art, above all in an age—here the physical reality of exile shows itself—which has lost a social frame of reference and needs a power to transcend the passing, imperfect, often meaningless moment of history. This timelessness resides in the realm of myth, source of 'the basic substance of the human soul',[46] and to this context of universal myths belongs his own new form of the novel. In the quality of myth lies also his attraction to Kafka, against whom he implicitly measured all contemporary literature. During the few years he lived after the publication of *Der Tod des Vergil*, he turned from 'Mythos' to 'Logos', setting intellect before imagination, science before art. Behind his last, unfinished novel, *Der Versucher*, lies a body of epistemological and political theory on what he called 'Massenpsychologie', and this trend to objectivity makes *Der Versucher* as epic in manner as *Der Tod des Vergil* is lyrical.

Writing in 1933 of his story *Verlorener Sohn* (also known as *Die Heimkehr*), one of the collection of Novellen which make up the novel *Die Schuldlosen* (1950), Broch referred to his efforts 'to discover a new mode for the expression of the unconscious, the subconscious'.[47] His 'new mode', seeking a universality to embrace the rational and the irrational, the creative and the destructive, the harmonious and the discordant, the true and the beautiful, within a simultaneity of time past, time present and time future, stands under the banner of 'Art as Morality'. It is to discovering whether his poetry can pass this supreme test that Broch's Virgil surrenders the last hours of his life. The final serenity, the resolution of all discord, the presence of the peace that passes all understanding, give him—and us—the answer.

The classification of works of art—for convenience—by other than the most obvious biographical or chronological principles is always exposed to the dangers of arbitrariness and distortion. But to identify 'types' in the literature, painting or music of the twentieth century has become an especially hazardous exercise. What from earlier periods might be acceptably treated in a tradition of the picaresque novel, or the biographical novel, or the historical novel, or even the social novel, has acquired so many features of so many traditions that new contexts seem called for—perhaps even a rejection of all contexts except the biographical, the personal. To unite Franz Werfel's *Verdi*, Hermann Broch's *Der Tod des Vergil* and Thomas Mann's *Doktor Faustus* in the familiar German category of *Künstlerroman* will conceal more of the meaning of these works than it will reveal. To join Ernst Jünger's *In Stahlgewittern* with Remarque's *Im Westen nichts Neues*, Ludwig Renn's *Krieg* and Arnold Zweig's *Der Streit um den Sergeanten Grischa* as *Kriegsromane* may seem reasonable; but to set Jünger's *Afrikanische Spiele* in the company of Thomas Mann's *Felix Krull* as *Abenteuerromane*, or his *Auf den Marmorklippen* in the realm of *politischer Roman* inhabited by Hans Grimm's *Volk ohne Raum* and Werner Bergengruen's *Der Grosstyrann und das Gericht* (can there, indeed, in the broad sense, be a 'non-political' novel in this age?)—such attempts at classification imply resemblances which, used as critical categories, tend rather to distort than to define.

To be sure, there may be similarities of subject in plenty, and the establishment of thematic relationships is a legitimate critical activity. To arrange a body of literary material from a chosen period in terms of themes often seems a particularly appropriate way of revealing the dominant concerns of that period and providing a framework for their discussion. But the critical mind can also be destructive, and one must not destroy a higher unity in the interests of constructing a private pattern of analogies and meanings, however plausible that pattern may appear.

Hermann Hesse's *Das Glasperlenspiel* (1943) shows what is at stake in this argument. On the one hand, as a kind of *Kunstlerroman*, it can be set alongside Thomas Mann's *Doktor Faustus*, published two years later. Mann himself wrote of his consternation at finding in Hesse's novel the same framework of the fictional biography, with its accompanying elements of parody, the same involvement of music, and the same intercalation of reflections on modern culture as in his own work. 'I often remarked', Mann said of the early section of *Das Glasperlenspiel* which had been published in the *Neue Rundschau*, 'that it seemed like a part of myself, so close was this prose to my own.'[48] On the other hand it can be seen as the presentation of a utopia, and thus as a companion of Werfel's *Der Stern der Ungeborenen* and Ernst Jünger's *Heliopolis*. Or should it be called, by the negative implications of utopism, a *zeitkritischer Roman*? Or, as the chronicle of the spiritual education of its hero Josef Knecht, a *Bildungsroman*—even, in its ultimate tendency and in its manner, a religious novel?

Das Glasperlenspiel is all these, sometimes in sequence, sometimes at one moment. In the setting of Hesse's own life, and through the explicit dedication of the book 'An den Morgenlandfahrer', it harks back to the strange, introspective story *Die Morgenlandfahrt* of 1933. Apart from a few small pieces, including the poetic idyll 'Stunden im Garten', he had written nothing new since that time but had been laboriously working out the stages of his *Glasperlenspiel*. And although he lived almost another 20 years, it remained, except for the occasional poem or prose fragment, and philosophical statements in personal letters, the last thing he wrote.

The thought to which *Das Glasperlenspiel* is devoted, and whose convolutions filled Hesse's mind in the 10 years he lavished upon it, had been expressed in the opening lines of the poem 'Besinnung', written in 1933:

> *Göttlich ist und ewig der Geist.*
> *Ihm entgegen dessen wir Bild und Werkzeug sind,*
> *Führt unser Weg; unsre innerste Sehnsucht ist:*
> *Werden wir Er, leuchten in Seinem Licht!*[49]

(Divine and eternal is the Spirit. Our path leads to Him, whose image and whose instrument we are. Our innermost longing is to become like Him, to shine in His light.)

Life in Hesse's utopian kingdom of Kastalien, ruled by both Classical and Christian values, where an élite is educated to attain this supreme existence in the spirit, stands under the sign of the glass-bead game, symbol of that blend of art and science which admits the initiated mind to the superior spiritual reality. As an instrument, the Glasperlenspiel embodies the Romantic union of music and mathematics, the least 'real', least corporeal of the arts and the most exact, most fully symbolical of the sciences. But this union itself only symbolises the supreme religious mystery of the Castalian ideals and of the élite that guard the Glasperlenspiel like Knights of the Grail. 'To play the Glasperlenspiel', runs Hesse's definition—if it can be called such—'is to play the entire gamut of meanings and values in our civilisation. As an organist plays an organ, so the Glasperlenspieler plays the ideals, the knowledge, the works of art created by man, the learned concepts and intellectual achievements of later ages—in short, the whole corpus of spiritual values in mankind'.[50]

Noble as these pursuits of the spirit are, and incontestable as is the duty of Kastalien to educate men in the outside world to a realisation of the new truth, there hangs over the land the threat of an inbred exclusiveness (the Stefan George Circle had shown what this meant in practice), the fear that virtuosity in the techniques of the Glasperlenspiel will become an end in itself. This fear is carried in the figure of Josef Knecht, who learns that the Glasperlenspiel is not the mere aesthetic game he at first suspected but the embodiment of values that can lead to a higher spiritual unity above the transience and the warring polarities of earthly life. This is the theme of unity in diversity found in *Peter Camenzind, Der Steppenwolf, Narziss und Goldmund* and others of Hesse's novels, the theme which in *Demian* and its successors comes in the form of a journey of self-discovery within the field of tension generated between the antithesis of God and the world, mind and nature.

It is the interaction of the ideal world of Kastalien and the self-exploratory career of Josef Knecht that gives *Das Glasperlenspiel* its significance as an allegorical statement about the condition of the modern world and its needs, and makes it the summit of Hesse's achievement as a novelist. From the time of World War I Hesse had insisted that the world of the mind had no right to an existence independent of the world of common human reality. However beautiful the achievements of the intellect, however perfect the life of the soul, man in the fullness of his existential reality was man who accepted his place in history and his responsibility as a servant of his age. Josef Knecht, Magister Ludi and Kastalien's most distinguished son, offers his spiritual experience to the world in the role of teacher and dies in the service of his people, seeking a harmony between Kastalien and the world, that is, between heaven and earth.

This achievement of harmony with the portrayal, in the action of his novels, of the processes by which discords are to be resolved—above all the dichotomy of *Natur* and *Geist*—fills Hesse's thoughts. And as discords do not resolve themselves, so Hesse's message, serene yet challenging, quietly presented but unwavering and insistent, demands of the individual the moral stamina to find his own path towards the harmony that marks the resolution of the discords. For there are no instant answers to the world's problems. When, in Hesse's parable *Zarathustras Wiederkehr*, the prophet returns to earth, he can offer only the most unyielding of responses when the masses clamour for a magic solution: 'Learn to live your lives! Learn to understand your destiny! . . . There is no other God but the God within you.'[51]

Self-knowledge cannot be attained without suffering, and the creative value of suffering makes great demands. 'To learn to suffer is hard', Zarathustra tells the young men around him.[52] But suffering forms part of the equation. Remove it, and the balance is destroyed, the harmony broken. And like suffering, despair too is the inseparable companion of the man who accepts his destiny and seeks his salvation, not in the serenity of theory and dogma, but in the fire of a personal, lived reality.

Harmony, the synthesis of *vita activa* and *vita contemplativa*, of Orient and Occident, of Classical and Christian, of rational and romantic, subject and object, mind and nature—this synthesis remained Hesse's dream right down to *Das Glasperlenspiel*. It is that dream of the indivisibility of things so often expressed by Goethe:

> *Teilen kann ich nicht das Leben,*
> *Nicht das Innen noch das Aussen,*
> *Allen muss das Ganze geben,*
> *Um mit euch und mir zu hausen.*

(I cannot divide life, separating it into an Inside and an Outside; I must give everyone the Whole, if I am to be able to live with you and with myself.)

And with this ideal of wholeness before his eyes Josef Knecht leaves Kastalien to serve the world through a Goethean *Humanität*:

> *Denn alle menschlichen Gebrechen*
> *Sühnet reine Menschlichkeit.*

(Pure Humanitarianism redeems all human frailties.)

In an oft-quoted phrase, Hugo Ball, Hesse's first biographer, called him 'the last nobleman in the shining train of Romanticism'. Ball died in 1927, and his characterisation was of the Hesse of *Peter Camenzind*, *Unterm Rad*, *Demian* and *Siddhartha*. But this is not the Hesse of *Das Glasperlenspiel*. Josef Knecht's conquest of intellectualism in the name of humanity leads to a new dynamism which drives life onwards after Knecht, having played his part, dies. Life is not Being but Becoming, and Becoming is a dialectical, existential process. To serve, to further this process was the goal of Hesse's life and art.

Art in our time—its nature, its possibility, its justification—is embedded in the substance of both Broch's *Der Tod des Vergil* and Hesse's *Das Glasperlenspiel*. Broch's Virgil, wrestling with the moral problem of whether to destroy the manuscript of his *Aeneid*, symbolises the dilemma of the modern artist beset by doubts about the legitimacy of 'das Spielerische des Kunstwerks', indeed, of the whole morality of art, in an age of atom bombs and gas chambers.[53] Hesse's Josef Knecht, master of the aesthetically perfect mathematico-musical 'Spiel mit sämtlichen Inhalten und Werten unserer Kultur',[54] moves from the Gelehrtenrepublik of Kastalien to the service of the world outside as an expression of his sense of obligation to his fellow-men. These two men are joined by a third, the hero of one of the great novels of the twentieth century, a man whose character was being moulded during the same war-years as Broch's Virgil and Hesse's Knecht, and who, German to the marrow yet born of his creator in Californian exile, came into the world two years after the former and four years after the latter—Adrian Leverkühn, the Faust-figure of Thomas Mann's *Doktor Faustus*.

'To write is to sit in judgment over oneself.' In *Doktor Faustus* Thomas Mann sets not only himself on trial, still less only his musician hero Leverkühn, but art itself, German art, and beyond this, Germany herself. The classic German antithesis of *Natur* and *Geist* is embodied already in the external form of the novel, as the humanist Serenus Zeitblom chronicles the career of his daemonic Faust-Nietzsche friend Adrian Leverkühn. But this antithesis is no longer manipulated in the suavely ironical, two-edged manner, of which the *locus classicus* is the confrontation of Naphta and Settembrini in *Der Zauberberg*. Instead it forms a passionate, tragic context, with its own tragic irony, which reaches both backwards and forwards in time from the years to which Leverkühn's biography belongs. And through these different strata of time—again one recalls *Der Zauberberg*, with its juxtaposition of sanatorium-time and 'Flachland'-time—which are produced by the interpolation of a fictional narrator between the events of the story and the author, Mann draws into his novel the catastrophic events of the 1930s in Germany, and of the war that followed. Like his narrator Zeitblom, Mann began writing in May 1943, the year of the German defeat at Stalingrad and the Allied victory in North Africa. Three-and-a-half years later, in January 1947, with Germany in physical and spiritual ruin, he wrote the final lines, the prayer with which he had long intended Zeitblom to commend his biography to the world: 'May God have mercy on both your souls—O my friend, O my fatherland!'

There can be few works in the history of literature whose genesis and growth we can follow in such detail. For in *Die Entstehung des Doktor Faustus. Roman eines Romans* Thomas Mann has left a diary on the composition of his novel—the books he read, the letters he received, the conversations he held, the thoughts and problems that filled his mind, everything that surrounded him during the years he was at work on the book. The *Faustbuch* of 1587, the works of Martin Luther, the letters of Hugo Wolf, David Friedrich Strauss' biography of Ulrich von Hutten, the dodecaphonic serialism of Schoenberg, Adorno's *Zur Philosophie der modernen Musik*, Nietzsche, Dürer, E.T.A. Hoffmann, Dante, Kierkegaard, Shakespeare, theory of music, theology and a host of other subjects and names make up the panorama of elements which, in the form of an intellectual autobiography, he passes in review as the raw material of his montage. Leading us through the channels of his thought, he describes his intentions and explains his techniques, doing the critic's work for him and making explicit the attitudes that his novels and short stories had long embodied.

Not, of course, that Mann believed, either naively or presumptuously, that the artist himself must needs be the best, or only true, interpreter of his creations. In a talk on his *Zauberberg* given at Princeton in 1939 he presented a view of the work of art as something which, once finished and given to the world, might well be more fully understood by others than by the author, and the more so with the passage of time: 'Only in moments of rare lucidity, composure and control do we really comprehend ourselves, and the often surprising modesty of important men may to a large extent be due to the fact that they simply do not understand themselves sufficiently, are not fully aware of themselves, and therefore rightly feel themselves to be everyday people.'[55] *Die Entstehung des Doktor Faustus* records what seems like three years of 'lucidity, composure and control' over the composition of the novel. Yet, like all great works, Doktor Faustus has gathered new strata of meaning with the passage of time, and has to that extent outstripped the meanings with which its author consciously invested it. Thomas Mann's *Entstehungsgeschichte* is the legitimate first word on *Doktor Faustus*, but it is certainly not the last.

The dominant concern of Mann's work, right from the days of *Buddenbrooks*, is the practice of art and the nature of the artistic vocation in modern society and in the modern world. These terms also encompass an earlier novel of his exile years, *Lotte in Weimar* (1939), a portrait of Goethe in 1816, the lonely genius confronting the realisation that greatness is a compulsive and amoral force which rides rough-shod over everything that stands in its way, and that his successes have often been bought at the expense of the suffering and unhappiness of those who crossed his path. To be great is to be guilty of causing such suffering and unhappiness, and only the guilty man himself can pass judgement on his guilt. How close is a world thus defined to the world of Adrian Leverkühn!

Mann's growing concern with the figure of Goethe dates from the end of World War I. Between 1922 and 1938 he wrote four substantial essays on him—*Goethe und Tolstoi*, 1922; *Goethe als Repräsentant des bürgerlichen Zeitalters* and *Goethes Laufbahn als Schriftseller*, both 1932; and *Goethes Faust*, 1938. It is the Goethean affirmation of life over death and the search for a Goethean humanism with which to confront that life which marks the climax of Hans Castorp's voyage of self-discovery in *Der Zauberberg* of 1925. By the time of *Lotte in Weimar*, finished within a few weeks of the outbreak of World War II, the theme of the greatness of a German genius had become set round with an anxious counterpoint of concern for the future of the German nation, and behind Goethe's reflections in the novel on the national character, above all on the weaknesses that had proved the nation's undoing in its recent history, lies Mann's vision of the hideous reality that gripped his country at the very moment he was writing.

But the serene, composed atmosphere of *Lotte in Weimar*, as the ageing Goethe looks out—or down—upon the world in his musing wisdom, is shattered as Thomas Mann returns in *Doktor Faustus* to his theme of the destructive power of art and leaves the Olympian humanist of Weimar for the daemonic, disease-ridden composer of Kaisersaschern (= Naumburg). He knew from the beginning precisely what task he was setting himself—'nothing less than the novel of my own time, disguised as the disturbing biography of an artist and sinner'.[56] In reply to Leonhard Frank's question, whether he had had any particular 'artist and sinner' in mind, he replied that Adrian Leverkühn was 'a kind of ideal figure, a "hero of our time", a man who bears the suffering of the age'.[57] Moreover *Doktor Faustus*, unlike *Buddenbrooks*, *Der Zauberberg* and the *Joseph*-tetralogy, all of which acquired their monumental proportions only in the course of being written, and in spite of their author's initial intentions, was from the beginning planned to have the expansiveness proper to his aim.

The Faust of the German legend was a scholar and teacher whose involvement with black magic sprang from a desire to experience what it was not given to man to experience. In the *Volksbuch vom Doktor Faust* published by Johann Spiess in 1587, and its later adaptations, as in Marlowe's *Tragical History of Doctor Faustus*, Faust's ultimate damnation is axiomatic and beyond question. By the rationalist eighteenth century, however, an unhampered quest for knowledge has become man's birthright, and it is unthinkable that he should be damned for seeking to experience the values that make man what he is. In Lessing's *Faust* the new morality calls for Faust's redemption, and this line leads on to Goethe. Heine's Faust-ballet follows the puppet-play, with the hero's final damnation, but Lenau's Faust commits suicide in a vain attempt to escape the Devil's clutches. Mann's Leverkühn too tries to commit suicide after being discharged from the mental asylum, but another 10 years of Nietzschean madness are to pass before he dies, his creative life being compressed into the 24 years of diabolically-sponsored activity that the Faust tradition allows him before the Devil returns to claim his own.

That Mann's Faust-figure is no longer a philosopher or a magician, but a composer—though there is both philosophy and magic in his music—represents one of Mann's most deeply-held convictions about music and its meaning for the German people. Music is the most abstract, the most un-real of all the arts. It is also the art in which, above all in the Romantic nineteenth century, the Germans have excelled. Schopenhauer raised music to the status of a metaphysical force, defining the world as 'embodied music', while Wagner created in his music-dramas works in which the Romantic values of the nineteenth century found their apotheosis.

'If Faust is to stand as a representative of the German soul', declared Thomas Mann, 'he must needs be a musician, for the Germans' relationship to the world is abstract and mystical—which is to say, musical.'[58] And the super-intellectual Leverkühn, living in a post-Wagnerian world in which there appears to be nothing vital left for music to say, but determined to rescue his art from mediocrity even at the cost of damnation, is a very German musician, the embodiment of that Romantic *Innerlichkeit* which Mann equates in *Deutschland und die Deutschen* with what he calls the 'musicality of the German soul'. The summit of this German musicality is represented by Richard Wagner, the significance of whose music as the practical manifestation, even vindication, of Schopenhauer's philosophy, and as the quintessential expression of German Romanticism, sustains Mann's essay 'Leiden und Grösse Richard Wagners', one of the pieces in *Leiden und Grösse der Meister* (1935), the last of his books to be published in Germany until after World War II.

It is in the lecture *Deutschland und die Deutschen* that one finds at its most explicit that philosophical statement of the inner nature of music as 'the territory of the Devil', as he puts it, which lies at the heart—the German heart—of *Doktor Faustus*. It was delivered, in English, in the Coolidge Auditorium of the Library of Congress on 29 May 1945, three weeks after the end of World War II. When it became known in Germany, many expressed indignation at its diagnosis of the fatal flaws in the German character which, as Mann portrayed them, had dragged almost the whole world into darkness and destruction, Mann, his critics protested, had no brief to pronounce judgement, from the cosy prosperity of his transatlantic sanctuary, on the fellow-countrymen he had deserted in Europe. The novelist Manfred Hausmann went so far as to refuse to join the *Deutsche Akademie fur Sprache und Dichtung* so long as Mann remained an honorary member of that body.

But sadly understandable as such attitudes may have been among the tensions, the cynicism, the resignation and the hesitant hopes of the post-war months, they do not reach to the heart of Thomas Mann's position. Refusing to separate a 'good' Germany from a 'bad' Germany, he posits in *Deutschland und die Deutschen* the inseparability of the constructive and the destructive, the positive and the negative, in the German character and puts his faith for the future in what he calls 'die Masse des Guten' in the German people. Luther and Riemenschneider, Goethe and Wagner, Lessing and Bismarck, 1848 and 1933—such polarities are part of German history and part of the national consciousness, and as such integral to expressions of the national will. Connoisseurs of the ironical have not failed to observe that the absorption of the 'Masse des Guten' in the service of a European humanism, as Thomas Mann now sees the challenge of the future, is just what his brother Heinrich had demanded 30 years earlier, only to be scorned as a 'Zivilisationsliterat' by Thomas, author at that time of the nationalistic *Friederich und die grosse Koalition* and the inward-looking *Betrachtungen eines Unpolitischen*.

All these different Germanys, or manifestations of the one Germany, play their part in the tragedy of Leverkühn's career—which is no less tragic for the irony of manner with which the author manipulates the events and characters of his story. Leverkühn is presented as the leading German composer of the day, but his music, a form of voluntary sweated labour dictated by the Devil, only shows how cold, remote, ultimately irrelevant modern art has become, a private game no longer to be taken seriously, in which the only goal is technical, that is, intellectual, perfection *sui generis*. So to describe his

hermetically-closed serialism, the dodecaphonic compositional principle codified by Arnold Schoenberg, Mann's fellow-exile in
California, Leverkühn says: 'There is not a single free note left.' This
technique,' Zeitblom recalls, 'did not admit a single note, a single
sound, whose presence and function were not motivated from within
the work as a whole.'[59] The inseparability of art and sickness had been
an abiding motif in Thomas Mann's work from the time of
Buddenbrooks, *Tristan* and *Tonio Kröger*, but in *Doktor Faustus* it is stated
with unrivalled intensity. 'Genius is a life-force steeped in sickness,
inspired by sickness and creative through sickness,' says Zeitblom.[60]
Yet if the creation of works of art has only become possible through
the agency of the Devil and by contracting syphilis, and if the works
thus created rest on an arid, self-centred intellectuality bereft of
human warmth and human appeal, what jusification is left for art in
the world? It is an ambivalence that tormented Thomas Mann—and
an ambivalence in which, as a writer, he revelled.

Doktor Faustus draws on the legend of a man from the age of
Reformation and Renaissance, a man at the turning-point of
medieval and modern. For *Joseph und seine Brüder* and *Der Erwählte*,
Thomas Mann went even further back into history and myth. The
latter work, based on a story from the *Gesta Romanorum* and the Middle
High German *Gregorius* of Hartmann von Aue, belongs to his post-
war years. The former, the first two volumes of which—*Die Geschichten
Jaakobs* and *Der junge Joseph*—had been written before he left
Germany in 1933, lived in his mind throughout his exile; the third
and fourth volumes—*Joseph in Ägypten* and *Joseph, der Ernährer*—were
both published abroad, the one (1936) in Vienna, the other (1943) in
Stockholm. Two days after finishing *Joseph, der Ernährer* he began
collecting material for *Doktor Faustus*. Such was the pressure on his
mind, such his discipline and his energy.

The foundations of the Joseph-story, which, like *Buddenbrooks*,
chronicles the history of successive generations, lay far back in
Thomas Mann's experience, and the subject occupied his thoughts,
he later recalled, for 16 years before the final volume—that which,
ironically, came to be most quickly and eagerly written—was
complete. 'A work has to have deep roots in my life', he said, 'and
there must be secret links between it and my earliest childhood
dreams, if I am to advance a claim for the justification of what I am
doing. To take up a subject arbitrarily to which, whether through
one's affection for it or knowledge of it, one has no longstanding
commitment, seems to me amateurish and pointless.'[61] Sterne's
Tristram Shandy and Goethe's *Faust*, he said, were the two books above
all that fed his thoughts during his years of work on the *Joseph*-novels,

and the underlying myth of dying and rebirth, the *Bildung* not only of Joseph but of the Jewish people, even of God Himself, is that of the Goethean 'Stirb und werde'.

Where the mood of *Doktor Faustus* is tense, dark, doom-laden, and becomes heavier and darker as the story moves towards its tragic goal, the atmosphere of the *Joseph*-novels grows lighter and more relaxed the nearer we come to the 'happy ending', the final image of the honoured and revered Joseph in Egypt, the servant of the community and saviour of human ideals. And where the medieval Faust-myth, heavy with evil and retribution, carries the motif of the destructive course of modern German history, the Biblical Joseph-story is set in deliberate humanistic opposition to Alfred Rosenberg's *Myth of the Twentieth Century*, pseudo-philosophical Bible of Nazism. Remaining within the framework of the account, part-historical, part-legendary, given in the Book of Genesis, Thomas Mann directs his hero towards a synthesis of intellect and emotion, mind and matter, egocentricity and social responsibility. Joseph, chosen servant of God, is no creature of flawless perfection. Yet his roguishness and his religious presumptuousness serve the process of his *Bildung* as openly as do his less controversial virtues, and Mann himself wrote to Karl Kerényi of the 'humorous slant'[62] of the theology behind the novel.

As there is an irony in building such picaresque traits into the personality of a man who is eventually to attain high office in the land, so also is there in the author's involvement of various spheres of scientific knowledge—archaeology, mythology, history, anthropology, theology, history of religion—in his narration of what is fundamentally a legend, and therefore not susceptible of verification in these or any other 'scientific' terms. Like *Der Zauberberg* and *Doktor Faustus*, the *Joseph*-tetralogy is technically a montage that reveals the great learning of its author, a learning that is made to serve, not the pursuit of scholarship but the psychologising of the events of the legend. Psychology may or may not be a science in the strict sense, but wherever there are human characters, there is psychology, and since there is no novel without characters, so psychological realities are integral to all novels. The novelist is thus the man to put the flesh of psychological motivation on to the bare bones of a sequence of historical or mythical events, and in so doing either to illuminate the processes of history or to reveal the psychological significance for the present of events in the past. Inasmuch as the story of Joseph is both history and legend, Mann holds in his hand material rich in personal, social, national and universal meaning, a meaning, or set of meanings, which in his familiar ironical pose of detachment he both transmits and observes himself transmitting.

Furthermore, in *Joseph und seine Brüder* he sets himself the task of exploring the tension between the psychological motivation of the individual, that is, what makes for originality, and the inescapable pressures of common validity, that is, what constitutes the typical, the 'mythological'. Already in *Der Zauberberg* Hans Castorp's vision in the snow, though proper to Castorp's personal circumstance, is a vision of mythological reality which gives his experience representative status. From the beginning of his years in exile, however, and hardly by chance, Thomas Mann invests his individual characters, conspicuously Joseph, Adrian Leverkühn and Gregory, the 'holy sinner', more and more with powers that make their representative meaning more important than their individual fates. Hence Mann's early picture of his *Joseph* as 'a mythical book' in which what in *Buddenbrooks* had been played out on a middle-class family plane is transported into the realm of 'humanity at large',[63] as he wrote from Zurich in 1935.

Thomas Mann was an indefatigable commentator on his own works. Indeed, his ironical tone provides a dimension of commentary within many of his novels and short stories themselves, so that his extraneous observations become, in part, commentaries on commentaries. He did not keep a diary of the composition of *Joseph und seine Brüder* as he did for that of *Doktor Faustus*, but he spoke on a number of occasions about the genesis of the novel, its position in his development as artist and thinker, and the purpose he intended it to fulfil. In the letter quoted above he defines it as marking a break with the concentration on individual fate and middle-class values that had characterised his work hitherto, and a rising concern with the characteristic and the mythical. This in its turn broadens the human basis of his sympathies and leads to what he calls 'the feeling of common humanity (*das Menschheitliche*)' which nurtured the pleasure his Joseph gave him. So all-embracing did this historico-mythical interest become that he spoke, with the first two volumes already published, of an ambition to turn the book into 'a kind of abbreviated history of mankind'.[64] This is another way of describing that exploration of the relationship between what is psychologically significant in the individual, that is, the unique, and what is mythologically binding on the whole community, that is, the representative and paradigmatic, which underlies the course of *Joseph und seine Brüder*. The past in the present, the beginning in the end, the fusion of personal and communal, intuition and intellectual perception—these are what Joseph stands for and what, to general admiration and gratitude, he finally brings to pass.

'Irony?' writes Erich Heller in his study of Thomas Mann. '*Joseph und seine Brüder* is, if nothing else, one of the greatest and friendliest conquests the imagination has ever made of irony.'[65]

It is perhaps appropriate that one should conclude a chapter on writers in exile from Hitler's Germany—indeed, should conclude an entire survey of German literature and society between the wars—with Thomas Mann. Partly it is a question of generation, for although, like his brother Heinrich, like Döblin, Brecht, Zuckmayer, Anna Seghers and others, he continued writing after the end of the war, his creative personality was formed, and his reputation laid—again like theirs—during these years between the beginning of one world war and the end of another. Partly it is a matter of stature, for Thomas Mann is arguably the greatest of these writers.

There is hardly a way in which one can summarise, conclude, epitomise—call it what one will—the confused, contradictory aspirations, the hidden yearnings, the desperate trials and agitations which emerge from the life of society, as from the individual mind and soul, to fill the literature of this quarter of a century. As in the 1920s, against the background of defeat in war, inflation, social instability and political inexperience, the first German attempt at Parliamentary democracy crumbled, so novelists, poets and dramatists write grimly of their disillusionments, of the human and social failings that had to be overcome by reference to new, above all different, values. Then, during the reign of Hitler in the 1930s and 1940s, the fabric of national culture was split when all but a few of the best-known figures fled, leaving behind those willing to serve the National Socialist cause and a handful of sad, withdrawn, almost silent inner protesters.

Yet if one great writer can contain these conflicting, often centrifugal forces, knowing what each means yet with the spiritual and intellectual power to transcend the particular, it is Thomas Mann. The whole nature and appeal of his work rests on a total concern with German culture and with the psychology of the German people.

The trauma of the Third Reich was not a condition forced upon the German nation from without, or an historical episode quite unmotivated from within the nation itself, but the destructive product of forces known, identified, even individually respected over centuries of national life. To explain rather than to condemn, to face an unpleasant reality rather than to turn sheepishly or truculently away from it, is the decision that Thomas Mann takes, and the unity that he affirms is the basis of his socio-cultural message, from the *Betrachtungen eines Unpolitischen* of 1918, through the years of the unhappy Republic and the pall of Nazi darkness, down to *Deutschland und die Deutschen* in 1945.

'The history of German *Innerlichkeit*,' he said, 'teaches us one thing—that there are not two Germanys, one good, one bad, but a single Germany whose goodness has been seduced by the Devil into the paths of evil. The bad Germany is the good Germany that has been led astray, the good Germany in time of misfortune, of guilt, of collapse.'[66] Misfortune—guilt—collapse: almost like chapter headings for a summary of the story of Germany between 1918 and 1945. Thomas Mann did not choose his words lightly.

Notes

1. Klaus Mann, *Der Wendepunkt* (Frankfurt, 1952), 304
2. Döblin, 'Abschied und Wiederkehr' (*Die Zeitlupe. Kleine Prosa*, Olten/Freiburg, 1962, 202)
3. Döblin, 'Die deutsche Literatur [im Ausland seit 1933]. Ein Dialog zwischen Politik und Kunst' (*Aufsätze zur Literatur*, Olten/Freiburg, 1963, 194)
4. Thomas Mann, *Briefe 1889–1936* (Frankfurt, 1961), 410
5. Thomas Mann, 'Warum ich nicht nach Deutschland zurückgehe' (*Reden und Aufsätze II*, Stockholmer Gesamtausgabe, 1965, 649)
6. H. Pross, *Literatur und Politik* (Olten/Freiburg, 1963), 289
7. *ibid.* 287
8. *Exile Literature 1933–1945* (Inter Nationes, Bad Godesberg, 1968), 37
9. see M. Wegner, *Exil und Literatur* (Frankfurt, 1967), 93
10. *Stücke III*, 266–7
11. Brecht, 'Kann die heutige Welt durch Theater wiedergegeben werden?' (*Schriften zum Theater VII*, 1964, 301)
12. 'Preis oder Verdammung des Galilei?' (*Stücke VIII*, 205)
13. *Stücke X*, 300
14. *Stücke VIII*, 408
15. *ibid.*
16. see p. 77 above
17. *Gedichte IV*, 145
18. *Gedichte I*, 148
19. *Auswahl in sechs Bänden* (Berlin, 1952), III, 485
20. ed. cit. III, 347
21. ed. cit. III, 176
22. M. Herrmann-Neisse, *Lied der Einsamkeit: Gedichte von 1914–1941* (Munich, 1961), 153
23. ed. cit. 182
24. J.R. Becher, ed. cit. I, 161
25. Wolfskehl, *Gesammelte Werke I* (Hamburg, 1960), 216
26. ed. cit. 220
27. from a letter quoted by Gisela Dischner in *Nelly Sachs zu Ehren: Gedichte, Beiträge, Bibliographie* (Frankfurt, 1966), 108

28. Werfel, *Gesammelte Werke: Das lyrische Werk* (Frankfurt, 1967), 493–4
29. ed. cit. 500
30. 'Rede zum 2. internationalen Schriftstellerkongress zur Verteigung der Kultur' (1937) (*Schriften zur Literatur und Kunst* 2, Frankfurt, 1967, 48)
31. 'Vom Sinn des historischen Romans' (*Neues Tagebuch* III, 1935, Heft 27, 641)
32. 'Der historische Roman und wir' (*Aufsätze zur Literatur*, Olten/Freiburg, 1963, 163ff)
33. Döblin, op. cit. 184
34. *Deutsche Literatur im Zeitalter des Imperialismus* (Berlin, 1950), 78
35. p. 490
36. G. Lukács, *The Historical Novel* (London, 1962), 292
37. *Die Jugend des Henri Quatre*: Heinrich Mann, *Ausgewählte Werke in Einzelausgaben* (Berlin, 1951ff), VI, 360
38. *Das Lied von Bernadette* (Frankfurt, 1959), 8
39. *Der veruntreute Himmel* (Amsterdam, 1948), 356
40. *Der Tod des Vergil* (Zurich, 1952), 150
41. op. cit. 153
42. *Briefe von 1929 bis 1951* (Zurich, 1957), 201
43. 'Bemerkungen zum Tod des Vergil' (*Dichten und Erkennen: Essays I,* Zurich, 1955, 265)
44. *Briefe*, ed. cit. 416
45. *Briefe*, ed. cit. 221
46. *Dichten und Erkennen: ESsays I*, ed. cit. 91
47. *Briefe*, ed. cit. 91
48. *Die Entstehung des Doktor Faustus* (*Gesammelte Werke in zwölf Bänden*, Frankfurt, 1960, XI, 193)
49. *Gesammelte Dichtungen* (Zurich, 1952), V, 740
50. ed. cit. VI, 84
51. *Zarathustras Wiederkehr* (*Krieg und Frieden*, Frankfurt, 1949, 115)
52. *ibid.* 124
53. Letter of November 14, 1947 (*Briefe*, ed. cit. 280)
54. *Das Glasperlenspiel* (ed. cit. VI, 84)
55. *Der Zauberberg* (Frankfurt, 1964), xiii
56. *Die Entstehung des Doktor Faustus* (ed. cit. XI, 169)
57. *ibid.* 203. Among the many symbolic 'coincidences' in the novel is that Leverkühn was born in the same year (1885) as Alban Berg.
58. 'Deutschland und die Deutschen' (ed. cit. XI, 1131–2)
59. *Doktor Faustus* (Stockholmer Gesamtausgabe, Frankfurt, 1965), 645
60. *ibid.* 472
61. 'Joseph und seine Brüder. Ein Vortrag' (*Gesammelte Werke in zwölf Bänden*, 1960, XI, 661)
62. a letter to Karl Kerényi (ed. cit. XI, 641–2)
63. *Briefe 1889–1936* (Frankfurt, 1963), 390
64. *ibid.*
65. *The Ironic German. A study of Thomas Mann* (London, 1958), 258
66. 'Deutschland und die Deutschen' (ed. cit. XI, 1146)

BIBLIOGRAPHY

(The two focuses of attention in the following selection of works have been the socio-political history of Germany from 1918 to 1945 and the literary responses to the social circumstances of this period by the principal authors on whom the book has dwelt. Books on general literary issues, as well as studies of stylistic, formal and other specifically 'literary' characteristics of the writers discussed, have not been included)

Albrecht, F. *Deutsche Schriftsteller in der Entscheidung,* (Berlin and Weimar, 1970)

Allen, W.S. *The Nazi Seizure of Power* (Chicago, 1965)

Angress, W.T. *Stillborn Revolution* (London, 1963)

――*Der antifaschistische Widerstand 1933–1945 in Bildern und Dokumenten. Von einem Autorenkollektiv* (Frankfurt, 1955)

Arendt, H. *The Origins of Totalitarianism* (New York, 1958)

Arnold, H.L. (ed.) *Deutsche Literatur im Exil 1933–1945* (Frankfurt, 1974)

Aron, R. *German Sociology* (London, 1964)

Baumont, M., Fried, J.H., and Vermeil, E. (eds.) *The Third Reich* (New York, 1955)

Berendsohn, W.A. *Die humanistische Front, Einführung in die deutsche Emigrationsliteratur,* 2 vols. (Zurich, 1946; 1976)

Berglund, G. *Deutsche Opposition gegen Hitler in Presse und Roman des Exils* (Stockholm, 1972)

Bergsträsser, L. *Geschichte der politischen Parteien in Deutschland* (Freiburg, 1965)

Bernstein, E. *Die Deutsche Revolution* (Berlin, 1921)

Bing, S. *Jakob Wassermann: Weg und Werk des Dichters* (Berlin, 1933)

Bischoff, A.M. *Elias Canetti—Stationen zum Werk* (Bern/Frankfurt, 1973)

Bithell, J. *Modern German Literature, 1880–1938* (London, 1946)

Bleuel, H.P. *Deutschlands Bekenner. Professoren zwischen Kaiserreich und Diktatur* (Berne, 1968)

Boulby, M. *Hermann Hesse* (Ithaca, 1967)

Bracher, K.D. *Die Auflösung der Weimarer Republik: Eine Studie zum Problem des Machtverfalls in der Demokratic* (Villingen, 1955)

――*Deutschland zwischen Demokratie und Diktatur: Beitrage zur neueren Politik und Geschichte* (Bern, 1964)

――*Die Deutsche Diktatur: Entstehung, Struktur und Folgen des Nationalsozialismus* (Cologne/Berlin, 1969); transl. *German Dictatorship: Origins, Structure and Consequences of National Socialism* (London, 1971)

Bracher, K.D., Sauer, W., and Schulz, G. *Die Nationalsozialistische Machtergreifung: Studien zur Errichtung des totalitären Herrschaftssystems in Deutschland, 1933–1934* (Cologne, 1960)

Bramsted, E.K. *Goebbels and National Socialist Propaganda* (London, 1965)

Braulich, H. *Max Reinhardt. Theater zwischen Traum und Wirklichkeit* (Berlin, 1966)

――*Die Volksbühne* (Berlin, 1976)

Brecht, A. *Federalism and Regionalism in Germany* (New York, 1945)

――*Prelude to Silence—The End of the German Republic* (New York, 1944)

Brenner, H. *Die Kunstpolitik des Nationalsozialismus* (Reinbek, 1963)

Brescianini-Turroni, C. *The Economics of Inflation: a Study of Currency Depreciation in Post-war Germany* (London, 1937)

Broszat, M. *Der Staat Hitlers. Grundlegung und Entwicklung seiner inneren Verfassung* (Munich, 1971)
Buchheim, H. *The Third Reich. Its Beginnings, Its Development, Its End* (Munich, 1961)
Bullivant, K. (ed.) *Culture and Society in the Weimar Republic* (Manchester, 1977)
Bullock, A. *Hitler, A Study in Tyranny* (London, 1952)
Burden, H.T. *The Nuremberg Rallies, 1923–33* (London, 1969)

Carsten, F. *The Reichswehr and Politics, 1919–33* (Oxford, 1966)
Cecil, R. *The Myth of the Master Race. Alfred Rosenberg and Nazi Ideology* (London, 1972)
Clarke, R.T. *The Fall of the German Republic* (London, 1935)
Conway, J.S. *The Nazi Persecution of the Churches, 1933–39* (London, 1968)
Coper, R. *Failure of a Revolution. Germany 1918–1919* (Cambridge, 1955)
Craig, G. *Germany 1866–1945* (London, 1978)
Croner, F. *Soziologie der Angestellten* (Cologne/Berlin, 1962)
Curtius, E.R. *Deutscher Geist in Gefahr* (Stuttgart, 1932)

Dahlke, H. *Geschichtsroman und Literaturkritik im Exil* (Berlin/Weimar, 1976)
Dahrendorf, R. *Class and Class Conflict in Industrial Society* (London, 1965)
———*Society and Democracy in Germany* (London, 1967)
Déak, I. *Weimar's Left Wing Intellectuals* (Berkeley, 1968)
Dehio, L. *Germany and World Politics in the Twentieth Century* (London, 1959)
Denkler, H. and Prümm, K. (eds.) *Die deutsche Literatur des Dritten Reiches* (Stuttgart, 1976)
Dittberner, H. *Heinrich Mann: Eine kritische Einführung in die Forschung* (Frankfurt, 1974)
Duhnke, H. *Die KPD von 1933 bis 1945* (Stuttgart, 1973)
Durzak, M. *Das expressionistische Drama. Carl Sternheim—Georg Kaiser* (Munich, 1978)
———(ed.) *Die deutsche Exilliteratur 1933–45* (Stuttgart, 1973)

Emrich, W. *Franz Kafka* (Frankfurt, 1960)
Erdmann, K.D. *Die Zeit der Weltkriege (1914–1945)* (Stuttgart, 1960)
Eschenburg, Th. and others *The Road to Dictatorship* (London, 1964)
Esslin, M. *Brecht: A Choice of Evils* (London, 1959)
Eyck, E. *A History of the Weimar Republic* (Oxford, 1962)

Fähnders, W. *Proletarisch-revolutionäre Literatur der Weimarer Republik* (Stuttgart, 1977)
Fähnders, W., Karrenbrock, H., and Rector, M. (eds.) *Sammlung proletarisch-revolutionärer Erzählungen* (Darmstadt, 1973)
———*Sammlung antifaschistischer sozialistischer Erzählungen* (Darmstadt, 1974)
Fähnders, W. and Rector, M. *Linksradikalismus und Literatur. Untersuchungen zur Geschichte der sozialistischen Literatur in der Weimarer Republik* (Hamburg, 1974)
Felix, D. *Walther Rathenau and the Weimar Republic* (Baltimore, 1971)
Fest, J.C. *The Face of the Third Reich* (London, 1970)
———*Hitler: Eine Biographie* (Frankfurt, 1973); transl. *Hitler* (London, 1974)
Feuchtwanger, E.J. (ed.) *Upheaval and Continuity. A Century of German History, 1871–1971* (London, 1973)
Flenley, R. *Modern German History* (London, 1953)
Flitner, A. (ed.) *Deutsches Geistesleben und Nationalsozialismus* (Tübingen, 1965)
Frischauer, W. *Himmler, The Evil Genius of the Third Reich* (London, 1953)
Fromm, E. *Escape from Freedom* (New York, 1941)

Gamm, H-J. *Führung und Verführung, Pädagogik des Nationalsozialismus* (Munich, 1964)
Garten, H.F. *Modern German Drama* (London, 1959)
Gay, P. *Weimar Culture* (London, 1968)
Geiger, T. *Die soziale Schichtung des deutschen Volkes* (Stuttgart, 1932)
Gerhard, D. *Antifaschisten: Proletarischer Widerstand 1933–1945* (Berlin, 1976)
Gilman, S.L. *NS-Literaturtheorie* (Frankfurt, 1971)
Glum, F. *Philosophen im Spiegel und Zerrspiegel* (Munich, 1954)
Goldston, R. *The Life and Death of Nazi Germany* (London, 1967)
Goguel, R. *Antifaschistischer Widerstand und Klassenkampf* (Berlin, 1976)
Gordon, H. *The Reichswehr and the German Republic 1919–26* (Princeton, 1957)
Graf, O.M. *Gelächter von Aussen: Aus meinem Leben, 1918–1933* (Frankfurt, 1966)
Gray, R.D. *The German Tradition in Literature 1871–1945* (Cambridge, 1965)
Grimm, R. and Hermand, J. (eds.) *Exil und Innere Emigration* (Frankfurt, 1972)
Groener, W. *Lebenserinnerungen* (Göttingen, 1947)
Grosser, A. *Germany in our Time* (London, 1972)
Grossman, K-R. *Emigration, Geschichte der Hitler-Flüchtlinge, 1933–1945* (Frankfurt, 1969)
Grosz, G. *A Little Yes and a Big No* (New York, 1946)
Grunberger, R. *Germany 1918–45* (London, 1964)
Grunfeld, F. *The Hitler File. A Social History of Germany and the Nazis* (London, 1974)
——— *A Social History of the Third Reich* (London, 1953)
Guardini, R. *Rainer Maria Rilkes Deutung des Daseins* (Munich, 1953)
Guillebaud, C.W. *The Economic Recovery of Germany 1933–39* (London, 1939)
——— *The Social Policy of Nazi Germany* (London, 1941)
Gumbel, E.J. *Zwei Jahre Mord* (Berlin, 1921)
——— *Vier Jahre politischer Mord* (Berlin, 1922)
——— *Verräter verfallen der Feme* (Berlin, 1929)
——— *Lasst Köpfe rollen* (Berlin, 1932)
Gundolf, F. *Stefan George* (Berlin, 1930)

Haas, W. *Die literarische Welt: Erinnerungen* (Stuttgart, 1960)
Haffner, S. *Germany: Jekyll and Hyde* (London, 1940)
——— *The Meaning of Hitler* (London, 1979)
Hale, O.J. *The Captive Press in the Third Reich* (Princeton, 1964)
Halperin, S.W. *Germany tried Democracy: A Political History of the Reich from 1918–1933* (New York, 1946)
Hannover, H. and E. *Politische Justiz, 1918–1933* (Frankfurt/Hamburg, 1966)
Hay, G. (ed.) *Literatur und Rundfunk* (Hildesheim, 1975)
Heberle, R. *From Democracy to Nazism* (Baton Rouge, 1945)
Heiber, H. *Goebbels* (London, 1973)
——— *Die Republik von Weimar* (Munich, 1966)
Heiden, K. *Geburt des Dritten Reiches* (Zurich, 1934)
——— *Der Führer* (London, 1945)
Heintz, G. (ed.) *Deutsche Arbeiterdichtung 1910–1933* (Stuttgart, 1974)
——— *Texte der proletarisch-revolutionären Literatur Deutschlands 1919–1933* (Stuttgart, 1974)
Heller, E. *The Disinherited Mind: Essays in Modern German Literature and Thought* (Cambridge, 1959)
——— *The Ironic German: A Study of Thomas Mann* (London, 1958)
Heller, H.B. *Untersuchung zur Theorie und Praxis des dialektischen Theaters. Brecht und Adorno* (Bern/Frankfurt, 1974)

Herald, H. *Max Reinhardt* (Hamburg, 1953)

Herzstein, R.E. *The War that Hitler Won* (London, 1979)

Hess, H. *George Grosz* (London, 1974)

Heuss, Th. *Erinnerungen, 1905–1933* (Tübingen, 1963)

Hilberg, R. *The Destruction of the European Jews* (Chicago, 1973)

Hofer, W. *Die Diktatur Hitlers bis zum Beginn des Zweiten Weltkrieges* (Konstanz, 1960)

Holborn, H. *History of Modern Germany*, 3 vols. (London, 1965–9)

Holthusen, H.E. *Ein deutsches Thema. Nazizeit und Nazischuld als literarischer Gegenstand* (Frankfurt, 1974)

Hug, H. *Erich Mühsam. Untersuchung zu Leben und Werk* (Glashütten, 1975)

Hunt, R.N. *German Social Democracy 1918–33* (London, 1964)

International Council for Philosophy and Humanistic Studies, *The Third Reich* (London and New York, 1955)

Jarman, T.L. *The Rise and Fall of Nazi Germany* (London, 1955); (New York, 1956)

Jonge, A. de *The Weimar Chronicle: Prelude to Hitler* (London, 1979)

Kaufmann, H. *Krisen und Wandlungen der deutschen Literatur von Wedekind bis Feuchtwanger* (Berlin/Weimar, 1969)

Kaufmann, W. *Monarchism in the Weimar Republic* (New York, 1953)

Kessler, H. *Graf Tagebücher, 1918–1937* (Frankfurt, 1961)

Kiaulehn, W. *Berlin: Schicksal einer Weltstadt* (Munich, 1958)

Klemperer, K.V. *Germany's New Conservatism: Its History and Dilemma in the Twentieth Century* (Princeton, 1957)

Klineberger, H.R. *The Christian Writers of the Inner Emigration* (The Hague/Paris, 1968)

Klönne, A. *Die Hitlerjugend* (Hannover/Frankfurt, 1956)

Koch, H.W. *The Hitler Youth: Origins and Development 1922–1945* (London, 1974)

Kochan, L. *The Struggle for Germany 1914–45* (Edinburgh, 1963)

Koenigswald, H. von *Die Gewaltlosen. Dichtung im Widerstand gegen den National sozialismus* (Herborn, 1962)

Kohn, H. *The Mind of Germany* (London, 1962)

Kolb, E. (ed.) *Vom Kaiserreich zur Weimarer Republik* (Cologne, 1972)

Kolinsky, E. *Engagierter Expressionismus* (Stuttgart, 1970)

Kortner, F. *Aller Tage Abend* (Munich, 1959)

Koestler, A. *Arrow in the Blue: An Autobiography* (London, 1952)

Kracauer, F. *From Caligari to Hitler* (Princeton, 1947)

Krausnick, H. *Anatomy of the SS State* (London, 1968)

Krieger, L. *The German Idea of Freedom: History of a Political Tradition* (Boston, 1957)

Krispyn, E. *Anti-Nazi Writers in Exile* (Atlanta, 1978)

Kuhnke, K. (ed.) *Lieder der Arbeiterklasse 1919–1933* (Ahrensburg/Paris, 1971)

Lämmert, E., Killy, W., Konrady, K.O., and Polenz, P.V. *Germanistik-eine deutsche Wissenschaft* (Frankfurt, 1967)

Landmann, G.P. (ed.) *Der George-Kreis* (Cologne/Berlin, 1965)

——*Vorträge über Stefan George: Eine biographische Einführung in sein Werk* (Düsseldorf, 1974)

Langsam, W.C. *Historic Documents of World War II* (London, 1959)

Laqueur, W. *Weimar: A Cultural History 1918–33* (London, 1974)

——*Young Germany: A History of the German Youth Movement* (London, 1962)

Laqueur, W. and Mosse, G.L. *German Intellectuals between the Wars 1919–1939* (London, 1962)

Laursen, K. and Pederson, J. *The German Inflation 1918–1923* (Amsterdam, 1964)

Lebovics, H. *Social Conservatism and the Middle Classes in Germany 1914–1933* (Princeton, 1969)

Lederer, E. *State of the Masses. The Threat of the Classless Society* (New York, 1940)

Lehmann-Haupt, H. *Art under a Dictatorship* (London, 1954)

Lerner, D. *The Nazi Elite* (Stanford, 1951)

Lethen, H. *Neue Sachlichkeit 1924–1932* (Stuttgart, 1975)

Lewy, G. *The Catholic Church and Nazi Germany* (London, 1964)

Lilge, F. *The Abuse of Learning: The Failure of the German University* (New York, 1975)

Lion, F. *Romantik als deutsches Schicksal* (Stuttgart, 1947)

Litt, T. *Das Verhältnis der Generationen* (Wiesbaden, 1947)

Lochner, L. *Tycoons and Tyrants: German Industry from Hitler to Adenauer* (Chicago, 1954)

Loerke, O. *Tagebücher 1903–1939* (Heidelberg, 1955)

Loewy, E. *Literatur unterm Hakenkreuz* (Frankfurt, 1969)

——*Literarische und politische Texte aus dem deutschen Exil 1933–1945* (Stuttgart, 1979)

Maas, L. *Handbuch der deutschen Exilpresse, 1933–45* (Munich, 1976)

Mammach, K. *Die KPD und die deutsche antifaschistische Widerstandsbewegung 1933–1939* (Frankfurt, 1974)

Mann, K. *The Turning Point: Thirty-five Years in this Century* (New York, 1942)

Manvell, R. and Fraenkel, H. *The Canaris Conspiracy* (London, 1969)

——*Hermann Goering* (London, 1962)

——*Doctor Goebbels* (London, 1960)

——*Heinrich Himmler* (London, 1965)

——*The July Plot* (London, 1964)

Mason, E.C. *Rainer Maria Rilke* (Edinburgh, 1963)

——*Rilke, Europe and the English-speaking World* (Cambridge, 1959)

Matthias, K. (ed.) *Heinrich Mann 1871–1971: Bestandsaufnahme und Untersuchung* (Munich, 1973)

Mayer, M. *They Thought They were Free* (London, 1955)

McGovern, W.M. *From Luther to Hitler. The History of Fascist-Nazi Political Philosophy* (Boston/New York/Chicago, 1941)

Meinecke, F. *The German Catastrophe. Reflections and Recollections* (Cambridge, Mass., 1950)

Melzwig, B. *Deutsche sozialistische Literatur 1918–1945* (Berlin/Weimar, 1976)

Michels, V. (ed.) *Materialien zu Hermann Hesses 'Der Steppenwolf'* (Frankfurt, 1973)

——*Materialien zu Hermann Hesses 'Das Glasperlenspiel'* (Frankfurt, 1973)

Milatz, A. *Wähler und Wahlen in der Weimarer Republik* (Bonn, 1968)

Mittenzwei, W. et. al. *Kunst und Literatur im antifaschistischen Exil 1933–1945*, 6 vols (Leipzig, 1978–)

Mohler, A. *Die konservative Revolution in Deutschland, 1918 bis 1932: Grundriss ihrer Weltanschauungen* (Stuttgart, 1950)

Mosse, G.L. *The Crisis of German Ideology* (New York, 1964)

——*Nazi Culture* (London, 1966)

Muschg, W. *Von Trakl zu Brecht: Dichter des Expressionismus* (Munich, 1961)

Myers, B.S. *The German Expressionists: A Generation in Revolt* (London, 1963)

Nationalgalerie, Berlin: Catalogue of exhibition *Realismus und Sachlichkeit* (Berlin, 1974)

Neumann, F.L. *Behemoth: The Structure and Practice of National Socialism* (London, 1942)

Neumann, S. *Die Parteien der Weimarer Republik* (Stuttgart, 1965); orig. title *Die politischen Parteien in Deutschland* (Stuttgart, 1932)

Neurohr, J.F. *Der Mythos vom dritten Reich: Zur Geistesgeschichte des Nationalsozialismus* (Stuttgart, 1957)

Nichols, A. *Weimar and the Rise of Hitler* (London, 1968)

Orlow, D. *The History of the Nazi Party* 2 vols. (Pittsburgh, 1969/1973)

Pape, W. *Joachim Ringelnatz. Parodie und Selbstparodie im Leben und Werk* (Berlin, 1974)

Pfeiler, W.K. *War and the German Mind* (New York, 1941)

Pickar, G.B. *Deutsches Schrifttum zwischen den beiden Weltkriegen 1918–1945. Bibliographie* (Bern/Munich, 1974)

Pinson, K.S. *Modern Germany* 2nd edn. (New York, 1966)

Piscator, E. *Schriften*, 2 vols. (Berlin, 1968)

Plessner, H. *Die verspätete Nation: über die politische Verführbarkeit bürgerlichen Geistes* (Stuttgart, 1959)

Politzer, H. *Franz Kafka: Parable and Paradox* (New York, 1962)

Pörtner, P. *Literatur-Revolution 1910–1925* (Darmstadt, 1960)

Prawer, S.S. *Marx and World Literature* (Oxford, 1976)

Preller, L. *Sozialpolitik in der Weimarer Republik* (Stuttgart, 1949)

Pridham, G. *Hitler's Rise to Power* (London, 1973)

Pross, H. *Literatur und Politik* (Olten/Freiburg, 1963)

Pulzer, P.J. *The Rise of Anti-Semitism in Germany and Austria* (New York, 1964)

Raabe, P. (ed.) *Expressionismus: Aufzeichnungen und Erinnerungen der Zeitgenossen* (Olten/Freiburg 1965); transl. *The Era of Expressionism* (London, 1974)

Rathenau, W. *Politische Briefe* (Dresden, 1929)

Rauschning, H. *Die Revolution des Nihilismus* (Zurich/New York, 1938)

——— *Hitler Speaks* (London, 1939)

——— *Die konservative Revolution* (New York, 1941); transl. *Make and Break with the Nazis* (London, 1941)

Reid, T.J. *Thomas Mann: The Uses of Tradition* (Oxford, 1974)

Reiss, H. *The Writer's Task from Nietzsche to Brecht* (London, 1978)

Reitlinger, G. *The SS* (London, 1956)

Ringer, K. *The Decline of the German Mandarins* (Harvard, 1969)

Ritter, G. *The German Resistance: Carl Goerdeler's Struggle Against Tyranny* (New York, 1958)

——— *The Sword and the Sceptre: The Problem of Militarism in Germany*, 4 vols. (London, 1972–3)

Roberts, D. *Artistic Consciousness and Political Consciousness. The Novels of Heinrich Mann 1900–1938* (Bern/Frankfurt, 1971)

Robertson, E.M. (ed.) *The Origins of the Second World War* (London, 1971)

Roloff, E-A. *Bürgertum und Nationalsozialismus* (Hanover, 1961)

Roseberry, R.L. *Robert Musil: Ein Forschungsbericht* (Frankfurt, 1974)

Rosenberg, A. *The History of the German Republic* (London, 1936)

Rothe, W. *Der Expressionismus* (Frankfurt, 1977)

——— (ed.) *Die deutsche Literatur in der Weimarer Republik* (Stuttgart, 1974)

——— *Expressionismus als Literatur* (Berne, 1969)

Rothfels, H. *Die deutsche Opposition gegen Hitler* (Hamburg, 1958)

Rühle, G. *Theater für die Republik 1917–1933* (Frankfurt, 1967)

Ryder, A.J. *The German Revolution of 1919* (Cambridge, 1967)

Samuel, R.H. 'The Origin and Development of the Ideology of National Socialism', *Australian Journal of Politics and History* IX (1963) pp. 59–77
Samuel, R.H. and Thomas, R.H. *Education and Society in Modern Germany* (London, 1949)
——*Expressionism in German Life, Letters and the Theatre* (Cambridge, 1939)
Sayler, O. (ed.) *Max Reinhardt and his Theatre* (New York/London, 1968)
Scheele, G. *The Weimar Republic, Overture to the Third Reich* (London, 1945)
Schlawe, G. *Literarische Zeitschriften 1910–1933* (Stuttgart, 1973)
Schneider, F.J. *Der expressive Mensch und die deutsche Lyrik der Gegenwart* (Stuttgart, 1927)
Schnell, R. *Literarische Innere Emigration 1933–45* (Stuttgart, 1976)
Schoenbaum, D. *Hitler's Social Revolution* (New York, 1966)
Scholl, I. *Students against Tyranny*, transl. Schultz, A.R. (Middletown, 1970)
Schonauer, F. *Stefan George in Selbstzeugnissen und Bilddokumenten* (Hamburg, 1960)
——*Deutsche Literatur im Dritten Reich* (Olten/Freiburg, 1961)
Schröter, K. *Heinrich Mann in Selbstzeugnissen und Bilddokumenten* (Hamburg, 1967)
Schulz, G. *Faschismus—Nationalsozialismus* (Berlin, 1974)
Schumacher, E. *Die dramatischen Versuche Bertolt Brechts 1918–1933* (Berlin, 1955)
Schwarz, W.J. *War and the Mind of Germany* (Bern, 1975)
Schweitzer, A. *Big Business in the Third Reich* (London/Indiana, 1964)
Sell, F.C. *Die Tragödie des deutschen Liberalismus* (Stuttgart, 1953)
Seydewitz, M. *Civil Life in Wartime Germany* (New York, 1945)
Shirer, W.L. *Berlin Diary* (London and New York, 1941)
——*The Rise and Fall of the Third Reich* (New York, 1960)
Snyder, L.L. *German Nationalism. The Tragedy of a People* (Harrisburg, 1952)
Sokel, W.H. *The Writer in Extremis: Expressionism in Twentieth-Century German Literature* (Stanford, 1959)
——*Franz Kafka: Tragik und Ironie* (Munich/Viena, 1964)
Sontheimer, K. *Anti-Demokratisches Denken in der Weimarer Republik: Die politischen Ideen des deutschen Nationalismus zwischen 1918 und 1933* (Munich, 1962)
——*Thomas Mann und die Deutschen* (Munich, 1961)
Speer, A. *Inside the Third Reich* (London, 1971)
Steffen, H. (ed.)· *Der deutsche Expressionismus: Formen und Gestalten* (Göttingen, 1965)
Steinert, M.G. *Hitler Krieg und die Deutschen* (Düsseldorf/Vienna, 1970)
Stephenson, J. *Women in Nazi Germany* (London, 1975)
Stern, F. *The Politics of Cultural Despair* (Berkeley, 1961)
Stern, J.P. *Hitler: The Führer and his People* (London, 1974)
——*Nietzsche* (Hassocks, 1978)
Sternfeld, W. and Tiedemann, E. (ed.) *Deutsche Exilliteratur 1933–1945* (Heidelberg, 1962)
Stirk, S.D. *The Prussian Spirit. A Survey of German Literature and Politics 1914–1940* (London, 1941)
Stolper, G. *The German Economy 1870 to the Present* (New York, 1967)
Strauss, R./Zweig, S.; *Briefwechsel* ed. Schuh, W. (Frankfurt, 1957)
Strothmann, D. *Nationalsozialistische Literaturpolitik* (Bonn, 1968)
Szczesny, G. *Das Leben des Galilei und der Fall Bertholt Brecht* (Frankfurt, 1966)

Taylor, A.J.P. *The Course of German History* (London, 1945)

Taylor, T. *Sword and Swastika: Generals and Nazis in the Third Reich* (New York, 1952)
Turner, H.A. Jr. *Stresemann and the Politics of the German Republic* (Princeton, 1963)
——(ed.) *Nazism and the Third Reich* (New York, 1972)
Tutas, H.E. *NS-Propaganda und deutsches Exil 1933–39* (Meisenheim, Glan, 1973)

Vermeil, E. *L'Allemagne contemporaine 1890–1950* (Paris, 1953) English transl. (London, 1956)
Verrina (pseud.) *The German Mentality* (London, 1941)
Viereck, P. *Metapolitics. The Roots of the Nazi Mind* (New York, 1941)
Vondung, K. *Völkisch-nationale und nationalsozialistische Literaturtheorie* (Munich, 1973)

Waite, R.G.L. *Vanguard of Nazism: The Free Corps Movement in Postwar Germany, 1918–1923* (Cambridge, Mass., 1952)
Walter, B. *Theme and Variations: An Autobiography* (London, 1946)
Walter, H.A. *Deutsche Exilliteratur 1933–50* (Darmstadt/Neuwied, 1972–4; Stuttgart 1979–): I. *Bedrohung und Verfolgung bis 1933* II. *Asylpraxis und Lebensbedingungen in Europa* VII. *Exilpresse I* IV. *Exilpresse* (1979)
Weigand, J. *Thomas Mann's Novel 'Der Zauberberg'* (New York, 1933)
Weisenborn, G. *Der lautlose Aufstand. Bericht über die Widerstandsbewegung des deutschen Volkes 1933–1945* (Frankfurt, 1953)
Wheeler-Bennett, J.W. *The Wooden Titan: Hindenburg in Twenty Years of German History 1914–1934* (London, 1936)
—— *The Nemesis of Power. The German Army in Politics 1918–1945* (London, 1953)
Willett, J. *The New Society 1917–1933: Art and Politics in the Weimar Period* (London, 1979)
Winkler, H.A. *Mittelstand, Demokratie und Nationalsozialismus* (Cologne, 1972)
Winkler, M. *Stefan George* (Stuttgart, 1971)
——*Der George-Kreis* (Stuttgart, 1971)
——(ed.) *Deutsche Literatur im Exil 1933–1945* (Stuttgart, 1977)
Wollstein, G. *Vom Weimarer Revisionismus zu Hitler* (Bonn, 1973)
Wulf, J. (ed.) *Literatur und Dichtung im Dritten Reich* (Reinbek, 1963)
——*Presse und Funk im Dritten Reich* (Reinbek, 1966)
——*Die bildenden Künste im Dritten Reich* (Reinbek, 1966)
——*Musik im Dritten Reich* (Reinbek, 1963)
——*Theater und Film in Dritten Reich* (Reinbek, 1966)

Zeller, B. *Hermann Hesse* (Harmondsworth, 1976)
Zeman, Z.A.B. *Nazi Propaganda* (Oxford, 1964)
Zimmermann, E. and Jacobsen, H.A. (eds.) *Germans against Hitler* (Bonn, 1960)
Ziolkowski, T. *The Novels of Hermann Hesse* (Princeton, 1965)
Zuckmayer, C. *Als wär's ein Stück von mir* (Vienna, 1966); transl. *A Part of Myself* (London, 1970)
Zweig, S. *Die Welt von Gestern* (London, 1945); transl. *The World of Yesterday* (London, 1943)

INDEX OF NAMES